The
MUSIC
of
SPAIN

Gilbert Chase

SECOND REVISED EDITION

DOVER PUBLICATIONS, INC.   NEW YORK

Manufactured in the United States of America

Dover Publications, Inc.
180 Varick Street
New York 14, N. Y.

TO MY MOTHER AND FATHER

Foreword to Second Edition

CIRCUMSTANCES have not made it possible for me to undertake a complete revision of the entire text of this book. It now appears, therefore, very much the same as in the original edition, except for minor corrections and the addition of a Supplementary Chapter reviewing the main developments since 1941. The original list of recordings has been deleted as obsolete, and no new list has been added, chiefly because of the plethora of current recordings of Spanish music, with a spate of new releases every month — surely a gratifying state of affairs for the readers of this book, as well as for myself.

With regard to the Bibliography, I have added the important publications of the Spanish Institute of Musicology, none of which were available when I first wrote this book; and also some other titles published since 1941, but without any attempt at compiling a complete bibliography of the subject.

This was my first book, and I am grateful to those readers who have kept the demand for it alive during the many years that it was out of print. Now that the book is in circulation again, I hope that my new readers will be as indulgent and as faithful as the older ones have been.

GILBERT CHASE

Chapel Hill, N. C.
May, 1958

Foreword

THIS is not so much a history of Spanish music as a panorama of its salient features from the Middle Ages to the present day. It is the first book in any language attempting to give a concise yet comprehensive account of Iberian music in all its aspects.

The gathering of material was begun in Spain some fourteen years ago and was continued during subsequent visits to that country, supplemented by research in the libraries of Paris, New York, and Washington. Yet it is obvious that no one can be a specialist in every branch of a subject as vast and complex as that of Spanish music, and my debt to various writers is considerable. It has, I trust, been duly acknowledged at all times, either explicitly in the footnotes or implicitly in the Bibliography.

Anyone working in the field of Spanish music must owe something to the pioneer historian of that subject, Rafael Mitjana, for his fundamental work published in the Lavignac-Laurencie *Encyclopédie de la Musique et Dictionnaire du Conservatoire* (for the sake of brevity this treatise is referred to in the notes as *La Musique en Espagne*). On the other hand, the work of Mitjana has been supplemented and in many places corrected by the more recent investigations and publications of such scholars as Higini Anglès, Emilio Cotarelo y Mori, José Subirá, Otto Ursprung, Peter Wagner, and Otto Kinkeldey.

The Bibliography does not pretend to be exhaustive. With

very few exceptions it includes only works that have actually been consulted by the author in the preparation of this volume. However, many of the works listed contain extensive, specialized bibliographies which may be consulted by those interested in following up any particular subject.

To various Spanish composers of the present day, among them Manuel de Falla and Oscar Esplá, I am grateful for useful information placed at my disposal. Helpful suggestions have also been received from Gustavo Durán and Joaquín Nin-Culmell. The sections on Portuguese music were written by Albert T. Luper, of the University of Texas, who has traveled and studied in Portugal.

Table of Contents

List of Illustrations

Introduction

HISTORY, the process of human culture, has a geographical basis. The destiny of the Iberian peoples is written in the shape and sinew of their land. This mountain-studded peninsula, thrust boldly forth into the sea, with one face turned eastward toward the source of civilization, the other westward toward a new world, was fated to be the meeting place of many cultures and the starting point of far-flung discoveries. South and east its shores are washed by the history-laden Mediterranean, whose waters Ulysses cleaved as he reached the "Pillars of Hercules"—what we now call the Straits of Gibraltar—which were both the gateway to the unknown and the connecting link between Spain and Africa. North and west its coasts are swept by the Atlantic, whose mysterious dangers Columbus defied in search of the fabulous Indies, discovering, instead, the incredible Americas. Accustomed to action and enterprise by eight centuries of combat against the Moslems, and further stimulated to adventure by the penuriousness of a parched and barren interior, the men of Spain and Portugal went forth in quest of El Dorado and ultimately attained a less illusory goal by spreading Iberian culture over two thirds of the Western Hemisphere.

Some three thousand years before Columbus and his caravels set sail from the port of Palos, other venturesome seafarers had pushed westward toward what to them was a distant and enticing land situated "in the furthest confines of the Occident." Traders from Tyre, and "the merchants of Sidon that pass over the sea," touched upon Iberian shores with their sharp-beaked galleys and became the first colonizers of Spain. Trade was the absorbing interest of these Phoenicians, but the arts of music were not foreign to them. Recall what the prophet Isaiah said of Tyre in the days of its shame: "Take an harp, go about the city, thou harlot that hast been forgotten; make sweet melody, sing many songs, that thou mayest be remembered" (Isaiah 23:16).

The songs of Tyre are not remembered. Yet one may fancy that some vestige of them, mingled with the melos of Greece and of Islam, lingers in the cantilena of an Iberian folk song whose beginnings are lost in the dimness of time. Certain it is that the lore of ancient Greece was implanted in the Iberian Peninsula after the Phoenician ascendancy had given way to Hellenic supremacy in the Mediterranean. The Greeks established colonies not only on the southeastern seaboard, but also in the north, on the Cantabrian coast and in Galicia. In Grecian temples and theaters built on Iberian soil, men worshiped Diana of Ephesus and sang their odes and dithyrambs to the accompaniment of the lyre and the aulos.

After the Greeks came the Carthaginians, only to yield in turn before the invincible, newly risen power of Rome. During the six centuries of Roman domination Spain was one of the most vital forces of the Empire. From her loins, adding their luster to the grandeur of Rome, sprang emperors, philosophers, and poets, among them Trajan, Hadrian, Seneca, Juvenal, and Martial. From one of the *Epigrams* of Martial, who often wrote glowingly of his native land, we learn that in his day the dancing girls of Cádiz were already famed for their seductive grace and their skill in playing the *crusmata* (castanets).

The Western Roman Empire ceased to exist in the year 476 A.D. Long before that time, however, barbarians from the north had penetrated into the Iberian Peninsula in large numbers, as military auxiliaries of Rome. As the Imperial authority weakened, they asserted their hold on the country with increasing independence, and upon the collapse of the Empire they assumed complete control. Thus the Visigothic monarchy in Spain came into being as an aftermath of Roman rule. The Ibero-Roman population of Spain had early been converted to Christianity, and so had the Visigoths previous to their arrival in the peninsula. But the latter professed the heresy of Arianism, so that for many years the new monarchy was torn by strife between the two factions. Catholicism finally triumphed, but scarcely had religious unity been achieved when Christianity itself was threatened by the impact of Islam.

Less than a hundred years after the death of Mohammed, who instilled into his followers an intense proselyting zeal, the Arabs had conquered the decadent nations around them—Syria, Byzantium, Persia, Egypt—had extended their sway along the northern coast of Africa, and had formed a vast empire extending from the Indus to the Atlantic, with its capital at Damascus. Spain was a tempting prize that seemed within easy reach. With the connivance of Count Julian, Governor of Ceuta, and with an army composed of Berbers from North Africa, Arabs, and Syrians, the Moslem general Tarik crossed the Straits of Gibraltar in the summer of the year 711, defeated King Roderic at Lago de la Janda, and swept the disorganized Visigothic monarchy to an ignominious downfall. Most of the country was soon subdued, only a small nucleus of Christian resistance remaining in the north.

The Moslems who conquered Spain were not a unified group. Arabs, Syrians, and Berbers engaged in bitter feuds among themselves. The authority of the central caliphate soon ceased to prevail, and for many generations the country was rife with turmoil and anarchy. Not until the establishment of the caliphate of Cordova in the tenth century was a semblance of order enforced. The caliphate reached its apogee of splendor during the reign of Abdurrahman III (912–961). Such cities as Seville, Granada, and Cordova were brilliant centers of scientific, literary, and musical culture, attracting scholars from all over Europe. The magnificent Mosque of Cordova—later made into a cathedral by the Christians—the Alcazar of Seville, and the Alhambra of Granada bear witness to the high achievements of Arabian architecture in Spain.

The defiant Spaniards who had rallied in the mountainous regions of the north after the defeat of Roderic formed tiny independent states—Aragon, Navarre, Castile, León—and gradually, as they grew in strength and boldness, they encroached upon the territory held by the Moslems. The Reconquest was a slow and arduous undertaking, lasting nearly eight centuries. It was not until the marriage of Ferdinand of Aragon to Isabel of Castile, in 1469, had brought the greater part of Spain under a single rule, that the Reconquest drew to a triumphant close with the capture of Granada in 1492.

Thus the same year that saw the discovery of America also brought about the reintegration of Christian Spain, which under Ferdinand and Isabel achieved national unity for the first time. An era of immense imperialistic expansion followed, due partly to the conquest of territories in the New World, and partly to the circumstances that linked the fate of Spain—not entirely for the better—to the policies of the House of Hapsburg. With the marriage of Juana la Loca (the mad daughter of Isabel and Ferdinand) to Philip the Handsome of Burgundy, Spain was thrust into the forefront of European power politics, soon winning a military and political hegemony, but at the cost of internal exhaustion. What is of primary interest to us is that the period of maximum political expansion—the sixteenth century—coincided with the period of maximum musical achievement, so that both artistic and material factors contributed to making widespread the musical influence of Spain.

It has become a truism to declare that Spain's musical superiority, after a brief moment of glory, dwindled as rapidly as her political hegemony in Europe. Actually, the "Golden Age" of Spanish music lasted for about two centuries, which is a long span in the history of any art in any nation. It is unquestionably true that throughout the eighteenth and nineteenth centuries Spain takes a secondary place in musical history. Yet this does not mean that the stream of Spanish music was stagnant. Rather was it like a river that flows underground for a certain distance, reappearing presently with all its strength and vitality undiminished.

In tracing the historical development of music there is a tendency to dwell too exclusively on the evolution of forms. Seldom do musical historians look beyond the conventional periphery of the church, the concert hall and the opera house. No doubt the values thus established have their special significance. But they do not represent the sum total of musical experience in its full range of social and human values. This can only be embraced by including every manifestation of the musical instinct among human beings, not only in its aspect of genuine folk music, but also in such hybrid manifestations as urban street music and popular theatrical music. Music in this wider sense, inseparably allied to its natural partner the dance, has always been the life breath of the Spanish people. Spanish music may have ceased to be formally impressive for a time; it has never ceased to be intensely alive.

To be offered a fandango for a fugue, or a seguidilla for a symphony, is an affront only to a pedant. Great composers of every nationality have drawn freely upon the rich store of Spanish folk music. Thus, even during the so-called period of decadence, Spanish music proved its vitality by providing endless transfusions of warm red blood to nourish the music of other countries. Scarlatti, Boccherini, Glinka, Liszt, Bizet, Rimsky-Korsakoff, Lalo, Chabrier, Debussy, Ravel—these are but a few of the composers who have looked across the Pyrenees for inspiration.

The interplay of popular and artistic elements has nowhere been more significantly revealed than in Spanish music. From the *Cantigas* of Alfonso the Wise in the thirteenth century, through the splendid vocal and instrumental literature of the "Golden Age," and up to the music of Manuel de Falla in our own day, this intimate interrelation remains unbroken. The following pages will aim to demonstrate the continuity of this living tradition—a tradition which through Hispanic roots in the New World becomes also a part of that vast American heritage whose immense potentialities for the future we are just beginning to comprehend.

CHAPTER I

Saints, Caliphs, and Kings

THE odor of sanctity is not generally associated with Spanish music. Yet the first Spanish composers of whom we have any definite knowledge were saints. They were the eminent churchmen who organized the Christian liturgy in Spain, writing its hymns and prayers, editing and arranging the religious chants when they did not actually compose the music. In the early Christian Church, music was a tremendously important factor. It was one of the chief means of weaning the people from their pagan customs and ceremonies. The appeal of communal singing was as potent in those times as it is today, and the church made capital of this by encouraging the populace to sing hymns at the religious services and festivals. Even dancing was admitted as an adjunct of worship. Occasionally, however, the indiscriminate practice of singing and dancing in religious ceremonies led to abuses that the church felt bound to condemn. Thus the Third Council of Toledo, in 589, condemned the introduction of "dances and unholy songs" into the festivities for saints' days, and also prohibited the singing of funeral songs by the people— *funebre carmen quod vulgo defunctis cantari solet*—perhaps because they were associated with a heathenish cult to the deity of death practiced in certain sections of Spain.

It was up to the Fathers of the Church to see to it that the emotional and artistic appeal of music should be utilized for the greatest good of the Faith. In Italy, St. Ambrose at Milan and St. Gregory at Rome took the lead in organizing the liturgical chant of the Western Church. In France and Spain the musical liturgies were developed with a certain amount of independence, which eventually disappeared as the central authority of Rome asserted itself within the Western Church, imposing the uniform observance of the Roman rite and the Gregorian chant. Not until 1076, however, were the Hispano-Gothic liturgy and chant officially supplanted by the *Lex Romana.*

The three great centers of musical culture in Visigothic Spain were Seville, Toledo, and Saragossa. Seville owed much of its intellectual prestige to the presence there of two famous brothers, St. Leander and St. Isidore, both of whom were musicians and scholars. Both were, successively, archbishops of Seville. The elder brother, Leander (died in 599), while still an archdeacon, made an extended sojourn in Constantinople, where he lived in the same house with St. Gregory the Great, who was also residing there at the time. Through St. Leander and other Spanish churchmen who visited Constantinople, the Byzantine influence made itself strongly felt in the Hispano-Gothic liturgy and chant. The fact that St. Leander is specifically mentioned as the composer of many pieces—*multa dulci sono composuit*—warrants the assumption that he must have taken a very active part in the musical development of the liturgy.

Isidore of Seville was one of the greatest intellectual figures of the early Middle Ages. Within his mind he stored up all the knowledge that was available at that time and then proceeded to classify it and disseminate it through his writings, which have been called "a literary Noah's ark." His main work is the *Etymologies,* a one-man encyclopedia. In Book III of this work St. Isidore deals with the theory of music, summarizing the doctrines of Cassiodorus (died *c.* 580), which in turn were derived from the ideas of the ancient Greek theorist Aristoxenos. He also gives a descriptive nomenclature of the musical instruments used in his time. In another work, *De Ecclesiasticis Officiis,* he writes about hymns, psalms, and other forms of church music. For about two hundred years Isidore of Seville was regarded as the standard authority on music theory.

THREE SAINTS OF TOLEDO

Notwithstanding the importance of Seville, the influence of Toledo was preponderant in determining the musicoliturgical forms of the Visigothic Church. Toledo was the capital of the Visigothic monarchy and the seat of the famous Councils that promulgated both civil and ecclesiastical laws for the entire kingdom. There a notable trio of musical saints—St. Eugene, St. Ildefonse, and St. Julian—was very active in composing, correcting, and coordinating the chants and hymns of the Hispanic liturgy. St. Ildefonse, a disciple of St. Isidore, was the composer of Masses and Alleluias and is credited with originating "new musical and literary forms in his hymns to the Virgin Mary." St. Julian is mentioned in contemporary accounts as having composed many fine pieces for the church. The role of St. Eugene, who died in 657, is comparable to that of St. Gregory the Great in Rome. And just as the Roman chant became known as "Gregorian chant," so the music of the Hispano-Gothic Church is often spoken of as "Eugenian chant."

It is probable that St. Eugene may also have been the composer of some of the earliest secular songs that have been preserved not only in Spain, but in the whole of Europe. In the so-called Codex of Azagra, a Visigothic manuscript of the ninth or tenth century, there are several secular songs with music, including a lament for the death of King Chindasvinthus, who died in 652, and another for the death of his wife, Queen Reciberga.[1] The words of both songs are known to have been written by St. Eugene, who had received his appointment as archbishop of Toledo from King Chindasvinthus. In view of his musical attainments, it is likely that St. Eugene also wrote the melodies, in which case he is entitled to be regarded as Spain's first-known composer of secular music.

Saragossa, the cultural center of Aragon, could boast, like Seville, of two eminent brothers who took the lead in ecclesiastical affairs there. These were Joannes (d. 631), who wrote both words and music for the songs of the church, and Brauli (d. 651), his successor as archbishop of Saragossa, who had the distinction of being St. Eugene's teacher.[2]

DRAMATIC QUALITY OF THE HISPANIC CHANT

Dramatism and the incorporation of popular elements were the outstanding traits of the Hispano-Gothic liturgical chant. The dramatic quality arose above all from the participation of the people in the prayers and hymns, alternating in their responses with the officiant. The device of *centonization,* that is, the expansion of the regular liturgical phrases by interpolations or additions, was widely practiced by the arrangers of the Hispanic liturgy and this had the effect of giving fuller scope to the dramatic element. For example, the *Pater Noster*—whose Hispanic melody is one of the oldest in Europe, dating perhaps from the fourth century—was sung with an "Amen" interposed by the congregation after each petition of the prayer. The effect must have been not only dramatic, but also highly artistic and profoundly religious.

Another type of religious singing in which the people joined in the response were the *preces* (literally, "prayers"), proper to the Lenten liturgy and the Office of the Dead. The melodies and modulations of these *preces* had to be clear and simple, so that the people might be readily able to sing them, and it is believed that they were to some extent based on folk music. In the *preces* quoted on the opposite page, a supplication to Christ, the people respond at the end of each verse with the words *Deus, miserere* (Lord, have mercy).

The Hispano-Gothic chant reached its apogee in the period from about 630 to 711. In the latter year the Moslem invasion

Example 1.

of Spain took place, causing a profound upheaval in the political, social, and religious organization of the country. It is true that the Spanish Christians who remained in Moslem-occupied territory were allowed comparative freedom of worship,[3] but the organization of the church naturally suffered, and the high standard of singing—which demanded as much as nine years' training for the principal singers—could not be maintained.

THE MOZARABIC PHASE

The Christian Spaniards (as distinct from those who adopted the Moslem faith) living in the occupied area were called "Mozarabes"; hence the term "Mozarabic" came to be applied to their liturgy and chant. The term "Mozarabic" is also often applied to the Hispanic liturgy and chant as a whole, both before and after the period of Moslem domination. As the Spaniards, advancing from the north, gradually reconquered their territory from the Moors and Arabs, the Mozarabic rite and its music had to contend against another hostile factor: the growing authority of the Holy See in Rome, which aspired to impose a uniform liturgy throughout the Western Church. In Portugal the Roman rite had been adopted as early as the sixth century, and in Catalonia it began to be introduced from the beginning of the tenth century. But in the rest of the peninsula the people clung more stubbornly to their native liturgy. Even after the official suppression of the Mozarabic rite in 1076, it persisted in many of the Spanish churches.

Toledo, the great center of Hispanic culture, seems to have been the chief point of resistance to the encroachment of the *Lex Romana.* Toledo was retaken from the Moors in 1086, and Alfonso VI of Castile immediately made the Roman rite obligatory there. According to an old chronicler, the people revolted and it was finally agreed to submit the issue to trial by fire. Copies of the Gregorian and the Mozarabic liturgical books were thrown into the flames. It was the Mozarabic that came out unscathed, while the Roman book was consumed by fire. Yet the king would not abide by the result, for he was under the influence of the monks of Cluny, who urged him to persist in his imposition of the Roman forms. We are also told of an attempt to decide the issue by a combat between two knights, the champion of the Mozarabic rite being the victor. Toledo gained at least a partial victory in this struggle of wills, for by special permission of the Pope six parishes in that city were allowed to retain the Mozarabic rite. After the thirteenth century, however, it died out even there.

Toward the end of the fifteenth century an attempt to revive the Mozarabic chant in Toledo was made by the famous Cardinal Francisco Jiménez de Cisneros. A Mozarabic Missal and Breviary were published under his direction in 1500, and new versions of the chant were inscribed in three *cantorales* dating from about the same time. But in the fifteenth century Spanish musicians could no longer decipher the old neumes in which the Mozarabic melodies were written, so that from the musical aspect the work initiated by Cisneros is arbitrary and inaccurate. Because the Mozarabic neumes do not show the intervals from one note to another, it has not been possible, even in the light of the latest musical research, to decipher the vast majority of the old Mozarabic melodies. Only some twenty-odd melodies that were copied in diastematic notation (showing intervals) in some codices of the eleventh century can now be transcribed. Scholars have also endeavored to "restore" some of the melodies collected by Cisneros, by deleting what appear to be extraneous elements. Excellent results have been obtained, musically, by this method, even though complete historical authenticity cannot be guaranteed. The "restored" melody of the *Gaudete populi*, from which we quote the first part, is truly, in the words of Germán Prado, "one of the most beautiful in all liturgies and a great musical achievement." [4]

Example 2.

MUSIC IN MOSLEM SPAIN

We must now return to the period of the Moslem invasion in order to see how this affected the musical life of Spain. The early followers of Mohammed, observing the precepts of the Koran, shunned both wine and music. But as the caliphs became accustomed to power and luxury, they began to indulge freely in the pleasures of the cup and the lute. In the time of Harun al-Rashid and his successors, large numbers of musicians and dancers were maintained at court. It is recounted that Harun al-Rashid once assembled two thousand female slaves to sing at a feast in his palace.

Similar conditions prevailed in Moslem Spain, whither the vocal and instrumental art of Damascus and Medina was transplanted by the local emirs and caliphs. The Arabs brought numerous musical instruments to Europe, including the lute, which came to occupy such an important role in European instrumental music of the Renaissance. Most famous of the Moslem-Andalusian musicians was Ziryab, who flourished at the court of

Abd ar-Rahman II (822–852) and who is credited with adding
a fifth string to the lute. Ziryab is regarded as the founder of the
Hispano-Arabic school of music, which attained to a very high
stage of artistic development. He had eight sons and two daughters, all of them musicians who helped to diffuse and transmit
his art.

The Arabs had renowned musical theorists, the most famous
being Al-Farabi (872–950), a native of Persia. Known as a
master of science and philosophy, he was also a practical musician,
and his writings on music, translated into Latin by medieval
theorists such as Gerard of Cremona, who was active at Toledo
in the twelfth century, exerted a far-reaching influence in Europe.
Al-Farabi's treatise on music, *Kitab al-musiqi al-kabir*, is considered by Farmer "probably the greatest work on music written
up to his day." The writings of Al-Farabi and other Arabic scholars were assiduously studied by the Hispanic school of philosophy
that flourished in Toledo in the twelfth and thirteenth centuries.

It is known that Spanish kings and nobles employed Moorish-
Arabian musicians in their palaces. Some of the miniatures of the
Cantigas of Alfonso the Wise of Castile, for example, show Moorish musicians playing various instruments together with Spanish
musicians. It is unwise, however, to conclude from such evidence,
as Ribera and others have done, that peninsular music was entirely dominated by Moorish-Arabian influences.[5]

THE *CANTIGAS* OF ALFONSO THE WISE

Alfonso X of Castile and León (1221–1284) was in many ways
an unwise king, for he got his subjects into trouble through his
inordinate ambition, and he often neglected affairs of state to indulge his passion for the arts and sciences. Yet he acquired such
extensive knowledge, and made such impressive contributions to
the literary and artistic culture of his country, that he has gone
down to posterity with the sobriquet of "el Sabio." It is no longer
believed that he wrote either the text or the music of all the
Cantigas de Santa María, the collection of over four hundred

songs in praise of the Virgin Mary with which his name is associated.[6] He gathered together at his court a notable group of writers, poets, and musicians, among them Moorish instrumentalists from Andalusia and troubadours and jongleurs from France, and guided them in the task of composing the *Cantigas*, which for the most part simply embodied in poetic form many traditional elements of the medieval Marianic literature. Narratives of miracles performed by the Blessed Virgin alternate with hymns of praise and thanksgiving, and some of the songs also deal with events in the life of the royal family.

One of the miniatures which accompany the manuscript of the *Cantigas* is evidently meant to portray the manner in which the songs were composed. The king sits in the center, directing the entire proceeding. On the extreme right and left are four instrumentalists. To the left of the king are four scribes, all obviously intent upon following the monarch's instructions, and one of them is in the act of writing. On the other side of the king is a group of troubadours. From this it would appear that the *Cantigas* were "tried out" as they were composed, perfection being achieved by actual performance.

Another miniature shows how the *Cantigas* were performed by the people, for whom they were written. The performers face a statue of the Virgin and Child, with St. Joseph kneeling at Her feet. Six musicians, sitting on a bench, play on various instruments, and another, standing behind them, plays the viol. Next to him, three persons are dancing, holding hands in a circle—one more indication of the importance that dancing has always had in popular religious worship in Spain. One curious circumstance is that no one is visibly singing in this picture. Have we to do, then, with a purely instrumental performance? That is not impossible. It is more likely, however, that those who dance also sing at the same time.

Another miniature of the *Cantigas* depicts a couple dancing while other men and women kneel in prayer or hold candles before an image of the Virgin and Child. Still another miniature shows a jongleur playing a viol in church while kneeling before a similar image.

The *Cantigas* are written in the Portuguese-Galician language which was then the chief medium for lyrical poetry in the peninsula (it was only gradually that the Castilian language acquired literary and political supremacy in Spain). Many of them consist of four-line stanzas (rhyme scheme, BBBA), with a refrain in the form of a rhymed couplet (AA) coming before and after each stanza. Others have a four-line refrain (ABAB) and a six-line stanza with alternating rhymes. In their musical structure most of the *Cantigas* follow the melodic pattern of the French *virelai* and *rondeau*, similar to the metrical forms of the medieval Latin song known as *conductus*, of which specimens are found in Spain (Ripoll) about a century before the time of the *Cantigas*.

The following *Cantiga* on the Resurrection of Christ has the musical structure of the *virelai*, consisting of three different melodic phrases arranged in this order: AB CCAB(AB). It is remarkable for its joyous expression of the spirit of Easter.

Example 3.

The *Cantigas de Santa María*, beautifully and clearly written in mensural notation, constitute one of the greatest monuments

of nonliturgical monodic music that have come down to us from
the Middle Ages. When a complete and accurate modern transcription is made available, the full richness and beauty of the
Cantigas will become apparent.[7]

It is interesting to note that one of the *Cantigas de Santa María*
(*Madre de Deus, ora por nòs*) recalls the melody of the *Song
of the Sibyl*, which in its earliest written version dates from about
the middle of the tenth century and which is possibly of Mozarabic origin. The *Song of the Sibyl* is a prophecy consisting of an
acrostic on the Greek words meaning "Jesus Christ, Son of God,
Saviour," and it was presented as a brief dramatic scene. Many
versions are extant in Spanish, French, and Italian manuscripts
from the eleventh to the sixteenth centuries (numerous musical
settings are reproduced by Anglès in his *La Música a Catalunya
fins al segle XIII*). Until very recently the *Song of the Sibyl*
still survived as a semidramatic religious ceremony in Mallorca.

The miniatures that adorn the text of the *Cantigas* are extremely interesting for the study of medieval musical instruments
in Europe. More than seventy musicians are depicted playing
various instruments, ranging from the lute to the hurdy-gurdy.
In our illustration (Plate I) are shown the lute, the triangular
psaltery (of which there were also rectangular forms),[8] the viol
(played with a bow), and two kinds of guitar, the *guitarra latina*
(with incurved sides) and the *guitarra morisca* (oval shaped).
Other miniatures depict the *rebec* (derived from the Arabian
rebab), a diminutive two-stringed fiddle that eventually became
the "kit" or *pochette* which dancing masters carried around in
their pockets; sets of bells struck with hammers; transverse flutes
and other kinds of wind instruments with finger holes; straight
and curved trumpets and horns; harps, bagpipes (with human
and animal heads carved on them), castanets, and the "pipe and
tabor," played by a single musician exactly as may be seen in Spain
at the present day (*cf.* Plate XIV). With one hand the musician
holds the pipe to his mouth, and with the other he beats the
diminutive drum which is attached to his left elbow.

The Portuguese-Galician lyrical school flourished with great vigor, producing a notable body of troubadour love poems in the vernacular. The only group of such songs that has been preserved with decipherable musical notation is the *Siete Canciones de Amor* (*Seven Songs of Love*), dating from the first half of the thirteenth century and attributed to a jongleur named Martim Codax.[9] These love songs reveal a vein of charming lyricism, evoking the sea and the mountains of the region near Vigo. But, unfortunately, a completely satisfactory transcription of the music has not yet been achieved (only six of the songs, incidentally, exist with notation).

PILGRIM SONGS

Galicia, the center of this rich lyrical movement, was also important as the site of the famous shrine of Santiago de Compostela, named after the patron saint of Spain, St. James the Elder, who was supposed to have first preached the Gospel in the peninsula. To this shrine pilgrims came in a steady stream from all over Europe, contributing in no small measure to the interchange of culture between Spain and the rest of the Continent. The *Codex Calixtinus*, dating from the twelfth century and preserved in the Cathedral of Santiago de Compostela, contains the text and music of Latin hymns that were sung by the pilgrims to this holy city. This codex is one of the earliest sources for European polyphony.

There was another Spanish shrine that could rival the fame of Compostela. This was the monastery of Montserrat, near Barcelona, picturesquely situated at the summit of a rocky hill and built in a strikingly beautiful architectural style. It has been claimed that this was the legendary site of the Holy Grail, the "Montsalvat" of which the troubadours and minnesingers wrote and sang. Certain it is that in the fourteenth century it was eagerly visited by pious bands of pilgrims who came particularly to do honor to Our Lady of Montserrat and who found there not only religious edification, but also the wholesome joys of music and communal dancing. To refresh themselves after their night-long vigil at the shrine, the pilgrims sang and danced in the square before the church, using for this purpose songs especially composed or arranged for them by the monks.

Ten of these pilgrim songs (*Cants dels Romeus*) from Montserrat have been preserved, with music, in the so-called *Llibre Vermell*, a codex from the fourteenth century. The texts are partly in Latin and partly in Catalan (both erudite and popular forms), and all but one are dedicated to the Virgin Mary. The first three songs are in the form of canons for two or three voices —*caça de duobus vel tribus*—these being among the earliest canons known in European music. The beautiful hymn *Stella splendens in monte* is set for two voices, as is also the *Imprerayntz de la ciutat ioyosa*, while the last song is for three voices.

From a popular viewpoint, special interest attaches to the song entitled *Ballada dels goytxs de nostra dona en vulgar cathalan, a ball redon*, that is, "Ballad of the Joys of Our Lady," written in the Catalan vernacular and in the style of a "round dance." The *goytxs* (modern form, *goigs*), celebrating the seven joys of Our Lady, are a type of Catalan folk song that has persisted to the present day. And *ball redon* (modern form, *ball rodó*) is the term for the communal choral dances, in which the participants hold hands and move around in a circle, akin to the modern Catalan *sardana* (*cf*. Chapter XVI). In addition, the term *ballada* as used here signifies a religious dance with singing, such as the pilgrims were encouraged to practice in seemly fashion under the eyes of the Blessed Virgin. This antiphonal *Ballada* is in two sections, the first, with Catalan text, recounting the seven joys, and the second, with Latin text, reciting the words of the *Ave Maria* (Hail Mary, full of grace, the Lord is with thee). It is in the first part above all that the unmistakable popular flavor of this ingratiating melody may be fully appreciated (see Example 4).

All the evidence points to the conclusion that these pilgrim songs were originally folk tunes to which sacred words were added by the monks of Montserrat. Some of these tunes were so

Example 4.

A - ve Ma-ri-a gra-ci-a ple-na do-mi-nus te-cum vir- go se-re-na

deeply rooted in the folk tradition that they persisted in the popular memory for many generations. More than two hundred years later, Francisco Salinas (*cf.* Chapter IV) noted down in Castile a tune which is practically identical with that of the *Polorum Regina* from the *Llibre Vermell*. No wonder it survived, for it is a fine tune.

Example 5.

Po - lo-rum re-gi-na om-ni-um no — — — stra
stel-la ma-tu - ti-na de - le sce - le - - ra

We come now to the only song in this collection that is not addressed to the Virgin. This is the Latin song *Ad mortem festinamus* (*Toward Death We Hasten*), whose gruesome message is emphasized by a realistic drawing of a skeleton in an open coffin, inserted by the monkish scribe in the *Llibre Vermell*. This is a musical version of the Dance of Death, which served as the theme for so many artistic and literary productions of the Middle Ages. Especially after the devastating plague of 1347–1348, the image of Death in a triumphant *danse macabre* took hold of men's minds. It is not known exactly when or where the idea of the Dance of Death originated, but recently a Latin version of the Dance of Death (without music) was discovered in a Visi-

Musicians of the Cantigas (*Thirteenth Century*)

gothic codex of the eleventh century, which is much older than any other known source for this text.

There is reason for believing that the musical Dance of Death in the *Llibre Vermell* did not originate at Montserrat, but was based on earlier versions known elsewhere in Spain. In any case, it is the earliest known musical treatment of the subject and, as such, has great cultural and historical interest.

Religious pilgrimages were by no means the only occasions in which music was prominently employed in medieval Spain. It was an indispensable adjunct to weddings, coronations, public festivities, and official ceremonies of every kind. The old chronicles contain numerous references to music at the Spanish courts (Spain at that time was divided into several kingdoms), though little of the actual music has survived. In the *Coronación de Reyes y Ceremonías que en ella se guardan* (*Coronation of Kings and the Ceremonies Observed Therein*), written by Ramón, Bishop of Osma, there is a description of the coronation of Alfonso VIII of Castile (twelfth century) which recounts that in the midst of the celebration of the Mass, after the Epistle and the Alleluia, *vengan donçellas que sepan bien cantar, et canten una cantiga* (there came forth damsels skilled in singing, and sang a *cantiga*). An illustration in the chronicle shows that the *donçellas*, of whom there are five, not only sang, but also accompanied themselves on instruments. To the right of the picture one of the damsels plays a viol, while at the left there are two with arms outstretched as though they were sounding a pair of cymbals.

Women took a very active part in the musical life of medieval Spain. The feminine counterpart of the *juglar* was the *juglaresa* or *juglara*, who sang, played, and danced for the entertainment of kings and nobles, and also, on a lower scale, for the amusement of the populace. In the Galician-Portuguese *Cancioneiro da Ajuda* (*cf.* Chapter XVIII), which together with the *Cantigas* of Alfonso the Wise is one of the chief pictorial sources for musical instruments of the peninsula in medieval times, twelve out of sixteen miniatures show women as well as men participating in the musical performance. Usually these *juglaresas* appear as singers, often accompanying themselves with castanets or tambourine.

THE *JUGLARES*

The *juglar* (Spanish equivalent of the French jongleur) was the chief propagator of secular music in the Middle Ages. He was the interpreter, while the troubadour, though he might sing his own songs on occasion, was primarily the creative artist, the composer. In a general sense, the term *juglar* was applied to all those who earned a livelihood by entertaining in public, whether with music and poetry, or with mummery and tumbling. Some of them were just "on the road," while others were retained by wealthy patrons. The former wore motley costumes, but the latter often had rich and elegant liveries. The musicians who played for the wedding of the Condestable Miguel Lucas in 1461 had doublets of blue velvet over which they wore green Florentine cloth, with silver necklaces.

The Provençal troubadour Giraut Riquier, who spent some time at the court of Alfonso the Wise, addressed to that monarch, in 1274, a *Suplicatió al rey de Castela per lo noms dels juglars* (*Supplication to the King of Castile Regarding the Names of Jongleurs*), in which he deplored the indiscriminate application of the term "juglar" to all sorts of public entertainers, even of the lowest and most disreputable kind, and made a plea for a more judicious classification. The reply to this petition was embodied in the *Declaratió del senhor rey N'Amfós de Castela* (1275) which, though written by Giraut, was undoubtedly based on conversations with the king. This "Declaration" points out that in Spain, unlike France, such a classification was already established: those who play musical instruments are called *juglares;* those who entertain with pantomime and mimicry are called *remedadores;* the troubadours who go from court to court are known as *segrieres;* and, finally, those without skill or manners, who perform in the streets with crude recitations or tricks, are disparagingly called *cazurros*.

There was a class of *juglar* who specialized in reciting or singing the *cantares de gesta*, the epic poems narrating heroic deeds and famous events. The prolonged struggle against the Moslems made it necessary to maintain the martial spirit at a high pitch; hence the interpreters of the *cantares de gesta* were esteemed above all others. The Archpriest Almela, in his *Compendio Historial*, written in 1479 but referring to an earlier period, records:

The kings and princes of those olden times, esteeming the very great splendor of the deeds and acts of war, commanded to have read to them the chronicles of famous deeds of chivalry accomplished by their ancestors; . . . and they also commanded the *menestrilles* and *juglares* to appear with their lutes and viols and other instruments so that they might play and sing the ballads that were composed about the famous deeds of knights.[10]

Alfonso the Wise of Castile was but one of many Spanish kings who held music in special honor at their courts. In the fourteenth century the outstanding musical monarch was probably Pedro IV the Ceremonious of Aragon (1335–1387), who had at his court singers and instrumentalists from England (famed for its harpists), France, Flanders, Italy, and Germany. He also employed Moorish musicians. Higini Anglès has found the names of some six hundred foreign jongleurs, cantors (church singers), and organists who were active in Aragon and Catalonia during the fourteenth century.

From the foregoing it should be clear that throughout the Middle Ages Spain was in the main stream of European musical activity, receiving enrichment from many sources, both Eastern and Western, and at the same time making distinctive contributions that rank with the best produced in that period.

CHAPTER II

Secular Songs of the Renaissance

THE chronicler Gonzalo Fernández de Oviedo, in his *Oficios de la Casa Real,* writes about the musical inclinations of the youthful Prince Juan, only son of Isabel and Ferdinand, in these terms:

This prince was by nature inclined toward music, and he understood it very well, although his voice was not always equal to the demands he wished to make on it. Every afternoon, especially during the summer, he assembled in his palace five or six young singers, together with his *maestro de capilla* Juan de Anchieta, all gifted with fine voices, and joined them in singing for two hours or longer. He sang the tenor part and was well acquainted with the resources of the art. In his chamber he had a clavi-organ, several organs, clavicembalos, clavichords, *vihuelas de mano* and *vihuelas de arco* [guitars and viols] and flutes, and he was able to play all these instruments.[1]

What songs did Prince Juan and his musicians sing to while away those long summer afternoons? The time, let it be recalled, was the closing decade of the fifteenth century, a few years after the completion of the Reconquest and the discovery of America. The Renaissance was in full florescence, the "Revival of Learning" had spread from Italy to Spain, and men turned eagerly toward the cultivation of new literary, artistic, and musical forms. It was largely a question of pouring new wine into old bottles, because, in Spain at least, the rich folk vein that permeated both secular and sacred music throughout the Middle Ages continued to invigorate the vocal and instrumental art forms that reached their highest development during the Renaissance.

The pastoral or amorous lyric stemming from the Galician-Portuguese school, and the ballads that sprang from the old *cantares de gesta*, remained the basic prototypes of the song literature to which so many eminent poets and musicians of the fifteenth and sixteenth centuries contributed. Often the poet and the musician were one and the same person, for poetry and music seemed inseparably allied at that time. The spirit of the medieval troubadours, who set their own poems to music, appears to have lingered longer in Spain than elsewhere.

JUAN DEL ENCINA

The most distinguished of the poet-musicians who flourished in the reign of Ferdinand and Isabel was Juan del Encina (1468–1529), the creator of the Spanish theater and the composer of songs revealing great harmonic beauty, power, and variety of expression. A native of Salamanca, he was the seventh son of a shoemaker named Fermoselle—he probably changed his name for poetic reasons—and was educated at Salamanca University. He received his musical training as a chorister at Salamanca Cathedral under Fernando de Torrijos, whom he later aspired to succeed as choirmaster, the position being given instead to another poet-musician of Salamanca, Lucas Fernández.[2]

At the university, where he studied law, philosophy, and theology, Encina enjoyed the protection of the chancellor, Don Gutierre de Toledo, a member of the powerful Alba family, through whose influence he was able to enter the household of Don Fadrique de Toledo, second Duke of Alba, as a sort of musico-poetic master of ceremonies. For the entertainment of his patrons and their noble or royal guests, Encina wrote a series of *Representaciones* (pastoral playlets) that are generally considered the first definite starting point of the Spanish secular drama. The first of these was performed on Christmas Eve, 1492, the last in 1498. In the latter year, or soon after, Encina, who had taken minor orders in 1490, went to Rome, where he was received with marked favor by Pope Alexander VI.[3] He continued to enjoy the favor of the two succeeding popes, Julius II and Leo X, obtaining from the latter a lucrative ecclesiastical post. From 1509 he was archdeacon and canon of Málaga, and ten years later was appointed prior of León. Before taking up his duties there, however, he made a pilgrimage to Jerusalem, where he was finally ordained a priest, celebrating his first Mass on Mount Zion.

Encina himself tells us that most of his compositions (both poems and songs) were written between his fourteenth and twenty-fifth years, which would make them fall within the period of his activities at Salamanca. The palace of the Dukes of Alba was not in Salamanca itself, but in the near-by village of Alba de Tormes. This residence, and the manner of life within it, was symbolic of the transitional phase through which Spain was then passing. Outwardly, the palace, with its huge circular donjon in the center flanked by six towers and its thick bastioned walls, had the aspect of a fortress—one of those fortified castles that gave Castile its name. Within, however, all was luxury, with gilded ceilings and elaborate art work, spacious galleries and sumptuous chambers. The Duke and Duchess had their private chapel, where religious eclogues by Encina were performed, and undoubtedly they held informal singing sessions such as those that Prince Juan delighted in. Prince Juan himself—whose untimely death in 1497, at the age of twenty-one, was a bitter blow from which Isabel of Castile never recovered—was among those who attended performances of Encina's plays at the Alba palace. Encina wrote an elegiac "tragedia trovada" on the death of this prince, and it is believed that his gravely beautiful song *A tal pérdida tan triste* (*For So Sad a Loss*) was inspired by the same sad event.

THE CANCIONERO DE PALACIO

The most extensive collection of court songs belonging to this period, the so-called *Cancionero de Palacio,* remained unknown to the world for nearly four hundred years, until it was discovered by the composer-musicologist Barbieri in the Madrid National Library in 1870.[4] This collection originally contained some five hundred and fifty songs, of which only four hundred and sixty remain today. They were copied at different periods, but all seem to belong to the last third of the fifteenth century and the first quarter of the sixteenth. The index shows that Encina was originally represented by seventy-five songs, but seven of these are now missing. Nevertheless, with the remaining sixty-eight songs, Encina has three times as many as any other single composer in the *Cancionero,* so that numerically, as well as artistically, he dominates the collection. This fact led Barbieri to conjecture that the *Cancionero* may have been compiled for the use of the Duke of Alba's household.

Several of the most eminent Spanish composers of that period, in addition to Encina, are represented in the *Cancionero de Palacio.* Among them are Juan de Anchieta—already mentioned as music master to Prince Juan—Lope de Baena, Juan Escobar, Alonso de Mondéjar, Francisco Peñalosa, Juan Ponce, Antonio de Ribera, and Francisco de la Torre. Others, again, are mentioned only by their surnames and remain rather mysterious. There is, for instance, a certain "Millán," with twenty-three compositions, of whom nothing is known; he is not to be confused with the celebrated poet-musician of Valencia, Luis Milán. Many of the songs are anonymous, and these are often the oldest.

In the *Cancionero* are songs of all kinds: amatory, pastoral, chivalresque, historical, religious, political, picaresque, humorous—and indecent. Most of the texts are in Castilian, but a few are in Italian, French, Portuguese, and Basque. The majority of songs are written for three and four voices. By far the greater number of compositions are called *villancicos.*

The term "villancico" means literally a rustic song, being derived from *villano*, a villager or commoner. Probably the term —and much of the form also—may have been adopted into Castilian usage from the Galician-Portuguese *cantigas de vilhao*, the dance songs used by the peasants in their village festivities. The name was also applied to the popular religious songs that stemmed from the tradition of the *Cantigas de Santa María*.[5] A poetic treatise of the late sixteenth century [6] defines villancico as "a kind of verse that is composed solely to be sung. . . . In the villancicos there is a head and feet; the head is a verse of two, or three or four lines . . . which it is customary to repeat after the feet. The feet are a stanza of six lines, being a sort of variant of the theme contained in the head." The real popular element in the literary villancico was the refrain or "head" (so called because it came at the head of the composition), and the literary form developed from the expansion or elaboration of this popular nucleus. Actually, there was considerable freedom and variety in the structure of the villancico, but its basic pattern rested on the device of the initial refrain and its guiding principle was the artistic treatment of traditional elements.

As a musical form, the villancico was to Spain what the madrigal was to the rest of Europe. As a secular part song it shared some of the polyphonic elements of the madrigal, but with less reliance upon contrapuntal and imitative writing. Though many of the composers of villancicos were masters of the contrapuntal style (as proved by their religious compositions),[7] all willful display of artifice was avoided in their song writing. They aimed rather at achieving the greatest expressiveness within the utmost simplicity of style. They sought always to make the music enhance and emphasize the meaning of the words. The poet that lurked in every musician resented any subordination of the text to a purely musical development. The tendency, therefore, was toward a homophonic and syllabic style of song writing, in which each vertical "block" of notes (what we would now call a chord) generally corresponds to one syllable of the text, melismatic prolongations being reserved for the cadences. The effect is much more "harmonic," in the modern sense, than most of the part writing of that time. The rhythmic element is also emphasized—and here one should bear in mind that the primitive *cantiga de vilhao* was always associated with dancing.

The following *villancico amatorio* by Encina, *Pues que jamás olvidaros* (*Whereas My Heart Can Ne'er Forget Thee*), from which we quote the first two lines, is typical of his more serious moods. It belongs definitely to the courtly school of gallant poetry, yet it has that grave and somewhat melancholy undertone that is characteristic of the Castilian temperament.[8]

Example 6.

In contrasting mood is the villancico *Romerico, tú que vienes*, which belongs in the popular tradition, being similar to Spanish folk tunes that may be found at the present day. In it the poet asks his newly arrived friend, Romerico, to give him news of his beloved.[9]

Example 7.

Encina was fond of stressing these contrasts, as when he recommends that the lively villancico *Levanta, Pascual, levanta,* in
which the poet urges his companion to mount in haste and ride
to Granada for news has gone forth that the city is taken, should
be sung immediately after the expressive ballad *Qué es de tí,
desconsolado,* which laments the fate of the Moorish king who
has lost Granada. The fact that Encina himself was present at the
siege of Granada indicates how close the Spanish poets and musicians of the Renaissance still were to the events out of which
they fashioned their songs and ballads.

The musical phrasing of the villancico always follows closely
the form of the verse, contributing to a very clear and logical
structure, divided into well-defined melodic periods. The melodies are smooth and flowing, without wide leaps, and give an
impression of absolute naturalness. At the point corresponding
to the poetic caesura there is either a semicadence or a full close.
Analogies with liturgical chant may be found in some of the
melodies.[10]

MUSICAL "SALADS" AND MADRIGALS

One also finds the terms *villanesca, endecha, estrambote* and
ensalada applied to the part songs of this period. It would be difficult to make a rigid distinction between the villancico and the
villanesca, but the latter tended to approximate the style of the
madrigal, being more artistically developed, with more rhetori-
cal emphasis, a freer melodic line, and frequent wide intervals
from one note to another, as may be seen in the following frag-
ment of a *villanesca* by Pedro Guerrero, one of the chief cultivators of this form.

Example 8.

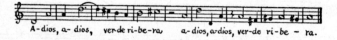

A-dios, a-dios, ver-de ri-be-ra,   a-dios, a-dios, ver-de ri-be - ra.

The *endecha* was a song lamenting the death of a friend or protector. The *estrambote* (from *estrambótico*, meaning odd, queer) was similar in form to the villancico, but generally had more bombastic and extravagant words, sometimes in a mixture of Spanish and Italian. The Italian *frottole* from Petrucci's collections included in the *Cancionero de Palacio* are called *estrambotes*.[11]

The humorous conception of a polyglot extravaganza reached its typical expression in the *ensaladas* (literally, "salads"), burlesque madrigals in which several popular tunes, with their corresponding texts, were contrapuntally combined. A typical example is the *ensalada* by Peñalosa in Barbieri's *Cancionero* (No. 438), for six voices, two of which sing the same text while the other four sing the words of as many different popular songs, including one in Latin. Some of the best-known *ensaladas* were written by Mateo Flecha and his nephew of the same name. A collection of their works in this form was published at Prague in 1581.

The term "madrigal" was used very little in Spain. It appears only in a few collections after the middle of the sixteenth century, mostly printed abroad and revealing foreign influences. The outstanding Spanish composer of madrigals was Pedro Vila, a native of Catalonia who in 1561 published at Barcelona a collection entitled *Odarum quas vulgo madrigales appellamus*, with texts in Castilian, Catalan, Italian, and French. Another madrigal collection printed in Barcelona was that of Joan Brudieu, who, though of French extraction, spent most of his life in Catalonia, being choirmaster at the Cathedral of Urgell. Other Spanish madrigalists were Pedro Ruimonte, Sebastián Raval, and Pedro Valenzola. A book of madrigals by Mateo Flecha the younger was printed at Venice in 1568.

Encina's most notable successor in the cultivation of the villancico was Juan Vázquez, a native of Badajoz, whose melodic vein is of the utmost vigor and freshness. He published two collections, the first at Osuna in 1551, the second at Seville in 1560, for three to five voices. Here we find a truly exquisite blending of popular and artistic elements. Like Encina and so many of the other Spanish composers, Vázquez can strike a note of grave yet poignant emotion, as he does in *Dúelete de mi, señora* (*Have Pity on Me, Lady*). To a lover's lament such as *Vos me matastes, niña en cabello* (*Thou Hast Slain Me, Maiden Fair*), he gives an intensity of expression surpassing anything in the contemporary song literature. In the words of Curt Sachs, "One cannot imagine a more moving or eloquent lamentation." [12] A charming song by Vázquez, whose text and melody proclaim a genuine folk inspiration, is *De los álamos vengo, madre* (*From the Poplars I Come, Mother*), which Manuel de Falla used in the first movement of his Harpsichord Concerto.[13]

The villancico continued to be cultivated as an art form during the seventeenth century, the representative collection of that period being the *Cancionero de Sablonara* (seventy-eight songs), originally compiled by Claudio de Sablonara and published in a modern edition by J. Aroca. The foremost composers in this collection are Mateo Romero and Juan Blas, whose work is discussed in Chapter VI.

THE BALLADS

Next to the villancico, the most widely used song form in Spain during the Renaissance was the *romance* (ballad), derived from the old epics of chivalry. The oldest peninsular ballads that have survived are those of the Carolingian cycle. The *romance* seems to have acquired an independent existence in the fourteenth century, at first as a popular form handed down by oral tradition (a tradition which has persisted to the present day), later taken up by cultivated poets and musicians. The first printed ballads appear in the *Cancionero General* compiled by Hernando del Castillo, of which the earliest edition was printed at Valencia in 1511. Of the thirty-seven ballads included there, nineteen are by known authors (among them Juan del Encina), while the rest are traditional. In the latter group are such famous ballads as *Conde Claros, Durandarte,* and *Triste Estaba el Caballero,* all of which acquired great musical importance in the sixteenth century through settings by eminent composers. The tune of *Conde Claros* became a favorite theme for instrumental variations.

The first collection devoted specifically to ballads was the *Silva de Romances* (Saragossa, 1550) compiled by Estebán de Nájera, in which is found the ballad of Don Gayferos and Melisendra, whose story Maese Pedro enacted for Don Quixote with his puppet show (*cf.* Chapter XII). In the early seventeenth century appeared the *Romancero General,* so that before long over a thousand ballads were available in print.

It was not customary to print music with these *Romanceros,* though the ballads (at least all the traditional ones) were definitely intended to be sung. Musical settings are to be found in collections such as the *Cancionero de Palacio,* and in the tablature books that began to be printed from 1535. The traditional melodies of the ballads consisted generally of a single period of thirty-two essential notes corresponding to the thirty-two syllables of the ballad stanza (two pairs of octosyllabic couplets with assonance rhyme). In some of the older ballads there was only one semiperiod of sixteen notes; this is the most primitive and archaic type. In either case the melody was repeated throughout the entire length of the ballad, which might be well over a thousand lines. When cultivated musicians took up the ballad, they condensed it and varied the musical treatment to secure a more artistic effect. An adept at this sort of transformation was Luis Milán, as may be seen from his setting of *Durandarte, Durandarte,* which is a perfectly organized art song in every sense of the term.

The ballads enjoyed an enormous popularity with all classes of society in Spain. The courtier in his palace and the peasant in his hut derived from them an equal delight. In the pages of Cervantes's immortal novel we find ample testimony of the extent to which these old ballads were part of the people's daily life.

Characters often carry on a conversation by quoting appropriate lines from familiar ballads (compare the scene between Don Quixote and the Innkeeper in Chapter II of Part I). When Don Quixote and Sancho Panza were approaching El Toboso, they encountered a peasant who, as he went to labor in the fields, sang the ballad that begins

> *Mala la hubistes, franceses,*
> *En esa de Roncesvalles.*

Don Quixote interprets this as a good omen, but Sancho remarks that the fellow might just as well be singing "the ballad of Calainos" for all the difference it would make to him.

This ballad, *Ya cabalga Calainos* (*Calainos Is Riding Forth*), is found in Valderrábano's tablature book, *Silva de Sirenas* (1547), where it is described as a *romance viejo* (old ballad), this term being applied to the ballads of traditional origin as distinguished from the ones written by known authors. The tune of this ballad, reproduced below, also proclaims its ancient origin. The liturgical influence is very pronounced (Albert Geiger compares it to the opening phrase of the Responsorium for Good Friday, *Caligaverunt oculi mei*).

Example 9.

Ya ca - val - ga Ca — la - y — nos a la som-bra de una ver-de oli - va, sin po - ner pié en el e - stri - bo.

The oldest Spanish ballad preserved with written notation is *Lealtad, O Lealtad* (*Loyalty, O Loyalty!*), included in a copy of the *Crónica del Condestable Miguel Lucas de Iranza* made in 1466. Barbieri reproduces it in the Appendix to his *Cancionero*, and so does Mitjana.[14] The ballad *Alburquerque, Alburquerque*

(Barbieri, No. 321) refers to a historical event of the year 1430 and may therefore be an older composition than the foregoing, though its actual source is later (manuscript from end of the fifteenth century).

Sometimes refrains are interpolated in the *romances*, as is the case with that famous ballad of the taking of Alhama, with its recurring lament, *Ay de mí, Alhama!* (*Woe Is Me, Alhama!*). Sometimes, following the villancico pattern, the refrain appears at the beginning and is repeated after each stanza. An example of this type is the ballad on the death of the prince Don Alfonso of Portugal (1491), which begins with the lamenting refrain *Ay, ay, ay, ay! que fuertes penas!* [15] The melody is thoroughly Spanish in its inflections, bearing some similarity to the *Song of the Sibyl* and the *Plaint of the Virgin* in the Mystery of Elche.

EMERGENCE OF THE SOLO SONG

Villancicos and *romances* composed or arranged as solo songs with instrumental accompaniment are found in the Spanish tablature books of the sixteenth century. It will readily be seen that the homophonic type of part song cultivated by the early Spanish composers lent itself admirably to instrumental setting, particularly for instruments such as the guitar and the lute, in which chord successions, alternating with single plucked notes, could blend with, and give support to, the vocal line. This type of accompanied monody, which the Spaniards handled with supreme mastery from the early decades of the sixteenth century, anticipated in its essential traits the "new style of music" sponsored by the Florentine *camerata* toward the end of that century. Many of the villancicos of Vázquez and the *ensaladas* of Flecha were transcribed as solo songs in the tablature books.

A master of the villancico who deserves to rank with Encina and Vázquez is Luis Milán, of whom we shall have more to say in the next chapter. The six Portuguese villancicos included in his book *El Maestro* (1535) are models of their kind. One feature of Milán's accompaniments deserves special mention. This is his practice of giving two versions of each song, one in slow tempo with a purely chordal accompaniment, and one in faster tempo with ornamental scale passages. As indicated by his own comment in the text, the slow version was to permit the singer to embellish the vocal part, which he calls *hacer garganta* (literally, "use the throat"). That this was a common practice at that time is indicated by various contemporary documents, among which we may cite Vicente Espinel's celebrated picaresque novel *Marcos de Obregón*, in which there are numerous references to music.[16] Describing an impromptu concert, Espinel writes:

> The tenor, whose name was Francisco de la Pena, began to make some very excellent vocal passages [*hacer excelentísimos pasajes de garganta*], which, as the accompaniment was slow, there was time for him to do.

This improvisational feature presents a problem to the modern interpreter or editor of these songs. Some have used their own judgment in inserting the embellishments, while others have ignored this aspect entirely.

Another question that arises with regard to the interpretation of the solo songs is whether the vocal part should also be included in the accompaniment. In the tablature (which is described in the next chapter) the notes to be sung usually appear in red, the others in black. Claiming that "it would have been a positive insult to a good singer to play his part for him on an instrument," J. B. Trend maintains that the voice part was not played on the accompanying instrument. Weighing the purely musical evidence, other authorities, notably Jesús Bal, who studied the problem with special reference to Fuenllana's *Orphénica Lyra*, conclude that the red notes should be played instrumentally as well as sung. We incline to share the latter view.

The interest of these early Spanish songs is threefold: musical, literary, and human. They owe no small part of their charm to the qualities of Castilian poetry, which both in its popular and erudite forms attained in the fifteenth and sixteenth centuries a

The Second Duke and Duchess of Alba, Patrons of Juan del Encina

From *La Música en la Casa de Alba*

variety and power of expression that has never been surpassed. From the sixteenth century onward, Spanish musicians began to set to music the poems of the finest contemporary writers, such as Boscán, Garcilaso, and Lope de Vega. A whole volume of contemporary settings of poems by Lope de Vega was issued at Madrid in 1935 on the occasion of the tercentenary of that poet's death. The setting of Boscán's *Claros y Frescos Rios* (*Rivers Fresh and Clear*) found in Mudarra's tablature book is truly a beautiful song. Mudarra also includes a setting of the *Coplas* of Jorge Manrique (the famous elegy which Longfellow translated into English), and of poems by Virgil, Ovid, and Petrarch. Before the middle of the sixteenth century, the solo art song with instrumental accompaniment had achieved surprising maturity in Spain.

From the human angle, we get a more vivid and intimate picture of Spanish life from these songs than from many ponderous tomes of history. Here are the Spanish people as they lived and loved, happily or unhappily, always intensely human. The girls make trysts with their lovers at the site of the popular pilgrimages (*romerías*) and naïvely confess their love affairs and heartaches to their mothers, as in that widely popular villancico *Aquel caballero, madre*, in which a young girl tells her mother that there is a *caballero* who is dying for love of her, and that she, too, is dying of the same pain:

> *También siento sus dolores,*
> *Porque de los mismos muero yo.*

Here a girl who cannot find a husband laments that she must bathe her face with sorrows and longings instead of with lemon-water as married women do. And there is the beautiful lady unhappily married, *La bella malmaridada*, who yet will not allow the gallant *caballero* to console her. This was one of the lyrical themes that was taken over into the ballad and became so popular as a subject for poetic and musical variations that a malicious writer declared the poor lady was more mistreated by poets and

musicians than by her husband. Here a village girl is being teased
by her companions to the liveliest of tunes, *Isabel, perdistes la tu
faja* (*Isabel, You Have Lost Your Sash*). And here is a rustic swain asking his girl to tell him in what part of the river she
is going to bathe, so that he may be there to watch, *Si te vas a
bañar, Juanica.* This villancico retains its full piquancy if we remember that it was then customary for Spanish women to bathe
in the rivers in a state of nature, not only in the country, but in
the cities also—the sight of women bathing in the Manzanares
invariably drew startled comment from foreign visitors to Madrid.

Spain may have been full of bigotry, fanaticism, persecution,
and oppression, as the historians assure us, but there is no trace of
that in these songs, which are a true national manifestation and
which express the joys and sorrows of life with a spontaneous and
unaffected simplicity that makes them, and the men and women of
whom they sing, live warmly and palpably for us today.

On the artistic side, as a final summing up we cannot do better
than quote the words of one of the keenest and best informed
among present-day historians of music,[17] who writes that these
songs "disclose a musical art of such grace and finish as elevates
Spain among the leading musical nations of the Renaissance."

CHAPTER III

Early Masters of the Guitar

IN the sixteenth century the guitar was not exactly the instrument that we know today. Yet essentially it was the same: a stringed instrument played directly with the fingers, having an incurved body or sound chest shaped like a figure eight, with flat top and bottom, and a long neck or finger board with frets. The type, in fact, goes back to remote antiquity, as witnessed by Egyptian bas-reliefs dating from the Eleventh and Twelfth Dynasties (3762–3703 B.C.). According to one theory, the guitar was introduced into Spain by the Arabs; but a more probable supposition is that the guitar was derived from the Roman cithara, of Greco-Assyrian origin, and that it was brought to the Iberian Peninsula by the Roman colonizers long before the Moslem invasion. Spanish texts of the Middle Ages mention two types of guitar, the *latina* (Latin) and the *morisca* (Moorish); the former, as may be seen in the illuminated manuscript of the *Cantigas* of Alfonso the Wise, has the incurved sides of the true guitar, while the latter has the rounded shape characteristic of the lute. It seems unlikely that an instrument borrowed from the Arabs would be known as a "Latin guitar." At any rate, the *guitarra latina* of medieval Spain is the precursor of the modern guitar.

Several kinds of guitar were current in Spain during the sixteenth century. They differed chiefly in size and in the number of strings. Guitars were made with four, five, six, and seven strings, or pairs of strings, the one with the most strings being the largest. Usually all the strings except the highest one were doubled at the unison. Gaspar Sanz, writing in the seventeenth century, states that it was customary to double most of the strings of the guitar in Spain, but not in Italy. He adds, however, that the doubling was optional, and that the single strings were more suitable for the *punteado* or contrapuntal style of playing, which was that practiced by the early masters of the guitar. In the old Spanish guitars the strings were of gut.

The Spaniards employed the term *vihuela de mano* (or sometimes simply *vihuela*) to designate the various types of guitar then in use. At first sight the word *vihuela* looks somewhat strange. But on closer examination it proves to be an old acquaintance slightly disguised. It is etymologically akin to the French *viole* and *vielle*, the Italian *viola*, the German *fiedel* (Old High German, *fidula*), and the English *fiddle*, all being derived from the Low Latin *vitula* (Latin, *fidicula*). The common derivation becomes quite clear when we compare the Provençal *viula* with the old Spanish *viuela*.

In Spain *vihuela* was also used as a general term for all kinds of stringed instruments with a neck, whether played with a bow, with a plectrum, or with the fingers. But in order to distinguish the three main types, a qualificative was usually added. Thus, the Archpriest of Hita, in the fourteenth century, mentions the *vihuela de péndola* (played with a plectrum) and *vihuela de arco* (played with a bow, that is, a kind of viol). Because it was played directly by the fingers, the guitar was called *vihuela de mano* (i. e., "of the hand"). The lute (*laúd*) was sometimes referred to as *vihuela de Flandes* ("vihuela of Flanders"), showing that it was regarded as an alien instrument in Spain, though it had originally reached the rest of Europe through that country, whither it had been brought by the Moslems.

SUPREMACY OF THE GUITAR IN SPAIN

It is a curious fact that during the Renaissance Spain should have rejected the lute, which figured so largely in instrumental music throughout other European countries, in favor of the guitar, which then had no artistic status outside the Iberian Peninsula. Perhaps the Spaniards felt a subconscious resentment toward an instrument which had been introduced by the Moslems and which, therefore, symbolized a hated subjugation. It is more likely that they found the guitar a handier and more practical instrument than the delicate and costly lute. Certain it is that they never wavered in their fidelity to the guitar, which they regarded as the king of instruments. Enriquez de Valderrábano wrote that "among earthly creatures, God placed music with the greatest reason and perfection in man, and among stringed instruments, in the vihuela." And a vignette in Luis Milán's *El Maestro* (1535) represents Orpheus, in a medieval setting and surrounded by a rapt audience of birds and beasts, playing, not the antique lyre, but a six-stringed guitar!

Some modern writers have persisted in referring to Spanish guitar music of the sixteenth century as lute music, on the ground that it was written in the same style as the music of the lutenists and that it bears little relation to the subsequent development of guitar music. This argument appears to us utterly fallacious. It leads, moreover, to a needless confusion. The illustrations in their books show clearly that the Spaniards played the guitar and not the lute; hence there is no justification whatever for calling them lutenists, even though they may have been influenced by the prevailing lute style of composition.[1]

Of the four types of guitar, the oldest was that with four strings. We do not know exactly when the guitars with five, six, and seven strings began to be made. The first mention of the six-stringed guitar is found in Luis Milán's *El Maestro*. Juan Bermudo, in his important *Declaración de Instrumentos* (1555), mentions all four types. Regarding the five-stringed guitar, he writes: "We have seen guitars in Spain with five strings, tuned in *la, re, sol, si, mi.*" His wording indicates that this instrument was somewhat of an exception in his time. At all events, his statement definitely undermines the persistent legend—based on a passage in Lope de Vega's *Dorotea*—that makes the poet-musician Vicente Espinel the "inventor" of the five-stringed guitar, for Bermudo was writing only four years after Espinel's birth. But it is quite likely that Espinel may have been the one who made the instrument popular.

Bermudo gives a drawing of the seven-stringed guitar and describes various ways of tuning it. He also includes a setting for this instrument of the old ballad *Mira Nero de Tarpeya,* and he tells us that a certain musician named Guzman wrote much for the seven-stringed guitar. But no works by this Guzman have been found, and the seven-stringed guitar does not figure in the extant tablature books. From other sources we learn that Francisco Guerrero, the famous composer of religious music, was also a skilled player of the seven-stringed guitar.

With regard to the four-stringed guitar, Bermudo says that it has two different tunings, one *a los nuevos* ("in the new style") and one *a los viejos* ("in the old style"). The former he gives as A-d-g-b; the latter as G-d-g-b, adding that this tuning is "more suitable for old ballads and strummed music (*música golpeada*) than for music of the present time." This is a very significant statement.

From medieval times, as we have seen, it had been customary to use the guitar for accompanying the singing of old ballads and dances. Bermudo indicates that the style of playing by strumming rather than plucking the strings was suitable for the old traditional type of music, but not for "music of the present time." By the latter phrase he meant the art of the polyphonic masters, the great contrapuntal art of the Renaissance which the lutenists were endeavoring to transfer to their instrument. It was doubtless a desire to emulate the art of the polyphonic lute that caused the Spaniards to add more strings to the medieval guitar, so as to increase its contrapuntal resources. Thus there came into existence the large six-stringed guitar, or *vihuela de mano,* often called simply *vihuela,* which was tuned in the same manner as the lute.

The four-stringed guitar, or *vihuela de cuatro órdenes,* remained the favorite instrument of the populace, who were less concerned with contrapuntal technique than with finding, in the words of Emilio Pujol, "a basis of tonality for their songs and dances." But the four-stringed guitar was not entirely neglected by cultivated musicians. Miguel de Fuenllana, one of the greatest masters of the sixteenth century, wrote some of his finest works for this modest instrument. Fuenllana also wrote for the five-stringed guitar, which, however, attained its greatest popularity in the seventeenth century.

DON LUIS MILÁN

It was perhaps not by mere chance that the first Spanish tablature book came to be printed at Valencia. In the third decade of the sixteenth century the Valencian court was a brilliant center of artistic culture. After the death of Queen Isabel, Ferdinand of Aragon had married Germaine de Foix, the beautiful young niece of the French king. Ferdinand himself died in 1516, and Germaine was made vicereine of the kingdom of Valencia. Her youth and beauty prevented her from remaining long a widow; her second husband was the Elector of Brandenburg, and after his death in 1525 she married the Italian-born Duke of Calabria, son of the former king of Naples, who ruled with her as viceroy. The Duke of Calabria, one of the most cultured noblemen of his time, had a large and valuable library, an important collection of musical instruments,[2] and reputedly the finest chapel of musicians, both vocal and instrumental, in all Spain. It was there that the versatile Isabel Coello, at the age of seventeen, astonished the court by her virtuosity on the clavier, the harp, the viol, and every manner of instrument then in vogue.[3]

As courtier, poet, musician, wit, and gallant, Don Luis Milán enjoyed a privileged position at the viceregal court. Born about 1500, he came of a noble Valencian family. Scarcely anything is known of his early life and final years; but he must have died after 1561, when his last book, *El Cortesano,* was published. This work, modeled after Baldassare Castiglione's *Il Cortegiano* (which Boscán had translated into Spanish in 1534),[4] gives a detailed picture of court life at Valencia, and from it we are able to reconstruct the milieu—a curious mixture of superficial pleasures, elaborate etiquette, and artistic sophistication—in which Milán passed the years of his maturity.

Milán also had relations with the Portuguese Court, though we have no record of any sojourns he may have made there. *El Maestro* is dedicated to King John III of Portugal, an ardent patron of arts and letters, who bestowed upon the author an annual pension of seven thousand *cruzados*—a striking proof that Don Luis Milán was esteemed abroad no less than at home.

In *El Cortesano,* Milán mentions music as one of the indispensable accomplishments of the perfect courtier. So in his *Libro de Vihuela de Mano intitulado El Maestro* his object was to provide a clear and practical instruction book for gentlemen desirous of learning the fashionable art of playing the vihuela. He himself, as he informs us in his preface, was entirely self-taught in music. But doubtless he felt that others less gifted and clever than himself would welcome the help of his method. Having explained the purpose of his book, Milán proceeds to give detailed instructions for tuning the instrument. The tuning he adopts is in fourths, with a major third between the third and fourth strings, thus: G-c-f-a-d'-g'. He then describes the system of tablature in which the music is written. This is based on quite a different principle from the musical notation to which we are accustomed. The essential difference is that tablature indicates finger position instead of note position.

Tablature makes use of parallel lines similar to those of our five-line staff, but the number of lines varies according to the number of strings of the instrument, since each string is represented by a line (in the case of organ tablature the number of lines corresponds to the number of parts in the music). In Milán's tablature the top line represents the highest string (in other Spanish tablature books this procedure is reversed: the top line represents the lowest string; but the principle remains the same). On the lines of the tablature, numerals (from 0 to 10) are placed, indicating the fret upon which the finger should be placed. For example, if the figure 3 appears on the fifth line (from the bottom), it means that the d string is to be played with the finger on the third fret. As all the guitars had their frets placed a semitone apart, the note indicated by any given numeral can be determined by counting the corresponding number of half steps above the note produced by the open string. Thus, in the instance given above, the note to be sounded would be three half steps above d, that is, f. The figure 0 signifies an open string, played without holding the finger on any fret. Time values are indicated by mensural notes placed above the tablature. In the case of songs, the vocal part is indicated by red numerals.

In addition to six Spanish and six Portuguese villancicos, and six Italian sonnets, Milán's book contains forty instrumental fantasias, four *tientos* (preludes), and six pavanes. He begins with pieces of a very simple character, suitable for beginners, and gradually progresses to more elaborate and difficult compositions, though with the exception of the six pavanes they all preserve the improvisatory nature typical of the instrumental music of that period. The early sixteenth-century composers for the lute and guitar had to create a type of music adapted to the resources of their instruments out of the material then available, which consisted on the one hand of vocal polyphonic music and on the other of traditional dance forms and folk tunes. By drawing upon both these elements they brought about a fusion of harmony and polyphony that resulted in the development of a distinctly instrumental style. When they transcribed vocal polyphonic music for their instrument, as they continually did, the result was necessarily harmonic, because their plucked strings could not sustain notes like the human voice. Yet by skillful manipulation and calculation they managed to achieve certain polyphonic effects which, though limited, added considerably to the variety and interest of their musical syntax.

If we examine one of Milán's fantasias, we find that it is rather loosely constructed as regards thematic development and division into fixed periods. The purpose seems to be to display the best resources of the instrument without overmuch concern for structural unity. Yet one can see how much of the composition grows organically out of thematic nucleuses, basic rhythmic patterns that are repeated in different forms and combinations. But in the course of the piece new thematic material makes its appearance, the initial themes are definitely abandoned, and tonality remains as the chief mainstay of unity. The composer is content to have traversed fields of harmonic beauty that were then new.

With regard to the pavanes, the form is more closely knit, following the pattern of a dance that had become largely conventionalized by this time. Milán himself tells us that he imitated the Italian style in these pavanes, and that in two of them he used Italian themes. These pavanes are termed "marvels of melodiousness and audacious harmony" by Curt Sachs, who discerningly observes that in spite of its foreign form "there is no mistaking the chivalrous and romantic spirit that stamps this music with a fundamentally Spanish seal." [5]

EARLIEST INSTRUMENTAL VARIATIONS

Hard on the heels of *El Maestro* came another tablature book for vihuela, *Los Seys Libros del Delphín de Música*, published at Valladolid in 1538. The author was Luis de Narváez, a native of Granada who became *maestro de vihuela* to Philip II and who was mentioned by Bermudo as one of the finest players of that time. It was said that to any piece of four-part music that was set before him he could improvise immediately four additional parts on the vihuela. He is assumed to be the Ludovicus Narvays several of whose motets, for four and five voices, are included in collections published by Jacques Moderne at Lyons in 1539 and 1543.

Like Milán, Narváez begins by giving the rules for reading the tablature and tuning the instrument, though his instructions are briefer. Unlike Milán, he includes transcriptions of vocal works by famous composers, such as Josquin Desprez, a practice widely followed by contemporary vihuelistas and lutenists. In his original fantasias Narváez relies less on chordal passages and more on contrapuntal imitation, generally in two or three parts.

The most notable feature of his book is that it marks the first appearance of the instrumental theme with variations, which the Spaniards called *diferencias*. Narváez has both purely instrumental variations and variations that take the form of different accompaniments for the same song. The harmonic texture of Narváez's instrumental variations has been aptly characterized in the *Oxford History:* "Instead of merely adding a counterpoint to the tune, the instrument skips nimbly through the whole compass of treble and bass, giving a kind of rapid sketch of the harmony implied."

Narváez gives twenty-one very brief variations on the tune of the old ballad *Conde Claros,* and four more extended variations on the popular air *Guárdame las vacas,* which became the favorite variation theme among Spanish composers of the sixteenth century.[6] As J. B. Trend has pointed out, this tune was also known in England: under the title of *The Sheepheard Carillo his Song* it was printed in *England's Helicon* (1600), with Spanish and English words. Here is the English version of the text:

> I pre-thee keepe my kine for me
> Carillo, wilt thou. Tell.
> First let me have a kiss of thee,
> And I will keep them well.

The next tablature book to appear in Spain was Alonso de Mudarra's *Tres Libros de Música en Cifra para Vihuela,* published in 1546 at Seville, where the author, who died about 1570, was a canon of the Cathedral. He was brought up in the household of the Duke of Infantado, and is said to have traveled in Italy. Mudarra reveals himself as a composer of excellent taste and genuine inspiration in his original fantasias, pavanes, galliardes, and variations, as well as in his settings of songs, both Spanish and Italian. Some of his variations present the peculiarity of a constant bass, a feature that is met with in later specimens of variation form, for example, among the English virginalists.

The features of a miscellany that the tablature books were tending more and more to assume are very noticeable in Enriquez de Valderrábano's *Silva de Sirenas*, printed at Valladolid in 1547. His book consists largely of songs and transcriptions of vocal music, so that we have little opportunity to judge of his qualities as an instrumental composer. Yet one of his pieces, written for two guitars, has impelled a modern critic to write that "this composition—which is bold at the same time that it is modest, and gentle at the same time that it is heroic—suffices, by reason of its musical quality, to ensure both for itself and its creator an unimpeachably valid place high in the music of all peoples and all times." [7]

We must pass briefly over Diego Pisador's *Libro de Música de Vihuela* (Salamanca, 1552), which is especially rich in vocal settings, so that we may deal with one of the finest and most important of the Spanish tablature books, the *Orphénica Lyra* of Miguel de Fuenllana (Seville, 1554). Fuenllana, blind from birth, was at first chamber musician to the Marquesa de Tarifa and later, like Pisador, entered the service of Philip II, to whom his book is dedicated. From 1563 he was chamber musician to Philip's third wife, Isabel of Valois. He died before 1591, when his heirs claimed certain sums owed to him by the court. [8] Bermudo praised Fuenllana as a *consumado tañedor* ("a most skillful player") and declared that his skill was so great he could even play on an instrument that was not tuned. As a composer he was no less remarkable. His book, besides the usual transcriptions and songs, contains eighty-eight original fantasias, including some for four- and five-stringed guitars.

VOGUE OF THE "SPANISH GUITAR"

Esteban Daza's *El Parnaso* (Valladolid, 1576) was the last of the tablature books written for the old six-stringed guitar. It was followed ten years later by Juan Carlos Amat's *Guitarra Española* [9] (Barcelona, 1586), which set forth a new system for playing the "Spanish Guitar" *de cinco órdenes*. As the "Spanish Guitar" came into vogue, the term "vihuela" fell into disuse, though later writers employed it occasionally, as did Pablo Nassarre in his *Escuela Música* (1724). The instrument described by Amat had four double strings (two tuned at the unison and two at the octave) and one single string, the highest. The method of tuning, in fourths with a third near the middle, remained the same. He also deals with the four-stringed guitar (three double strings and one single).

Although the story that credits Vicente Espinel with having added a fifth string to the guitar has been shown to be without foundation, this remarkable figure merits attention here, for in addition to being poet, novelist, soldier, vagabond, and priest, he was also a composer and a celebrated guitarist. Born at Ronda in 1550, Espinel studied at Salamanca, joined a military expedition that was frustrated by an outbreak of the plague, entered the service of the Conde de Lemos, went to Seville and fell into disreputable ways of life. With the aid of powerful protectors he made a fresh start, accompanying the Duke of Medina Sidonia to Genoa in 1578. He then went to Flanders, returned to Italy, and three years later was back in Spain, where he studied for the church, was ordained a priest, and became *maestro de capilla* to the Bishop of Palencia. He died at Madrid in 1624.

Out of this variegated experience Espinel drew the material for his famous picaresque novel, *Vida del Escudero Marcos de Obregón*, which served as a model for Le Sage's *Gil Blas*. In this novel he not only mentions well-known musicians with whom he was acquainted, among them Francisco Salinas and Bernardo de Clavijo, but also gives a very detailed and vivid picture of musical life in those days. We do not need to consult a learned treatise to discover that in the popular style of playing the guitar was strummed, not plucked. Espinel reveals this in one small incident. He writes of a young man who was always playing the guitar, and he says that he did this "not so much to show his skill, but rather to scratch his wrists with the movement, for they were covered with a kind of rash." His characters are continually stopping to make music and to talk about it—and this no matter to what station of life they belong, from barber to marquis. Though none of Espinel's compositions has survived, his novel, like Milán's *El Cortesano*, provides a living background for the musical treatises we have been discussing.[10]

As the seventeenth century advanced, the vogue of the Spanish guitar spread rapidly over the rest of Europe. In France its popularity was furthered by the publication of Luis de Brizeño's *Método para Aprender a Tañer la Guitarra a lo Español* (Paris, 1626), and in Italy it received an impetus from the appearance of Nicolas Doisi de Velasco's *Nuevo Método de Cifra para Tañer Guitarra* (Naples, 1630).

The next guitar treatise to appear in Spain was the *Instrucción de Música sobre la Guitarra Española* (Saragossa, 1674) of Gaspar Sanz, a native of Calanda in Aragon who held the degree of bachelor of theology from Salamanca University. The drawing of the guitar in his book shows an instrument with the top of the neck bent back at a sharp angle.[11] He gives instructions for two types of playing, *tañer rasgueado* (strumming) and *tañer de punteado* (plucking), and includes compositions for both types. Sanz implies that the *rasgueado* style of playing was used especially for dancing. His book has considerable folkloric value, for it gives many of the dance tunes that were popular in his day. He also continues the tradition of writing *diferencias* on popular themes.

Other works on the same order are the *Luz y Norte Musical para Caminar por las Cifras de Guitarra Española* (Madrid, 1677) of Lucas Ruiz de Ribayaz, the *Poema Harmónico* (Madrid, 1684) of Francisco Guerau, and the *Resumen de Acompañar la Parte de Guitarra* (Madrid, 1714) of Santiago de Murcia. This was the last of the treatises in which tablature was used. It also marked the end of the career of the five-stringed guitar as an artistic instrument.

The epoch of the modern six-stringed guitar may be said to begin with the publication, at Madrid in 1799, of the *Principios para Tocar la Guitarra de Seis Órdenes,* written by a naturalized Spaniard of Italian birth, Federico Moretti. He was a pupil of Padre Miguel García Basilio, who also wrote for the six-stringed guitar, and whose playing proved so fascinating to Boccherini (*cf.* Chapter VII). Moretti's treatise established the fundamental principles of modern guitar technique upon which subsequent methods were based. Spain continued to produce famous masters of the guitar, whose art we shall discuss in a later chapter. Present-day masters of the instrument, such as Emilio Pujol and Andrés Segovia, have revived the contrapuntal style of playing, thus giving new life to the music of their great predecessors of the sixteenth century.

CHAPTER IV

Organists and Theorists

THE art of organ building and organ playing acquired great impetus in Spain from the fourteenth century onward. Splendid instruments, in their outward form magnificent specimens of Spanish Renaissance art, were built in the cathedrals of the leading cities, such as Salamanca, Tarragona, Barcelona, and Saragossa. By the early part of the sixteenth century Spain could boast of organs and organists that could rival, if not excel, the best of Europe.

The artistically towering figure of the blind organist Antonio de Cabezón dominates the first half of the sixteenth century. Not only does he loom head and shoulders above his contemporaries, but at his best he leaps forward almost two hundred years to anticipate the grandeur of conception and force of expression that we find in the music of Johann Sebastian Bach. It was Pedrell who first termed Cabezón "a sixteenth-century Spanish Bach," and the comparison has been found valid by subsequent commentators, such as the musicologist Willi Apel, who has developed the analogy in terms that cannot be bettered:

To associate Cabezón with Bach, as we have casually done, signifies more than the expression of an unconsidered admiration. It points to an inner relationship that links the Spanish master more closely to the great German than perhaps to any other musician. In any event, I know of no one among the clavier and organ composers of all time

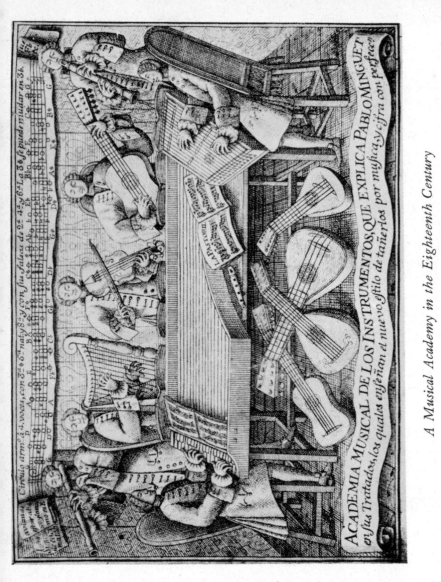

A Musical Academy in the Eighteenth Century

By Courtesy of the *Library of Congress*

who, by reason of musical spirituality, profundity and exalted serious-
ness of purpose, austerity and sublimity of thought, and—last but
not least—complete contrapuntal mastery, more properly belongs in
his company.[1]

Interesting also is the opinion of the eminent nineteenth-
century German musicologist Siegfried Dehn, who took the
trouble to master the old organ tablature in order to study the
music of Cabezón. That he considered himself amply repaid is
attested by the following passage from a letter he wrote to Franz
Liszt in 1853:

Much more than in the Italian contrapuntists, I am interested in
the Spanish composers of the 16th century, and above all in Cabezón.
. . . The discovery of his works (from the year 1578) has caused
me to adopt an entirely new point of view, not only with regard to
the origins of instrumental music, but also with regard to the origins
of figurative music in general. For example, triplets and quintoles
are already to be found in the compositions of the old Spanish master.
Unfortunately, one has to have a very strong head, capable at need of
battering through a wall, in order to contemplate and appreciate the
marvels hidden therein, for, in truth, the notation employed by the
old Spanish musicians was for me, at first, an impassable barrier. . . .[2]

Another prominent German musical historian, the late Karl
Krebs, expressed similar feelings of admiration in a letter to
Pedrell:

Studying the compositions of Cabezón I was amazed at the perfection of their musical form, at the beauty and profundity of the ideas,
and at the facility of the creative technique that seemed to lend itself
to all the dictates of the composer's artistic imagination. . . .[3]

And Pedrell himself summed up the historical importance of
Cabezón by remarking that in his compositions "are found all
the germinal elements of instrumental music that, passing
through Frescobaldi, lead eventually to the orchestra of Haydn."

CABEZÓN'S LIFE AND ART

Antonio de Cabezón was one of a notable triumvirate of blind Spanish musicians who flourished during the sixteenth century, the other two being Miguel de Fuenllana and Francisco de Salinas. He was born in 1510 at Castrojeriz near Burgos, and was blind from early infancy. It is believed that he studied under Tomás Gómez at Palencia. He must have been an accomplished musician at eighteen, for that is the age at which he became organist and clavichordist to the Emperor Charles V. His life thereafter was one of devotion to his art and his family. An old chronicler records that "he married for love, which was a great marvel in a blind person" (*Casó por amores, que fué gran maravilla, en un ciego*). He had two daughters and two sons, one of whom, Hernando (d. 1602), acquired some reputation as a musician and succeeded to his father's posts at court.

Cabezón continued in the royal service under Philip II, who came to the throne in 1556 after having married Mary Tudor, Queen of England, two years previously. Cabezón accompanied the king on at least one of his trips to England,[4] and he also traveled with the court to Italy and Flanders (Philip, it will be recalled, was King of Naples and sovereign of the Low Countries). Thus the fame and influence of the Spanish organist spread far beyond the limits of his own country, and there is evidence that his style left its traces not only upon the English virginalists, but also upon the compositions of such important organists as Trabaci in Naples and Sweelinck in Holland.

The reader may have noticed that Dehn refers to Cabezón's works as dating from the year 1578. That is the year in which they were first published, by his son Hernando, under the title of *Obras de Música Para Tecla, Arpa y Vihuela.*[5] But this was twelve years after Cabezón's death, and historically this music must be placed somewhat earlier, in the period (1530–1560) corresponding to the composer's creative maturity. Cabezón's compositions may be divided into three main categories: short liturgical pieces (versicles) used in connection with the Mass; more extensive pieces in contrapuntal style called *tientos* (a term approximately equivalent to "prelude"); and—perhaps the most interesting of all—pieces in the form of a "theme and variations." In the preface to his edition of his father's works, Hernando de Cabezón is careful to inform us that these compositions are to be regarded as "crumbs fallen from the table" rather than as deliberate artistic creations, because they were intended for the instruction of his pupils and therefore represented not so much the skill of the master as the aptitude of the pupil. Be this as it may, we owe to Hernando's filial piety the preservation of some of the most remarkable keyboard music that has come down to us from the sixteenth century.

At first sight, Cabezón's shorter pieces, which are grouped together in series according to the eight ecclesiastical modes, may seem too slight and simple for the purposes of effective artistry. Yet in reality they are models of concise and forceful utterance, concentrating in the most compact form a wealth of varied expression. And, at a time when vocal technique held sway over nearly all musical thought, they are conceived in a purely instrumental style.

As we observed in the previous chapter, Spanish composers took the lead in developing the instrumental variation form. Cabezón must be considered one of the prominent pioneers in this field, for his keyboard variations, though not published till later, were doubtless composed at about the same time as those of Mudarra and Narváez. Nine sets of *diferencias*, or variations, are to be found among Cabezón's works. Three of them are variations on that favorite popular tune *Guárdame las vacas*. Others are *Diferencias sobre la Gallarda Milanesa* and *Diferencias sobre el Canto del Caballero*, the theme of the latter being that of a folk song which is said to have given Lope de Vega the idea for his play *El Caballero de Olmeda*. Both of these compositions reveal that mastery of form and power of expression which is characteristic of this master's art.

Antonio de Cabezón died at Madrid on March 26, 1566, and his passing was deeply mourned by the entire court. On his tomb was inscribed a glowing epitaph in Latin, describing him as "the first organist of his time, whose fame fills the world."

THREE CELEBRATED THEORISTS

A worthy disciple of Cabezón was Fray Tomás de Santa María (d. 1570), a Dominican monk, whose compositions for organ show great purity of style. But he is most important as the author of a treatise on musical interpretation, *Arte de Tañer Fantasía, Assi Para Tecla Como Vihuela* (Valladolid, 1565), in which he gives rules for improvisation and for the technique of keyboard instruments (fingering, ornaments, position of the hands, varieties of touch, etc.). He recommends the use of all five fingers—a practice not generally adopted until much later.

In the previous chapter we had occasion to mention Fray Juan Bermudo, of the Minorite Order, whose *Declaración de Instrumentos Musicales* (Osuna, 1549 and 1555) is an invaluable compendium of information concerning musical instruments of the sixteenth century and methods of musical performance. The book also contains many illuminating references to famous contemporary musicians and throws light on various musical practices of the time. The hue and cry against arrangements that rises perennially in our own day was also raised by Bermudo, who fulminates against the indiscriminate practice of making *glosas* or arrangements of works by noted composers. In Chapter XLVI of Book IV he writes: "Here comes my Cristóbal Morales, who is the light of Spain in music, and a Bernardino de Figueroa, whose skill is unique, and after prolonged study they spend much time in composing a motet, and then someone who does not even know plain song . . . wishes to improve on it."

Bermudo was also the author of a theoretical treatise, *El Arte Tripharia* (Osuna, 1550), written for the use of the nuns of the Convent of Montilla. With reference to this work, Pedrell wrote of Bermudo: "Not only is he the most methodical, the most thorough and the most clear of all the theorists writing in the vernacular—not only is he admirable for this and for the lucidity of his ideas, but he also aspires with all his might . . . to remove from music all trace of sophistry." [6] Bermudo had an exceedingly open mind, as evinced by his remark that there was no novelty in music to which men might not become accustomed in time. He foresaw clearly the immense forward strides that music was to take.

Medieval scholastics had concerned themselves largely with mulling over the remnants of ancient Greek theory as transmitted in the writings of Boethius and Cassiodorus, who flourished in the sixth century. It was a Spaniard, Bartolomé Ramos de Pareja, who gave the deathblow to the outworn theories of Boethius and prepared the way for an essentially modern conception of musical theory and practice. Born at Baeza in 1440, Ramos de Pareja became lecturer on music at Salamanca University, where a chair of music had been established by Alfonso the Wise in the thirteenth century. He also spent some time at Bologna, where his Latin treatise *De Musica Tractatus sive Musica Practica* was published in 1482. There he had as a pupil the able theorist Giovanni Spataro, who later came to his defense (like all iconoclasts, Ramos de Pareja aroused violent opposition from those whose pet theories he had disturbed). The date of his death has not been ascertained, but it must have been after 1491, in which year he is known to have been in Rome.

Ramos de Pareja abandoned the old hexachordal system of solmization invented by Guido d'Arezzo in the eleventh century, and in its place substituted the new and modern system of solmization based on the octave. By establishing the mathematical ratios 4:5 and 5:6 for the major and minor third, and 3:5 and 5:8 for the major and minor sixth, he completed the definition of the consonant triad and laid the foundation for our modern harmonic system. But the most revolutionary and far-reaching tenet of his doctrine was that which set forth the theory of equal temperament, that is, the division of the octave into twelve equal semitones. It has been suggested that Ramos de Pareja derived this theory from the practice of the Spanish guitarists, who placed the frets on their instruments a semitone apart, thus forming a scale of equal semitones. Considering the fact that theory invariably codifies practice, this explanation is very likely; but it does not detract from the merit and boldness of Ramos de Pareja's conceptions, especially when we consider that it was not until the eighteenth century that the adoption of equal temperament was definitely advocated, the way having been prepared by Bach's *Wohltemperirtes Clavier*.

THE EARLIEST COLLECTION OF SPANISH FOLK SONG

Bermudo and Santa María were but two among many Spanish theorists who continued along the progressive path indicated by Ramos de Pareja. From the fifteenth to the seventeenth century about one hundred theoretical works were published in Spain, notable as much for quality as for quantity. To us, the most interesting of all these works is *De Musica Libri Septem* (Salamanca, 1577) by Francisco de Salinas, not primarily for its theoretical value, great as that may be, but because it contains the earliest collection of Spanish folk music that has come down to us. To call Salinas a collector of folk songs would be to credit him with an intention that was surely far from his mind. He reproduced these specimens of folk song merely to illustrate certain points in his discussion of rhythm and meter in relation to classic prosody. Nevertheless, the fact remains that in noting down these melodies and their texts, even in fragmentary form, he performed a task of the utmost value for posterity.[7]

From the examples given by Salinas we are able to observe how certain tunes persisted in the popular memory from one century to another. He quotes, for instance, a Castilian folk song, *Yo me iba, mi madre, a Villa Reale*, which is practically identical with the tune of the Catalan pilgrim song *Polorum Regina*, contained in the fourteenth-century *Llibre Vermell* of Montserrat (*cf.* Chapter I). Salinas also quotes a tune with the words *Rey don Alonso, Rey mi señor*, of which he says that he thinks it came originally from the Moors, "for it is still sung to Arabic words:

Calvi vi calvi, calvi aravi."

These syllables have no meaning in any language, but it has been assumed that they represent the Arabic

qalbi bi qalbi, qalbi 'arabi
("Heart, my heart, 'tis the heart of an Arab"),

the Spanish tendency being to confuse the "b" and "v" in pronunciation. The Archpriest of Hita gives another phonetic variant of the Arabic text in his *Libro de Buen Amor*, where he speaks of a rebec "playing the tune of *Calbi garabi*." This proves, in any case, that the tune was already well known in the fourteenth century.

Sir John Hawkins, the famous English musical historian, writing in the second half of the eighteenth century, devoted three entire chapters of his *History of the Science and Practice of Music* (Book IX, Chapters 85–87) to Salinas's book, translating the preface, which contains autobiographical data, and summarizing his theories. He calls Salinas's work "one of the most valuable books on music now extant in any language" and praises the sagacity and independence of the author's mind, so far removed from all "credulity."

Francisco de Salinas, born at Burgos in 1513, was blind from the age of ten. Nevertheless, he distinguished himself as a student at Salamanca and was taken into the service of Cardinal Sarmiento, whom he accompanied to Rome in 1538. About 1553 he went to Naples and became organist to the great Duke of Alba, the Spanish viceroy there. Returning to Spain in 1561, he was appointed professor of music at Salamanca six years later, retaining that post until his retirement in 1587. Salinas died at Salamanca in 1590. He was an intimate friend of the poet Fray Luis de León, who dedicated to him the beautiful *Ode to Music* that embodies the sixteenth-century Spanish philosophy of musical mysticism.

While Salinas was organist at the viceregal court of Naples, another notable Spanish musician was *maestro de capilla* there. This was Diego Ortiz, a native of Toledo, who in 1553 (at Rome) published a book entitled *Tratado de Glosas Sobre Cláusulas y Otros Géneros de Puntos en la Música de Violones* (*Treatise on the Ornamentation of Cadences and Other Kinds of Notes in the Music for the Bass Viol*). This work is of fundamental importance for the study of early instrumental music. As Arnold has shown in his exhaustive history of thorough bass, the treatise of Ortiz proves "that the practice of improvising an accompaniment over a given bass was known nearly fifty years before the publication of the figured basses of Peri, Caccini and Cavalieri, or of the *Cento Concerti* of Viadana." [8] Ortiz gives numerous musical examples to demonstrate his method of instrumental improvisation, and these rank among the earliest specimens of concerted instrumental music. He demonstrates three different ways of playing, the most interesting being that in which a piece for several voices (madrigal or motet) is transposed for the cembalo, while the bass viol plays variations on one of the parts. At other times an ornate melody is played by the viol, while the cembalo provides an accompaniment over a given bass. Again, both players may improvise on their respective instruments. Thus the artistic possibilities of the variation form were still further developed by a Spanish musician, who through the publication of his work in Rome exerted considerable influence upon the course of Italian music.

It was also at Naples that the most celebrated musical treatise in Spanish was published. This was *El Melopeo y Maestro* (1613), by Domenico Pietro Cerone, an Italian who had gone to Spain in 1592 and joined the court choir in Madrid. From 1610 he held a similar position in Naples. His work is a compendium of early musical theory.

THE SUCCESSORS OF CABEZÓN

Returning to Spain, we find a notable succession of organists following Cabezón. Contemporary with that master was Luis Venegas de Henestrosa, organist to Cardinal Tavera at Toledo. His *Libro de Cifra Nueva Para Tecla, Harpa y Vihuela* (Alcalá, 1557) is the earliest extant Spanish book of organ music, as distinguished from theoretical works with musical examples. It contains sixty-nine pages of music in organ tablature, including many compositions by a mysterious composer identified only as "Antonio." Pedrell assumed that this composer was identical with Antonio de Cabezón, but Anglès can find no grounds whatever for this assumption. Among other composers represented in the collection are Francisco Pérez Palero of Granada, Pedro Vila of Barcelona, Luys Alberto, and Venegas de Henestrosa himself. Their compositions offer positive proof that Spain possessed a flourishing organ school with its own characteristic features based on a well-established tradition.

Sebastián Aguilera de Heredia (born in Aragon, 1570), from 1603 organist at Saragossa, was especially notable for his masterly use of chromatic alterations (*falsas*). The power and freedom of his style may be seen in the *Obra de Octavo Tono* published by Joseph Bonnet, which is called an *Ensalada* because of the diversified character of the themes it employs. Aguilera's works mark the transition from the comparative simplicity of sixteenth-century organ music to the more complex style of the seventeenth century, which is represented in the compositions of Francisco Correa de Araujo (*c.* 1581–1663), organist at the Collegiate Church of San Salvador in Seville, whose *Facultad Orgánica* was published at Alcalá in 1626. This volume contains seventy original compositions for organ, the majority of them by Correa de Araujo himself. He was a bold and original genius whose innovations marked a great stride forward in writing for organ. The tumultuous energy of his *Tiento a Modo de Canción* (reprinted by Bonnet), with its undercurrent of passionate melancholy, bespeaks the hand of a master to whom technique serves as a means for the most profound expression of human emotions.

Greatest of the Spanish organ masters after Cabezón was Juan Bautista José Cabanilles, born at Algemesí (province of Valencia) in 1644. From 1665 until his death in 1712 he was organist at the Cathedral of Valencia. He became a priest in 1668. An amazingly prolific genius, it has been estimated that his complete works would fill thirty octavo volumes; but, strange to say, none of his works appears to have been published during his lifetime. Like Cabezón, he shows exceptional mastery in his use of the variation form, both on popular and liturgical themes. He does not share the tormented mysticism of Correa de Araujo, but reveals a serene and soaring strength. His fugal developments display magnificent workmanship. Speaking of a *Tiento de 5° Tono* by Cabanilles, "with its air of pride and energy," Joseph Bonnet writes: "This is the song of the real, enduring Spain. The mark of time disappears from this incomparable work: it is music of eternity." 9

CHAPTER V

"The Eternal City"

THE results of modern research make it necessary to rectify long-prevalent conceptions regarding the origin and development of the Spanish polyphonic school. It was previously thought, and repeatedly asserted, that Spain did not possess a native school of religious polyphony until the advent of the Flemish musicians in the time of Philip the Handsome and Charles V had introduced this art into the peninsula. The discovery of abundant musical documents from the fourteenth to the beginning of the sixteenth centuries reveals that Spain had a flourishing polyphonic school long before the arrival of the Flemings who were employed in the chapel of Charles V.

The composers who lent their talent to the simple song forms of the *Cancionero de Palacio* were thoroughly versed in contrapuntal technique and most of them also cultivated the larger polyphonic forms that were used in the church. Limiting ourselves to the composers of the *Cancionero*, we find that they produced many impressive examples of sacred polyphony. More than twenty-five religious works by Juan Escobar have been found, while at Tarragona there are over forty works by Francisco de Peñalosa, including six Masses. By Juan Almorox there is a Mass for three voices that has been described as a marvel of counterpoint, while Alonso (who has eleven songs in the *Cancionero*) has left a magnificent setting for five voices of the psalm *Super flumina Babylonis.* Among the many sacred compositions of Juan de Anchieta may be mentioned two Masses, the *Credo* of the second bearing a resemblance to the tune of a song, *Ea judíos, a enfardelar,* that was popular about the time the Jews were expulsed from Spain (1492). Religious works by Madrid, Alonso de Mondéjar, Juan Ponce, Antonio Ribera, Juan Sanabria, Pedro Tordesillas, and Francisco de la Torre have also been found. Higini Anglès, who discovered most of this music, points out that it reveals a combination of the homophonic style with elements of florid counterpoint derived from the Flemish school, and he emphasizes its marked quality of religious mysticism.

This is a quality that the world has not been slow to recognize in Spanish religious music of the sixteenth century. In fact, it has sometimes been overstressed by certain commentators to the point of obscuring all other qualities. The chief point to be made here is that the great Spanish polyphonic religious school of the sixteenth century that reached its culmination in the art of Morales and Victoria was not an offshoot of the contemporary Franco-Flemish school, but rather a further growth of the native school that had already been implanted, with all its characteristic features, by previous generations of Spanish composers. It is not our purpose to deny the enrichment that may have resulted from contact with the Flemish musicians who came to Spain in the sixteenth century; but it is necessary to see this Flemish influence in its true historical perspective, as a continuous parallel process from the beginning of the fifteenth century, constantly conditioned and modified by the strength of native traditions.

The focal center of Spanish religious music in the sixteenth century was not Madrid, with its Flemish chapel, but Rome, where Spanish musicians had entrenched themselves in full force from the beginning of the century. The case of Juan del Encina, who stood in such high favor at the Papal Court, was not an isolated instance. Riaño [1] gives a list of more than thirty Spanish musicians who were active in Rome during this period, some of them as members of the Papal Choir, and all of them prominent in the musical life of the Eternal City. Included in the list are two of the most famous composers whom Spain has produced: Cristóbal Morales and Tomás Luis de Victoria, who has paid the penalty for his Roman sojourn of going down in most musical histories as "da Vittoria." The lives of these two composers span the entire sixteenth century, and in their music they sum up all the spiritual fervor, the austere passion, the supreme faith and ardent sincerity that the world admires in Spanish mysticism.

"THE LIGHT OF SPAIN IN MUSIC"

Cristóbal Morales was born in Seville about 1500. His teacher was Pedro Fernández de Castilleja, choirmaster of Seville Cathedral, called "the master of Spanish masters" because he had so many illustrious pupils. In 1526 Morales was appointed choirmaster at Avila, remaining there until 1530. In 1535, having entered the priesthood, he was at Rome as a singer in the Papal Choir, where he was soon joined by two other notable Spanish composers: Bartolomé Escobedo (in 1536) and Pedro Ordóñez (in 1539). The esteem in which Morales was held is attested by the fact that he was chosen to compose a cantata to celebrate the conclusion of the peace treaty that Pope Paul III had successfully negotiated at Nice between Charles V and Francis I in 1538. The following year he was again honored by being chosen to compose a cantata for the elevation of Ippolito d'Este to the dignity of cardinal. This princely churchman, who built the famous gardens of the Villa d'Este at Tivoli, was noted as a munificent patron of art and music—he was later Palestrina's patron—and, consequently, his seal of approval meant that Morales enjoyed the highest sort of reputation in Rome. In 1540 Morales visited Spain on leave, and in 1546 he returned to his native land for good, spending his remaining years at Toledo, Marchena, and Málaga. His death occurred in 1553, probably at Málaga.

Morales is the outstanding representative of the Andalusian school. His place in music has been aptly summed up by Mitjana:

"His austere, severe and profound genius, his lofty and noble inspiration, his remarkable expressive power, and his bold yet impeccable technique, cause him to occupy a pre-eminent place in the evolution of vocal polyphony." [2] The published works of Morales comprise Masses, magnificats, lamentations and motets, with a few madrigals in collections of the period; many religious works are in manuscripts in various Spanish churches.[3] In setting the religious texts, he aimed at dramatic truth and emotional expression rather than at academic correctness. As Prunières writes, "He discovers the dramatic ideas in the text and then illustrates them by powerful contrasts. . . . With vigorous strokes he portrays the inward world, the drama of the human conscience." [4]

One of Morales's finest motets is *Lamentabatur Jacob*—Jacob mourning for his two sons—for the third Sunday in Lent, which Fuenllana transcribed for vihuela. Adami da Bolsena, the historian of the Papal Choir, writing in 1711, calls this work *"una maraviglia del'Arte"* and *"la piu preziosa composizione che abbia il nostro archivio."* With his intensely expressive setting of the phrase *Heu me, dolens sum*, Morales makes us feel the father's desolation, and then he gradually depicts the transition to hope and confidence based on faith in God's goodness. Even more striking in its dramatic power is the motet *Emendemus in melius*, for the first Sunday in Lent, an injunction to make amends for our sins. While four voices sing the words of penitence, a fifth (tenor) sings the awesome words of warning, *Memento homo quia pulvis es, et in pulverem reverteris*, as a *cantus firmus* repeated with increasing insistence and leading to an imposing climax, followed once more by the calmness of faith. This device of having one voice sing a text different from the others is frequently employed by Morales to bring out those dramatic contrasts that give such emotional force to his music. Truly, Juan Bermudo was justified in calling Cristóbal Morales *"luz de España en Música"* ("the light of Spain in music").

Another representative of the Andalusian school who deserves mention here is Francisco Guerrero. Born in 1527, he, too, was a native of Seville and a pupil of Fernández de Castilleja, whom he succeeded as choirmaster in 1574 (having previously been his assistant). But no sooner had he succeeded to this post than he applied for leave of absence and followed the trend to Rome, where he remained so long that a substitute had to be appointed in his stead. Like Encina, he rounded off his life with a pilgrimage to the Holy Land (in 1588) and wrote an account of his journey that was widely read for more than a hundred years after his death, which occurred in Seville in 1599. Several volumes of his religious music were printed in Rome, and to Soto de Langa's *Secondo Libro di Laudi Spirituali* (Rome, 1583) he contributed a setting of Lope de Vega's *Si tus penas no pruebo* (*If I Share Not Thy Pain*).

Because of his suave and melodious style, Guerrero has been called "the Murillo of Spanish music," and the analogy is strengthened by the fact that both artists did their best work when inspired by a common cult for the Virgin Mary. Murillo is famed for his painting of the Assumption, and Guerrero for his hymns to the Blessed Mother, both works being the expression of a sincere religious faith and executed with impeccable technique, if not with much character or originality. Francisco Guerrero had one of the purest souls of any man who ever sang the praises of God in music; there is something extremely touching in his naïve joy upon first beholding, at the age of sixty, the place of the Saviour's birth. He was a veritable saint, giving all his substance to the poor and filled with true humbleness and charity. This serenity of soul is reflected in his music, a little too tame for our taste, but within its limitations showing an admirable alliance of skill and expression.

VICTORIA OF AVILA

Notable as was the Andalusian school, it remained for Castile to produce the greatest of all the Spanish religious composers.

Avila, the city of Saint Teresa, was also the birthplace of Tomás Luis de Victoria. He was born about 1548 and was probably a chorister in the Cathedral of Avila until his departure for Rome in 1565 to prepare for the priesthood at the Collegium Germanicum there.[5] This seminary had been founded by Victoria's fellow countryman, Saint Ignatius de Loyola, for the training of German students for the priesthood, but later the regulations were extended to include students of other nationalities. It is interesting to note that in 1565 Giovanni Perluigi da Palestrina had become music master of the Collegium Romanum, or Roman seminary, and as the two schools maintained close relations it is not improbable that young Victoria, who was about the same age as Palestrina's two sons, Rodolfo and Angelo (both studying at the Collegium Romanum), may have received lessons from the Italian master at this time. Some support is given to this hypothesis by the fact that when Palestrina resigned his position in 1571 he was succeeded by Victoria—perhaps a case of a master recommending a talented pupil (we offer this suggestion with due caution; in any case it is sounder than Riemann's assertion that Victoria studied in Rome with Morales, who had left that city some twenty years before Victoria's arrival!).

Victoria had left the seminary in 1569 to become organist and choirmaster at the Church of Santa Maria di Monserrato, a position he continued to hold after his appointment as maestro at the Collegium Romanum. But by the summer of 1573 he was back at the Collegium Germanicum again, this time as music master instead of student. In 1575 he was ordained a priest, having received the preliminary orders *extra tempore* (that is, without the usual intervals of waiting). He had already received a benefice from the Pope earlier that year, and another was added in 1579 (both were in Spain, but did not require residence). In 1578 he gave up his post at the Collegium Germanicum (though he continued to take a prominent part in

José Herrando, Author of the First Spanish Violin Method

Spanish Student Playing the Guitar

musicoreligious ceremonies there, as well as in the Spanish church of San Giacomo) and became a resident priest at the Church of San Girolamo della Carità, famed as the birthplace of the Oratorio of St. Philip Neri.

This great spiritual figure, of whom it was said that "his apostolate extends from the Pope to the smallest urchin in the street," had been living at San Girolamo for many years, and out of the religious meetings held there under his guidance— meetings in which music, especially the singing of hymns or *Laudi spirituali,* played such a prominent part—had grown the Congregation of the Oratory, officially created in 1575, its membership consisting of secular priests and clerics. In 1578 the Congregation moved to the Church of Santa Maria in Vallicella, but St. Philip himself continued to live at San Girolamo della Carità until 1583, so that for five years he and Victoria lived under the same roof and in daily contact. This intimate association between the greatest exponent of religious mysticism in music and the greatest spiritual leader of his time is inspiring to contemplate.

Though he was not a member of the Congregation, Victoria must have taken some part in its musical and spiritual exercises, at least while its headquarters were at San Girolamo.[6] We know, in any case, that St. Philip's principal musical collaborator (after the death of Giovanni Animuccia in 1571) was a Spaniard, Francisco Soto, called "de Langa" from the name of his birthplace. He had come to Rome at an early age, had entered the Papal Choir in 1562, and at the same time became a follower of St. Philip, being formally admitted to the Congregation shortly after its creation. From 1583 to 1598 he published five books of *Laudi spirituali* for the use of the Oratory, often using Italian and Spanish folk tunes for the settings of the religious texts. Sometimes Spanish words were used, as in the one beginning *Esclarecida madre,* which is a paraphrase of a Spanish villancico, *Esclarecida Juana,* preserved in a manuscript of the Medinaceli Library at Madrid. Soto had a fine singing voice, and it is said that he preserved it to the age of eighty. He died at Rome in 1619, in his eighty-fifth year.

It will be seen that Spanish musicians were conspicuously active in Rome at a period when that city was the musical center of the world. It is true that for many years Victoria held no official position in Rome commensurate with his genius and his importance as a composer. But there is every indication of the high fame and esteem in which he was held, and a tangible proof of this is that he was able to bring out his works in sumptuous editions, thanks to the backing of royal, princely, and churchly patrons. The fact that Victoria left his post as music director at the Collegium Germanicum to become a simple priest at San Girolamo indicates that he took his religious state very seriously and was truly, as Ancina called him, *Servus Christi ardens*—"an ardent servant of Christ." In the preface to his *Cantica B. Virginis per annum*, published in 1581, he declares that his whole ambition is to employ music as a means of raising the soul to the contemplation of divine truth. As a composer he enjoyed the luxury of fame and handsome folio editions, but as a servant of God he was content to walk humbly in the path of duty.

In the dedication of a book of Masses published in 1583, addressed to Philip II, Victoria expresses a desire to return to his native land after so long an absence. Nevertheless, he appears to have remained in Rome for another ten years or so. In 1592 he mentions for the first time his appointment as chaplain to the widowed Empress Mother María, sister of Philip II. His return to Spain probably took place in 1594 or 1595, and the remainder of his life was spent in Madrid, where, in addition to his attendance upon the empress, he was choirmaster at the Convent of the Descalzas Reales. He died on August 27, 1611.

As far as is known, Victoria composed only religious music—about one hundred and eighty works in all. From the very outset of his career the individual qualities of his style are apparent. His first book of motets, published in 1572, contains some of his finest and best-known compositions, *O quam gloriosum* and *O vos omnes,* the former, according to a practice frequently followed by Victoria, later used as the basis for a Mass included in the volume of 1583. Unlike most composers of the period, Victoria hardly ever took secular songs as themes for his Masses, using themes either from his own motets or from the liturgical chant. Most of Victoria's works were published in Rome, but after his return to Spain there appeared, in 1605, a work that has been called "the greatest triumph of his genius." This was the *Officium defunctorum,* a Requiem Mass for six voices composed in memory of the Empress María and dedicated to her daughter, the Princess Margaret. In addition to the parts of the Requiem that it was then customary to compose (the *Dies Irae* is not among them), the volume included a motet, *Versa est in luctum;* the responsorium *Libera me;* and a four-part setting of the Second Lesson of the Vigil Office, *Taedet animam meam.* This was the last work published by Victoria, and it is fitting that he should have closed his creative career with a composition that marks the culminating point of his art.

VICTORIA AND PALESTRINA

Victoria and Palestrina are often mentioned together as the two outstanding representatives of the so-called "Roman School." But a comparison between them is fruitless unless it serves to emphasize the differences both in their art and their character. We cannot accept Proske's opinion that Victoria "among all the Roman contemporaries of Palestrina stood next to him in spiritual nobility." Spirituality was not a dominant trait of Palestrina's character. As E. J. Dent writes, "The whole course of Palestrina's life shows clearly that he was not only a great religious composer but also a very successful business man." [7] Toward the end of his life, when momentarily overwhelmed by personal bereavements, he thought of entering the priesthood, but soon changed his mind, married a wealthy widow instead, and embarked upon a lucrative business career as a dealer in furs, with real estate as a profitable side line. Twice when negotiations for an important post were under way they were broken off because Palestrina demanded such exorbitant terms from his prospective employers. And one of his biographers suggests that it is very unlikely he ever served as musical director for St. Philip's Oratory, because he was not the man to offer his services free, as Animuccia and Soto had done. If we contrast these traits with those of the man who gave up an important musical post to become a humble priest at the Church of San Girolamo della Carità, and who even contemplated giving up composing in order that it might not interfere with his religious devotions, we must admit that the shoe does not fit where Proske thought it did. In spiritual nobility Victoria was second to none.

We have no desire to detract from the artistic merit of Palestrina, whatever his spiritual shortcomings may have been. There is every probability that he was Victoria's teacher, and the younger man—young enough to be his son, let it be remembered—unquestionably imbibed the best qualities of his style. It is natural that the elder man should have influenced the younger; what is remarkable is that the latter, in turn, influenced the former. In some of the later motets of Palestrina there is evidence that he was emulating the more ardent and vehement style of his young Spanish colleague. Romain Rolland [8] was one of the first to point out the significance of Victoria's expressive and dramatic tendency in foreshadowing one of the principal elements of lyrical tragedy through its musical projection of the inner spiritual life of man. And another perspicacious French writer, Henry Prunières, underlines this tendency in his summary of the Spanish master's art:

He makes use of the madrigalesque style and of all the musical symbolism then current in Italy, in order to express mystical emotions of such poignancy and tragic grandeur as none before him had attained. Every idea suggested by the text is in some manner illustrated by the music with an extraordinary inventiveness, force and colour.

The Passions in the Office for Holy Week (1585) are perhaps the works that reveal most characteristically the vehement and passionate genius of Victoria. Already, by their vigour and realistic detail, they announce the Passions of Bach, which they often surpass by the intensity of their mystical emotion.[9]

Palestrina is the Raphael of music, Victoria the El Greco. Each is great and unique in his own way.[10]

Some writers claim that Victoria's teacher in Rome was Bartolomé Escobedo, but this is impossible, because Escobedo left Rome eleven years before Victoria arrived there. Nevertheless, Escobedo merits some attention in his own right. He was born in Zamora about 1510, joined the Papal Choir in 1536, and in 1554 returned to Spain to become choirmaster at Segovia, where he died some ten years later. His works, similar in style to those of Morales, include a six-part Mass, *Philippus Rex Hispaniae,* written for the accession of Philip II, several motets, magnificats, and a Miserere. Salinas praises him highly, and from the examples of his work published by Eslava [11] we can appreciate the contrapuntal skill that he brings to the expression of his mystic fervor.

About the time that Victoria went to live at San Girolamo della Carità, a question of considerable importance was claiming the attention of musical circles in Rome. This was the question of the reform or revision of the traditional music of the Catholic Church (Gregorian chant or plain song) as embodied in the Roman gradual. In 1578 Pope Gregory XIII had commissioned Palestrina to undertake the preliminary groundwork for such a revision, in conjunction with Annibale Zoilo. Great as were the artistic merits of Palestrina and his colleagues, they lacked a historical and critical knowledge of Gregorian chant, and this "revision" meant, in effect, a distortion of the plain song to conform to sixteenth-century ideas on the subject. At this juncture a decisive step was taken by a Spanish musician who had for some years been resident in Rome, and who to his creative ability as a composer added a gift for disputatious theology and a talent for diplomatic intrigue. His name was Don Fernando de las Infantas. Born at Cordova in 1534, of a noble family, he had become known as a composer through several motets commemorating solemn or glorious events of the time, such as the death of Charles V in 1558 and the victory of Lepanto in 1571. He settled in Rome in 1572.

When Infantas learned of the intended revision of the gradual he decided that something ought to be done to circumvent this tampering with tradition. He at once sent a long report on the subject to Philip II, who replied with instructions to the Spanish ambassador in Rome to take the necessary steps in the matter. In doing this his religious zeal was doubtless heightened by the fact that the Spanish Crown had a monopoly on printing the graduals used in churches throughout the empire. The publication of a revised gradual authorized by the Roman pontiff would have rendered the Spanish books obsolete and thereby entailed a considerable loss to the Crown. If the motives that prompted Philip II to enforce his veto on the revised gradual were not entirely disinterested, the result was in any case fortunate, and Infantas may be longer remembered for his part in this affair than for his music, which, while revealing a remarkable science, is not exempt from traces of pedantry.

RELIGIOUS MUSIC IN SPAIN

Though the outstanding Spanish composers of church music were chiefly active in Rome, it must not be imagined that there was any lack of religious musical activity in Spain itself. Both Charles V and his successor Philip II were music-loving monarchs and took a keen interest in fostering all phases of the art. The Emperor Charles V, a member of the House of Burgundy, had learned to play the organ and the spinet in his youth. Educated entirely under Flemish influences, he naturally formed his chapel in Madrid with Flemish singers. But it is curious to observe that after his abdication and retirement to the Monastery of Yuste (in Extremadura) he separated himself completely from his Flemish chapel and surrounded himself with Spanish musicians, mostly Hieronymite monks, who sang for him daily at the religious services. He prided himself on being able to detect the slightest error or negligence in their singing and was continually keeping his ear cocked for false notes. He also emulated the critics of our own day who are always detecting what one composer has "borrowed" from another. Once, after hearing the choir sing some motets by Guerrero, from a book presented to him by the composer, the emperor, using his favorite—and barely translatable—expletive, exclaimed, "Oh, what a subtle thief is this Guerrero, for he has stolen this passage from So-and-so, and that one from So-and-so." Doubtless poor Guerrero was innocent of any deliberate musical thieving, though appearances may have been against him. The composition of a motet for four voices, *Ecce sic benedecetur homo,* has been attributed to Charles V.

Philip II continued to maintain his father's Flemish chapel in Madrid, but after he had begun to build (in 1562) his famous monastery of the Escorial, his musical interests became centered there, and even before it was completed he had a special choir installed (1573). After the completion of the monastery (1586), the choir numbered one hundred and fifty monks—as compared to forty singers in the Flemish chapel of Charles V.

Spain at that time was full of churches, monasteries, convents, and private chapels of the nobility, and in all of them music was given the utmost importance. Judging by the types of composition that were written for them—such as Victoria's Mass for twelve-part chorus written for the Convent of the Descalzas Reales—they must have possessed musical resources of a really exceptional order.

In Valencia, where the Duke of Calabria maintained a notable chapel under his *maestro de capilla* Pastrana, there existed a flourishing polyphonic school that preserved its vigor well into the seventeenth century. There we find the interesting figure of

Saint Francis Borgia, Duke of Gandia, who to his saintly virtues added the accomplishments of a musician: he composed a Mass and some motets, which were sung at a solemn religious festivity celebrating the Mystery of the Resurrection, consisting in part of an outdoor procession, as in the early *autos sacramentales* (*cf.* Chapter VI).

The most illustrious representative of the Valencian school was Juan Bautista Comes (1568–1643), whose works are characterized by a profound spiritual exultation and an imposing grandeur of form. In the masters of the Valencian school, with their tendency toward grandiose conceptions and violent contrasts, we encounter elements of the baroque style that left such marked traces in other branches of Spanish art during the seventeenth century. One of the most characteristic works of Comes is a Miserere for four choruses, a richly ornamented and magnificently developed composition that forms a worthy counterpart to the baroque altarpieces of the great Spanish cathedrals.

Another outstanding Valencian composer was Juan Gínez Pérez, from 1585 choirmaster of Valencia Cathedral, of which he was made a canon in 1595. Pérez was one of the composers who had a hand in the polyphonic setting of the celebrated Mystery of Elche, the mystery play on the Assumption of the Virgin Mary performed annually on August 14 and 15 at Elche, near Alicante. According to tradition, the text, music, and ceremonial of this liturgical drama, together with a miraculous image of the Virgin, were brought to Elche by an ark which drifted to the coast in the year 1266 (some accounts say 1370). Thereafter it was performed every year until 1568, when it was forbidden by Philip II following the death of his son Don Carlos. Revived in 1603, with new musical settings by Pérez, Antonio de Ribera, and Lluis Vich, it has continued to be given up to the present time. The part of the Virgin Mary is taken by a boy, and his long monodic passages are sung in a floridly ornate style that seems to go back to a much earlier period than that of the polyphonic settings. It was from the medieval tradition of the liturgical drama, combined with the new polyphonic and monodic vocal art, that the secular lyric theater of the sixteenth and seventeenth centuries was to emerge.

CHAPTER VI

Growth of the Lyric Drama

IT was under the direct influence of Virgil's *Eclogues* that Juan del Encina, toward the end of the fifteenth century, was led to undertake the composition of those pastoral dialogues or *Representaciones* that form the first definite starting point of the Spanish theater. For the element of dramatic presentation, however, his immediate precedent was to be found in the religious plays that stemmed from the medieval mysteries, such as the *Auto* [1] or *Misterio de los Reyes Magos,* performed at the feast of the Epiphany, whose text goes back perhaps to the middle of the twelfth century. A definite precursor of Encina may be found in the person of Gómez Manrique, who, like his more famous nephew Jorge Manrique, was both soldier and poet. His *Representación de Nuestro Señor,* the earliest extant example of a dramatic treatment of the Officium Pastorum in Spain, written between 1467 and 1481 for performance by the nuns at the Convent of Calabazanos, is the prototype of the *Representaciones* that Encina wrote and produced for the entertainment of his ducal patrons at Alba de Tormes.

In those of his *Representaciones* written for religious feasts, such as Christmas and Easter, Encina was following a well-established tradition. But in those dealing with secular themes he broke fresh ground. The two secular eclogues in which Encina comes nearest to achieving a definite dramatic form are those entitled *The Squire that Turns Shepherd* and *The Shepherds that Turn Courtiers*. The first tells of a shepherdess, Pascuala, who is wooed by a shepherd named Mingo. A squire appears, falls in love with the shepherdess and invites her to come to the court. Pascuala finally consents to accept the squire as her husband, on condition that he will turn shepherd, to which he agrees. The piece ends with all three singing a villancico (Manrique's *Representación*, let it be noted, ended with a villancico also).

In the second eclogue we find the squire, married to his shepherdess, already bored with life in the country. He tries to persuade the shepherds to give up their pastoral existence and turn courtiers. After much argument pro and con, the squire prevails upon his wife to enter the palace and don courtly dress, whereupon the others follow her example. In the middle of this eclogue the characters sing the villancico *Gasajémonos de hucía* (Barbieri, No. 353), and at the conclusion they sing another one, *Ninguno cierre las puertas* (Barbieri, No. 354), in praise of love. Both of these are jolly, spirited tunes.

Of Encina's fourteen plays, all but two conclude with a villancico, usually accompanied by a dance. This poet-musician was therefore not only the creator of the Spanish drama, but of the Spanish lyric theater as well.

His first imitator in Spain was that same Lucas Fernández with whom he had disputed the choirmastership of Salamanca Cathedral. Fernández (1474–1544), who in 1522 succeeded Encina's brother Diego Fermoselle as professor of music at Salamanca University, was the author of a volume of *Farsas y Églogas al Modo y Estilo Pastoril y Castellano* (Salamanca, 1514) which contains a "Dialogue To Be Sung" that marks a further advance toward the conception of "opera," poor though it is in dramatic elements. The significant feature here is that the dialogue is intended to be sung throughout. It is therefore a very early example of quasi-dramatic monody, and without doubt an instrumental accompaniment for the performance may be assumed.

The dialogue, consisting of one hundred and fifty-four lines,

is between two shepherds, Bras and Blas; the former is down-
cast, and upon learning that the cause of his chagrin is unrequited
love, Blas tries to console him. The author directs that it be sung
to the *tono* (tune) of *Juan Pastor*, a well-known villancico beginning

> *Quién te hizo, Juan pastor,*
> *sin gasajo y sin placer?*
> *Que tú alegre solías ser.*
> (Who has made you, shepherd John,
> Lose your mirth and gaiety,
> When you so joyful used to be?)

This villancico is found in Barbieri's *Cancionero* (No. 360), in a
three-part setting ascribed to a certain Badajoz, who has been
identified as a musician in the service of King John III of Portugal (*cf.* Chapter XVIII). It is also included in Esteban Daza's
tablature book *El Parnaso* (1576), considerably modified and
arranged as a solo song with guitar accompaniment.[2]

The tune is very simple, and it is probable that the singers in
the *Diálogo* varied the air to avoid monotony, in the manner
of the *diferencias* on popular airs found in the sixteenth-century
tablature books.

MUSIC IN THE PLAYS OF GIL VICENTE

The customary villancicos occur in plays by other followers of
Encina, notably Fernán López de Yanguas and Bartolomé de
Torres Naharro. But music figures more prominently in the
plays of the most important dramatist of the period, the Portuguese Gil Vicente, who flourished as a writer for the stage from
1502 to 1536. In spite of his Portuguese nationality, Gil Vicente
looms large in the history of the early Spanish drama, and, of his
forty-two works, twenty-five are written entirely or partly in
Castilian. Like so many of the poets of that time, Vicente was
also a musician and wrote the music for some of the songs in his
plays. In the *Barca de la Gloria* (1519) and the *Comedia de
Rubena* (1521) there are several choruses. And in the tragi-

comedy *La Fragua del Amor* (1525), we find the following
curious stage directions: *Entra un Negro na fragoa, e andaon de
martellos todos cuatro em seu compasso, e cantaon as serranas a
quatro voces a o compasso dos martellos esta cantiga seguiente.*
(Enter a Negro into the forge, and all four keep time striking
with their hammers, and the shepherdesses, to the rhythm of the
hammer strokes, sing the following song in four voices.) Here is
an "anvil chorus" that anticipates *Il Trovatore* by more than four
centuries!

Another curious stage direction occurs in *La Barca do Purga-
torio* (1518, in Portuguese): *Sahem os diablos do batel i com
huma cantiga muito desacordada levaon o taful; e os anjos cantando lavaon o menino.* This is a primitive example of musicodramatic realism: the devils carry off the gambler to the accompaniment of a "very discordant" song, while angels sweetly
singing bear the child to heaven.

In an *Auto da Fe* by Gil Vicente dating from 1510—it is really
an allegory in which Faith explains to the shepherds the mysteries
of Christianity—we encounter the term *ensalada* for the first
time: *Cantaon huma ensalada que veio de Francia, e assi se vaon
com ella, e acaba a obra.* (They go off singing an ensalada, which
came from France, and so the play ends.) From this passage, it
has been rashly concluded that the *ensalada* (*cf.* Chapter II) was
of French origin. But as Menéndez y Pelayo pointed out, the
phrase simply means that this particular *ensalada* was not written
by Vicente himself.[3]

Another piece by Gil Vicente that deserves mention is the *Auto
of the Sibyl Cassandra*, an eclogue for Christmas morning. The
heroine, Cassandra, is wooed by the shepherd Salamon, but she
is determined not to marry, for she has had intimations of the
approaching birth of the Saviour and cherishes the hope that she
is to be the virgin mother of this Holy Child. Salamon appeals to
Cassandra's three uncles for help in his courting, and all four
enter singing a *folía* (*cantando todos quatro de folía a cantiga
seguinte*):

Sañosa esta la nina!
Ay Dios, quién le hablaría?
(She is wild! She is wild!
Who shall speak to the child?)

This is probably the first mention of the so-called *Folies d'Es-pagne* (which, according to Salinas, was of Portuguese origin),[4] the dance that later became famous through its use by celebrated European composers such as Lully, Corelli, and Vivaldi. Vicente's eclogue was written about 1505 and therefore antedates by several decades the *Farsa del Juego de Cañas* by Diego Sánchez de Badajoz (*c.* 1550), which Cotarelo cites as containing the first mention of the *folías* as a special way of singing and dancing.[5]

RISE OF THE POPULAR THEATER

The plays of Encina and Vicente were written for private patrons, in whose homes they were performed before invited audiences. The theater had yet to become a public and commercial entertainment. This transition was accomplished largely through the enterprise and talent of a goldsmith from Seville named Lope de Rueda (fl. *c.* 1544–1567), who achieved wide success as playwright and actor-manager. He formed a company of strolling players with which he toured the country, producing his own plays for popular audiences. His material equipment was extremely primitive.

In the time of this celebrated Spaniard [wrote Cervantes, recalling the activities of Lope de Rueda] the whole apparatus of a manager was contained in a large sack, and consisted of four white shepherd's jackets . . . four beards and false sets of hanging locks, and four shepherd's crooks, more or less. . . . The theater was composed of four benches, arranged in a square, with five or six boards laid across them. . . . The furniture of the theater was an old blanket drawn aside by two cords, making what they call a tiring-room, behind which were the musicians, who sang old ballads without a guitar.[6]

The reference to the singing of old ballads in the theater is interesting. Lope de Rueda himself used to come before the audiences at the beginning of the performance and sing a sort of prologue, accompanying himself on a guitar.

These early performances took place in a public square, or in the courtyard of some large house. In the course of time certain courtyards (called *corrales*) came to be permanently fitted out as theaters, with a rude stage and benches, an awning for the actors, but no roof for the spectators. Two theaters of this type were set up in Madrid in 1579 and 1583, taking their names from the streets in which they were located ("Príncipe" and "Cruz"). When the court was transferred to Madrid in 1561, making that city the permanent capital of the country, theatrical activity began to be concentrated there. By the beginning of the seventeenth century this activity had expanded enormously, for the theater was truly a passion with the Spaniards. Before the middle of the century there were as many as forty companies of actors in Madrid. They had their special quarter in the city, near the Prado (in the streets now appropriately named after Cervantes and Lope de Vega), which served as a general gathering place not only for the actors themselves, but also for playwrights, poets, managers, and the whole motley tribe of theatrical hangers-on. It was one of the most animated quarters of the city, and also one of the rowdiest, for the stage folk were inclined to be riotous and unruly. Here it was, on a summer afternoon in 1629, that a comedian named Pedro Villegas stabbed and killed the brother of Pedro Calderón de la Barca, and then took refuge in the near-by Convent of the Trinitarias, which was forthwith assaulted by an angry mob that included the great Calderón himself.

Calderón was then only twenty-nine, and his greatest achievements were still to come. At that time the most celebrated figure in the Spanish drama was Felix Lope de Vega (1562–1635), an amazingly prolific genius who wrote over two thousand plays. His popularity with the common people was overwhelming, and he was no less successful in pleasing the noble society of the court. For, while the drama became a popular pastime, it did not cease to develop simultaneously as a courtly entertainment. When

Philip IV, an affable and pleasure-loving monarch, ascended the throne in 1621, at the age of sixteen, there commenced a period of lavish dramatic entertainments at the Spanish Court, with music playing a role of ever-increasing prominence.

THE FIRST SPANISH OPERA

Spain, indeed, was the second nation to follow the example of Italy in the performance of "opera," that is, of plays set entirely to music. In 1627 Heinrich Schütz had introduced this Florentine novelty into Germany with his setting of a translation of Rinuccini's *Dafne*, which Peri had set to music in 1594 as the first "opera." And toward the end of 1629, Philip IV and his court were regaled with a similar novelty, in the form of a "pastoral eclogue that was sung at a festivity in honor of His Majesty." The work was entitled *La Selva sin Amor* (*The Forest Without Love*), and the author was none other than Lope de Vega. Unfortunately, we do not know who wrote the music, nor has any trace of the score been found. The musical character of the work must be deduced from the internal evidence of the text, and from certain passages in the dedication, addressed to Don Juan Alonso Enriquez de Cabrera, Admiral of Castile. In this dedication Lope de Vega writes,

Your Excellency not having seen this Eclogue, which was sung in performance [*que se representó cantada*] before their Majesties and Highnesses, a new thing in Spain, I thought it opportune to print it, that in this manner Your Excellency might the more easily picture it to himself, though the least part of it was my verses. The machinery for the stage was made by Cosme Lotti, a Florentine engineer, for whom His Majesty sent to Italy to enter his service in the planning of gardens, fountains and other things in which he has a rare and excellent talent.

The dramatist goes on to describe the "machinery," which was extremely elaborate and ingenious. Then he speaks about the music:

Luigi Boccherini

Domenico Scarlatti

The instruments occupied the front part of the theater, without being seen, and to their harmony the actors sang the verses; all the effects, such as surprise, lamentation, love, anger, being expressed in the composition of the music itself.

Writing as a literary man, Lope de Vega here pays a significant tribute to the expressive and emotional power of music as it appears in the Spanish lyric drama from the very beginning, the aim being always to emphasize poetic and dramatic expression, rather than to display technical skill and virtuosity for its own sake.

La Selva sin Amor is in one act and consists of some seven hundred lines.[7] It deals with the amorous difficulties experienced by two shepherdesses and their swains, with a happy denouement effected through the intervention of Venus and Cupid. The concerted vocal numbers comprise a trio, a duet, and the final chorus; otherwise, the characters sing as soloists. Pedrell maintained that this work was sung only in part, and that spoken dialogue alternated with the singing. But Cotarelo points out that if it had not been entirely sung it would have been no novelty (for plays in which singing and speaking alternated had long been known in Spain), and it would have been nonsense for Lope de Vega to write that this performance was "a new thing in Spain."

Lope de Vega was surrounded by a host of brilliant contemporaries—including Tirso de Molina, Guillén de Castro, Ruiz de Alarcón, Cervantes, and Quevedo—who brought the Spanish theater to a high level of achievement. In most of their plays music intervened more or less prominently. But it was Lope de Vega's most notable successor, Calderón de la Barca, who united music and poetry in an indigenous form that was to take permanent root in Spain. He did this by creating the zarzuela.

BIRTH OF THE ZARZUELA

This musicodramatic form, characterized by the division into two acts and the alternation of singing and dancing with spoken dialogue, derived its name from the palace of La Zarzuela,[8] originally a hunting lodge built by the Infante Don Fernando in the royal domain of the Pardo near Madrid. After Don Fernando's departure for Flanders in 1634, Philip IV enlarged the building, adorned it with gardens, fountains, and statues, and used it as a kind of rustic retreat. The king, of course, had to have his entertainment there as well as in Madrid, so it became customary for the comedians to present short pieces, with music and singing, which at first were called "fiestas de zarzuela" and later simply zarzuelas. The early fiestas de zarzuela were probably of an improvisatory character, with a very slight literary basis. At any rate, the first-known text described as a fiesta de zarzuela is Calderón's *El Golfo de las Sirenas,* performed at the Palace of La Zarzuela on January 17, 1657. It was called a "Piscatory Eclogue," because the scene was by the sea and some of the characters were fisherfolk. It consisted of only one act, preceded by a *loa* [9] and followed by a *mojiganga.*[10]

Closer to the zarzuela pattern, because it was in two acts, was an earlier work by Calderón, *El Jardín de Falerina (The Garden of Falerina)*. This was performed at the royal palace in Madrid in 1648 (not at La Zarzuela, as originally affirmed by Vera Tassis, Calderón's friend and biographer, and repeated by later writers). Pedrell—followed in this by Mitjana—fell into a curious error with regard to the date of this performance and the authorship of the music, fixing the former in 1629 and attributing the latter to a composer named José Peiró. This Peiró (or Peyró) was in fact a Catalan or Mallorcan musician who flourished in the first part of the eighteenth century, and he was therefore certainly not the composer of the music for the first performance of *El Jardín de Falerina,* even though that took place nearly twenty years later than Pedrell supposed.[11]

Paradoxically, the work that stands as the real prototype of the zarzuela, Calderón's *El Laurel de Apolo,* was likewise not performed at the palace of La Zarzuela, but at the Buen Retiro palace in Madrid (built in 1630; the Coliseo del Buen Retiro, or royal theater, was built in 1639). The piece, however, had been originally commissioned for La Zarzuela in the autumn of 1657, and its transference to Madrid was due to extraneous circumstances, namely the birth of a royal heir, which took place on November 28 of that year. The king returned to Madrid to be present on this auspicious occasion, and, as he remained in the capital, Calderón's two-act zarzuela was performed at the Buen Retiro on March 4, 1658. The score has not been preserved, but the musical numbers were as follows:

1. Chorus of shepherds and shepherdesses; 2. musical dialogue between Apollo and Cupid; 3. chorus of nymphs and solo of Apollo; 4. rustic song and dance; 5. solo of Iris, accompanied by double chorus; 6. dialogue, partly sung and partly spoken, between Apollo and Daphne; 7. chorus of shepherds, with a shepherdess singing a seguidilla; 8. final chorus.

From this it may be seen that even in the mythological concoctions demanded by courtly taste, the rustic and popular note was not lacking. It will be noticed that one of the best known of Spanish popular song-and-dance forms, the seguidillas, was already in vogue at this time. Like Don Quixote, the seguidillas came from La Mancha—Cervantes mentions them in the second part of his famous novel (Chapter 38).

CALDERÓN AS OPERA LIBRETTIST

The term "opera" was not used in Spain until the end of the seventeenth century, when we hear of a "fiesta de ópera" taking place in Madrid (1698); but the form itself, contrary to the belief of Pedrell and Mitjana, was by no means unknown. Calderón himself wrote the text of two Spanish operas. The first of these was *La Púrpura de la Rosa,* in one act, written to celebrate the marriage of the Infanta María Teresa to Louis XIV of France. Like *El Laurel de Apolo,* this work was originally intended for La Zarzuela (whence on the title page of the edition of 1664 it is called a "Fiesta de la Zarzuela"), but was instead performed at the Buen Retiro on January 17, 1660. There can be no question that the piece was entirely sung, for in the *loa,* or introduction, Calderón expressly states that the play *habrá de ser toda música* ("will be all in music"). Thereupon one of the characters objects that the Spanish temperament will never put up with a whole comedy entirely sung. The objection is answered by the assurance that this is not a comedy (which would be in three acts), but simply a small one-act piece.

We do not possess any of the music written for *La Púrpura de la Rosa,* but we are more fortunate with respect to the second of Calderón's operas, *Celos Aun del Aire Matan,* music by Juan Hidalgo, performed in the Coliseo del Buen Retiro on December 5, 1660. The musicologist José Subirá, while working among the archives of the Palacio de Liria, the home of the Dukes of Alba in Madrid, was lucky enough to discover the music for the first act of this opera. He devoted a chapter of his book *La Música en la Casa de Alba* (Madrid, 1927) to this important discovery, and in 1933 he published the score in a separate volume, together with a detailed critical commentary.

By this time Calderón was apparently convinced that the Spaniards could take their opera in larger doses, for *Celos Aun del Aire Matan* was a full-length comedy in three acts.[12] As the play opens, the nymph Aurora is brought before Diana, charged with having been unfaithful to her vows by falling in love with the shepherd Erostrato. The penalty for this crime is death, which Diana and her nymphs forthwith prepare to administer. Cephalus and his servant Clarin, attracted by Aurora's cries of distress, appear upon the scene and Cephalus endeavors to save Aurora's life, if necessary by the sacrifice of his own. Aurora, however, is saved by the supernatural intervention of Amor, who transforms her into a nymph of the air. Erostrato vows to be revenged for his frustrated love. Here the first act ends. Thereafter the nymph Procris, who had been strongest in her condemnation of Aurora's dereliction, becomes herself the victim of her love for Cephalus and learns to her sorrow that "jealousy, even when it comes from the air, can kill." But, as this is a comedy, there must be a happy ending. So Venus, at the request of Aurora, prevails upon Jupiter to transform Procris into a star and Cephalus into a zephyr.

Juan Hidalgo, who composed the music for this opera, was one of the most famous Spanish musicians of his time. He was harpist of the Royal Chapel from 1631 and is described as an eminent composer of *tonos divinos y humanos* ("of sacred and secular songs"). The Duke of Infantado, the most distinguished patron of music among Spain's grandees of that period, calls him "unique in the faculty of music." Hidalgo lived to a very advanced age, dying at Madrid in 1685. It was he who wrote music for Calderón's last comedy, *Hado y Divisa de Leonido y de Marfisa*, in 1680. He also wrote music for Calderón's *Ni Amor se Libra de Amor* (1662) and for *Los Celos Hacen Estrellas* by Juan Vélez, probably dating from the same year.[13] Pedrell printed a four-part chorus with instrumental accompaniment from *Ni Amor se Libra de Amor* (*Love Frees Not Itself From Love*), a comedy dealing with the love of Cupid and Psyche. This chorus, *Quedito, pasito* (*Softly, quietly*), is sung off stage while Cupid is sleeping. It is, in effect, a sort of sophisticated lullaby. The music is beautifully expressive; the poetic idea is conveyed with exquisite sensibility and with an infallible feeling for the most appropriate harmonic effect.[14]

Most of the early Spanish theatrical music that has been preserved is in the form of choruses or concerted vocal numbers. But the first act of *Celos Aun del Aire Matan*, while including several brief concerted numbers, offers the most extensive example of monody in the early Spanish theater that has come down to us. Unfortunately, in the manuscript discovered by Subirá, only an outline of the instrumental accompaniment (*basso continuo*) is given with the voice part, so that we cannot form an exact idea of the harmonic texture of the music. Nevertheless, in Hidalgo's arias and recitatives we can perceive the same freedom and variety of expression that we previously found in the Spanish solo songs of the sixteenth century, based on a very advanced sense of tonality. Compared with Italian opera of the same period, Hidalgo's music reveals less development in the formal structure of the aria, but more variety and flexibility in the treatment of the recitative, as well as greater rhythmic animation in the melodic line. Interesting is the presence of a sort of leading motive, the lament of Aurora, which recurs throughout the act, modified on successive appearances in order to stress the changes in the dramatic situation. Certain traits, such as the use of the metric pattern of the seguidilla, give the music a definitely national character.

Though the manuscript gives no indication of the instrumentation, an orchestra, of course, was used in the performance. The theatrical companies usually had only harps, violins, and guitars; but the Royal Chapel had several wind instruments: bassoons, *chirimías* (a kind of clarinet), and trumpets. These were doubtless available for performances at the royal palace, and on occasion they were augmented by other instruments, as indicated by the following passage from the prologue to the comedy *Celos Vencidos de Amor,* dating from 1698: "The singing . . . in addition to the harps and guitars, violins and basses, trumpets, and kettledrums, was accompanied by the orchestra that has come from Flanders, consisting of very fine instruments, such as the viol [*vigüela de arco*], the viola d'amore, etc." Castanets are also mentioned in this text.[15] Here, then, we have a complete orchestra comprising strings, wind, and percussion.

OTHER DRAMATIC COMPOSERS

Most of the Spanish composers of the seventeenth century appear to have been actively engaged in writing for the theater. Cotarelo gives the names of more than a hundred who were writing stage music between the years 1615 and 1730, and there were many whose names have not come down to us. Besides Hidalgo, the outstanding dramatic composers of the seventeenth century were Juan Blas de Castro, Mateo Romero, Carlos Patiño, José Marín, Francisco Navarro, Miguel Ferrer, and Juan de Navas.

Two others, Manuel Machado and Manuel Correa, were of Portuguese origin, though active in Spain.

Juan Blas de Castro was a close friend of Lope de Vega, who frequently mentions him in his writings and who wrote a eulogy on his death. Castro was a member of the Royal Chapel from 1605 and was blind for the last twenty years of his life (he died in 1631). The manuscripts of most of his works were lost in the fire of 1734 that destroyed the archives of the royal palace, but twenty of his compositions, for three and four voices, are included in the *Cancionero de Sablonara*. The majority of these appear to have been sung in plays.

Mateo Romero, called "El Maestro Capitán" because he had served with the army in Flanders, became a member of the Royal Chapel in 1594 and was made maestro in 1598. He was ordained a priest in 1609. In 1633 he retired on a pension and was succeeded by Carlos Patiño. Romero died in Madrid in 1647. The *Cancionero de Sablonara* contains twenty-two compositions by him, including settings of poems by Lope de Vega.

The century is brought to a close by José Marín (1619–1699), whose career reads like a picaresque novel (he seems to have combined murder and highway robbery with composing and singing in church choirs). He was imprisoned and sentenced to the galleys, but managed to escape, and ended his days in an exemplary manner. His song *Corazón que en prisión* (*Heart That in Duress*), is supposed to refer to the period of his imprisonment.[16] He wrote music for zarzuelas by the dramatist Juan Bautista Diamante, one of the followers of Calderón.

SOME MINOR THEATRICAL FORMS

Now a word about the minor theatrical forms, in which music was a paramount factor. Theatrical performances usually began with a *cuatro de empezar*, that is, a four-part chorus sung to the accompaniment of guitars and harps. This was followed by the *loa* or prologue, which was sometimes also sung. After the first act came an *entremés*, in which there was singing and sometimes dancing. The second act was followed by a *baile*, in which, as its name indicates, dancing was featured. After the third act the performance was concluded by a *fin de fiesta* or a *mojiganga*. The entire show lasted about two hours, and there were no intermissions.

There was another minor form, known as *jácara*, which had no fixed place in the performance, but was interpolated more or less at will. The *jácara* was originally a picaresque interlude describing the discomfiture of some villainous character—always a source of amusement to the gallery. Later it became more elaborate and was called *jácara entremesada*, combining spoken dialogue, singing, and dancing. By the end of the seventeenth century it was thus a sort of miniature comic opera with a strong popular tang.[17]

Insignificant as these minor forms were in themselves, the music written for them—even when composed by anonymous hacks such as were employed by every theatrical troupe—is full of charm and verve. After hearing or playing some of this music, one can understand the admiration expressed by a contemporary theologian, Padre Ignacio Camargo, in his *Discurso Theológico sobre los Teatros y Comedias de este Siglo* (Salamanca, 1689): [18]

Theatrical music in Spain is today so advanced and so highly developed in all its aspects, that it seems impossible it could go any further. For the rich harmony of the instruments, the skill and smoothness of the voices, the ingenious invention of the melodies, the verve and spirit of the choruses, the gracefulness of the ornaments, the sustaining of the trills and the weaving of the counterpoint, produce such a harmonious effect that it keeps the hearers spellbound in suspense. To the least verse or air sung in the theater they give such charm and zest, that Hidalgo, that great and celebrated musician of the Royal Chapel, confessed with admiration that he could never compose anything of such perfection, and used to say, in jest, that without doubt it was the devil who conducted in the theaters.[19]

Hidalgo was too modest in disclaiming the ability to match the perfection achieved by his colleagues in the theater. As for Padre Camargo, that worthy theologian was in reality penning an attack upon the theater on the grounds of morality. How irresistibly fascinating the lyric theater in Spain must have been, when it could draw forth such a glowing tribute even from a professed enemy!

CHAPTER VII

In the Orbit of Scarlatti

IF Spanish musicians invaded Italy in full force during the
sixteenth century, the tables were turned during the eighteenth, when Italian musicians swarmed into Spain, captured
the lyric theater by assault, and comfortably installed themselves
in the seats of the mighty. This situation was largely the result
of a change in the ruling dynasty of Spain. The House of Austria became extinct with the miserable and sickly Carlos II, who
died in 1700 without issue, reluctantly naming as his heir the
grandson of Louis XIV, the Duc d'Anjou. The latter consequently ascended the Spanish throne in 1701 as Philip V, a youth
of seventeen, entirely ignorant of the country and its language. To
make matters worse, he at once proceeded to marry a thirteen-
year-old Italian princess, Marie Louise of Savoy, whose igno-
rance of Spain was as complete as his own. She died in 1714, but
Philip immediately enmeshed himself still more deeply in the
trammels of Italianism by marrying Elizabeth Farnese, Duchess
of Parma, a forceful and ambitious woman who quickly became
the real ruler of Spain. As prime minister she chose an Italian up-
start, Alberoni, who was said to have served the Duc de Vendôme
in the triple capacity of secretary, buffoon, and cook.

In a court infested with Italian favorites, Italian music naturally held the place of honor. Italian opera troupes had begun to

appear in Spain from the beginning of the century. According to Cotarelo, no new lyrico-dramatic works in Spanish were produced in Madrid between the years 1700 and 1707. All was Italian opera. In 1730 a mediocre Neapolitan musician named Francesco Coradini came to Madrid and was soon appointed official court composer. But the Italian faction achieved its major triumph with the arrival, in 1737, of the famous male soprano Carlo Broschi, better known as Farinelli.

This singer, reputed to have had the most beautiful voice ever heard, had aroused unbounded enthusiasm throughout Europe. He intended to make only a flying visit to Madrid between engagements in Paris and London, but circumstances completely upset his calculations. Philip V had sunk into a state of melancholy and indifference from which apparently nothing could arouse him. Without his knowledge, the queen arranged for Farinelli to give a concert in a room next to the king's. The unhappy monarch was so delighted with Farinelli's singing that he sent for the artist and offered to give him any reward he might name. The upshot was that the celebrated *castrato* was retained at the Spanish Court at a huge salary, having agreed to renounce his public career and to sing only for the pleasure of his royal master. Thereafter, until the king's death nine years later, Farinelli sang the same four songs to him every night. By thus rendering himself indispensable to the king, the Italian singer was able to make himself a powerful figure at the Spanish Court. So cleverly did he insinuate himself that even after Philip's death his influence continued and increased; during the reign of Ferdinand VI he was a political personality of the first magnitude, consulted on affairs of state, courted by foreign diplomats, and enjoying all the privileges of a royal favorite. It was not until the advent of Carlos III in 1759 that Farinelli, after more than twenty-five years of uninterrupted sway, was obliged to leave Spain, though still preserving his princely salary in his enforced retirement at Bologna.

Of the Italian influence on the lyric theater in Spain we shall

speak in the next chapter. For the present our primary concern is
with instrumental music. Opera, as the most ostentatious of musical forms, has always been the center of attraction in circles where
enjoyment of music is inseparable from social distractions, scenic
display, and vocal virtuosity. Most of the Italian musicians at the
Spanish Court were concerned with opera, either as composers or
as performers. The disparity between worldly appreciation of
vocal and instrumental music may be seen by comparing the position of Farinelli at the Spanish Court with that of another Italian
musician who also spent a large portion of his life in Madrid. We
refer to Domenico Scarlatti.

SCARLATTI IN SPAIN

Scarlatti's sojourn in Spain was not a mere episode in his life,
as some writers seem to regard it. It was the dominant factor of
his whole existence and artistic career. In the first place, we now
know that Scarlatti, having settled in Madrid in 1729, at the age
of forty-four, remained there for the rest of his life, instead of returning to his native city of Naples to spend his last years, as had
previously been supposed.[1] Moreover, Scarlatti had been living
in the Iberian Peninsula since 1720, when he was called to Lisbon
as maestro of the Royal Chapel there and music master to the
Princess Maria Barbara. With the exception of a brief visit to his
father at Naples in 1724, Scarlatti did not quit the Iberian Peninsula after taking up his post at Lisbon.[2] During the ten years he
had previously spent in Rome, he composed several operas that
are now quite forgotten; during the thirty-seven years that he
lived on Iberian soil he gave to the world those unique keyboard
pieces that form a landmark in the development of instrumental
music and that continue to delight us by their grace and vivacity,
their sparkle and freshness.

It was for his royal pupil, the Princess Maria Barbara, that
Scarlatti composed those harpsichord pieces, which we usually
refer to as sonatas, but which he himself modestly entitled *Eser-
cizi*—"exercises." The first volume of these, containing thirty

pieces, was published at Madrid in 1728 or 1729, about the time that Scarlatti arrived in the Spanish capital in the suite of the Princess Maria Barbara, who had married the heir to the Spanish throne, the future Ferdinand VI. Scarlatti retained his position as music master to the princess, who was a sincere and accomplished musician. When she became queen in 1746 she made him her *maestro de camara*, while her husband conferred upon him the title of *Caballero del Hábito de Cristo*. Thus Scarlatti's position at the Spanish Court was secure and pleasant, for his royal patroness appreciated his qualities and took pains to show it. Yet his position was a modest one compared to that of Farinelli. His relative obscurity is indicated by the paucity of information that has come down to us concerning his life in Madrid. It has been suggested that he was befriended and protected by Farinelli, but there is no evidence to support this view.[3] Had this been so, it is reasonable to suppose that some of Scarlatti's operas would have been produced in Madrid; yet there is no record of any such performance.

If details of Scarlatti's life in Spain are lacking, we can at least evoke the atmosphere in which he lived. Under the Bourbons, the Spanish Court was very different from what it had been in the time of the Hapsburgs. The somber austerity of the Escorial was a perfect manifestation of the temperament of Philip II, but the character and tastes of Philip V and his successors found expression in palaces of quite another type. The combination of French taste and Italian ingenuity produced elaborately ornate palaces such as those of Aranjuez and La Granja, built in the neighborhood of Madrid. Here every artifice that human skill could contrive and every whim that wealth could satisfy were united to achieve marvels of artificial preciosity and lavish display. The palace of La Granja, built by Philip V on a spot nearly four thousand feet above sea level, had three hundred and fifty acres of gardens and twenty-six monumental fountains, considered by some authorities superior to those of Versailles. The crowning glory of this architectural-aquatic extravaganza was the fountain called *Los Baños de Diana,* showing the goddess emerging from the water surrounded by twenty naked nymphs. This was the favorite residence of Philip V, as of his successor, Ferdinand VI.

Scarlatti's time, then, was passed between the royal palace in Madrid and the royal residences of La Granja and Aranjuez. In these palaces the atmosphere was strictly rococo and utterly superficial. But La Granja and Aranjuez were situated in the country. In going to them from Madrid, one drove along the open road, where muleteers might be passing; by fields, where farmers might be singing at their work; through hamlets, where peasants might be dancing and making merry. In Madrid itself one heard the cries of the street vendors and night watchmen, the songs of the blind beggars, and the strains of the ubiquitous guitar from every open doorway. Scarlatti was a Neapolitan and as such possessed an innate love for popular music. We may be certain that he lent a more attentive ear to the popular songs and dance tunes of Spain than to the trite conventionalities of the Italian opera in Madrid. The proof is in his music.

Dr. Burney, the pioneer English historian of music, writing in Scarlatti's own century, observed that in the Neapolitan master's music there were many passages "in which he imitated the melody of tunes sung by carriers, muleteers and common people." Subsequent commentators, likewise noting this popular element, have been more specific regarding its origin. One of Scarlatti's distinguished countrymen, the modern composer Francesco Malipiero, goes straight to the heart of the matter when he writes: "Whoever observes his [Scarlatti's] life by means of his works, must remain impressed by the influence popular Spanish music exerted on him."

THE HISPANISM OF SCARLATTI

The rhythmic verve and variety of Scarlatti's style are a continual reminder of his sojourn in a land where rhythm is the essence of every musical impulse. Among the six hundred or more sonatas written by Scarlatti, one might cull a delightful album of "Spanish Dances," redolent both of courtly and popular atmosphere, stylized with exquisite grace and infallible artistry. Conspicuous in such a collection would be a Sonata in D major (No. 208 of the Longo edition), which, though editorially labeled a minuet, is in reality a *jota aragonesa*, in lively 3/8 time, with the characteristic triplets; and a Sonata in G minor (Longo No. 338), which is a typical dance of the province of León.

Examples of sonatas that utilize the basic rhythm and figuration of the *jota* are too numerous to mention. Generally speaking, whenever the time signature is 3/8 or 3/4 the influence of the *jota* is usually apparent. A particularly interesting example of the *jota* style, which happens to be in 6/8 time, is the Sonata in C major (Longo No. 104). This bears a pronounced rhythmic analogy to the theme used by Lalo in the Rondo of his *Symphonie Espagnole*. The same basic rhythmic pattern is also observable in the last movement, so thoroughly Scarlattian in spirit, of Manuel de Falla's Harpsichord Concerto. The alternation of 3/4 and 6/8 rhythms, so typical of Spanish music, is often to be met with in Scarlatti; likewise the frequent use of syncopation.

The Sonata in B flat (Longo No. 498) is replete with Catalonian popular rhythms; but here Scarlatti is nearer home, for these rhythms in turn show an analogy to the popular music of Sicily, with which Catalonia long had the closest relations. Essentially cosmopolitan in form, but with a Spanish touch that has caused it to be called the *Bourée d'Aranjuez*, is the Sonata No. 263.

Since the tonadilla was coming to the fore in Madrid during the later years of Scarlatti's life (*cf.* Chapter VIII), it is not surprising to find him writing sonatas that bear unmistakable reflections of the tonadilla style. Such is the Sonata in G minor (No. 128), from which we quote a few measures of marked Hispanic character:

Example 10.

The influence of the guitar upon Scarlatti's style is manifested in many details of his music. One of the most prominent of these guitaristic effects is the internal pedal point, derived from the practice, it would seem, of steadying the player's hand by dwelling on one or two notes while the other notes of the harmony are changed. Throughout Scarlatti's sonatas there are passages that are strongly reminiscent of the style of the early Spanish guitarists. The most striking example is probably the Sonata No. 324, especially from measure 14 onward, which is absolutely in the *punteado* style, and again from measures 27–30, in which the combination of arpeggio chords and single detached notes, and the typical cadence, might have stemmed directly from any of the old guitar books. Other sonatas that show kinship with the classical guitar style are Nos. 57, 310, and 400.

The popular guitar style, on the other hand, is illustrated in the Sonata No. 449, with its harmonization of a melody by descending to the octave below, and its chordal passage work lying between the widely spaced march of the two outer parts:

Example 11.

Further evidence of the guitar technique is found in Scarlatti's predilection for building up chords with fourths instead of thirds (a conspicuous instance, among many, is the Sonata No. 58, espe-

Manuel García as Othello

María Malibran

By Permission of Columbia University Press

cially in the version of the *Codice Veneziano*). Of frequent occurrence is the typically Andalusian melodic descent A-G-F-E; the Sonata No. 61 offers an interesting example of this melodic descent in the bass.

Francesco Malipiero observed of Scarlatti that "there are themes in his works that seem to be written by modern Spanish composers of our own day." This is very true, and the explanation for it is threefold. In the first place, Scarlatti was astoundingly modern in his innovations; secondly, he drew upon the common source of Spanish folk music; thirdly, modern Spanish composers feel strongly attracted toward Scarlatti, who stands as the embodiment of their artistic ideal by virtue of his sublimation of the best qualities of Hispanic music.

Among modern Spanish composers who owe allegiance, tacit or avowed, to Domenico Scarlatti are Albéniz, Granados, Falla, Turina, Joaquín Nin, and the Halffter brothers, Ernesto and Rodolfo. From the many parallels between Scarlatti and later Spanish composers we choose one of the most striking instances, as demonstrated in the following juxtaposition of a passage from Scarlatti's Sonata No. 429 with a passage from Turina's *Andaluza Sentimental:*

Example 12a. Scarlatti.

Example 12b. Turina.

The Sonata in F major (No. 384), replete with guitaristic effects, bears a fundamental resemblance to the style of Albéniz, especially in the latter's *El Albaicín.* Both composers have utilized the characteristic guitar interval of the fourth in rapid "plucked note" effects with brusque rhythmic punctuations, and with chromatic inflections peculiar to Andalusian folk music.

Professor Trend suggests that it would be no more unreasonable to describe Scarlatti as a Spanish composer than it is to describe El Greco as a Spanish painter. The point is well taken. Certain it is that Domenico Scarlatti, both for what he received and for what he gave, belongs in a very real sense to the history of Spanish music.

SOLER, PUPIL OF SCARLATTI

In the same year that Scarlatti was summoned to Madrid, there was born a Spanish musician who was destined to become his pupil and to carry on his tradition. This was Antonio Soler, born in the Catalonian town of Olot de Porrera on December 3, 1729. Admitted to the Escalonía of Montserrat at the age of six, he made rapid progress in his musical studies. In 1752 he took Holy Orders and entered the monastery of the Escorial, there to spend the rest of his life as organist and choirmaster, at the same time composing copiously. In addition to his harpsichord sonatas—of which some seventy-five are extant—he wrote a large quantity of religious music; six concertos for two organs and many other works for organ; six quintets for strings with organ or harpsichord obbligato; and much dramatic music, including not only the *autos sacramentales,* whose sacred character made them appropriate to his priestly calling, but also such purely secular forms as comedies, *entremeses,* tonadillas, and *sainetes.*

The fact is that the Escorial, in spite of its austere exterior and its grim associations as the burial place of Spanish kings, was not exclusively a place of prayer and penitence. Music and the drama were held in honor there, and the seminarians studying within those forbidding walls had ample opportunity to acquaint themselves with the classics of the Spanish drama, from whose performance music was inseparable. These plays, for which Soler wrote music, were performed only within the Escorial, as part of the cultural, educative program. In the catalogue of Soler's works, preserved in the archives of the Escorial, we find such entries as "Music for the *loa* of the comedy entitled *The Daughter of the Air*, presented by the class in Fine Arts of this Royal College."

Between Soler's arrival at the Escorial and Scarlatti's death in 1757 there was an interval of five years. This, then, was the period when Soler received instruction from the Neapolitan master. The evidence that he did so hinges not only upon the fact that on the title page of a collection of his sonatas he is described as "discepolo de Domenico Scarlatti," but also on the testimony of a contemporary music lover, Lord Richard Fitzwilliam (1745–1816), whose valuable musical collection is preserved in the Fitzwilliam Museum at Cambridge University. In that collection is a volume of twenty-seven sonatas by Soler, bearing the following note written and signed by Lord Fitzwilliam: "The original of these harpsichord lessons was given to me by Father Soler at the Escorial, 14th February, 1772; Father Soler had been instructed by Scarlatti." The English nobleman undoubtedly had this information from Soler himself.

By their spirit and structure the sonatas of Soler proclaim him a disciple of Scarlatti on every page. The Spanish musician makes no innovation in form, being content to accept the simple, one-movement form as cultivated by Scarlatti. But he shows progress and originality in his modulations, which break new ground. Soler was indeed a master of modulation. He wrote an important theoretical work on the subject, entitled *Llave de modulación y antigüedades de la música* (Madrid, 1762), which reveals his advanced ideas and his deep knowledge of musical science. While continuing the Scarlattian tradition more successfully than any other composer, Soler speaks with a voice that is more than a mere echo of his predecessor's idiom. He has a charm and a wit of his own, and for that reason his sonatas find a welcome place on piano programs of the present day. They are, however, generally played in the arrangements by Joaquín Nin; the *ur*-text should be made available in a modern edition.

Padre Antonio Soler is the most luminous and vital Spanish composer of his period. Some of his works—sonatas and quintets —have evinced their vitality in the modern concert hall, but much of his vast output remains unknown. He cultivated every field of music save opera, and whatever he touched proved fruitful in his hands. As a composer for the organ he carried on the classical Spanish tradition, being a worthy follower of Cabezón and Cabanilles, especially in his masterly use of the variation form. The variation is also the structural backbone of his quintets for strings and organ, which, although they prefigure the ultimate sonata form to a lesser extent than the compositions of the Mannheim school, reveal a complete freedom from all scholastic rigidity and a notable advance toward the emancipation of the individual instruments of the quartet. Least known of all his output is Soler's religious music; yet the portions of the Requiem for eight voices printed by Eslava in the *Lira Sacro-Hispana* show that he is one of the last upholders of a tradition that had already lost much of its pristine glory.

Then, as now, Spanish composers found difficulty in having their music published in their own country. In the eighteenth century London appears to have been the publishing center for Spanish composers, very much as Paris has been for the modern Spanish school. It is curious to observe that some of the collections of sonatas by Scarlatti published in London, such as the set printed by Johnson in 1752, bear Spanish titles and give the composer's name in Hispanized form as "Señor D. Domingo Scarlatti." The only contemporary printed collection of sonatas by Soler that has come down to us was published in London by Robert Birchall (four copies are extant). It contains twenty-seven sonatas.

Though Soler was the most original and most gifted of the

eighteenth-century Spanish composers who wrote for harpsichord or piano, he was by no means alone in this field. Joaquín Nin, to whom the modern public owes the revelation of Soler's keyboard pieces, has also published a representative selection of similar works by eight of Soler's contemporaries and immediate successors. Thanks to these two volumes of Nin, *Classiques Espagnols du Piano,* such names as Mateo Albéniz, Mateo Ferrer, Rafael Anglés, Vicente Rodriguez, Narciso Casanovas, Felipe Rodriguez, and José Gallés—like Soler, they are nearly all clerics and Catalans—have been rescued from the semioblivion of reference books to the living light of concert programs. The most notable of this group are Mateo Albéniz (d. 1831) and Mateo Ferrer (1788–1864), the latter choirmaster of Barcelona Cathedral for fifty years.

To these should be added the name of Manuel Blasco Nebra (1750–1784), organist of Seville Cathedral and nephew of the eminent composer José de Nebra (*cf.* Chapter VIII), who published at Madrid a set of six admirable sonatas for piano.[4]

It is an interesting fact that whereas in the realm of vocal music the Italian influence predominated in Spain, in the domain of instrumental music the Spanish idiom exerted a strong influence upon Italian composers. The explanation is probably that the Spaniards are not primarily singers, but dancers and instrumentalists—masters, above all, of that fascinating instrument the guitar, whose potent and far-reaching influence has never been fully recognized. The rhythms of the Spanish dance and the instrumental effects of the guitar could not fail to captivate the imagination of composers, such as Scarlatti, whom long residence in Spain brought into firsthand contact with these Hispanic elements. After Scarlatti came another Italian, Luigi Boccherini, who spent nearly forty years in Spain.

BOCCHERINI IN SPAIN

The name of this prolific and unjustly neglected composer is generally coupled with that of Haydn in the early development of chamber music. He composed more than four hundred and sixty instrumental works, including one hundred and two string quartets, sixty string trios, and twenty-one sonatas for piano and violin. Yet to the modern public he is best known for his famous Minuet, taken from one of his quintets (second series, written in 1771). This piece, incidentally, was composed some two years after his arrival in Spain and bears traces of Hispanic influence, as evidenced in its syncopations and its pizzicato accompaniment, the whole giving a guitaresque effect.

Having made a name for himself as composer and cellist in Italy—he was born at Lucca in 1743—Boccherini went to Paris in 1768 and there met with immediate success. Soon he was persuaded by the Spanish ambassador to visit Madrid, which was then a center of attraction for virtuosi from all over Europe. Owing to the intrigues of a certain Brunetti, an Italian violinist established in Madrid, Boccherini did not fare as well as he had hoped at the Spanish Court. Nevertheless, he found a patron in the king's brother, the Infante Don Luis, and, except for a brief period as court composer to the king of Prussia, he settled in Madrid for the rest of his life, dying there in 1805.[5]

The eminent French musicologist Georges de Saint-Foix, who has pleaded eloquently for wider recognition of Boccherini's genius, is of the opinion that his works offer an array of Spanish dance forms "of a beauty and richness without equal." The same writer speaks of "the imperishable, the warm and precious musical treasure of Spain" that Boccherini has assimilated and transmitted in his compositions. Boccherini himself tells us that some of his music was inspired by hearing the celebrated Padre Basilio (*cf.* Chapter III) play fandangos on the guitar.

That Boccherini had a thorough acquaintance with the technique of the guitar is demonstrated by his three quintets for strings and guitar, in which he employs the resources of the latter instrument with exceptional skill. The third of these quintets has a finale which is in the rhythm of the fandango.

Boccherini's *Spanish Ballet* is an interesting example of his

Hispanism. The score and parts of this work, which was probably written for the composer's brother-in-law, the choreographer Onorato Vigano, are preserved in the Hessische Landesbibliothek at Darmstadt. The ballet was performed at Vienna and at Moscow in 1775. It consists of four brief movements: *Larghetto*, *Minuet-Andantino*, *Allegretto*, and *Contredanse*. One wonders why Boccherini did not employ specific Spanish dance forms in his ballet, but it is evident that he intended to convey an impressionistic rather than a realistic effect. Instead of imitating actual dances, he suggests Spanish atmosphere by the use of roulades, syncopations, and pizzicato passages.

Boccherini further associated himself with Spanish music by writing a zarzuela to a libretto by Ramón de la Cruz, entitled *Clementina*, which was privately performed at Madrid in 1778.

SPANISH COMPOSERS OF CHAMBER MUSIC

In the eighteenth century, chamber music was widely and assiduously cultivated in Spain. King Carlos IV was a keen amateur and often played the second violin in quartet performances at his palace. Nobles and dignitaries vied with men of letters in giving musical soirees at which the chamber music of Haydn and Boccherini was given the place of honor. The poet Tomás de Iriarte (1750–1791), not content with singing the praises of music in a long and famous poem entitled *La Música*, learned to play the violin and the viola and composed string quartets, *symphonies concertantes*, and tonadillas. He was a pupil and friend of the eminent composer Antonio Rodríguez de Hita.

Manuel Canales (1747–1786) is credited with having written the first string quartets to be published in Spain. His Opus I, consisting of six quartets, was published about 1774.[6]

José Herrando, a pupil of the famous Italian master Corelli, became first violin in the chapel of the Convent of the Incarnation at Madrid and wrote one of the earliest violin methods to come out of Spain, the *Arte y Puntual Explicación del Modo de Tocar el Violín con Perfección y Facilidad*, which was printed at

Paris in 1756. In 1754 he composed six sonatinas for violin alone, dedicated to the singer Farinelli; these have been preserved in a manuscript in the Library of the Liceo at Bologna. His *Eighteen New Spanish Minuets* for violin were printed at London in 1760 (not all the pieces in the collection, however, are by Herrando). Among his unpublished works are twelve sonatas for violin and bass written for the Duke of Alba, whose home in Madrid, the Palacio de Liria, was a notable center of musical activity in the eighteenth century. These sonatas are noteworthy for their melodic vigor and their freshness of invention.[7]

It was also to the Duke of Alba that Luís Misón, whom we shall meet in the next chapter as a composer of tonadillas, dedicated his twelve sonatas for transverse flute and viola with *basso continuo,* of which only the flute and bass parts have been preserved (in MS.). The sixth sonata of this set includes a *Zamorana* —a dance from the region of Zamora—in 6/8 time, with a double pedal point representing the drone of the *gaita gallega,* the Galician bagpipe. In Spain, musically speaking, a ducal palace was never very far removed from the village square.

CHAPTER VIII

Rise of the Popular Zarzuela

THE Calderonian mythico-legendary zarzuela continued as the predominant type of the Spanish lyric theater during the first half of the eighteenth century. The chief literary continuators of the Calderonian school were the Conde de Clavijos, Francisco de Bances Candamo, Antonio de Zamora, and José de Cañizares. Though their works have fallen into complete desuetude, they merit mention here because their plays were set to music by the leading Spanish composers of the period, such as Sebastián Durón, Antonio Literes, and José de Nebra.

Sebastián Durón has been erroneously credited with having introduced violins into the Royal Chapel in Madrid, of which he was appointed maestro in 1691. Violins were used there before his time, but he gave them added importance and in general gave a rather unfortunate impetus to the "theatricalization" of Spanish church music by cultivating the new florid Italian style with instrumental accompaniment. Durón seems to have had an essentially dramatic temperament, which made him feel more at home in the theater than in the chapel. The story is told that once, after he had conducted a performance in the Royal Chapel with rather unsatisfactory results, the king went up to him and said, "Tell me, Durón, why is it that things always go much better when you conduct in the theater than when you conduct in church?" To which the unabashed musician replied, "Sire, in the theater it is the devil who leads the musicians, while in the Royal Chapel it is only myself."

A typical zarzuela of this period is *Veneno es de Amor la Envidia* (*Envy Is the Poison of Love*), music by Durón, text by Zamora, dating from about 1700. The plot deals with the love of Glaucus and Scylla, which arouses the jealousy of Circe; the latter obtains her revenge by transforming Scylla into a siren. It provides an opportunity for the usual scenic effects, as when Apollo and Circe make their first appearance in a chariot drawn by white steeds. The music of Durón, consisting of airs, recitatives, and concerted numbers, reveals the characteristics of this transitional period, when the Spanish lyric theater was hesitating between loyalty to native forms and an inclination to adopt the seductive Italian style, the result almost invariably being a compromise between the two elements. While arias and recitatives generally tended to follow the Italian pattern, a pretext for bringing in the native seguidillas and villancicos could always be found in the pastoral or rustic episodes that customarily found a place in the classical zarzuela. It must be said that the Italian influence is very obvious in Durón's music, though at the same time he was capable of unconventional rhythmic touches whose freedom and boldness reveal the vivifying undercurrent of popular sources.

Durón's career in Madrid was cut short by political circumstances. In 1705 he left the service of Philip V and went over to the party of the Archduke Charles of Austria, a rival claimant for the Spanish throne. He probably spent some time in Barcelona, where the archduke had obtained a foothold and was encouraging the production of Italian opera. But after the archduke's defeat Durón was forced into exile; he died in France about 1716.

Antonio Literes, like nearly all his contemporaries, was equally active as a composer for the church and for the theater. In 1696 he became bass violist in the Royal Chapel, and later was second organist there, still holding that position in 1752. He composed both zarzuelas and operas "al estilo Italiano," in the latter category being *Los Elementos*. The poet-moralist Padre Feijoo praised the sweetness and loftiness of his style. His genuine melodic gift may be judged from the song *Confiado Jilguerito* (*Too Trustful Goldfinch*), reprinted by Pedrell and Mitjana. It is taken from the heroic zarzuela *Accis y Galatea* (performed on December 19, 1708), a work that is interesting because it shows a tendency to acquire quasi-operatic status by increasing the proportion of musical numbers in relation to the spoken scenes.

THE ''LOPE DE VEGA'' OF MUSIC

The third important zarzuela composer of this period was José de Nebra, whose talent and fecundity caused Cotarelo y Mori to dub him "the Lope de Vega of Spanish music." After being organist at the Convent of the Descalzas Reales, he obtained a similar position at the Royal Chapel in 1724 and was appointed maestro there in 1739. He lived to be over eighty, dying at Madrid on July 11, 1768.

In addition to about one hundred religious works—including the admirable Requiem [1] for the funeral of Queen Barbara (Scarlatti's patroness) in 1768—Nebra wrote the music for a large number of plays, beginning with Calderón's famous *auto La Vida es Sueño* (*Life Is a Dream*). One of Nebra's earliest and most successful zarzuelas was the one bearing the challenging title *De los Encantos del Amor la Música es el Mayor* (*Of Love's Enchantments, Music Is the Greatest*), produced on October 23, 1725.

Nebra was obliged to yield to the prevailing fashion in writing music for pseudohistorical or legendary plays imitated from the Italian poet Metastasio, whose librettos were enjoying a huge vogue. But he revenged himself by parodying the stilted Italian mannerisms in his comic scenes. And in one such work, *Aquiles en Troya* (1747), dealing with the siege of Troy, he has two comic characters singing seguidillas before the walls of that ancient city, thus emphasizing with a glaring anachronism his determination to flaunt the popular element in the face of artificial fashions.

A man of energy and resourcefulness, possessing a complete mastery of his art, José de Nebra held his own even against the favored court composer Coradini, who attempted to replace talent by intrigue. Yet, by the nature of their subjects, Nebra's dramatic works still adhered to the post-Calderonian, legendary-mythical tradition, and it is only in the year of his death, 1768, that we encounter the first really popular zarzuela, a product of younger and more venturesome spirits.

THE ZARZUELA COMES DOWN TO EARTH

The title alone of this new work—*Las Segadoras de Vallecas* (*The Reapers of Vallecas*)—is enough to indicate the beginning of another phase in the evolution of the zarzuela. Instead of gods and nymphs, kings and legendary heroes, we have here ordinary human beings of a humble station in life: the *segadoras* are a group of peasant women who earn their living by reaping in the fields at harvesttime, going from farm to farm. This particular band of reapers is hired to reap the fields of a wealthy young landowner who happens to be a widower. He falls in love with one of the reapers—who turns out to be of gentle birth—and ends by marrying her, though not before the intrigues of a former lover, of a jealous rival, and of a spiteful housekeeper have created the necessary dramatic interest and suspense.

The music of this zarzuela was written by Antonio Rodríguez de Hita, the text by Ramón de la Cruz. These two men played a crucial role in the development of the Spanish lyric theater. To Ramón de la Cruz (1731–1794) belongs the merit of having provided, with unflagging verse and the keenest observation of life, precisely the kind of texts that were needed for a truly popular lyric theater. It is true that he had begun by writing mythological zarzuelas: his first effort, dating from 1757, bore the bombastic title *Quien Complace a la Deidad, Acierta a Sacrificar* (*Whoso Pleases the Deity Has Made a Worthy Sacrifice*). And on July 11, 1768—the very day of Nebra's death —he produced the heroic zarzuela *Briseida,* with music by Rodriguez de Hita. This work met with notable success, yet Cruz and his musical collaborator, as if impatient to be pioneers in the breaking of fresh ground, turned almost immediately to the popular field with *Las Segadoras de Vallecas.*

A year later they followed this up with another popular zarzuela, *Las Labradoras de Murcia* (*The Workingwomen of Murcia*), produced at the Teatro del Príncipe on September 16, 1769. The plot shows no striking originality as compared to its predecessor, but it offers a pretext for a succession of picturesque scenes, laid in the silk-growing district of Murcia, which forms a background for a love story complicated by the usual difficulties and culminating in the inevitable happy ending. An opportunity for humorous characterization is offered by such types as the old coquette, the pedantic student, and the two rustic louts.

The most effective popular scene in this zarzuela, that closing the first act, takes place in the silk nursery during a thunderstorm. According to a local superstition, the silkworms will die of fright if they hear the noise of thunder. So when a storm breaks all the workers come rushing in with their traditional instruments—guitars, mandolins, tambourines, and castanets— playing as loudly as they can and singing at the top of their voices to drown out the noise of the thunder. They sing and dance a *Jota Murciana,* that is, a variety of the *jota* typical of the region of Murcia. This type of scene, with its array of popular instruments on the stage and its basis of pure folk music, was to remain a characteristic feature of the zarzuela.

The thunderstorm gives the composer a chance to display his descriptive powers in the orchestra. As Mitjana writes, "Rodríguez de Hita, in this superb scene, which is far in advance of its time, has painted a marvelous picture, transforming the folk element into a work of art." There, in a nutshell, was the problem that the creators of the popular zarzuela had to solve: that of making an art work from the raw material of musical folklore and native traditions. The essential step in the solution of that problem was provided when Ramón de la Cruz began to furnish Spanish composers with plays that drew their inspiration from the actual life of the people. For as long as playwrights adhered to the artificial and high-flown conceptions of the pseudoclassical drama, the musical folk element was bound to remain about as incongruous as the singing of seguidillas before the walls of ancient Troy.

Las Labradoras de Murcia stands out as the masterpiece of the Spanish popular lyric theater in the eighteenth century. The complete score of this work is preserved in the Municipal Library in Madrid, but the only numbers that have been made conveniently available are Narciso's Minuet from Act I and Teresa's expressive air from Act II (*De pena, de susto*), neither of which represents the popular aspect of the work.² Proof that it is more than an archaic curiosity or a historical document was provided by a performance given at the Madrid Conservatory, on the initiative of Felipe Pedrell, on May 28, 1896, to commemorate the centenary of the death of Ramón de la Cruz. Mitjana, who was present, bears witness that "this delightful score has lost nothing of its original freshness and remains a little marvel of grace and picturesque color."

Rodríguez de Hita (d. 1787), who in addition to writing for the stage was an eminent church musician and theorist, does not appear to have continued his collaboration with Ramón de la Cruz; but other composers followed the path that he had so successfully blazed, all of them utilizing the texts of the same prolific and inimitable playwright. Typical of the new orientation given to the zarzuela by Cruz are such works as *Los Jardineros de Aranjuez* (*The Gardeners of Aranjuez*), music by Pablo Esteve (1768); *Los Zagales del Genil* (*The Peasant*

Lads of Genil), music also by Esteve (1769); *Las Foncarraleras* (*The Girls of Fuencarral*), music by Ventura Galván (1772); and *El Licenciado Farfulla* (*The Lawyer Farfulla*), music by Antonio Rosales (1776). In this last-named work the popular element reaches its climax in a copious offering of seguidillas, *folías, jácaras, caballos*—a whole array of native airs and dances.

Not only because of its intrinsic merit, but also because it inaugurated a genre that was to attain an enormous vogue in Spain, mention must be made of the one-act "zarzuelita" (little zarzuela) *La Mesonerilla* (*The Hostess of the Inn*), words by Cruz, music by Antonio Palomino (1769), which Cotarelo calls "a gem of a zarzuela." The score comprises six sets of seguidillas, besides two arias (one with recitative), a minuet, a trio, and a final chorus. In the nineteenth century the "little zarzuela," in one act, came to be known as the *género chico*. To this day it remains the quickest and surest vehicle of commercial success in the Spanish theater.

TEMPORARY ECLIPSE OF THE ZARZUELA

It must be admitted that the career of the popular zarzuela in this first phase of its existence was extremely brief, lasting barely two decades. Though Cruz lived almost to the end of the century, he wrote scarcely any more zarzuela texts after 1776 (two were privately performed in 1786), and there was none to replace him in this field. He found that the best outlet for his talent lay in the cultivation of the *sainete*—one-act play of a satirical or humorous tendency—to which he henceforth devoted his unique gifts. After 1787 the zarzuela vanished from the Spanish stage, to return only after a lapse of more than half a century.

Two factors contributed to the eclipse of the zarzuela. One was the ever-increasing preponderance of Italian opera, which had continued to extend its sway over the lyric theater in Spain ever since Farinelli, shortly after his arrival in Madrid, had converted the royal theater of the Buen Retiro into a stronghold of

Italianism. The other was the rise of the *tonadilla escénica*, a popular lyrico-dramatic form that began to develop toward the middle of the eighteenth century and soon achieved an astonishing success, becoming a rallying point for all the adherents of Spanish music in the theater.

Etymologically, the word "tonadilla" is the diminutive of "tonada," meaning song or tune. But in musical morphology what actually happened was that the diminutive term came to stand for a larger and more complex form than was implied in the original conception of a simple solo song. The primitive tonadilla was, in effect, a "little song" appended to one of the minor theatrical forms, such as the *jácara,* the *entremés,* or the *sainete,* sung by an actor to the accompaniment of the guitar, as described in the following lines:

> Yo me acuerdo, señores,
> Cuando cantaba
> Tonadillas a solo
> Con mi guitarra.

("I remember, sirs, when I used to sing *tonadillas a solo* with my guitar.")

COMIC OPERA IN MINIATURE

When tonadillas began to be sung by two characters in dialogue, they already contained the seeds of an independent dramatic form. Gradually they broke away from the interludes or sketches to which they originally were appended and assumed a separate existence. Soon they came to be written for several characters, and sometimes for the entire company (in which case they were called *tonadillas generales*), with orchestral accompaniment and with action to suit the situation, resembling at their apogee a sort of miniature comic opera, having a maximum duration of twenty minutes. To this theatrical form of the tonadilla we apply the term *tonadilla escénica,* to distinguish it from the type that is merely a solo song.

El Baile (*The Dance*), *Tapestry Design by Goya*

The assertion, made by Mitjana on the dubious authority of the anonymous *Memorial Literario de Madrid* (1787), that the *tonadilla escénica* was "invented" by Luís Misón in 1757 has no foundation in fact. The form, as we have seen, was a gradual development, and it began to take definite shape about 1750. By 1757 both Antonio Guerrero and Luís Misón were writing tonadillas, though the latter must be given credit for giving the new form its greatest impetus and establishing its popularity on a firm basis. Misón, of Catalan origin, was flutist in the royal orchestra from 1748, being appointed conductor in 1756. He wrote about one hundred theatrical tonadillas, all strongly imbued with national color.

Other Spanish composers, such as Pablo Esteve, Ventura Galván, Antonio Rosales, Jacinto Valledor, José Palomino, and Blas de Laserna, were quick to take up the tonadilla, since it offered the best popular medium for the stage and the only escape from the bonds of Italianism. Some idea of the vogue attained by the scenic tonadilla in its heyday may be gathered from the fact that in the Madrid municipal archives there are preserved no less than two thousand of these works, all of them performed at only two theaters, the Príncipe and the Cruz. If we add all the works that have presumably been lost, and those that were performed at other theaters, we can readily see that it would make an impressive total. Yet the tonadilla, with all its popularity, was essentially an ephemeral form. The public was avid for tonadillas, but the rate of consumption was terrific. The maximum life of a tonadilla was seven days. Fecundity and facility were prerequisites for the composer of tonadillas, who was obliged to drive his talent to the utmost in order to earn a living and satisfy an eager but insatiable public.

The scenic tonadillas dealt with a wide variety of subjects, but most of them were of a satirical or picaresque nature, and nearly all of them depicted typical phases of popular life. Subirá mentions the following categories: amorous, patriotic, historical, autobiographical, magical, allegorical, and *costumbrista* (based on local customs). The favorite character types were drawn from the lower strata of society: petty tradesmen, artisans, hawkers of all kinds, washerwomen, seamstresses, barbers, lackeys, coachmen, soldiers, friars, and, above all, those *majas* and *majos* whom Goya has immortalized in his canvases—the swashbuckling gallants of Madrid and their gay ladies, ever ready for a deadly brawl or a passionate rendezvous, as quick with their wit as with their swords. In fact, the *majas* and *majos* became such a fixture of the tonadilla that in the end they were satirized along with other conventions. That was the essence of the tonadilla: a continuous effervescence of wit and satire against everything that tended to crystallize in conventional patterns, be it the fashions of foreign opera or the effusions of local color.

"THE SPANISH IDIOM"

While not a form to which permanent artistic value of a high order can be assigned, the scenic tonadilla is nevertheless musically interesting from several points of view. For one thing, it marks the definite emergence of what for the sake of convenience we may call "the Spanish idiom" in music. It is, of course, possible to find traces of this idiom long before the appearance of the scenic tonadilla. It exists in the villancicos and in the *jácaras, bailes,* and *mojigangas* of the early lyric theater, which drew so much of its substance from popular sources. But by the term "Spanish idiom" we designate more specifically the product of a process of fusion and amalgamation that reached its culmination in the second half of the eighteenth century and the early part of the nineteenth. The elements so fused and amalgamated, largely under the influence of the scenic tonadilla, were threefold: first, there was the element of pure folk music, essentially of rural origin; secondly, the element of urban street music, essentially popular but more heterogeneous in texture; and, thirdly, the conventional apparatus of instrumental and vocal technique, by this time developed to a point that might be called "modern."

Most of the foreign composers who helped to conventionalize
and spread the "Spanish idiom" abroad drew their material not
from firsthand folk sources, but from the more accessible arsenal
of the *tonadilla escénica*. Thus it was that the Italian operatic
composer Mercadante used the theme of Blas de Laserna's celebrated *Tirana del Trípili* in the overture of his opera *I due
Figaro* (1835), causing it to become known all over Europe.
We quote the *copla* and refrain of this song, because it is typical
of the tonadilla style, and also because we shall have occasion
to refer to it again in connection with the *Goyescas* of Granados.

Example 13.

Another case in point is that of Bizet, whose immensely successful exploitation of Spanish atmosphere in *Carmen* is partly
derived from the tonadillas of Manuel García (*cf.* Chapter
XIX). Rossini, Liszt, and, more recently, Ernesto Halffter (*cf.*
Chapter XIII) have also utilized the theme of García's celebrated *polo*, *El Contrabandista*, which was inserted in the tonadilla entitled *El Poeta Calculista*.[3]

Manuel García, known to the world as a singer and as the
founder of a dynasty of celebrated singers, began his career as a
composer of tonadillas, his works in this form including *La Maja
y el Majo* (1798) and *La Declaración* (1799). In the autumn of
1806 he obtained a position as assistant conductor to Blas de

Laserna at the Teatro de la Cruz in Madrid, but in the following year left Spain to seek his fortune abroad. We shall meet
him again among the great Spanish virtuosi (*cf.* Chapter XIV).
García has been called "the last of the *tonadilleros*," but he might
also be called "the first of the *operetistas*," because the works
written in the years immediately preceding his departure from
Spain (1802–1807) tended to desert the style of the tonadilla
for that of the operetta. His operettas, in fact, contributed to the
decline of the tonadilla, which languished and waned after the
first decade of the nineteenth century, soon disappearing entirely.

The early nineteenth century was a period of great vicissitudes
for Spain. She was dragged into disastrous wars, she became the
prey of Napoleonic invasion and the victim of a vile and treacherous monarch, the unspeakable Ferdinand VII. Revolution, anarchy, and reaction kept the country in a constant turmoil, broken
only by the dull apathy resulting from tyrannical suppression.
During the whole of this dark period the Spanish lyric theater
continued to decline, but Italian opera continued in the ascendancy, firmly consolidating its power in Spain. The Italian affilia-
tions of the Spanish Court remained almost as preponderant as
they had been during the early years of the Bourbon dynasty.
The fourth wife of Ferdinand VII, María Cristina of Naples,
was an Italian, a lover of *bel canto* and a warm admirer of Rossini, who became the new operatic idol in Spain. It was under the
auspices of this Italian queen that the Madrid Conservatory—
originally known as the Conservatorio de María Cristina—was
founded in 1830. The first director of the new institution was,
of course, an Italian, a singer named Francesco Piermarini. And
the language used in the classes for singing and declamation was
not Spanish, but Italian.

In the eighteen thirties, then, Spain's native lyric theater was
virtually nonexistent. The zarzuela had vanished from the stage.
The tonadilla had run its meteoric course. Imitations of French
operetta on the lighter side, and of Italian opera on a more
pretentious scale, scarcely relieved the bleakness of the theatrical

horizon. The point at which the emergence of a national lyric drama might be perceived seemed far off indeed. Yet, within the next decade or two, an amazing transformation was to take place.

TRIUMPH OF THE RESURGENT ZARZUELA

Even when the situation appeared most hopeless, there was not lacking a nucleus of resistance against the Italian domination of the lyric theater. While Spanish musicians were apparently defeated for the moment, the spirit of opposition found a vigorous spokesman in the person of a writer named Manuel Bretón de los Herreros, who published a widely read poetic satire against Italian opera. Wishing to carry his attack into the theater, he sought the collaboration of a musician and, strangely enough, chose for this purpose an Italian, Basilio Basili, who had come to Madrid in 1827.[4] The resulting opus, *El Novio y el Concierto* (*The Fiancé and the Concert*), in one act, with a plot designed to pit Spanish popular music against the Italian operatic style, was described as a "zarzuela-comedia." Its performance on March 12, 1839, marked the first appearance of the term "zarzuela" on the billboard of a Spanish theater since the time of Ramón de la Cruz. Before the century was over it was to appear countless times on hundreds of billboards, beckoning eager crowds to the only spectacle in Spain that could rival the attraction of a bullfight.

Through Basili's collaboration with Bretón de los Herreros, we have the paradoxical situation that the revival of the zarzuela received its initial impulse from an Italian musician. But Basili, who had come to Spain as a young man, had evidently been impressed with the possibilities of exploiting native Spanish music in the theater. The native popular forms had been allowed to languish so completely that, as Basili was clever enough to realize, their revival would have the full force of novelty. And so it proved, for his "Spanish opera" *El Contrabandista,* performed in

1841, was hailed as "the first Spanish production of this kind in modern times." In the rediscovered field of the zarzuela, he achieved an encouraging success that same year with *El Ventorrillo de Crespo* (*The Tavern in Crespo*), in which he intercalated García's *polo, El Contrabandista,* and the song *El Charran* by Yradier (the composer of *La Paloma*). Continuing his collaboration with Bretón de los Herreros, he produced another zarzuela, *Los Solitarios* (*The Solitary Ones*), in 1843. He also attempted, in association with Barbieri, to organize a Spanish opera company in Madrid. But the time was not yet ripe for such a venture and the enterprise had to be abandoned. Nevertheless, the experiment demonstrated that Basili, like Scarlatti and Boccherini, was fully alive to the musical potentialities of his adopted land.

It was toward the middle of the century that the resurgent zarzuela really came into its own. A group of young composers, of whom the most prominent were Joaquín Gaztambide, Emilio Arrieta, Rafael Hernando, Cristóbal Oudrid, and Francisco Asenjo Barbieri, all born in the eighteen twenties, found in the zarzuela an immediate and welcome outlet for their talent. The modern zarzuela was firmly established by the resounding success of such works as *Colegiales y Soldados* (*Students and Soldiers*) by Hernando (1848), *La Mensajera* (*The Messenger*) by Gaztambide (1849), *Jugar Con Fuego* (*Playing With Fire*) by Barbieri (1851), *Buenas Noches, Don Simón* (*Good Night, Don Simon*) by Oudrid (1852), and *El Dominó Azul* (*The Blue Domino*) by Arrieta (1853). The production of zarzuelas soon attained the same momentum that the production of tonadillas had assumed in the previous century, with this important difference: the tonadilla's day of glory was brief whereas the nineteenth-century zarzuela acquired a permanent hold on the public. To give some idea of the rate of production, Oudrid wrote over a hundred zarzuelas, Barbieri seventy-seven, Arrieta about fifty, and Gaztambide forty-four (these figures include works written in collaboration with other composers—a practice frequently followed by the *zarzuelistas*).

Though the tonadilla was not revived in name, its spirit lived in the new zarzuela, which owed much more to it than to the classical zarzuela of the Calderonian school. Nothing of the latter, indeed, survived, save the name and the presence of spoken dialogue. Whatever, in the nineteenth-century zarzuela, was not a reflection of Italian opera or French operetta drew its substance from the savory folk vein of the tonadilla. The humorous element, the types from everyday life, the array of popular songs and dances—all these were derived from the theatrical tonadilla. In its most authentic manifestations, the modern zarzuela was an expanded and elaborated version of the eighteenth-century tonadilla, which in turn had its origins in the minor lyrical forms of the primitive Spanish theater.

FRANCISCO ASENJO BARBIERI

This authentic Spanish tradition found its most genuine embodiment in the zarzuelas of Francisco Asenjo Barbieri (1823–1894), and especially in his two masterpieces *Pan y Toros* (*Bread and Bulls*) and *El Barberillo de Lavapiés* (*The Little Barber of Lavapiés*), dating respectively from 1864 and 1874. Born at Madrid in humble circumstances, and thrown upon his own resources at an early age, Barbieri at first earned his living by playing the clarinet in military bands, in second-rate theaters, at public dances, and even in strolling street bands; later he became conductor of itinerant opera troupes, and more than once financial failure obliged him to make his way back to the capital on foot. Wherever he went his skill in playing the *bandurria* (mandolin), his fine singing voice, and his spirit of camaraderie made him welcome among the populace.

Drawing upon this wide and varied experience, imbued with a determination to make Spain's popular music prevail in the lyric theater, aesthetically nourished and fortified by his historical investigations—he was the most eminent Spanish musicologist prior to Pedrell—Barbieri instilled into such works as *Pan y Toros* and *El Barberillo* the essence of all that was colorful and picaresque, radiant and ebullient, vivid and palpitating, in the Spain of Goya's time.

It is the Madrid of this period, with its bullfighters, *majos* and *majas*, blind beggars, jovial clerics and plotting patriots, that he summons to life in *Pan y Toros*, in which Goya himself is one of the chief characters. The episode of the election of the director for the *plaza de toros*, with its celebrated chorus and march accompanied by guitars and *bandurrias* on the stage, is replete with true popular zest, while the seguidillas, *Aunque soy de la Mancha* (*Though I Come from La Mancha*), are full of the most captivating grace and spirit.

By bringing these authentic Spanish songs and dances into the domain of the lyric theater at a time when the latter was almost completely overrun by foreign influences, Barbieri decisively influenced the future course of Spanish music. His best works were to prove intensely stimulating to such composers as Albéniz and Manuel de Falla.

THE ZARZUELA IN RECENT TIMES

No such significance can be claimed for the vast majority of zarzuelas that have flooded the Spanish stage during the past hundred years. The most that can be said is that all of them brought pleasure to audiences who sought amusement rather than elevation in the theater, and that some of them, to a greater or lesser degree, succeeded in capturing some vital spark of the popular spirit that gives them a certain folk value. Among the zarzuelas whose immense popularity has made them part of the fabric of Spanish life must be mentioned *Marina* (1855) by Arrieta, *El Duo de la Africana* (1893) by Fernández Caballero, *La Gran Vía* (1886) by Federico Chueca [5] and the elder Valverde, and *La Verbena de la Paloma* (*The Feast of Our Lady of the Dove*) by Bretón.

This last work, dating from 1893 and belonging to what is known as the *género chico* (one-act zarzuela), has obtained a deeper hold on the Spanish public than any other zarzuela of modern times. It deals with a typical aspect of popular life in Madrid and is full of catchy tunes like the *habanera concertante*, "Where are you going with that shawl from Manila?" One has only to hum a few bars of this melody in order to awaken an immediate response in the breast of any Spaniard.

Example 14.

Don-de vas con manton de Ma,-ni-la, don-de vas con ves-ti--do chi-né?

In addition to the composers already mentioned, outstanding cultivators of the modern zarzuela include Pedro Marqués (1843–1918), Jerónimo Jiménez (1854–1923), Vicente Lleó (1870–1922), Amadeo Vives (1871–1932), José Serrano (1873–1941), Pablo Luna (b. 1880), Francisco Alonso López (b. 1887), Federico Moreno Torroba (b. 1891), Jacinto Guerrero (b. 1895), and Joaquín ("Quinito") Valverde (1875–1918), whose output of two hundred and fifty zarzuelas (some in collaboration with other composers) is probably a record even in a field where fecundity is taken for granted. The two last-mentioned composers cultivated chiefly the *género chico*, a type that has often degenerated into the most trivial and ephemeral concoction, scarcely more dignified than a vaudeville sketch and resembling a cosmopolitan cocktail in its indiscriminate mixture of musical ingredients ranging from the bubbling froth of Viennese operetta to the synthetic "hooch" of tin-pan alley.

It can be seen that the term "zarzuela" is very elastic. While it may cover a multitude of trivialities, it may also aspire, both in its remote antecedents and in its more ambitious modern manifestations, to the estate of genuine lyric drama.

CHAPTER IX

Toward a National Opera

"SPANISH opera does not exist; Spanish opera has never existed"—so wrote the Spanish musical historian Antonio Peña y Goñi in the eighteen eighties. Nevertheless, he undertook to write a history of Spanish opera in the nineteenth century, devoting a substantial volume to this nonexistent subject. As a historian he took cognizance of what he denied in theory, resolving the paradox by declaring that Spanish opera, regarded as a distinct national entity, could not exist because the continual interpenetration of artistic elements from one country to another resulted in the elimination of all distinctive local traits.

What Peña y Goñi set out to describe in his book was opera as composed by Spaniards, with no implication of a characteristic national label attached thereto. Here was a bedrock of fact not affected by the shifting sands of theory: Spanish composers were writing operas, and had been writing them for a long time. Upon this elementary factual foundation we may, for the moment, base our retrospective survey of "Spanish opera."

The two most notable Spanish opera composers of the eighteenth century, Domingo Terradellas and Vicente Martín y Soler, had almost no connection with their fatherland save that of birth. Terradellas (his name is frequently Italianized as Terradeglias), born at Barcelona in 1713, was sent to Naples as a boy, became a pupil of Durante there, began his career as a dramatic com-

poser at the age of twenty-three, and continued it with uninterrupted success until his death fifteen years later, ending his days
as choirmaster of the church of San Giacomo degli Spagnuoli in
Rome.[1] His works, most of them with texts by the two most
famous Italian librettists of that time, Metastasio and Apostolo
Zeno, were performed not only throughout Italy, but also in
London, whither he went in 1746 to witness the production of
his operas *Mitridate* and *Bellerophon*. Dr. Burney praises his
music, and the English publisher John Walsh brought out several
collections of "Favourite Songs" from his operas.

A RIVAL OF MOZART

Still more brilliant was the cosmopolitan career of Martín y
Soler, a native of Valencia (born in 1756), who, after a period as
organist at Alicante, went to Florence in 1780 and the following
year achieved an immediate success with his first opera, *Ifigenia
in Aulide*. Going to Vienna in 1785, he made the acquaintance of
Mozart's librettist, Lorenzo da Ponte, who provided him with
the text of *Il Burbero di Buon Cuore*, the first of his Viennese
triumphs. His most sensational success was obtained with *Una
Cosa Rara* (November 11, 1786), which for a time completely
eclipsed Mozart's *Le Nozze di Figaro*, produced six months
earlier. But *Una Cosa Rara* is remembered now chiefly because
Mozart borrowed a theme from it for the second finale of his
Don Giovanni.[2] Martín y Soler left Vienna in 1788 and went to
St. Petersburg as director of the Italian Opera. He died there
in 1806, without ever having revisited his native country.

In that country, during the decades that followed the death
of this illustrious expatriate, other composers, less widely traveled
but almost equally Italianized, continued to write operas showing scarcely any trace of their geographic origin.

The representative figure of this period in Spain is Ramón
Carnicer (1779–1855), who as the first teacher of composition
at the newly founded Madrid Conservatory (1830) exercised
considerable influence upon the rising generation of Spanish com-

posers. A Catalan by birth, he began his theatrical career as director of the opera in Barcelona, but in 1827 transferred his activities to Madrid, where he endeavored to emulate the success of the Italian Mercadante, who had gathered fresh laurels in the Spanish capital about this time. While yielding to the prevailing fashion in his Italian operas, Carnicer seems to have preserved a nostalgic longing to "go native," since he occasionally intercalated Spanish songs of a marked popular character into these works. It is curious to note that among Carnicer's operas (all in Italian, of course) there is a setting of the Don Juan legend, *Don Giovanni Tenorio, ossia Il Convitato di Pietra* (1822)—a subject which was given its first dramatic form by the Spanish playwright Tirso de Molina in the seventeenth century.

The Italianized operas of Baltasar Saldoni (1807–1889) and Miguel Hilarión Eslava (1807–1878) enjoyed their moment of fleeting success, though in the long run they could not compete with the genuine Italian product of such composers as Bellini, Donizetti, and Rossini, who were complete masters of the operatic stage in Spain. Eslava, like Carnicer, attempted to inject some local color into his operas, notably in *Il Solitario* (1841), where he introduces an accompaniment of rhythmical handclapping for one of the choruses, borrowing the idea from the Andalusian *cuadro flamenco* (*cf.* Chapter XV). Eslava derives his claim to lasting fame not from his operas, but from his historical investigations, culminating in the publication of his monumental anthology of Spanish sacred music, the *Lira Sacro-Hispana*. Saldoni, who was professor of singing at the Madrid Conservatory, deserves to be cited primarily because, when appointed to be director of the Teatro del Príncipe (later called the Teatro Español) in 1848, he rallied the younger generation of composers around the banner of nationalism, urging them to accomplish through the medium of the reborn zarzuela what he himself had failed to do—to write works with Spanish texts and with a definite national character.

As we observed in the previous chapter, the most gifted member of the group that responded to this call was Francisco Asenjo Barbieri, whose *Pan y Toros* (1864) is an unsurpassed model of the three-act "zarzuela grande." From "zarzuela grande" to "grand opera" is but a step, and it seems strange that Barbieri, who lived almost to the end of the century and therefore experienced the full force of the controversy that seethed around the question of Spanish opera, should not have taken that step. His failure to do so is all the more strange because he was not a mere opportunist like most of his contemporaries, but a man who devoted a great part of his energies to completely disinterested historical researches and to building up public taste by presenting the finest masterpieces of symphonic music in the pioneer concerts that he organized and conducted in Madrid from 1859.

BARBIERI ON SPANISH OPERA

Barbieri, however, did give considerable thought to the burning question of Spanish opera, as evinced in his letters and other writings. The following passage from a letter to Felipe Pedrell, written in his sixty-sixth year, indicates that operatic ambitions were not entirely alien to him: "Though my character or the circumstances of the moment caused me to work in the purely comic field of the zarzuela, I assure you that, old as I am, I would still venture to try my powers in the field of opera, if I could find an author with whom I could come to an understanding." [3] What Barbieri might have done in the field of "serious" opera remains in the realm of conjecture; but it must be recognized that his genius lay more in the direction of comedy than of serious drama or tragedy. Moreover, his conception of a national lyric theater was firmly vinculated in popular sources, both in its origins and in its aims. That is to say, he held that the lyric theater should not only draw its inspiration from the songs and dances of the populace (and for him this meant an urban rather than a rural populace), but should also make the most immediate and direct appeal to that same populace, reducing to a minimum the process of artistic rarification or sublimation. It will be noticed that in the passage quoted above he refers to the zarzuela as a "purely comic" form, and we cannot help concluding that his views in this matter were subconsciously conditioned by the special limitations and bent of his temperament.

Elsewhere in the same letter Barbieri expresses himself quite definitely on the subject of Spanish opera:

> The general taste of the Spanish people has always manifested itself in the theater by the approval bestowed upon those works which, to their historical or fictional interest, whether comic or serious, have united a variety of entertaining and picturesque incidents. We can only conclude that our much-desired Spanish opera, if it is to have a distinctly national character, must be above all *varied* and *picturesque*, without excluding, even in the most serious subjects, the comical and popular elements.

According to this conception, the Spanish lyric theater might produce a *Carmen*, but not a *Tristan und Isolde*.

AN OPERATIC CRUSADER

Barbieri's views were sound as far as they went, but obviously they could not satisfy the partisans of a national opera in the most transcendent acceptation of the term. There were composers who felt that Spain should be endowed with an indigenous opera equaling, or aspiring to equal, the loftiness and grandeur of the most impressive foreign products. Unfortunately, the technical equipment of these operatic crusaders was seldom on a par with their lofty aims. Such was the case of one of the earliest and most vociferous champions of Spanish opera, Joaquín Espín y Guillén, who gave further proof of his pioneer spirit by founding and editing the first musical periodical in Spain, *La Iberia Musical* (1842–1845). This worthy person composed a Spanish opera based on a well-known episode in the national history (the revolt of the *comuneros* in 1520), entitled *Padilla, o El Asedio de Medina* (*Padilla, or the Siege of Medina*), and at the cost of Herculean efforts succeeded in having the first act performed in 1845.

He was never able to have the entire work produced, but both by word and deed he focused attention on a question that was to agitate Spain's musical life for several generations to come: how to achieve that elusive ideal referred to by Barbieri as "our much-desired Spanish opera."

There were, to be sure, plenty of ready-made answers to that question. After the middle of the nineteenth century, when the revived zarzuela had thoroughly established itself in popular favor, the idea began to prevail that by taking the larger type of zarzuela, in two or three acts, and replacing the spoken dialogue with recitatives, a full-fledged Spanish opera could be produced. This procedure was applied by Emilio Arrieta, Barbieri's exact contemporary, in the case of his highly popular zarzuela *Marina* (1855). Enlarged to three acts instead of two, and with some additional arias, it was given as an opera at the Madrid Royal Theater on March 16, 1871, with a cast that included the famous tenor Tamberlick (at whose suggestion, it is said, the transformation was undertaken). The artistic worth of *Marina* was not increased an iota through its operatic metamorphosis, and it remained what it had always been: a skillfully written and attractive work, but so thoroughly saturated with the Italianism Arrieta had imbibed during his years of study in Milan that its only connection with Spain lies in the language and the setting. Arrieta made quite a stir in his day with the ambitious operas *Ildegonda* (1849) and *La Conquista de Granada* (1850), but he was not a progressive element in Spain's national lyric drama.

A FOE OF ITALIANISM

In sharp contrast to the irradicable Italianism of Arrieta was the attitude of a composer who came into prominence during the last years of Arrieta's life with a five-act opera entitled *Los Amantes de Teruel* (1889). This was Tomás Bretón, born at Salamanca in 1850. In spite of having been a pupil of Arrieta at the Madrid Conservatory and of having spent a year in Italy on a stipend from the Spanish government, he became an outspoken foe of the Italian musical influence in Spain, which he denounced as "stupid and disastrous." He declared that from the time of Farinelli up to his own day, Spanish music had suffered from a grave disease, chronic *Italianitis*. "This Italianism stifles and degrades our art," he exclaimed in a discourse before the Spanish Royal Academy.

Having once thrown down the gauntlet, Bretón continued to be a militant champion of Spanish national opera throughout his life. He protested strongly against the use of Italian librettos by Spanish composers. "The national opera is embodied in the national language," he declared. He fought against the virtual monopoly that Italian composers and singers exercised over the lyric theaters of Spain, and in particular over the Royal Theater of Madrid, which should have been the chief mainstay of the national school. His energetic campaign culminated with a motion in favor of a "National Lyric Theater" presented to the first Artistic Congress held at Madrid in 1919, three years before his death.

Bretón spoke with the prestige of personal success, for his opera *Los Amantes de Teruel,* after being acclaimed in Madrid and Barcelona, had been received with favor in Vienna and Prague, while his next opera, *Garín,* with a Catalan setting, had won an enthusiastic reception at Barcelona in 1892. Still more impressive was the success achieved by his three-act regional opera *La Dolores* (1895), which in its first season received sixty-three consecutive performances in Madrid and one hundred and twelve in Barcelona. Later it was given at Milan and Prague and throughout South America. To these should be added the phenomenal triumph of his one-act zarzuela *La Verbena de la Paloma* (*cf*. Chapter VIII). He never equaled these early triumphs in his later works, but he had acquired enough glory to last him a lifetime and over.

Bretón's closest competitor in the operatic field was Ruperto Chapí (1851–1909), whose admirers hailed him as "the Spanish Massenet." Like Barbieri and Bretón, he rose from humble begin-

Tomás Bretón

Felipe Pedrell

nings to win fame and fortune via the theater. As a writer of zarzuelas he enjoyed great popularity, his masterpiece in this genre being the one-act zarzuela *La Revoltosa* (1897), which aroused the keen admiration of Saint-Saëns. When Chapí's "serious" zarzuela, *La Tempestad* (*The Storm*), based on the play *Le Juif polonais* by Erckmann-Chatrian, was produced in 1882, some persons raised the old fallacious cry, "Suppress the spoken dialogue, and here is our Spanish opera!" As a matter of fact, Chapí's partisans had no difficulty in persuading themselves that he was the veritable creator of the modern Spanish lyric drama, on the strength of his operas *Roger de Flor, La Bruja, Circe,* and *Margarita la Tornera* (this was produced at the Royal Theater the day before Chapí died). But his superficiality, his lack of sustained dramatic power, and his weakness in characterization disqualified him for the highest flights of opera, and he will be remembered chiefly as a delightful miniaturist.

Since we have mentioned the view of those who believed that the zarzuela could be raised to the category of "grand opera" simply by suppressing the spoken dialogue, we should also set forth the views of those who maintain that the "serious" zarzuela is an artistic product sufficient unto itself, containing all the necessary attributes of a national lyric drama. The chief spokesman for this group is the erudite historian Emilio Cotarelo y Mori, who writes of the zarzuela:

> There is no valid foundation whatever for the idea of inferiority that some persons attribute to this class of genuinely Spanish lyric drama. . . . The zarzuela was and is dramatic, and even tragic, because it is a complete lyrico-dramatic form just as much as the opera, and without limitations of any sort. It differs from the opera only in that a considerable portion of the text is not sung but spoken.[4]

A composer who began by writing legendary operas on Pedrellian principles and later veered to the more remunerative field of the zarzuela was Amadeo Vives (1871–1932), a native of Catalonia who lived most of his life in Madrid. His most serious claim to recognition as a dramatic composer rests on the two-act "lyric eclogue" *Maruxa* (1913), produced at the Madrid Royal Theater. But his great popular successes were achieved with the zarzuelas *Bohemios* (one act) and *Doña Francisquita* (three acts, 1923). The latter, considered a modern classic in Spain, was also performed hundreds of times in South America.

THE IDEALISM OF PEDRELL

All of the foregoing composers wrote both zarzuelas and operas, relying on the latter for prestige and on the former for cash. We come now to a composer who wrote no zarzuelas (one or two youthful pecadilloes excepted), but who concentrated all his efforts upon the creation of a national lyric drama on the most grandiose conceptions. Needless to say, he won much prestige but little cash. His operas were produced only after long and arduous campaigns undertaken on their behalf. They enjoyed no more than a fleeting *succès d'estime* and were withdrawn after a few performances. Nevertheless, Felipe Pedrell (1841–1922) remains a great figure in the history of Spanish music, and one whose regenerative influence will long continue to be felt.

The significance of Pedrell's work is epitomized in the following appreciation by César Cui of his dramatic trilogy *Los Pirineos:*

> Its nobility of style, the strength of its conviction, the avoidance of any and every concession to the prevailing taste, together with its originality and maturity, render this work a grateful phenomenon amid the commercialized products of modern opera-music. It is the creation of a great and high-minded artist of the loftiest idealism.[5]

Pedrell's ambition was to raise Spanish music from the picturesque to the sublime while adhering to a basically national tradition.

Throughout his long life Pedrell labored indefatigably, not only as composer, but also as writer, lecturer, editor, historian, and teacher, for the elevation of Spanish music. From his earliest years, when as a boy he sang the music of Victoria in the cathedral of his native Tortosa, or listened to the songs of the blind beggars as he played in the streets, he was fascinated by the richness of Spanish music in its double aspect of folk song and artistic tradition. Delving into the priceless store of Spain's musical treasure, he rescued from semiobscurity the works of Cabezón, Victoria, Morales, Guerrero, and the other great Hispanic masters of polyphony whose compositions are included in the eight volumes of his *Hispaniae Schola Musica Sacra*. And in the third and fourth volumes of his *Cancionero Musical Popular Español* he included compositions of such men as Encina, Milán, Vázquez, Romero, Navarro, Hidalgo, and Marín, to show how the classical Spanish school affirmed its national character by the technical procedure of composing nearly always on the basis of the popular melody.

Drawing his inspiration both from his historical studies and from the living folklore that he studied and gathered no less assiduously, he sought in his work as a creative artist to unite these two elements of artistic and popular tradition, fusing them into a complex but homogeneous entity. Backing his views with the authority of a principle formulated by the Spanish theorist Padre Antonio Eximeno [6] in the eighteenth century—"Each people should construct its musical system on the basis of its national folk song"—Pedrell carried on with vigor his campaign for the rehabilitation of Spanish music, earning warm praise and enthusiastic encouragement from the foremost critics of Europe, who by his efforts were induced for the first time to take modern Spanish music seriously. Coining an epithet that was quickly taken up by other writers, Moritz Moszkowski, in the *Berliner Tageblatt*,[7] called Pedrell "the Spanish Wagner."

The only point at which Pedrell can be placed on the same level as Wagner is in his intentions. He aspired to do for Spanish opera what Wagner did for German opera. The fatal difference was that he lacked Wagner's genius. So Pedrell's music still awaits its Bayreuth, and the chances are that it will continue to wait in vain. Pedrell was a good musician, but the times and the task demanded a colossal genius whose music would sweep all before it in a triumphant surge of creative force. The phrase that Ernest

Newman applied to Berlioz is even more applicable to Pedrell; he was, as a creative artist, "a pathetic monument of incompleteness."

Pedrell set forth his theories on the national opera in a manifesto entitled *Por Nuestra Música* (*For Our Music*), published at Barcelona in 1891 as a theoretical pendant to his dramatic trilogy *Los Pirineos*, which he envisaged as the cornerstone of modern Spanish opera. Drawing largely upon the ideas of a contemporary Catalan critic, José Ixart, he tried to formulate, in rather obscure and involved terms, the basic principle that Spanish opera must go beyond the exterior forms of language, national setting, and borrowings from folk music in order to assimilate and re-create the essence of the Spanish spirit as embodied in a synthesis of all its most authentically characteristic manifestations. He summed up his views in the dictum that "the character of a truly national music is to be found not only in the popular song and in the instinct of the primitive ages, but also in the genius and in the masterpieces of the great centuries of Art."

Pedrell's chief aesthetic failing was probably that he interpreted his own doctrine too literally. In attempting to give a national color to his operas he often borrowed entire passages from the works of the old Spanish masters (in *Los Pirineos*, for example, he uses a *fauxbourdon* taken from Tomás de Santa María); and the popular themes that he uses in his operas, while exquisitely harmonized, are not always sufficiently integrated into the texture of the work. He came closest to achieving the great Spanish opera of which he dreamed in his *La Celestina* (1904), based on a famous Spanish literary classic of the fifteenth century, the *Comedia de Calisto y Melibea*, dealing with the tragic love of a young couple who are brought together by the machinations of an evil old procuress named Celestina. This work was hailed by Camille Bellaigue as a Spanish *Tristan und Isolde*. With all its shortcomings, it remains a milestone in the history of Spanish opera.

Edgar Istel points out that the distinctive characteristics of Pedrell's music "are never to be sought in the orchestra, but always in the singers' parts, which are set in masterly fashion for vocal effect." The best qualities of Pedrell's art have been summed up as follows by Manuel de Falla: individuality in the means of expression, serene emotional strength, and extraordinary evocative power.[8]

Barbieri and Pedrell represent the two main currents that have gone into the making of modern Spanish music. Composers such as Albéniz, Granados, and Falla, whose contributions to the lyric theater will be discussed in subsequent chapters, have succeeded in combining the colorful vitality of Barbieri and the profound nationalism of Pedrell in works whose appeal is all the more universal because they are truly Spanish.

CHAPTER X

Albéniz and Granados

IN any discussion of modern Spanish music the names of Albéniz and Granados are almost certain to be mentioned together. This casual juxtaposition finds some justification in the parallelism of their careers. Both were born in Catalonia, and in the same decade. Both were pupils of Pedrell and exponents of his doctrine of nationalism in music. Both were famed as virtuoso pianists and as interpreters of their own compositions for piano. As composers, both won their widest and most enduring renown with piano pieces, yet cherished the ambition of winning laurels in the field of opera. Both were cut off in the full tide of their creative maturity, and at exactly the same age: forty-eight. Most important of all, these two put modern Spanish music on the map of the world and made the average music lover conscious of it for the first time. When Pedrell distributed copies of his works, the critics took notice and praised him in their writings. When Albéniz and Granados sent forth their unpretentious little piano pieces into the world, people played them; they found their way into virtually every home that had a piano.

Albéniz had none of the Catalan localism that showed itself in Pedrell. To his intimate friends he used to confide, "I am a Moor," perhaps because he really believed he had Moorish blood in his veins, more likely to emphasize his affinity with the exotic and colorful atmosphere of Andalusia. He declared that the place in Spain where he felt most at home was the Alhambra. Nearly all his best music was of Andalusian inspiration. Yet circumstances made him a native of Catalonia, where his father, who came from Vitoria, was employed as tax collector. Isaac Manuel Francisco Albéniz was born at Camprodón, in the province of Gerona, on May 29, 1860. Incredibly precocious, he began to learn the elements of piano playing from his sister when he was scarcely out of the cradle, and at the age of four he gave a concert in public. His father, determined to make Isaac a successful child prodigy, forced him to practice on the piano continually, to the exclusion of all other studies. When he was six years old his mother took him to Paris, where he studied for nine months with the celebrated pedagogue Marmontel. An attempt was made to enter him as a pupil of the Conservatoire, but the story goes that although he passed his examinations brilliantly he chanced to smash a mirror while playing with a ball, whereupon the jury postponed his admission for two years. His father then recalled him to Spain, where, together with his sister, he was hailed on the concert stage as an infant wonder.

THE ROAD TO ADVENTURE

Following the revolution of 1868, the Albéniz family moved to Madrid and Isaac entered the Conservatory there as a pupil of Mendizábal. But the boy was restless. Reading the tales of Jules Verne, he felt the enticements of adventure. He ran away from home and began a concert tour "on his own" all over northern Spain. His most exciting adventure was being robbed by highwaymen on the road from Zamora to Toro. The death of his sister caused him to return home, but not to remain for long. Southern Spain lured him this time. While he was visiting Cádiz the governor threatened to arrest him if he did not return to his father; panic-stricken at the thought, Albéniz embarked as a stowaway on the steamship *España*, bound for Puerto Rico. Since he could not pay for his passage, even though a collection for his benefit was taken on board, he was set ashore at the first port of call, Buenos Aires. For a while he lived from hand to mouth, sleeping out of doors, eating when he could. Finally he was given help in organizing a concert tour, and a year later he embarked for Cuba with a considerable sum of money in his pocket. He was now thirteen years old. By a strange twist of fate, his father had been transferred to Havana as a customs inspector, and when the elder Albéniz heard of his son's arrival he made another attempt to assert his parental authority. But when he saw that Isaac was not only independent but rich, he resigned himself to the inevitable and let the boy go on his own way.

Isaac's money, however, did not last long. He went to New York and was obliged to work there as a dock porter, also playing the piano in water-front dives. Eventually he attracted attention by playing the piano with the backs of his fingers while turning his back to the piano; with this stunt he made enough money to tour as far as San Francisco, and to pay his way back to Europe. He went first to England, and thence to Germany, studying for a while with Jadassohn and Reinecke at Leipzig. When his money was all gone, he returned to Spain and sought the patronage of Count Guillermo Morphy, private secretary to Alfonso XII and a noted musical amateur. With the count's help he obtained a royal stipend for study at the Brussels Conservatoire, where he had as a fellow pupil the violinist and conductor Enrique Fernández Arbós.[1] After winning a first prize for piano playing, in 1878, he left Brussels in order to receive lessons from Liszt in Weimar and Rome. Then, at the age of twenty, he began to tour Europe and America as a mature virtuoso.

But Albéniz's active career as a pianist—apart from his boyhood exploits—lasted little more than a decade. From 1892 he devoted most of his time to composition. Long before this he had been writing pieces with no marked Spanish character— waltzes, mazurkas, barcaroles, études, sonatas—most of them in a facile *salon* style. This he continued up to about his twenty-third year. It was then, in 1883, that he began to study composition with Felipe Pedrell in Barcelona. Pedrell himself has told us that there was very little formal instruction in these so-called lessons, which were really more in the nature of conversations. Albéniz, he affirms, was recalcitrant to rules and theories and could only understand music intuitively, and exclusively through the medium of the keyboard, not as an abstract conception to be heard "inwardly." What Albéniz derived from Pedrell was above all a spiritual orientation, the realization of the wonderful values inherent in Spanish music.

The year 1883 was also important for Albéniz in another way. He married one of his pupils, Rosina Jordana, and this marked the end of his Bohemianism. Henceforth he devoted himself to his music and his family (he had three children) and gradually, as we have seen, he even gave up concertizing. In 1893 he settled in Paris, where a new phase of his career began. He was thrown into the company of "serious" musicians with high ideals and complete mastery of their medium, and it was natural that he should strive to emulate them. He was a frequent guest at the home of Ernest Chausson, where he met such composers as Fauré, Dukas, d'Indy, and Charles Bordes. Through the two last-mentioned he was brought into the inner sanctum of the Schola Cantorum, where he taught piano for a while and where, above all, he imbibed an atmosphere of lofty aspiration. He needed this stimulus to his better instincts as a composer, for he had come perilously near to selling his artistic soul to the devil.

"THE PACT OF FAUST"

The trouble began in London, where Albéniz had made the acquaintance of a wealthy English banker, Francis Money-Coutts, whose foible was to write poetic dramas. Harmless enough—were it not for the fact that he liked to have them set to music and publicly performed. Worse still, he had the material means to satisfy this whim. He offered Albéniz a handsome annuity if the latter would consent to set his dramas—and his only—to music.

Yielding to the tempting prospect of financial security, Albéniz signed the contract—"the pact of Faust," as he himself called it, half-jestingly.

On top of being an utterly mediocre poet and playwright, Money-Coutts chose subjects that were far removed from the personal inclinations and interests of his musical bondsman. At the banker's behest Albéniz commenced to write music for a dramatic trilogy based on the Arthurian cycle, involving himself in a quagmire of pseudo-Wagnerism from which his improvisational gifts were powerless to extricate him. He finished only the first opera, *Merlin,* and part of the second, *Lancelot.* Even more uncongenial was his next operatic chore, *Henry Clifford* (performed at Barcelona in 1895), a bombastic historical romance.

Finally Albéniz was able to persuade his financier-librettist to choose a Spanish subject. This was *Pepita Jiménez,* adapted from the well-known novel by Juan Valera. The heroine of this story is a young and wealthy Andalusian widow who falls in love with the son of one of her elderly suitors, Don Luis, a student for the priesthood. Luis, whose blood is hot enough to involve him in a duel for her sake, is caught in a struggle between love and duty, and in the end it is the worldly passion that triumphs. There is a dearth of dramatic material in the story, and Money-Coutts's heavy-handed treatment kills whatever life and charm the original tale had. Albéniz is more himself in this work, through which runs an attractive vein of melody, but the defects of the libretto are insurmountable. Nor is the music itself entirely integrated, streaked as it is with Germanic, French, and Italian elements, while the score reveals that Albéniz thought primarily in terms of the piano rather than of the orchestra, a medium he never thoroughly mastered. Nevertheless, *Pepita Jiménez* remains noteworthy among modern Spanish operas, and it obtained a considerable European success, receiving performances in Barcelona (1896), Prague (1897), Brussels (1905), and Paris (Opéra-Comique, June 18, 1923).

Our chief concern is with Albéniz as a composer for the piano, the instrument for which he wrote his most original and most inspired compositions. We cannot even mention, let alone describe, the hundreds of piano pieces he turned out with such fluency in his earlier years. Among them is much that is trivial and character-less, though seldom without charm, and also much that, while simple in form and expression, strikes a new and individual note in piano music. Taking the guitar as his instrumental model, and drawing his inspiration largely from the peculiar traits of Anda-lusian folk music—but without using actual folk themes—Albéniz achieves a stylization of Spanish traditional idioms that, while thoroughly artistic, gives a captivating impression of spontaneous improvisation. Such pieces as the *Seguidillas, Córdoba, Granada, Sevilla, Cádiz,* and the Tango in D have entered the public domain of universal popularity.[2] *Córdoba* is the piece that best represents the style of Albéniz in this period, with its hauntingly beautiful melody, set against the acrid dissonances of the plucked accom-paniment imitating the notes of the Moorish *guzlas.* Here is the heady scent of jasmines amid the swaying palm trees, the dream fantasy of an Andalusian "Arabian Nights" in which Albéniz loved to let his imagination dwell.

GENESIS OF A MASTERPIECE

After Albéniz came under the influence of Bordes, Dukas, d'Indy, and his other Parisian friends, he began to feel that his earlier piano pieces were not "solid" enough and that he should attempt something more ambitious, something of greater archi-tectural scope and more impressive dimensions. The change began to manifest itself in *La Vega* (1889), with its complex polyphony, and reached its culmination in the last works that he completed before his death, the "twelve new impressions" for piano collec-tively entitled *Iberia,* published in four books from 1906 to 1909.[3] Works of formidable technical difficulty, taxing the resources of the best-equipped virtuosi, these twelve "impressions"—so they are called in the subtitle—constitute an imaginative synthesis of Spain (though in truth most of the pieces have Andalusia for their locale) as seen through the nostalgic evocations of the composer in his Parisian exile.

Each of these pieces utilizes Spanish dance rhythms in a freely artistic and idealized manner, the rhythms of the dance alternating with the vocal refrain or *copla*. *Evocación*, the opening number of *Iberia*, is a *fandanguillo* (literally, "little fandango"), with an intensely lyrical *copla* that appears first in the bass and latter returns in the upper register marked *très doux et lointain* ("very soft and distant"). This melody, with its characteristic cadence on the dominant and its thoroughly guitaristic accompaniment, is typical of Albéniz in his most idyllic mood. Technically, this is the least difficult of all the pieces in *Iberia*.

In the next number, *El Puerto* (*The Port*), we are at once plunged into the dazzling sunlight and irresistible animation of a *día de fiesta* in a southern seaport—Puerto de Santa María, on the river Guadalete. Three Andalusian dances, the *polo*, the *bulerías*, and the *seguiriya gitana* (Gypsy seguidillas), lend their rhythmic variety and harmonic piquancy to this pulsating evocation of a popular holiday. The piece begins with the *polo*, brusquely interrupted at the top of the second page by the *bulerías*, with the almost savage incisiveness of their harsh minor seconds and the vehement insistence of their accented offbeats. The entry of the *seguiriyas*, with their dissonance-provoking syncopations, is marked *souple et caressant*, for this is a supple and caressing rhythm, insinuating and provocative like the swaying hips of the *bailarina*. At the end all this exuberance and gaiety vanish in one of those fade-out codas to which Albéniz is so partial.

Seville is famous for the pageantry and intensity of its religious celebrations, especially those of Holy Week and Corpus Christi. It is the latter feast day that Albéniz depicts in *Fête-Dieu à Seville*, the third number of *Iberia*. As the procession bearing the Sacred Host makes its way through narrow, spectator-thronged streets, voices will suddenly be raised in a *saeta*—literally, an "arrow" of song—piercing the tumult of the celebration with the vibrant intensity of its lamentation. The *saeta*, a semi-improvisational manitestation of popular religious feeling, sometimes addressed to the Virgin Mary and sometimes invoking the sufferings of Her Son, is taken up by one group of spectators after another, passing from balcony to balcony as the procession moves along. *Fête-Dieu à Seville* begins with a marchlike theme, heard at first from a distance and growing louder as the procession approaches. Then the poignant melody of the *saeta* enters in fortissimo octaves, to be taken up later by a single voice, attenuated by distance. The marchlike theme is then developed to a tremendous climax—Albéniz uses three staves to obtain his far-flung sonorous effects—followed by a tranquil coda built over tonally shifting pedal points, the melody of the *saeta* appearing once again like a faint echo.

The second book of *Iberia* opens with *Triana*—the name is that of a popular quarter of Seville—based on the rhythm of the ubiquitous *paso-doble* ("two-step"), alternating, and at times combined, with a *marcha torera* ("toreador march"). The cross rhythms and unexpected modulations are extremely effective. The treatment of the themes is more rhapsodic than is usual with Albéniz, corresponding somewhat to the æsthetic concept of Liszt's Hungarian Rhapsodies. *Triana* is the most frequently played of all the pieces in *Iberia*, and with reason, for the lilt of its melodies and the verve of its rhythms are irresistible.

In *Almería* we have the languorous, nonchalant rhythm of the *tarantas*, a dance peculiar to the town and region of Almería, a Mediterranean seaport, whence the piece takes its title. There is an interesting incursion into the Lydian mode, and the expressive melody of a *jota* as sung in Almería makes its entry at the bottom of page five, in the key of C major. The next piece, *Rondeña*, takes its name from a dance, one of the variants of the fandango, which in turn is called after the town of Ronda, in Andalusia. Its rhythm is characterized by the alternation of measures in 6/8 and 3/4, a nervous, staccato rhythm, interrupted at the section marked *Poco meno mosso* by the lyrical refrain of a *malagueña-rondeña*, which is later contrapuntally blended with the theme of the dance.

Book III opens with what we consider the most beautiful and

original of all the pieces in *Iberia*. This is *El Albaicín,* named for the Gypsy quarter of Granada, so picturesquely situated on a hill facing the Alhambra. The music is marked to be played *Allegro assai, ma melancolico,* for it follows the pattern of the *bulerías,* one of those melancholy yet passionate dance themes so beloved by the Andalusian Gypsies. The *copla* has the sinuous, semi-Oriental contours of *cante hondo,* the "deep song" of Andalusia, moving within the characteristic compass of a sixth. The nostalgic poetry of the lyrical refrain is set off by the tense and pungent guitar figurations of the accompaniment. Debussy particularly admired *El Albaicín,* declaring that few compositions could compare with it. Certainly there is nothing quite like it in all piano literature.

Scarcely on the same height is *El Polo,* based, of course, on the well-known Andalusian song of that name, which always seems to have a burden of sorrow. Albéniz directs that the music should be played *toujours dans l'esprit du sanglot,* as though the rhythm were broken by sobs. In complete contrast is *Lavapiés* (named for a popular quarter of Madrid), at the head of which the composer writes: "This piece should be played joyfully and with freedom." It is in the same spirit as *Triana,* but less successful because the harmonic complexity and elaboration of detail are carried to a somewhat disconcerting extreme.

THE FOURTH BOOK OF *IBERIA*

In the opinion of Henri Collet, French biographer of Albéniz, the fourth book of *Iberia* contains "the most beautiful jewels of the collection." Yet these three pieces, *Málaga, Jerez* and *Eritaña,* are comparatively little known. As its title indicates, the music of *Málaga* stems from the *malagueña,* one of the popular forms related to the fandango. A simple but attractive theme is carried through a succession of unconventional modulations and is later contrapuntally treated in combination with the graceful theme of the *copla. Jerez,* which Collet calls *"la plus belle"* of all the pieces in *Iberia,* takes its name from the famous wine-producing town of Andalusia, in English corrupted to "Sherry." It is constructed on the pattern of the *soleares*, another favorite dance of the Spanish Gypsies. But perhaps "constructed" is too mechanical a term to use in connection with this composition, in which the most exuberant fantasy has free play, disporting itself in soaring arabesques and subtle fluctuations of tonality prepared by the prevailing Hypodorian mode (corresponding to A minor without the leading tone). The vibrantly expressive *cante hondo* melody weaves its way amid a fascinating wealth of exquisite filigree, like the delicate and complex ornamentation of the Alhambra.

Eritaña is named for a celebrated tavern on the outskirts of Seville. It evokes the gay rhythm of the *sevillanas* (related to the seguidillas), and as an exception this alluring dance is not interrupted by any lyrical refrain. The music has great harmonic boldness and modulates with marvelous audacity. Claude Debussy wrote enthusiastically of this piece:

> *Eritaña* is the joy of morning, the happy discovery of a tavern where the wine is cool. An ever-changing crowd passes, their bursts of laughter accompanied by the jingling of the tambourines. Never has music achieved such diversified, such colorful, impressions: one's eyes close, as though dazzled by beholding such a wealth of imagery.[4]

No more fitting epilogue to our summary of *Iberia* could be found than this dictum of Debussy: "Never has music achieved such diversified, such colorful, impressions."

With *Iberia*, Albéniz wrote his swan song. He died at Cambo-les-Bains, in the Basses-Pyrénées, on May 18, 1909, the year in which the fourth volume of *Iberia* appeared. His body was taken to Barcelona for burial. He was in the prime of life, but his early nomadic existence had undermined his health. It is tempting to speculate on what he might have done had he lived longer, but more rewarding to improve our acquaintance with the imperishable masterpieces he has left us.

ENRIQUE GRANADOS

Enrique Granados had none of the wanderlust that dwelt in Albéniz. He disliked traveling, especially by water. So distasteful was sea travel to him that even the short trip from Barcelona to Mallorca, a matter of some six or seven hours, he regarded as an ordeal: he spent the time looking at his watch and longing for the moment of disembarcation. When one of his friends asked what he would do if he had to give a concert in America, he replied with determination, "I would not go!"

Had Granados adhered to that early impulsive decision, the story of his life might have had a very different and less tragic ending. As it was, he finally did make up his mind to visit America, not primarily to give concerts, but to attend the world première of his opera *Goyescas* in New York. Ironically enough, he had then to brave not only the ordinary discomforts of a sea voyage, but also the far more terrible menace of submarine warfare, for it was in the midst of the first World War. On March 24, 1916, Granados and his wife, returning from America to Spain, perished in the sinking of the steamship *Sussex*, torpedoed by a German submarine in the English Channel.

Enrique Granados y Campiña, the son of an army officer, was born at Lérida on July 29, 1867. Early signs of musical inclination led to his receiving lessons from the local bandmaster until the family moved to Barcelona, where he studied with Francisco Jurnet and J. B. Pujol. Like most Spanish musicians, he wished to continue his studies in Paris and applied for admission to the Conservatoire. But before he could take the entrance examination he fell seriously ill, and by the time he recovered he had passed the age limit for admission. He had to content himself with taking private piano lessons from Charles de Bériot, one of the chief professors of the Conservatoire.

From 1889 Granados made his home in Barcelona, giving recitals in Spain and Paris, earning high repute as a piano teacher, and composing assiduously. He married Señorita Amparo Gal in

Isaac Albéniz

Enrique Granados, from the Portrait by Nestor

1892. By this time he had already composed some of those *Spanish Dances* for piano that became so deservedly popular. Having studied composition with Pedrell, he proceeded to put into practice, but in a thoroughly personal way, that master's principles of musical nationalism.

What the Alhambra was to Albéniz, Madrid was to Granados. Not the modern, bourgeois Madrid, but the Madrid of the days of Goya and Ramón de la Cruz, of the tonadillas, of the *majos* and *majas*, and of the gay *manolería*.[5] His admiration for Goya was boundless and permeated his whole imaginative and creative activity—he even undertook to make drawings, rather successfully, too, of *majos* and *majas* in the style of Goya.[6] His most significant compositions, the suite *Goyescas* for piano (later expanded into the opera of the same title) and the *Tonadillas al Estilo Antiguo* for voice and piano, are the result of his efforts to give musical expression to scenes and characters inspired by the paintings and sketches of Francisco Goya. The dominant aesthetic trait of Granados is his *madrileñismo*, his feeling for the spirit of Madrid at the most colorful and romantic moment of its history.

It must not be imagined, however, that Granados was impervious to the fascination of Andalusian music. On the contrary, he drew upon this material for some of his finest and most effective compositions, notably the *Spanish Dance* No. 5—the piece that made him famous—and *El Fandango de Candil*, from the first part of *Goyescas*, for piano. The *Spanish Dances* No. 2, No. 11, and No. 12 are likewise of Andalusian character. But Granados does not respond to the vibrations of *cante hondo* and the excitement of the flamenco dances in the same intimate and sympathetic way that Albéniz does. He is more restrained and aristocratic. The "naturalism" of Albéniz and Falla is not congenial to him. His temperament is profoundly romantic, and his imagination is stimulated not so much by the impact of sensuous imagery and primitive feelings as by the visions of sublimated love and tragic passion viewed in the emotional perspective of the past. In the list of his works for piano we find such titles as *Romantic Scenes*,

Poetic Scenes, Poetic Waltzes, Waltzes of Love, Romeo and Juliet (Poem)—all redolent of romantic atmosphere. We also find him writing a symphonic poem entitled *Dante*, in which the main episode deals with the tragic love of Paolo and Francesca.[7] In his cult for Goya he tended to disregard the realistic and satiric aspects of that master's art, and to concentrate upon its romantic and picturesque aspects. Granados, in a word, was somewhat of a sentimentalist. Nowadays he might be called an escapist.

THE OPERA *GOYESCAS*

Although the *Goyescas* for piano preceded the opera of the same title, it will be advisable to describe the opera first, because familiarity with the plot that Granados and his librettist, Fernando Periquet, wove around these scenes from Goya will enable the reader to enter more readily into the spirit of the pianistic *Goyescas*. The setting of *Goyescas* is in Madrid and its environs, toward the end of the eighteenth century. The curtain rises upon a scene inspired by one of Goya's best-known tapestry cartoons, *El Pelele*,[8] which depicts the tossing of a dummy by four *majas*. While the crowd is engaged in this popular pastime, a flirtation is going on between the bullfighter Paquiro and the beautiful Rosario. He invites her to attend the *Baile de Candil*, a popular ball. The invitation is overheard by Rosario's suitor, the captain Fernando, who obliges Rosario to swear that she will not attend the dance without him. Paquiro's action has also aroused the jealousy of his sweetheart, Pepa, who vows to be revenged on Rosario. Act II is the scene of the ball, at which Fernando and Paquiro come into conflict; they agree to fight a duel. The third and last act has Rosario's garden as its setting. The nightingale sings as Rosario and Fernando indulge in an impassioned love scene. In the duel with Paquiro, Fernando is mortally wounded. Rosario, grief-stricken, falls prostrate over the dead body of her lover.

Goyescas had been accepted for performance at the Paris Opéra, but the outbreak of the first World War put an end to that project.

Instead the work was produced at the Metropolitan Opera House in New York on January 28, 1916, in the presence of the composer. It marked "not only the first time that Spanish had been the language of a performance at the Metropolitan, but also the first production of an authentically Spanish work, in any language, in that auditorium." [9] The opera received five performances that season and thereafter was not given again. The critics praised the beauty of the music and lauded its authentic Spanish atmosphere. The New York *Times* spoke of "this full-blooded, passionate utterance, sometimes stirring in its characteristic rhythms and frank melody, sometimes languorous, poetical, profoundly pathetic, subtly suggestive. . . . His [Granados's] harmonic scheme is elaborate and gives a peculiar distinction, warmth and brilliancy to his style. This music has a haunting power." The music of *Goyescas* has indeed all these admirable qualities, yet as an opera it hangs together loosely and lacks the dramatic force by which works live in the theater. The famous *Intermezzo* from the opera, which has become so popular as a concert piece because of its strikingly beautiful melody, does not figure in the original score of the work, but was added by Granados at the last minute, in order to allow time for a change of scenery.[10]

THE *GOYESCAS* FOR PIANO

For those who like to have their music provided with a literary background, the libretto of *Goyescas* may serve as a programmatic guide to the piano suite of the same name, complementing the descriptive titles that Granados himself gave to these pieces, which bear the collective subtitle *Los Majos Enamorados* (*The Majos in Love*). The suite consists of six pieces, published in two volumes (1912–1914). An analysis of the first number, *Los Requiebros* (*Compliments*), reveals the musical *madrileñismo* of Granados in some of its most characteristic manifestations. The composition is directed to be played *con garbo y donaire*—gracefully and with spirit. Its two main themes are taken from the celebrated *Tirana del Trípili* by Blas de Laserna (*cf.* Chapter VIII), a song that enjoyed enormous popularity and was inserted in various theatrical pieces of the eighteenth century. Granados uses the word "Tonadilla" to mark the presence of these themes in *Los Requiebros* because he employs the word in its current meaning of "song," having probably little conception, if any, of its historical meaning as a musicodramatic form. The first theme used by Granados is taken from the first four measures of the refrain (*estribillo*) of Laserna's song (*cf.* p. 131), with a triplet substituted for the penultimate sixteenth note to enhance the artistic effect. This theme makes its appearance in the eighth measure (*molto a piacere*) and is later emphatically articulated in octaves at the section marked "*tonadilla—con gallardía.*" The second theme is based on the initial phrase of the second part of the refrain ("Anda, chiquilla") and is treated by Granados in a variety of ways, culminating in an *allegro assai, con fuoco,* leading to a section marked *molto capricioso,* in which the theme passes freely from one voice to another.

The second number of *Goyescas* is *Coloquio en la Reja* (*Lovers' Meeting at the Window*), with a very expressive *copla*. A footnote directs that the bass notes should imitate the tones of a guitar. The third number, *El Fandango de Candil,* is, of course, a fandango. This is followed by *Quejas ó la Maja y el Ruiseñor* (*The Maja and the Nightingale*), marked *andante melancolico*. This piece has no popular element at all, but is one of Granados's most personal and most poetic utterances. In spite of the fact that this is an entirely original melody, with no national basis, Pedro Morales declared that "rarely has the Spanish soul manifested itself so clearly in cultured music as in the initial theme of *La Maja y el Ruiseñor*." [11]

The second volume opens with the most dramatic and brilliant of all these pieces, *El Amor y la Muerte* (*Love and Death*), subtitled *Balada,* in which themes from the preceding numbers reappear. The suite concludes with an Epilogue, *Serenata del Espectro* (*The Specter's Serenade*), which presumably evokes the ghost of Fernando, singing his ghostly serenade, mingled with echoes of the fandango, to the muffled accompaniment of his spectral guitar. Not published together with the suite, but nevertheless closely associated with it, is a seventh piece, *El Pelele* (*The Dummy*), based on the music of the opening scene of the opera *Goyescas,* a lively and strongly rhythmed composition depicting the "man of straw" being tossed in the air by the *majas.* Though written last, it really forms a sort of introduction to the suite.

Unlike *Iberia,* which is simply a series of detached pieces that may be played in any order, the *Goyescas* are a suite in the strict sense of the word, bound together by both poetic and thematic unity. Although his technique and his aesthetic approach stem from Chopin and Liszt, Granados achieved a truly original work with the *Goyescas,* which together with *Iberia* mark the highest peak of modern Spanish piano music. Ernest Newman, who in 1917 called *Goyescas* "the finest piano music of our day," has summed up the qualities of Granados's art with his customary insight and felicity of expression: [12]

The *Goyescas* are indeed a fascinating work. The music, for all the fervor of its passion, is of classical beauty and composure. The harmony is rich but never experimental. The melodies have new curves, the rhythms new articulations. Informing it all is a new grace, a new pathos, a new melancholy. Not only the separate pieces themselves but the themes of them have a curious poetic individuality, so that to meet in a later piece with a theme from an earlier one is like seeing a definite personality step across the scene; but, above all, the music is a gorgeous treat for the fingers, as all music that is the perfection of writing for its particular instrument is. It is difficult, but so beautifully laid out that it is always playable: one has the voluptuous sense of passing the fingers through masses of richly colored jewels. . . . It is pianoforte music of the purest kind.

CHAPTER XI

Regionalism and Romanticism

SPAIN, said Ortega y Gasset, is not a nation, but a series of watertight compartments. By this the eminent philosopher meant that each region of Spain thinks, feels, and acts in terms of its own particular interests and inclinations. National unity in Spain has never been a natural, organic growth. Rather has it been an extraneous concept imposed by the political and cultural hegemony of Castile, and arduously enforced by the monarchist policy of centralism. Whenever that centralizing power has been weakened by the rise of liberalism, there has been a corresponding acceleration of the separatist tendency throughout Spain. Such was the case during the years of the Second Republic (1931–1939), when the Catalans, the Basques, the Galicians, and the Asturians made rapid strides toward autonomy.

This regional isolationism of Spain is the result of numerous factors, both psychological and physical. Natural barriers—rivers and mountains—divide the country into well-defined sectors. Moreover, the Spaniard is a stubborn individualist, and this individualism manifests itself collectively in the various regions, which do not wish to lose their identity even for the sake of a common nationhood. Separatism has manifested itself most strongly in Catalonia, which has been called "the Ireland of Spain." [1] Had the Republican instead of the Nationalist side been victorious in the civil war of 1936–1939, Catalonia would in all probability have become just as much of an independent nation as Eire is today. For the time being her separatist ambitions have been thwarted by the centralist policy of the Franco regime, but the latent nationalism of Catalonia is a powerful force that must always be reckoned with, both politically and culturally.

It is an ironic fact that when Pedrell wrote his dramatic trilogy *Los Pirineos,* purporting to lay the cornerstone of a Spanish "national" opera, he not only chose a Catalan subject, but also used a libretto written in the Catalan language, whose beauty and musicality he warmly extolled. Furthermore, the subject of the opera made a strong appeal to local patriotism, for it dealt with the successful struggle of the Catalonians to free themselves from the domination of the Papacy in the thirteenth century (Pedro II of Aragon and Catalonia had enfeoffed his domains to the Pope against the will of his subjects). The work is indeed replete with national sentiment, but that sentiment is Catalan, not Spanish.

In the light of Catalan nationalism, it becomes necessary to view Pedrell's creative activity in another aspect. He was not only the regenerator of modern Spanish music, but also the creator of the modern Catalan national school of music. Not only in *Los Pirineos,* but likewise in the lyric drama *El Comte Arnau,* the cantata *La Glosa,* and the symphonic scenes *Lo Cant de las Montanyas,* he produced works that were thoroughly Catalonian both in spirit and substance. Pedrell's posthumous fate as a composer depends largely on the extent to which Catalan nationalism can be kept alive in the midst of the political vicissitudes that it must suffer. Should Catalonia ever become and remain an independent nation, then Felipe Pedrell may find his Bayreuth after all—his native Tortosa might become a shrine to honor the memory of the first great modern Catalan composer.

Among other composers who were native sons of Catalonia, none has attained the world-wide fame that befell Albéniz and Granados, in whose music very little that is specifically Catalan can be found — Albéniz's suite for piano and orchestra, entitled *Catalonia,* is one of his less-inspired works. Local if not international eminence was attained by Antonio Nicolau (1858–1933) and Enric Morera (b. 1865). Both were born in Barcelona and both were very active, as conductors and educators, in promoting the musical life of that city. Nicolau lived for eight years in Paris, where his symphonic poem *El Triunfo de Venus* was performed in 1882. Although he wrote some stage works, including the opera *Constanza*, he is best known as a composer of choral works to Catalan texts. His masterpiece in this genre is *La Mort del Escolá*, a work that according to Pedro Morales "ought to be in the repertoire of every choral society throughout the world."

Morera, a pupil of Pedrell and a solid technician, was strongly influenced by the modern French and Belgian schools. Possessing a more robust and vigorous talent than Nicolau, he obtained considerable success as a dramatic composer, notably with the operas *Emporium* (Barcelona, 1902), *Bruniselda,* and *Tassarba.* A prolific composer, he has written some fifty stage works, besides many orchestral works, piano pieces, songs and choral arrangements of Catalan folk songs, some of which have been performed by the Schola Cantorum of New York. He composed a symphonic poem on the epic *La Atlántida* by Verdaguer, which Manuel de Falla has also set to music as a cantata.

A CATALAN MODERNIST

Morera's most important pupil is Jaime Pahissa (b. 1880), who until his departure for Argentina in 1937 was a leading figure in the musical life of Catalonia. His opera *La Princesa Margarida* was received with enthusiasm upon its production at the Liceo of Barcelona on February 8, 1928, and was subsequently given in other cities of Catalonia. This opera has an interesting musical history. The plot and some of the thematic material are derived from a Catalan folk song, *La Presó de Lleida* (*The Prison of Lerida*), of which Pahissa had made a choral arrangement early in his career. In 1906 he was commissioned to write incidental music for a lyrico-dramatic work based on this folk song; the work was so successful that it received one hundred consecutive performances at the Teatro Principal of Barcelona. Some twenty years later Pahissa decided to expand this musical and dramatic material into a three-act "Catalan romantic opera," which he entitled *La Princesa Margarida* after the unhappy protagonist of the story. The princess loves a shepherd who is unjustly imprisoned and sentenced to death; failing to obtain a pardon for her beloved from her father, she disguises herself as a man, mingles with the prisoners, and is put to death with them. Upon realizing the result of his obduracy, the father dies of grief.

Pahissa had previously created somewhat of a sensation with his opera *Gala Placidia* (Teatro Liceo, January 19, 1913), to a libretto by the famous Catalan dramatist Angel Guimerá, set in the time of the invasion of Roman Spain by the Visigoths. More melodically ingratiating and less uncompromising in harmonic structure were two other operas, *La Morisca* (one act, 1919), libretto by Eduardo Marquina, and *Marianela* (three acts, 1923), libretto by the brothers Alvarez Quintero. He has also composed many large orchestral works—including the symphonic poem *El Camí* (*The Path*)—chamber music, piano pieces, choral works and songs, most of them of definite Catalan inspiration. Pahissa cultivates a "vertical" or "linear" style of writing in which harmony plays a secondary role. He considers himself the inventor of a "system of pure dissonance" which is neither tonal, nor atonal, nor polytonal. His *Suite Intertonal* for orchestra was written to illustrate this system. Another orchestral work, *Monodia*, is intended to demonstrate that a composition can be based exclusively on melody, without regard to harmony or rhythm. The bulk of his music, however, does not partake of this experimental nature.

So abundant is the musical productivity of the modern Catalan school that even to list the names of the outstanding composers would require more space than we can afford. Mention may be made of the distinguished precursor Francisco Alió (1862–1908), one of the first to collect and harmonize Catalan folk melodies; of Joaquín Cassadó (1867–1926), composer of over two hundred works, of which the most popular is the fantasy *Hispania* for piano and orchestra; of Joan Manén, famed as a violin virtuoso, among whose works in neoclassic vein are found some of Catalan character, such as the symphonic poems *Nova Catalonia* and *Camí del Sol*; and of the composers of religious music, Domingo Mas y Serracant, J. B. Lambert, and Cumellas Ribó. Most notable of the composers born in the eighteen nineties are Frederic Mompou and Robert Gerhard. The former studied in Paris and lived there for many years, producing a limited but highly personal body of piano music that reveals a sensitive and original artistry. Gerhard, born in Catalonia, but of Swiss parentage, was Pedrell's last pupil. He also studied with Schönberg in Vienna for five years and was strongly influenced by that composer's theories. Neither his modernism nor his foreign extraction has caused him to abandon his musical ties with Catalonia, as witnessed by such works as the cantata *L'Alta Naixença del Rei En Jaume* (for solos, mixed chorus, and orchestra), the *Albada, Interludi i Dansa* for orchestra (performed in London, 1937), or the six *Cançons Populars de Catalunya* for soprano and orchestra. As a result of the civil war, Gerhard left Spain and went to England, where he found a haven at the University of Cambridge.

No account of music in Catalonia would be complete without mention of the Orfeó Català, the famous choral society founded by Luis Millet and Amadeo Vives in 1891. In reviving the masterpieces of the polyphonic period, in fostering the performance of Catalan folk music, and in bringing out works of the modern Catalan school, this society accomplished a task of the highest significance. In 1908 the Orfeó Català inaugurated its own concert hall in Barcelona, the Palau de la Música Catalana. It also published the excellent musical periodical *La Revista Musical Catalana*. The precursor of the choral movement in Catalonia was Anselmo Clavé (1824–1874).

OUTPOSTS OF "GREATER CATALONIA"

The Balearic Islands are considered a part of "greater Catalonia," though separatist feeling does not seem to run so high there. The initiator of the modern musical movement in Mallorca was Antonio Noguera (1860–1904). A fervent cultivator of Balearic folk music, he has been called "a Mediterranean Grieg." He wrote fine melodies and excellent choral works and also harmonized Mallorcan folk songs. His piano music includes *Three Dances on Popular Airs from Mallorca*. A similar tradition has been carried on by Baltasar Samper, born at Palma de Mallorca in 1888, who studied piano with Granados and composition with Pedrell. Among his compositions are *Dues Suites de Cansons i Danses de l'Illa de Mallorca* for orchestra; the choral works *L'Estiu, Cansó Trista*, and *Jocs de Nins*; and *Danzas Mallorquinas* for piano. He has collected and harmonized many Balearic folk songs (some published in the *Obra del Cançoner Popular de Catalunya*).

Also included in the concept of "greater Catalonia"—that is, the old historical domain of Catalonia as distinct from the modern provincial demarcation—is the contiguous one-time kingdom of Valencia, lying further south along the Mediterranean coast. The language—or rather dialect—spoken there is a variant of Catalan; yet the Valencians, with true Iberian individualism, resent the idea of cultural or political dependency upon Catalonia and prefer to develop their own regional personality along independent lines. The patriarch of Valencian music was Salvador Giner (1832–1911). Possessing a facile talent and a fluent technique, he wrote copiously in all forms, including operas of Meyerbeerian tendency, many zarzuelas, symphonic poems, and church music. Becoming director of the Conservatory of Music at Valencia, he taught many of the newer generation of Valencian composers, among them Vicente Ripolles (b. 1867), best known as a composer of religious music.

The present leader of the Valencian school, Eduardo López-Chavarri (b. 1881), studied with Pedrell in Barcelona and became prominent not only as a composer, but also as a poet and a writer on music. Active, in addition, as educator (he taught Aesthetics and History of Music at the Valencia Conservatory) and as conductor (of the Conservatory Orchestra), he has been able to advance the musical culture of his native province along a wide front. Master of a solid technique, he has expressed his reaction to the Valencian milieu in such compositions as *Valencianas* for orchestra, *Acuarelas Valencianas* for string orchestra, *Legenda* for chorus and orchestra, *Rapsodia* for piano and orchestra, and *Danzas Valencianas* for piano. Francesch Cuesta, Manuel Palau,[2] José Moreno Gans,[3] and Joaquín Rodrigo [4] are other composers who have helped to enhance the prestige of the Valencian school.

Proceeding southward along the Mediterranean coast, we come to the region of Murcia and Alicante, known as El Levante. The cities of Murcia and Alicante, capitals of the respective provinces of those names, are not large enough to support a local musical activity such as we find in Barcelona and Valencia. Politically, the autonomous feeling is dormant, because these regions passed directly from the domination of the Moslems to that of Valencia, without knowing an independent existence like the kingdoms of the North. In modern times each of these provinces has produced an important composer through whose art the music of each region has attracted attention throughout Spain and abroad. Though Bartolomé Pérez Casas, born in Lorca (province of Murcia) in 1873, has spent the greater part of his life in Madrid as conductor of the Philharmonic Orchestra, which he founded in 1915, he recalled the scenes of his birthplace in his *Suite Murciana: A mi Tierra* (*To My Land*) for orchestra, which received a prize from the Academia de Bellas Artes in 1905 (together with Falla's *La Vida Breve*). Debussy, who heard this work at Paris in 1913, wrote that it was "of a poetry impregnated with Oriental languor, and containing very novel instrumental combinations in which the persistent search for colorful effects is nearly always justified by the sincerity of the expression." [5] Pérez Casas has also written a Quartet in D minor for piano and strings, and a symphonic poem, *Calisto y Melibea,* based on the same subject that Pedrell treated operatically.

A PHILOSOPHER-ENGINEER-COMPOSER

Oscar Esplá, born at Alicante in 1886, is one of the most interesting personalities in modern Spanish music. He first prepared for the career of a civil engineer and later studied philosophy, obtaining a doctorate in the latter subject. Though he showed musical aptitude from childhood, he received scarcely any systematic instruction in music. In his youth he spent several years in Germany, where he studied composition with Max Reger for a short time. In 1909 he won an international prize at Vienna with a suite for orchestra, and from 1913, when Arbós performed his symphonic poem *El Sueño de Eros* with the Madrid Symphony Orchestra, he began to take his place as a composer with something distinctive to say. By the advent of the Republic in 1931 he was a figure of national importance. He was made president of the Junta Nacional de Música and director of the Madrid Conservatory. But during the civil war he left Spain and settled in Brussels.

Esplá's approach to musical composition is conditioned by his intellectual background. As an engineer he was trained to think primarily in terms of structure. As a philosopher he was given to developing abstract ideological systems. His contact with Germanic influences at a formative period of his life strengthened his tendency toward grandiose conceptions. The speculative trend of his mind manifested itself in such writings as *Art and Musicality* and *The Activities of the Spirit and Their Aesthetic Foundation.* In contrast to the spontaneous creative exuberance of an Albéniz, Esplá has the type of mind that needs to formulate a system before it can create art.

Esplá's musical system is based on the folk music of his native region, but he has taken only certain characteristic traits and evolved from them a scale of his own invention, as follows: C,

D flat, E flat, E, F, G flat, A flat, B flat. This scale lends itself to a dominant-tonic relationship, and it is possible to form a minor tonic chord. But apart from this its harmonic functions are very limited, and the lack of definite tonal contrasts produces a certain monotony that is perhaps the chief defect of Esplá's music. The use of this scale is first met with in the Sonata for piano and violin (Opus 9), a work of huge proportions in the "cyclic" style, and it reaches its maximum development in the symphonic poems *Ciclopes de Ifach* (1916), *El Ámbito de la Danza* (1924), and *Las Cumbres* (with chorus, completed in 1924). The scale is also used in the piano pieces entitled *Crepúsculos, Evocaciones, Ronda Levantina*, and *Cantos de Vendimia*.

Esplá does not believe in any sort of musical "nationalism," nor in the reproduction of folk themes to obtain local color. By the application of his musical system he claims that he gives "universal character to that which would otherwise be simply picturesque and regionally limited." Hence it is difficult to detect any specific Spanish element in his music, though one thoroughly familiar with the folk music of the Levante might recognize certain rhythmic and melodic characteristics. This is true in particular of the *Canciones Playeras* for voice and piano (also orchestrated), which are stylizations of the songs of fishermen from Alicante, and of some of the pieces in the suite *Levante* for piano.

The only one of Esplá's orchestral works that has been published and widely performed is the "symphonic episode" entitled *Don Quijote Velando las Armas* (*Don Quixote's Vigil at Arms*), originally written for small orchestra and later rewritten for full modern orchestra with augmented percussion. In the latter version it was first performed by Arbós at Madrid in 1927, and a year later (March 30, 1928) it received its first hearing in New York under the same conductor. The only programmatic indication given by the composer is: "Meditations and hopes of Don Quixote during the night of his vigil at arms.—Adventures, fancies and landscapes." The three connected movements are entitled *Prelude, Dance,* and *Final Scene.* The dance takes the form of the *seguidillas manchegas*—that is, from the region of La Mancha in Castile. The recurrent theme associated with Don Quixote is a simple rhythmic figure, a sort of martial fanfare, which unfortunately lacks the stirring quality of the knightly theme that Richard Strauss invented for his *Don Quixote*. The work is extremely poetic, but somewhat lacking in cohesion and vitality.

In contrast to the elaborate complexity of some of his larger works, Esplá has written many piano pieces in a vein of delightful simplicity. Among these are his five musical impressions entitled *Cuentos Infantiles*, composed in 1905 for a children's party and illustrating well-known fairy tales such as "Little Red Ridinghood" and "Cinderella." He also returns to childhood scenes in the tone poem *La Nochebuena del Diablo* (1921), in which he quotes from traditional Spanish children's songs.

Another phase of Esplá's work is represented by his compositions for the theater, comprising the ballet *El Contrabandista* (produced by La Argentina at Paris in 1934), the fairy opera *La Bella Durmiente* (*The Sleeping Beauty*), and the ballet opera *La Belteira*, with a libretto by Irene Lewisohn of New York.[6] In 1939 he completed a *Sonata del Sur* for piano and orchestra.

TURINA OF ANDALUSIA

The extent to which the Andalusian idiom becomes a passport to international success may be seen in the case of Joaquín Turina (b. 1882), whose reputation abroad is considerably in excess of his intrinsic merits as a composer. Turina achieved fame with his orchestral tone poem *La Procesión del Rocío*, first performed in 1913. This is a brilliant but superficial descriptive piece, evoking a popular religious celebration in Seville, replete with realistic details of local color. Turina, however, does not appear to have acquired a taste for Andalusian atmosphere in his native Seville, but rather in Paris, where he studied composition with Vincent d'Indy at the Schola Cantorum from 1906. How completely he came under the post-Franckian atmosphere of the Schola is demonstrated by his Sonata for violin and piano and his Quintet for piano and strings (1907). Albéniz, friendly and helpful as ever, aided him in getting these works published, and—what was even more valuable—urged him to turn his attention to the popular music of his native land.

Having thus been set upon the right path by Albéniz, Turina proceeded to turn out, in rapid succession, a large quantity of compositions, mostly of a descriptive nature and dealing with the Andalusian scene. His harmonic syntax, however, continued to show traces of his sojourn in the Rue Saint-Jacques, and he retained a predilection for the "cyclic" method of composition so dear to the school of d'Indy. The blending of Andalusian atmosphere with scholastic science may be seen in his String Quartet (1911), performed in the cenacle of the Société Nationale de Musique. More frankly picturesque are his suite *Sevilla* for piano, his *La Oración del Torero* (*The Bullfighter's Prayer*) for string quartet, his *Sinfonía Sevillana* for orchestra (1920), and his *Canto a Sevilla* for soprano and orchestra. Among his numerous pieces for piano, some of the best are the *Sonata Romántica, Tres Danzas Andaluzas, Mujeres de España, Cuentos de España* (two series), and *Jardines de Andalucía.* His *Danzas Fantásticas* for orchestra (1920) have been widely performed.

An excellent pianist (pupil of Tragó and Moszkowski), a critic of some influence (for many years critic of *El Debate* in Madrid), and a member of the Royal Academy of Fine Arts, Turina is a personality of importance in the contemporary Spanish musical scene. But as a composer he has shown no capacity for development or creative renewal. His style is not an organic growth, but a series of mannerisms that he repeats ad infinitum. He writes effectively in any medium—except for the stage, in which he has had no conspicuous success [7]—and his piano pieces undeniably have much charm. Yet his artistic stature has diminished rather than increased with time.

The composer who has written the best Andalusian music is Manuel de Falla, to whom we devote a separate chapter. Here we may mention Angel Barrios (born in Granada, 1862), who

Joaquín Turina

Oscar Esplá

became known both as a guitar virtuoso, specializing in the flamenco style, and as a composer (he studied with C. del Campo in Madrid and A. Gédalge in Paris). Impregnated with Andalusian atmosphere are his symphonic poem *Zambra en el Albaicín,* the *Danzas Gitanas* for orchestra, and the zarzuela *Granada Mía.* Another Andalusian composer whose piano pieces have attained considerable popularity is Manuel Infante (born in Osuna, near Seville, 1883). Though living in Paris from 1909, Infante has never forgotten the musical attractions of his native province, which he has recalled in such works as *Gitanerías, Pochades Andalouses, Sevillana,* and *El Vito* (variations on a popular theme and original dance), all for piano. Effectively written for two pianos are his *Three Andalusian Dances* (*Ritmo, Gracia, Sentimiento*).

REGIONAL COMPOSERS OF THE NORTH

The province of Extremadura, bordering on Portugal, does not appear to have developed any regional school. Galicia, in the northwest corner of the peninsula, has produced a few regional composers, of whom the most notable is Juan de Montes, a native of Lugo. His works include a *Fantasia on Galician Popular Airs* for orchestra, *Seis Baladas Gallegas* for violin and piano, and *Sonata Descriptiva* for string quartet. Following the provincial periphery along the Atlantic coast we come to the titular principality of Asturias, which is rich in folk music but poor in composers. The best known "Asturian" composition is an orchestral suite on popular airs of that region written by Ricardo Villa, a native of Madrid.[8]

Lying between Asturias and Castile is the ancient kingdom of León, whose chief modern representative in music is Rogelio Villar (1875–1937). His romantic regionalism is modeled on the style of Grieg. Besides publishing five volumes of folk songs from León with his own harmonizations, he has written an *Eclogue* for orchestra, six string quartets, songs, and piano pieces, of which the most typical are the *Danzas Montañesas.* The prevailing mood of his music is one of pastoral simplicity and elegiac melancholy, expressed with a technique that is purposely naïve. His art is intimate and subjective.

The musical banner of Navarre has been held aloft by Joaquín Larregla (born in Lumbier, 1865), whose *jota* entitled *Viva Navarra!* attained enormous popularity.[9] He has also composed a *Rapsodia Vasco-Navarra* for orchestra and many effective piano pieces, which he himself has interpreted on concert tours throughout Spain. He is a member of the Royal Academy of Fine Arts.

The Basque country vies with Catalonia both in the strength of its autonomous inclinations and in the richness of its musical activity. The Basque language is less highly developed as a literary medium than the Catalan, but in pride of race and independence the Basques are second to none. The national hero of Basque music, so to speak, is Juan Crisóstomo de Arriaga y Balzola (1806–1826), after whom the principal theater of Bilbao is named. Extraordinarily gifted, at the age of thirteen he wrote an opera, *Los Esclavos Felices* (*The Happy Slaves*), which was successfully produced in Bilbao. He was then sent to study at the Paris Conservatoire, where he astonished the worthy Fétis by his mastery of counterpoint. He wrote a Mass, a Salve Regina and other church music, cantatas, songs, symphonies and chamber music, of which three admirable string quartets were published in his lifetime (Paris, 1824). But his frail constitution could not support the strain of such intense creative effort and he died in Paris just after reaching his twenty-first birthday.

In many ways a modern counterpart of Arriaga was José María Usandizaga (1887–1915), born in San Sebastián, where a monument in the Plaza de Guipúzcoa honors his memory. After local studies he went to Paris, becoming a piano pupil of Planté and studying composition with d'Indy at the Schola Cantorum. Returning to San Sebastián, he threw himself wholeheartedly into the Basque musical movement, winning local prizes with the Basque fantasia for orchestra, *Irurak Bat*, and the overture *Bidasoa* for band. His ambition to create a Basque opera was realized when his opera *Mendy-Mendiyan* was produced at Bilbao in 1910. Not satisfied with local acclaim, however, he moved to Madrid, where his opera *Las Golondrinas* (*The Swallows*), libretto by Martínez Sierra, was produced at the Teatro Price (February 5, 1914) with sensational success. It achieved an almost unprecedented triumph throughout Spain, and the young composer was hailed as the bright hope of the Spanish lyric theater.

The subject of *Las Golondrinas* bears a resemblance to that of *I Pagliacci,* for it deals with the loves and tragic jealousies of a group of circus folk. Cecilia, Lina, and Puck, the clown, belong to an itinerant troupe of jugglers and acrobats. Puck is Cecilia's lover, but Lina is secretly in love with him. Cecilia abandons the troupe in order to satisfy her worldly ambitions. Meanwhile Puck and Lina achieve success in their own field and are apparently happy together. But Puck has never forgotten Cecilia, and when she appears at one of his performances he seeks her out and attempts to win back her love. She protests that she still loves him, but when he is finally convinced of her faithlessness he kills her in a moment of desperation.

Well equipped with instrumental and vocal science, possessing a genuine melodic gift and a keen sense of the theater, Usandizaga was able to make a strong emotional appeal to the public while maintaining a high level of artistry. His music partakes of the serious yet emotional fervor of César Franck, which he imbibed at the Schola Cantorum, and of the more theatrical emotionalism of Puccini. Had he lived longer, he might have attained to a deeper dramatic impact, for his gifts were great. But he was of a very frail physique and he died of tuberculosis at the age of twenty-eight.

Usandizaga's last dramatic work was the opera *La Llama* (*The Flame*), produced at Madrid in 1915, the year of his death. Among other works, thoroughly Basque in character, should be mentioned *Umezurtza* (*The Orphan*) for soprano, tenor, chorus, and orchestra; *Ytzaia* for mixed chorus; a Basque Quartet for strings; and a Basque Rhapsody for piano.

A close contemporary of Usandizaga is Jesús Guridí (born in Vitoria, 1886), who studied with d'Indy in Paris, Jongen in Brussels, and Neitzel in Cologne. He composed the successful Basque operas *Mirentxu* (1910) and *Amaya* (1920), and the very popular zarzuela *El Caserio* (1926). His choral arrangements of Basque folk songs are noteworthy, as are also his symphonic poems *Una Aventura de Don Quixote* and *Leyenda Vasca*.

Padre José Antonio de San Sebastián,[10] an assiduous collector of Basque folk songs, has made a reputation as a musical landscapist of sensitive perception and delicate expression, in particular with his piano pieces, *Preludios Vascos* and *Acuarelas Vascas* (also orchestrated).[11]

AN EXPONENT OF "STURM UND DRANG"

Almost an unknown quantity to the outside world, yet esteemed in Spain as one of the country's most eminent composers, is Conrado del Campo (born in Madrid, 1879), cultivator of the larger dramatic and symphonic forms, and of chamber music. He attended the Madrid Conservatory, but was largely self-taught in composition, coming at first under the influence of César Franck and later of Richard Strauss. Scarcely any of his works have been published, or performed outside of Spain, though the list of his compositions is impressive in its bulk and scope: thirteen operas, seven symphonic poems, eight string quartets, a symphony with chorus, a Mass for eight-part chorus with orchestra, and songs. Strangely enough, he has written nothing for piano save a set of impressions entitled *Paisajes de Granada* (*Landscapes of Granada*). Of his operas, the most definitely Spanish in character are *El Final de Don Alvaro* (one act, 1910) and *El Avapiés* (three acts, 1919), written in collaboration with Angel Barrios. The former is a passionate love drama, the latter a picturesque evocation of Madrid in the period of the *majos* and *majas*. An out-and-out Romanticist, he has drawn much of his musical inspiration from literary sources such as *The Divine Comedy*, the plays of Shakespeare, and the verses of the Spanish Romantic poets Zorilla and Bécquer. One of his best and most widely known string quartets, entitled *Caprichos Románticos,* is inspired by the celebrated *Rimas* of Gustavo Adolfo Bécquer, the nineteenth-century Sevillian poet who wrote of love with such intense and tumultuous ardor. In the words of Adolfo Salazar, "Chromaticism, national lyric drama, and *Sturm und Drang* are the terms that define the artistic personality of Conrado del Campo." [12] Like Oscar Esplá, Conrado del Campo is a living proof that contemporary creative trends in Spanish music are much more varied than is generally supposed.

CHAPTER XII

Manuel de Falla

IT is difficult to imagine a figure more Spanish in type than this slight man, thin and alert, whose face seems delicately sculptured in wood; not an atom of fat under the skin of this animated visage; eyes of flame that reveal the intense emotion burning within. Manuel de Falla is the incarnation of passion, enthusiasm, imagination, although an iron will disciplines his emotions." [1]

As the man, so the music. Not a superfluous note, not an ounce of padding, in the finely wrought, muscular texture of his scores. The sinews of his art are tense, yet flexible; they pass from meditative repose to dynamic action with dramatic rapidity. His creative reflexes respond with sensitive alertness to every emotional impact, yet the process of musical transmutation is achieved with the most painstaking care, with a ceaseless, disciplined striving for perfection.

Albéniz and Granados were masters of the piano. With Falla, Spanish music finds complete orchestral utterance. This is an orchestra that has exactly the right speech for every emotion, for every imaginative flight, for every situation, from the spectral apparition of a Gypsy lover to the clumsy gait of a foolish Corregidor, from the perfumed intoxication of Andalusian nights to the mad chivalry of Don Quixote. This orchestra has all the raciness of a guitar in the hands of an Andaluz, together with the subtle distinction of a Ravel or a Debussy. The music of Manuel de Falla is the true *cante hondo* of Spain—the deep song welling up from an immemorial past through the heart and mind of an artist who embodies the finest qualities of his race.

Manuel María de Falla y Matheu was born in the sea-girt Andalusian city of Cádiz on November 23, 1876. His father's family was of Valencian origin, while his mother was of Catalan extraction; but both families had been settled in Cádiz for several generations. The household was musical. Manuel's first piano teacher was his mother, with whom, at the age of eleven, he took part in a public performance of Haydn's *Seven Last Words of Our Saviour*, a work originally composed for one of the churches in Cádiz. The rudiments of theory he acquired from two local musicians, Odero and Broca, who, in Falla's own words, "initiated me in harmony and counterpoint, which I afterwards continued to study by myself, at the same time analyzing with avid curiosity every piece of music that held a real interest for me because of its affinity with certain secret aspirations whose realization, nevertheless, seemed to me scarcely possible." [2] A pity that Falla did not specify what works he studied with such avid curiosity. Yet, reading between the lines, we can see that he already was forming mental habits of self-discipline, and that he instinctively reacted to every higher stimulus that presented itself in his musical path.

Barbieri's musical instincts were awakened by listening to opera in the theater of which his grandfather was caretaker, Pedrell's by singing the music of Victoria as a cathedral chorister. Falla's experience lay midway between these two extremes and was equally symbolic of his destiny as a composer. It was after hearing a series of symphonic concerts in the Museum of Art at Cádiz that he determined to devote himself entirely to music. A further spur to his creative ambitions was provided by the private concerts of chamber music held in the home of a local amateur, Don Salvador Viniegra, in which Falla participated as pianist and at which his earliest compositions—later destroyed—were performed.

Madrid was the next step in Falla's artistic odyssey. He was sent to study piano with José Tragó at the Conservatory there and made encouraging progress on the instrument, though he had no desire to be a virtuoso pianist. He wanted to be a composer. But in order to be a successful composer in Madrid at that time, one had to write zarzuelas. Yielding to circumstances, and hoping to make enough money to continue his studies in composition, Falla tried his hand at a couple of these. The first was a flat failure, the second was not even produced.[3] At this crucial juncture he met the man who was to exert a decisive influence upon his artistic career: Felipe Pedrell. Falla studied with Pedrell in Madrid for about three years, and he has left it on record that to this experience he owed his definite orientation as a creative artist. Technically, perhaps, Falla did not learn much from Pedrell. But he emerged aesthetically fortified, and with a vivid realization of the creative values inherent in the music of Spain. From Pedrell he imbibed that historical sense which, in the words of T. S. Eliot, "involves a perception not only of the pastness of the past, but of its presence." [4]

With his convictions strengthened and his idealism rekindled, Falla eagerly welcomed the first challenge to his new-found powers. This came when the Royal Academy of Fine Arts, in 1904, offered a prize for the best lyric drama submitted by a Spanish composer. Setting immediately to work, he composed the two-act opera *La Vida Breve* (*Life Is Short*), to a libretto by Fernández Shaw, wisely utilizing the Andalusian background with which he was familiar. The following year his opera won the Academy's prize. And in that year (1905) he also won, in a national competition, the Ortiz y Cussó prize for pianists. The Academy award entailed no production of his opera, yet this double triumph as composer and executant enabled him to establish himself as a successful teacher in Madrid and soon provided him with the means for carrying out a long-cherished ambition: a visit to Paris. In the summer of 1907 he boarded the train for

France. He went ostensibly on a seven-day excursion; he remained seven years.

When the history of modern Spanish music comes to be written, a full chapter should be devoted to the role that Paris played in its development. All that a great, noble, generous, and beautifully civilized city could do for the promotion of art was done by Paris, the modern Athens, in those decades before and after the first World War. This beneficent influence was exerted not by the imposition of any rigid academic system, but by the sympathetic interest of individuals who knew how to inspire and guide by precept and example. On the material side, the great majority of works by modern Spanish composers were first published in Paris, and in the concert halls of that capital these works always found a cordial welcome.

The French musicians who befriended Falla in Paris—Debussy, Dukas, Ravel—were keenly appreciative of the values inherent in Spanish music, to which they themselves reacted with such sensitive intuition.[5] Moreover, many of the seemingly novel processes associated with Impressionism were familiar adjuncts of Spanish folk music—for example, the open strings of the guitar form in themselves quite an "Impressionistic" chord (other common features include the tendency toward modal melodies and harmonies; tonal ambiguity resulting from frequent "false relations" and "deceptive cadences"; systematic use of successive fifths; use of unresolved appoggiaturas; metric complexity, involving frequent changes of time signature and simultaneity of different rhythms). Thus, it is hardly accurate to speak of Falla as having become "Frenchified" in Paris through the adoption of Impressionistic methods. Rather did he acquire there a technique that was eminently suited to express the musical idioms of his native land.

In acquiring this orchestral technique he was guided mainly by the informal tutelage of Debussy and Dukas. Another stimulating influence was that of Albéniz, who was living in Paris when Falla arrived there. Writes Falla: "To Isaac Albéniz, whose music I barely knew when I arrived in Paris, and to whom I was presented by Dukas, I also owed valuable advice and warm stimulus for my work. I shall never forget the welcome he gave me; for this reason I dedicated to him the *Four Spanish Pieces*." Falla had begun these piano pieces in Madrid and finished them in Paris, where they were first performed by Ricardo Viñes in 1908. The set, consisting of *Aragonesa, Cubana, Montañesa,* and *Andaluza,* was published by Durand in 1909. The most interesting of these pieces, because it most clearly foreshadows the future course of Falla's art, is the *Andaluza,* with its skillful use of modal harmonies. In contrast to the languorous lilt of the *Cubana* is the harsh, almost metallic clang of the chords in *Andaluza,* marked to be played *avec un sentiment sauvage*—a direction that shows Falla's determination to break away from the sentimental conception of Spanish music so dear to foreign composers. There is poetry in this music, mysterious, elusive, but no softness.[6]

THE GARDENS OF SPAIN

In the same year that the *Four Spanish Pieces* were published, Falla began to compose the "symphonic impressions for piano and orchestra in three parts" entitled *Nights in the Gardens of Spain,* which he completed seven years later.[7] This work may properly be called a tone poem, though it has no "program" beyond the indications given in the titles of the respective movements: *In the Generalife* (the summer palace of the Moorish kings in Granada), *Distant Dance,* and *In the Gardens of the Sierra de Córdoba.* It evokes scenes, memories, emotions, whose exact nature the composer does not wish to specify—Falla is no lover of "program music"—but whose poetic emanations are felt throughout the music, with its haunting beauty and its undercurrent of passionate melancholy, mysteriously throbbing even through the wild revels of a Gypsy *zambra* such as is depicted in the last movement. Regarded merely as a picturesque evocation, the work impresses itself vividly on the senses; yet whoever listens with a more profound perception cannot fail to realize that in this music, with all its charm and sensuous power, there palpitates that "tragic sense of life" which Unamuno has shown to be latent in the most essential manifestations of the Spanish soul.

Though written for piano and orchestra, these nocturnes are by no means a concerto in the conventional meaning of the term. The solo instrument has a difficult and important role, but a display of pianistic virtuosity is no part of the scheme. The piano is intended to blend with the orchestra as one of its component units. The composition as a whole embodies those traits of Andalusian music that we touched upon in discussing Albéniz's *Iberia*, translated into terms of the orchestra yet still preserving many peculiarly guitaristic effects. The blending of folk elements with an intensely personal emotional expression is perhaps best exemplified in the last movement of the *Nights*, in which a typical *polo* rhythm alternates with freely lyrical passages in a manner that is both exciting and deeply moving. This movement probably represents the ultimate sublimation of the Andalusian style in symphonic music.

Following the outbreak of the first World War in 1914, Falla returned to Spain. Meanwhile, France had proved hospitable to his opera *La Vida Breve*, which was produced at Nice on April 1, 1913, and at the Paris Opéra-Comique on December 30 of the same year.[8] The libretto of this two-act opera has been much criticized for its lack of dramatic qualities. The plot is indeed simple, almost commonplace. Salud, a Gypsy girl of Granada, is forsaken by her lover, Paco, after he has sworn to be eternally faithful. In the second act Paco and his new sweetheart, Carmela, are about to be married. Salud appears in the midst of the wedding festivities, denounces her faithless lover, and then falls dead at his feet. Pedro Morales has pointed out that Salud, rather than Carmen, is the true Spanish feminine type. This does not, of course, make *La Vida Breve* a better opera than *Carmen*, for the latter is above all dramatically effective, whereas the former is dramatically weak. Nor has Falla completely solved the problem of finding a characteristically Spanish declamation and melody for the more lyrical and dramatic situations of the opera, such as the love duet between Salud and Paco, in which he has recourse to a more or less conventional idiom reminiscent of Massenet. But in evoking the Andalusian background of his opera, and in the marvelously effective dances of the second act, Falla achieves a higher degree of artistry and ethnic authenticity than is to be found in any previous manifestation of the Spanish lyric drama.

From the year 1914 date the *Seven Spanish Popular Songs* for voice and piano, which are not, as Falla is careful to explain, a literal transcription of folk tunes, but a subtle artistic transmutation of their essential values.[9] Folk songs in their pristine state are not suitable for the concert hall. It is not so much a question of the melodic line as of the harmonic and instrumental support that the melodies should receive. Folk melodies in their natural state are sung either unaccompanied, or else accompanied by various popular instruments that do not correspond to those customarily employed in "art" music. The average harmonization for piano of a folk song, based on conventional academic procedures, is neither ethnically accurate nor artistically effective. For Falla, a folk song is not a simple tune to be arbitrarily adorned. Each folk song, he believes, conceals a deep musical meaning, a latent wealth of expression, that the arranger should endeavor to fathom and extract. Complex and difficult as are some of his accompaniments, they represent the re-creation on an artistic plane of the inherent *melos* of each song. Such a feat can only be accomplished when a great artist and a profound folklorist are found in the same person.

A GYPSY BALLET

This ability to extract the highest artistic essence from the folkloric substance is conspicuously demonstrated in Falla's next work, the ballet *El Amor Brujo,* which he composed shortly after his return to Spain, in 1915. The famous dancer Pastora Imperio asked him to write a work in which she could both dance and sing. This was the point of departure for *El Amor Brujo* (*Love, the Sorcerer*), whose scenario, by Martínez Sierra, was based on a story told by the dancer's mother, an old Gypsy versed in the lore of her race. The scene is in Granada. Candelas, a beautiful Gypsy girl, is courted by Carmelo and is disposed to return his affection. But she is pursued by the specter of her dead lover, a wild and dissolute Gypsy whose ghost continually arises between her and her new sweetheart. Finally Carmelo decides to frustrate the specter by a ruse. He persuades Lucía, an attractive friend of Candelas, to attempt to lure the ghost from his persecution of the latter. Lucía is on hand the next time that the specter appears, he is fascinated by her charms, and while he presses his attentions upon her Candelas and Carmelo are able at last to exchange the perfect kiss of love, freed forever from the haunting obsession of the past.

El Amor Brujo was written at white heat. Scored originally for chamber orchestra, each section of the work was put into re-hearsal as it came fresh from the pen of the composer. The first performance took place at the Teatro Lara in Madrid on April 15, 1915, with Pastora Imperio taking the role of Candelas. Later the work was revised and scored for a normal theater or-chestra. As early as 1916 the music began to be popular in concert programs, but as a ballet, save for a few performances given by Adolf Bolm in the United States, it did not really begin to hold the stage again until 1925, when it was mounted at the Théâtre des Arts in Paris. In 1928 it was given at the Opéra-Comique in Paris, with La Argentina in the leading role. It was a great pity that this remarkable dancer died just before she was about to produce *El Amor Brujo* in the United States, because, as Profes-sor Trend justly observes, "the music alone can give little idea of how effective, how overwhelming, the ballet is on the stage."

And yet the music itself is tremendously effective. For sheer, overwhelming, dynamic effectiveness, scarcely anything in modern music can compare with the *Ritual Fire Dance,* which Candelas dances at midnight to exorcise all evil spirits.[10] No less impressive in its portrayal of fear is the *Dance of Terror,* in which the emotion becomes almost plastic before our eyes. In contrast to the primitive force of these dances is the entrancing beauty of such scenes as *The Magic Circle* and the *Pantomime,* so exquisitely scored. The extraordinary way in which Falla has assimilated the essence of *cante hondo* is strikingly evident in the vocal sections, such as the opening *Canción del Amor Dolido* (*Song of Sorrowful Love*), laden with that fatalistic quality which imbues the deep song of Andalusia. Yet Falla has nowhere used an actual folk tune in this ballet, which is a supreme example of what might be called creative realism.

THE THREE-CORNERED HAT

In his next work, the ballet *El Sombrero de Tres Picos* (*The Three-cornered Hat*), Falla depicts an entirely different aspect of Andalusian life: the vivacious and somewhat sardonic humor of the peasantry. The scenario is based on a well-known story by Alarcón, which in turn is drawn from popular tradition.[11] The central theme is the discomfiture of a fatuous Corregidor (chief magistrate of the village) who attempts to make gallant advances to the miller's pretty wife. She literally "leads him a dance," and though the situation looks rather compromising at one point the Corregidor in the end is thoroughly ridiculed and humiliated—in fact, he is tossed in a blanket as the *majas* tossed the dummy in Goya's picture—and the miller and his wife are mutually assured of each other's fidelity. Falla originally wrote this work as *El Corregidor y la Molinera* (*The Corregidor and the Miller's Wife*), under which title it was given at Madrid in 1917. The revised version was produced by Diaghilev's Ballet Russe in London on July 22, 1919, with choreography by Leonide Massine—who scored a triumph in the "Miller's Dance"—and with scenery and costumes designed by Picasso. It was an immediate success and remains to this day one of the brightest jewels in the Russian ballet's repertoire, while the three dances extracted from the ballet are perennial favorites in the concert hall.

In *The Three-cornered Hat* Falla does make use of folk tunes, but only in an incidental manner, as topical allusions, so to speak. Toward the end of Part One, when the Alguacil (bailiff) appears menacingly, a catchy little tune, known to all Spaniards, is heard. It is sung to the words *Con el capotín, tin, tin, tin, que esta noche va a llover* ("With my little cape, cape, cape, cape, for tonight it will rain")—a humorous allusion to the fact that the Corregidor has ordered the miller to be arrested that night. Elsewhere he uses a phrase from the accompaniment of the popular song *El Paño Moruno*, and a phrase from the *jota* of Navarre, the latter associated with the miller's wife. But the main dances, such as the miller's *farruca* and his wife's fandango, and the spirited *jota* of the finale, with its fascinating cross rhythms, are free artistic creations. With regard to the orchestration of *The Three-cornered Hat*, Falla writes, "My intention has been to evoke, by means of the instrumentation in specific passages, certain guitaristic values." Having said so much on this subject already, it is unnecessary to elaborate on the nature and significance of these "guitaristic values." Suffice it to remark that they are also apparent in the orchestration of *La Vida Breve* and *Nights in the Gardens of Spain.*

The last of Falla's compositions in the Andalusian idiom is the *Fantasía Bética*, for piano, dating from 1919. "Provincia Baetica" was the ancient Roman name for Andalusia; hence this work is simply an "Andalusian Fantasy," utilizing the same basic material that is found in the early *Andaluza* for piano. But in the *Fantasía*, Falla has so rarefied the material that it would probably not be recognized as "Andalusian" at all save by those capable of analyzing its component elements. Here are the prevailing Phrygian mode (with a lovely lyrical interlude in the Aeolian mode, also very prevalent in Spanish folk music); the *cante hondo* type of melody over a guitaristic accompaniment; characteristic dance rhythms like those of the *sevillanas* in the opening section, and so

forth. But the total effect is unlike anything hitherto associated
with Spanish music. This is because Falla is drawing away from
the local, picturesque aspects of Andalusian music, toward a more
universal and stylized concept. On the technical side, the modernism of the composition tends to overshadow the local traits; Falla
carries his harmonic syntax to a more "advanced" state than in
any previous work. One finds here a superposition of tonalities—
what is generally known as polytonality, though Falla himself
repudiates the use of that term.

DON QUIXOTE IN A PUPPET OPERA

The large number of operas written on the subject of Don
Quixote, from Purcell to Massenet, indicates the attractiveness
of the theme for musicians. But when Falla turned his thoughts
to Cervantes's hero he conceived a musical setting along quite
novel and distinctive lines. He chose one of the most significant
episodes, one which makes visible the confusion between reality
and imagination that was at the core of Don Quixote's noble madness, and he fashioned it into a chamber opera to be performed
by puppets, intending it for the private marionette theater of the
Princesse de Polignac in Paris. The episode is from the second
part of *Don Quixote* and recounts how the knight and his squire,
while resting at an inn, were entertained by a certain Maese
Pedro with his puppet show, enacting the story of Don Gayferos
and Melisendra, based on an old Spanish ballad that tells how a
beautiful Christian princess was delivered from the power of the
Moorish king in Saragossa by one of Charlemagne's knights.

The *mise en scène* of *El Retablo de Maese Pedro* (*Master
Peter's Puppet Show*) is rather complicated, for there are two sets
of puppets, one large sized, representing the characters in Cervantes's novel, the other small sized, representing the characters
in Maese Pedro's show. It is, therefore, "a puppet show within a
puppet show." There are only three singing characters: Don
Quixote (*basso cantante* or baritone), Maese Pedro (tenor), and
the Boy (boy-soprano or mezzo-soprano), who tells the story of

Manuel de Falla

Manuel Frères

the action performed by the small puppets. Real actors, of course, placed in the orchestra pit, sing the three principal parts, the movements of the large puppets being synchronized with the music. It was in this form that the work was first produced at the home of the Princesse de Polignac in Paris on June 25, 1923.[12]

When it came to performing the work in a large theater, such as the Opéra-Comique, where it was given in 1928, the difficulties of *mise en scène* proved very troublesome, although the scenery and the puppets were designed by the eminent Spanish painter Zuloaga and the rehearsals were supervised by the composer himself. In earlier performances of the work, at Bristol in 1924, advantage had been taken of the composer's note to the effect that "the puppets representing real persons may be replaced by living actors; but in that case they should wear masks." With living actors taking the three principal roles, the action became much clearer and easier to follow. Since masks were found to hamper the singers, these were discarded also and ordinary make-up was used. *El Retablo* challenges the best skill and ingenuity of any producer; but it is a challenge worth taking up.

The climax of the performance comes when the Moors are pursuing Don Gayferos and Melisendra, and Don Quixote, in whose deranged mind the puppet show has suddenly become real, rushes forth furiously, sword in hand, and begins to hew and hack at the villainous puppet-Moors, not stopping until he has cut them all to pieces. He then turns to the spectators and delivers a stirring speech in praise of knight-errantry; for what, he asks, would have become of Don Gayferos and Melisendra had he, Don Quixote, not been present at that moment? Maese Pedro's business is ruined, of course, but Don Quixote has been faithful to his vow of chivalry.

Scored for a small orchestra of about twenty-five players, *El Retablo* reveals Falla's ability to achieve a wide variety of effects —and of very subtle and telling effects—with an extreme economy of means. The music is certainly far removed from any conventional conception of operatic effectiveness, for its primary appeal is to a sophisticated and exceptionally cultured audience. More than with any previous work by Falla, *El Retablo* calls for a knowledge of the historical background of Spanish music if it is to be fully understood and appreciated. Without rigid archaism, but with profound historical feeling, Falla has depicted this scene with absolute fidelity to Cervantes's novel and to the spirit of seventeenth-century Spanish music. As usual, he employs actual folk material sparingly, the most notable instance being the slow melody that accompanies Melisendra's reverie in the second scene, which is based on an old ballad tune. The realism of the whole performance is stressed by having the Boy sing in a voice "which is nasal and rather forced—the voice of a boy shouting in the street, rough in expression and exempt from all lyrical feeling." Don Quixote, on the other hand, has a nervous, rather high-flown declamatory style, with frequent leaps of wide intervals, which attains a dramatic and vigorous climax in his peroration in praise of knighthood. Falla has seized upon the precise combination of austerity and dry humor, of the sublime and the ridiculous, that constitutes the essence of *Don Quixote*.

THE HARPSICHORD CONCERTO

Falla's endeavor to express the spiritual essence of Spain in his music reaches its profoundest and most intense phase in the Concerto for harpsichord (or piano), flute, oboe, clarinet, violin, and cello (1923–1926), which may be regarded as an "abstract" presentation of the musical values inherent in *El Retablo* (where there is also an important harpsichord part).[13] Falla has always written with conciseness and directness, but in the Concerto he carries these qualities to the nth degree, applying a strict principle of artistic "depuration." This music is both austere and sensuous, both harsh and ingratiating, both archaic and modern. In it Falla affirms his aesthetic kinship with Domenico Scarlatti, and at the same time employs a thoroughly modern syntax in which the simultaneous appearance of different tonalities is carried much further than in the *Fantasía Bética*. Yet the emphatic perfect cadence that brings the work to an end proclaims that Falla still builds on the solid foundation of tonality.

It is interesting to observe that one of the themes in the first movement of the Concerto is taken from a sixteenth-century villancico by Juan Vázquez, *De Los Alamos Vengo, Madre,* which, as we remarked in Chapter II, is undoubtedly of popular origin. The theme makes its appearance very strikingly, played by the violin and the cello in octaves, marked *intenso sostenuto,* with the oboe entering, *forte,* in the second measure and the harpsichord sustaining the whole with sonorous, strongly accented arpeggios. This is the theme (note the characteristic syncopation in the sixth measure):

Example 15.

The Concerto is in three brief movements—*Allegro, Lento, Vivace*—and takes only about ten minutes to perform; but within those few minutes, and with only six instruments, Falla achieves magnificent effects of sonority, especially in the slow movement, in which the harpsichord plays big, sweeping arpeggios against the sharp, biting, staccato chords of the supporting instruments. The effect of spaciousness, as though one were in the interior of some vast cathedral, is amazing. There is a joyous solemnity, an atmosphere of incense and exultation, about this movement, as though it evoked a great religious festivity—the music, in fact, was finished on the day of the Feast of Corpus Christi. The last movement, marked *flessibile, scherzando,* with its characteristic alternations of 3/4 and 6/8 time, possesses the utmost zest and sparkle; it is very Scarlattian, yet only Falla could have written it.

In 1927, to mark the Góngora tercentenary, Falla made a setting of that poet's *Soneto a Córdoba* for voice and harp. This composition has been almost entirely neglected by singers, yet those who have followed the evolution of Spanish music and lingered over the song literature of the Golden Age will readily understand from what noble lineage Falla's music springs, and will appreciate the purity and strength of his conception. This austere yet eloquent declamation, supported by strong, rich chords, stems from the vocal settings of the old *vihuelistas* such as Milán, Mudarra, and Fuenllana.

In addition to its poetic qualities, this sonnet probably attracted Falla because of the fact that it was written in Granada, where he had settled in 1921. Granada—the city of the Alhambra, of the Albaicín and of the Catholic Kings (Ferdinand and Isabel are buried in the cathedral there)—was bound to appeal strongly to Falla both because of its associations and its beautiful natural setting. He bought a small cottage—a *carmen*, as they are called there—close by the Alhambra, and there he quietly lived and worked, his tranquil existence broken only by visits to Paris, to London, and other European cities, chiefly to conduct "festivals" of his own compositions. He remained undisturbed in Granada throughout the Spanish civil war, and in the fall of 1939 went to South America, settling temporarily in the province of Cordova, Argentina. He has never been in the United States.

Falla has produced little since 1927.[14] His chief creative effort has been concentrated on the composition of a large cantata for solos, chorus, and orchestra, entitled *La Atlántida*, which he began in 1928. This work is based on an epic poem by the Catalan writer Jacinto Verdaguer; Falla has condensed the text and arranged it as rhythmic prose instead of verse, but he has kept the original Catalan language. In the poem the legend of the lost continent of Atlantis, which sank into the sea, is linked to the discovery of America by Columbus. In the Introduction, Christopher Columbus as a young man has just been shipwrecked and cast upon an island. There he meets an old hermit who tells him the story of Atlantis, with which are intertwined various ancient myths centering about the figure of Hercules, the great legendary hero of Spain who was supposed to have opened up the Straits of Gibraltar. His imagination aroused by the tale, Columbus determines to set forth in search of a new world. He obtains help from Isabel of Spain and the poem ends as he sails out toward the unknown.[15]

Unfortunately, this chapter must close with a question mark. Up to now, the score of *La Atlántida* has neither been published nor performed, because Falla is still seeking that ultimate perfection which, like the vision that drew Columbus onward, beckons him toward an illusive ideal. Always ready to answer friendly questions on other phases of his life and work, Falla prefers to keep silent regarding work in progress; hence the musical content of *La Atlántida* must remain a mystery until such time as he sees fit to disclose it to the world.

CHAPTER XIII

The Younger Generation

ALL vital and enduring artistic creation is based on the process of historical continuity that we call tradition. This does not, of course, mean a mere imitation of the past. The artist who has the deepest understanding of the true meaning of tradition will also be the one, as T. S. Eliot puts it, who is "most acutely conscious of his place in time, of his own contemporaneity." The music of Manuel de Falla, for instance, so deeply rooted in tradition, is also thoroughly modern.

It must be admitted that the Spanish composers who came to maturity toward the turn of the century, as Falla did, found themselves in an atmosphere quite unpropitious to the development of their highest creative potentialities. The field of the commercialized zarzuela loomed as the only practical opening for a talented young composer. Most of them had to go abroad before they could find their right path. The mere fact that Falla's pupil, Ernesto Halffter, without ever having studied abroad, began his career at eighteen with symphonic works showing a complete command of modern orchestral technique indicates that the musical climate in Spain had undergone an important transformation. When we add that these *Symphonic Sketches* were performed in Madrid soon after they were completed, the extent of the transformation becomes all the more apparent.

The composers of Halffter's generation not only find it natural to write symphonic works rather than zarzuelas and potboilers, but they are also able to bring their works before the public immediately. These composers, musically speaking, breathe an entirely different air. They no longer feel stifled by incomprehension and commercialism. They have the confidence that comes from being well equipped technically and from feeling themselves to be part of a thriving and integrated musical organism. They know where to turn for guidance, for inspiration, for the materials of their art. They know themselves to be the inheritors of a glorious musical tradition and at the same time they are fully conscious of their own contemporaneity. They organize concerts at which they perform compositions by Cabezón, Salinas, Milán, Valderrábano, Soler—names which a generation ago were known only to a handful of scholars. They also perform the latest works of Stravinsky, Shostakovitch, Schönberg—and they listen to lecture recitals on Gregorian Chant. One of them dedicates a piece "to the vihuela of Luis Milán"; another sets to music the poems of Jorge Manrique; a third writes incidental music to Guillén de Castro's *Las Mocedades del Cid*. And they can make these historical gestures without the self-consciousness, the somewhat strained effort, that handicapped a Pedrell. They have reached the point where the past and the present meet on equal terms. Their tradition has once more become a living force.

This does not mean, of course, that all Spanish composers born since 1900 are automatically in a position to produce masterpieces. Tradition and culture are not substitutes for genius. The case of Ernesto Halffter is perhaps as unique for this generation as was the case of Falla for the previous generation.

ERNESTO HALFFTER

Ernesto Halffter-Escriche, of German extraction on his father's side, was born at Madrid in 1905. His early musical background was rather unusual. In his own words:

No one in my family was musical, except my maternal grandmother, a Spanish lady who was steeped in the then fashionable Italian operas and played the piano. It is from her that I got the musical aptitudes I possess and she alone urged me on in my earliest efforts. When about four years old I started with the piano all alone, and I had no lessons until I was eight. I remember playing, when I was five, a transcription of the overture to *Tannhäuser* and composing music of the type of *The Bride of Lammermoor*. My parents, who had no taste for music and whose interests were foreign to any artistic career, had no wish to encourage my natural inclination, so much so that from the time I entered school up to the age of sixteen, I was able to have music only on Sundays. While the other members of the family went out for walks or to the theater, I spent my Sundays in playing the piano, trying, without any special method, to transcribe musical ideas which came to me. At that age I felt no doubts and I even composed Italian operas according to the Italian taste.[1]

His first revelation of modern music was in hearing a visiting pianist play Debussy's *L'Isle Joyeuse*.

His gifts attracted the attention of Manuel de Falla, who took him as a private pupil. The same qualities of self-discipline and striving for perfection that characterize Falla are apparent in Halffter. He does not take advantage of his facility in order to turn out music indiscriminately, nor did he foist his juvenile compositions upon a world always ready to applaud the feats of a prodigy. He made his official bow as a composer at eighteen with the *Two Symphonic Sketches* (*Dead Landscape* and *The Lamplighter's Song*), but he worked over this composition two years more before considering it really finished and ready for publication. Similarly, his *Sinfonietta* in D major, which won a National Prize in 1925, was revised over a period of four years, the printed score bearing the dates "1923–1927."

In the *Two Symphonic Sketches* one may already observe the refinement of instrumentation, the subtle balancing of sonorities, the economy of means that distinguish the orchestral writing of Halffter. Brilliant in style is the *Sinfonietta*, consisting of four movements: *Pastorella* (*Allegro*), *Adagio*, *Allegretto vivace* (*Minuetto*), *Allegro giocoso*. This work follows approximately the pattern of the "sinfonia concertante" of Haydn's day, in which certain instruments are given important solo parts, supported by the main body of strings and percussion. But the idiom is thoroughly modern, with frequent incursions into polytonality, though the feeling of a basic key is never lost. The essential charm of the music lies in its unfailing zest and sparkle; it is buoyantly lyrical, with an unforced gaiety. Here are clarity, sunshine, wit and laughter, and the spirit of youth. Audacity is never divorced from good taste and the utmost liveliness of fancy is controlled by the utmost perfection of execution.

In 1928, Antonia Mercé (La Argentina) produced Halffter's one-act ballet *Sonatina* in Paris. The title is that of a poem by Rubén Darío, upon which the scenario is based. The music is scored for a small orchestra and, like the *Sinfonietta*, relies largely upon a group of solo instruments. But the composition is of a more intimate and delicate character; it has the subtle grace and refinement of texture that mark the best pages of Ravel and, like that composer's *Tombeau de Couperin*, evokes the dances of a past age: *Rigaudon, Zarabanda, Giga*. Particularly attractive is the delightful fandango danced by the maidens (*Las Doncellas*).

Ernesto Halffter has also written a string quartet, a *Sonatina-Fantasia* for string quartet, three sonatas for piano, about half a dozen songs, a Portuguese Rhapsody for piano and orchestra (1939), and a four-act tragic opera, *La Muerte de Carmen* (*The Death of Carmen*). This operatic score was originally written for a film version of Mérimée's *Carmen* produced in France in 1926 with Raquel Meller in the title role. In its original version the score was as long as Wagner's *Tristan und Isolde*, indicating that Halffter, at twenty years of age, had no desire to emulate the modernistic purveyors of capsule operas. It was, of course, cut down considerably for the film.

The opera retells the story of Carmen with more fidelity to Mérimée's tale than was observed by Bizet's librettists. It is respectfully—and audaciously—dedicated to the memory of Bizet. Interesting to note is the effective use in Halffter's score of the theme of Manuel García's *polo*, *El Contrabandista*, closely akin in melodic and harmonic structure to the other *polo* by García, *Cuerpo bueno, alma divina*, used by Bizet (*cf.* Chapter XIX). Halffter also uses another well-known Spanish folk tune, *El Vito* (which likewise figures in the finale of Falla's *Three-cornered Hat*.) While influenced by Falla and Debussy, Halffter's music reveals a remarkable craftsmanship and a creative talent both robust and sensitive.

In 1924, at the age of nineteen, Halffter became conductor of the Orquesta Bética of Seville, a chamber orchestra founded by Manuel de Falla, with which he performed many modern works for the first time in Spain. In 1934 he was appointed director of the National Conservatory of Seville, holding this position until the outbreak of the civil war in 1936. Following a brief visit to New York in 1937, he settled in Lisbon, where he has since made his home (his wife is Portuguese).

Ernesto's elder brother, Rodolfo Halffter (born in Madrid, 1900), has also made a name as a composer. He was largely self-taught in music, with some advice from Falla. His works include a suite for orchestra (1928), *Obertura concertante* for piano and orchestra (1933), *Prelude and Fugue* and *Two Sonatas of the Escorial* for piano, and a one-act ballet, *Don Lindo de Almería* (Paris, 1936), with scenario by José Bergamín (the work is scored for two string orchestras). Rodolfo Halffter is more cerebral in his conceptions than his brother. He began by showing Schönbergian tendencies and, while he subsequently veered toward greater tonal clarity, he has retained a mordant and ironic quality reminiscent of Stravinsky's middle period. In one of his most characteristic works, the ballet *Don Lindo de Almería*, he adopts a humorously ironic attitude toward the conventional Spanish tunes and types. Like all the younger composers, he has the historical elements of Spanish music at his finger tips, and in one episode of this ballet (*Nuptial Ceremony*) he draws upon some organ music of the eighteenth-century Spanish organist Francisco Llisá. At the same time he feels emancipated from any conscious nationalism, and he therefore employs the popular and traditional material in a detached and objective manner, which in this case is emphasized by the humoristic element.

Rodolfo Halffter was prominently associated with the musical activities of the Spanish government during the last years of the Second Republic. He was a member of the Superior Council of Music and edited the review *Música*. Obliged to leave Spain after the downfall of the Republic in 1939, he migrated to Mexico and announced his intention of becoming a Mexican citizen.

"THE MADRID GROUP"

Ernesto and Rodolfo Halffter formed part of a group of young composers who banded themselves together at Madrid in the spring of 1930. Other members of the group were Salvador Bacarisse, Julián Bautista, Juan José Mantecón, Gustavo Pittaluga, Fernando Remacha, and Rosa García Ascot, who provided the sole feminine touch. Of these, the oldest was Mantecón, who, like Adolfo Salazar [2] (a sort of "big brother" to the group), was primarily a writer on music rather than a composer. Gustavo Pittaluga (born in Madrid, 1906) undertook to define the point of view of his associates in a brief lecture (afterward printed in *La Gaceta Literaria*) [3] whose most significant feature was that it did not discuss the problem of nationalism or folklorism, with which musicians of the previous generation had been so largely preoccupied. Instead, Pittaluga insisted upon the necessity of writing "authentic" music in an entirely nonethnical sense, that is, music whose worth is to be measured solely by its *musical* qualities, without admixture of any literary, philosophical, or metaphysical associations. For the rest, "no Romanticism, no chromaticism, no divagations—and no chords of the diminished seventh!"

Gustavo Pittaluga prepared himself for a legal and diplomatic career, but at the same time studied music, becoming a pupil in composition of Oscar Esplá. His reputation was established by the performance at Madrid in 1930 of his ballet *La Romería de los Cornudos* (concert version), which in 1933 was staged by Argentinita's ballet company in the same city. Besides *La Romería de los Cornudos*, he has written the "zarzuela antigua" *El Loro* (*The Parrot*), *Concerto Militaire* for violin and orchestra (1933), *Petite Suite* for ten instruments (1933), *Six Spanish Dances* for piano (1936), *Capriccio alla romantica* for piano and orchestra (1936).[4]

Considerably older is Salvador Bacarisse (born in Madrid, 1898), who studied the piano with Alberdí and composition with Conrado del Campo at the Madrid Conservatory. He has written about forty works, scarcely any of which have been published, or performed outside of Spain. In his own country, however, he won several National Prizes, notably for his symphonic poem *La Nave de Ulises* in 1921 and for his orchestral *Música Sinfónica* in 1931. The National Prize was also awarded to him in 1934 "for the merit of his work as a whole." From 1925 to 1936 he was musical director of the broadcasting station "Unión Radio" in Madrid. In his cultivation of the larger symphonic forms and of chamber music, Bacarisse appears to have followed in the footsteps of his teacher, del Campo. Except for the ballet *Corrida de Fiesta* (Madrid, 1934), there is nothing specifically Spanish in his music. However, his settings for voice and piano of three poems by the Marquis of Santillana reveal at least a bowing acquaintance with the great Spanish classics (these songs have been published as Opus 5).

Also a pupil of Conrado del Campo was Julián Bautista (born in Madrid, 1901), whose ballet *Juerga* (1921) obtained a marked success when it was produced by La Argentina at the Opéra-Comique, Paris, in 1929. His String Quartet in F sharp minor won a National Prize in 1923, and in 1933 he won first prize for his *Obertura para una Opera Grotesca* in the International Competition sponsored by the "Unión Radio." In 1936 he was appointed professor of harmony at the Madrid Conservatory, but after the civil war, in the course of which several of his musical manuscripts were destroyed, he left Spain, going to Belgium and thence to Argentina. Such works as his *Preludio* for orchestra (1929), *Sonatina Trio* for violin, viola, and cello (1925), *La Flûte de Jade* for voice and piano or chamber orchestra (1921), and *Colores* for piano (1922), reveal a modernism divorced from any deliberate nationalism.

Fernando Remacha, born in Tuleda (Navarre) in 1898, obtained a National Prize in 1934 for his quartet for piano and strings. He has also written a string quartet, a suite for orchestra, and a ballet, *La Maja*.

The remaining member of the group, Rosa García Ascot, studied piano with Granados and composition with Falla. Her principal works are a suite for piano and a concerto for piano and orchestra. She settled in Mexico.

Not officially a member of the erstwhile "Madrid Group," but closely associated with some of its members, is Gustavo Durán (born in Barcelona, 1906; lived in Madrid from 1910). He studied piano with Tragó and composition with Turina at the Madrid Conservatory. His ballet *El Fandango*, produced by La Argentina in 1927, was performed in various European capitals. Most of Durán's compositions were destroyed in 1939. Since then he has composed four songs on poems by Rafael Alberti and two songs on poems by Lope de Vega. During the Spanish civil war of 1936–1939, Durán distinguished himself as commander of the XX Army Corps in the Republican Army. At the present writing he is living in New York.

Another young composer possessing a fresh and original talent is Enrique Casal Chapí, grandson of Ruperto Chapí and a pupil in composition of Conrado del Campo. While still a student at the Madrid Conservatory (from which he graduated in 1936), he founded and directed a male quartet specializing in the performance of Castilian folk music and vocal classics of the "Golden Age." In 1933 he was appointed musical director of the Teatro Escuela de Arte in Madrid, for which he wrote incidental dramatic music. He believes in writing Spanish music that comes *from within*, not from the use of folkloristic accessories. His three songs on poems by Lope de Vega reveal a clear and elegant style, authentically Spanish in the classical sense. Following the civil war he lived as a refugee in France and then migrated to Santo Domingo.

JOAQUÍN RODRIGO

The most talented of the younger composers outside of the "Madrid Group" is Joaquín Rodrigo, born in the ancient city of Sagunto, near Valencia, in 1902. He has been blind since the age of three. A pupil first of Francisco Antioch at Valencia, he traveled extensively in Europe from 1920, and in 1923 composed his first important work, the symphonic sketch *Juglares* (Valencia Symphony Orchestra, 1924). In 1925 he obtained the National Prize for his *Cinco Piezas Infantiles* for orchestra, and in 1927 he went to Paris, where he studied composition with Paul Dukas. His orchestral *Prelude for a Poem to the Alhambra,* composed in 1926, was first performed in Paris at a Straram Concert in 1931.

Rodrigo's most important work is the symphonic poem *Per la Flor del Lliri Blau* (*By the Flower of the Blue Lily*), composed in 1934. The title is taken from the last line of a Valencian folk song, whose theme he has embodied in the score (there is also a march theme derived from the Catalan folk song *Els Tres Tambors*). This is the only one of Rodrigo's compositions that has a definite regional character. For the rest, his nationalism is mainly of the nontopical kind stemming from Falla's second period (beginning with *El Retablo*), revealing a sensitive perception of traditional values. This may be observed particularly in his *Tres Canciones* for voice and piano and *Zarabanda Lejana y Villancico* for strings (there are versions also for piano, and for guitar). An intimate lyricism pervades his music.

We began this chapter in an optimistic tone which does not, alas, correspond to the desolating reality of today. We were speaking in a figurative present tense that corresponded to the nineteen twenties and early thirties. That bright activity, those splendid programs, those groups of eager youth, that atmosphere of common accomplishment—all were shattered by the fratricidal struggle of 1936–1939, which was but a prelude to the frightful conflict in which the world is now engaged. Nearly all the composers whom we have mentioned in this chapter are now living in exile. Will these young composers ever be able to reincorporate themselves into the musical life of Spain? Will they not rather be absorbed into the cultural stream of the countries in which they are now residing? These questions the future must decide.

CHAPTER XIV

The Virtuosi

SCANNING the annals of the Spanish lyric theater, one might cull the names of sundry actors and actresses who, in times gone by, delighted the public of their day by singing in operas, zarzuelas, or tonadillas. The history of the Spanish theater has been studied with such all-embracing thoroughness by Emilio Cotarelo y Mori that the most minute details of the lives and careers of these once-admired players and singers are available for the perusal of the curious. We cannot encumber our pages with such a profusion of detail, nor can we undertake to call the roster of those more or less obscure stage folk, from the comedians of Lope de Rueda's troupe to the prime donne of the Royal Opera, who at one time or another won applause as interpreters of the lyric drama. But here and there a name or two stands out, recalling some theatrical figure who in his or her time made such a stir in the world as still to defy oblivion—and not always solely by reason of vocal or dramatic talent. As long as there is a Spaniard left to exclaim "Caramba!", there is likely to remain some memory of a singer named María Antonia Fernández, who was the idol of Madrid about the time when Ramón de la Cruz was infusing new life into the Spanish drama. And as long as men admire the art of Francisco Goya, they will gaze with admiration upon his portrait of another famous actress-singer of that period, María del Rosario Fernández, better known as "La Tirana."

Joaquín Rodrigo

Ernesto Halffter

After the death in 1767 of the incomparable María Ladvenant
—who had almost as many titled admirers as there were grandees
in Madrid—these two actresses, whose rivalry was notorious, held
the theatrical spotlight unchallenged for several decades. "La
Tirana," so called because her husband generally played the role
of tyrant (*tirano*) in the first company to which they belonged,
was primarily a dramatic actress; but María Antonia Fernández,
nicknamed "La Caramba," made her reputation as a singer of
tonadillas. The origin of her nickname—*caramba* is a euphemistic
expletive used by all Spanish-speaking peoples—is shrouded in
conflicting theories. Cotarelo, however, is certain that it derives
from the last line of a tonadilla that she sang shortly after her
arrival at Madrid in 1776, in which she tells how a young dandy
came to her house one morning and asked her to be his sweetheart.
The refrain was:

> I replied to him with my ditty,
>> With my song, my dance and my blush:
> How droll you are, *señorito*,
>> You ask me . . . *caramba! caramba!*

The song made such a hit that henceforth she was known as "La
Caramba." And she, in turn, gave her nickname to an extravagant
headdress whose distinguishing feature was a huge, brightly
colored bow. She launched this mode in 1778 and it soon became
the rage in Madrid. "La Caramba" invariably set the town agog
with the extravagance of her attire as well as with the notoriety
of her love affairs. But the Junta that controlled the municipal
theaters of Madrid did not dare take disciplinary action against
her for fear of provoking a riot, so tremendous was the hold she
had upon the public.

A native Andalusian—she was born at Motril, near Granada,
in 1751—"La Caramba" seems to have been one of the first
exponents of the style of singing that came to be known as flamenco
(*cf.* Chapter XV). Her singing is described as *gitanesco* ("Gypsy-
like") and replete with "all the voluptuousness of Andalusia."

What fascinated her hearers more than anything else was the way she had of prolonging the syllable *ay* in seemingly interminable cadenzas delivered with great intensity of feeling—and this is one of the most characteristic traits of *cante flamenco*.

Except for a brief marital interlude in 1781, "La Caramba" continued to delight the Madrid public until 1786, when she suddenly left the stage and changed her mode of life completely. While walking in the Prado one day she had taken refuge from a storm in a church, and so impressed was she by the priest's sermon that she decided to make amends for her past life by devoting herself henceforth to poverty, penitence, and prayer. She died, however, the following year.

THE GARCÍA FAMILY

Manuel del Popolo Vicente García [1] was not only a prolific and talented composer—we have already mentioned him as a writer of tonadillas—but was also the most famous of all the singers whom Spain has produced and the founder of the most remarkable family of singers the world has ever known, if we take into account not only their artistic ability but also their profound influence upon vocal science and pedagogy. Born in Seville in 1775, Manuel García became a chorister in the magnificent Cathedral there at the age of six, receiving his first musical instruction from the choirmaster, Antonio Ripa. By the time he was seventeen he had already established a local reputation as singer, actor, composer, and conductor. Before long his tonadillas and operettas were being performed with extraordinary success all over Spain. Nevertheless, he decided to try his fortune abroad and in 1807 went to Paris, making his debut at the Opéra-Bouffe on February 11, 1808, in Paer's *Griselda*. In spite of the fact that he had no serious operatic training, he triumphed by reason of his immense natural gifts, united with his native force of character and magnetic personality. His greatest popular success, however, was achieved in his own compositions, especially in the monodramatic tonadilla *El Poeta Calculista*, which he first presented in Paris in 1809. The exotic Spanish coloring of the music—which at that time came as a complete novelty to the Parisians—as well as García's spirited and expressive singing (he accompanied himself on the guitar) aroused the utmost enthusiasm. One number in particular, *El Contrabandista* (*The Smuggler*), made a tremendous impression and had to be sung three times at each performance. This was the piece that really launched "the Spanish idiom" on its way around the world (*cf.* Chapter VIII).

In 1811 García went to Italy, singing in Turin, Rome, and Naples, where he won the favor of Murat, then King of Naples, who appointed him first tenor of his Royal Chapel (García was originally a tenor, though in later life he became a baritone). At Naples he perfected his vocal technique under the tutelage of the tenor Ansani, and there, at the Teatro San Carlo, he obtained a brilliant success with his opera *Il Califfa di Bagdàd*. Returning to Paris in 1816, he was engaged as leading tenor of the Théâtre Italien, of which the famous soprano Catalini was then manager. He was also acclaimed in London.

It was for Manuel García that Rossini wrote the part of Count Almaviva in *The Barber of Seville* (1816), and the story goes that the Spanish singer even had a hand in composing the opera. At all events, Rossini used the theme of García's *El Contrabandista* in the first scene of his opera. There are other traces of Spanish influence in *The Barber of Seville*, notably in the chorus, "Mille grazie," of Act I, which is a kind of bolero, and in part of the variations on Figaro's theme, "Di si felice inesto" (Act II), which utilize the rhythm of the *sevillanas*.[2]

GARCÍA IN NEW YORK

In 1825, at the height of his fame as singer, composer, and teacher, García sailed from Liverpool to New York at the head of his own opera company, which included his son Manuel and daughter María. On November 16, 1825, the following advertisement appeared in the New York *American:*

Signor García respectfully announces to the American public, that he has lately arrived in this country with an Italian troupe [3] (among whom are some of the first artists of Europe), and has made arrangements with the Managers of the New-York Theatre, to have the house on Tuesdays and Saturdays: on which nights the choicest Italian Operas will be performed, in a style which he flatters himself will give general satisfaction. [4]

García's confidence was well founded, for the opening performance on November 29 was, in the words of a reviewer, "most completely successful." The opera chosen for this historic occasion was *The Barber of Seville*—this was "the first long opera ever sung in New York in the Italian or any other foreign tongue." [5] The bright star of the performance was García's seventeen-year-old daughter María, who sang the role of Rosina, in which she had made her debut at London in June of the same year. *The Barber* was given five times in succession.

On February 7, Rossini's *Otello* was produced, with the elder García as the Moor and María as Desdemona. The famous Shakespearian actor Edmund Kean, who was then appearing in New York, attended the performance, and "after the second act, when García left the stage, he was accosted by Mr. Kean, who introduced himself, as he said, for the satisfaction of expressing his admiration at the excellent manner in which the part of Othello had been represented and of complimenting the artist who had so well delineated a most difficult character." [6] García replied that "the approbation of so distinguished a master in his art was the most satisfactory tribute and the most pleasing recompense that could be made."

Later, García moved his company to the Park Theater. The farewell performance of the troupe took place on September 30, 1826 (they ended, as they had begun, with *The Barber*). In all, García gave seventy-nine performances, introducing eleven new operas to New York, among them Mozart's *Don Giovanni*, which received its American première on May 23, 1826. [7]

From New York, García took his troupe to Mexico, where

they spent eighteen months and met with many adventures.[8] Shortly before leaving the country they were robbed by brigands, who made off with the bulk of their earnings. But García was the sort of man who took such things in his stride. His energy and resourcefulness were inexhaustible. Going back to Paris, he re-appeared at the Italiens with continued success. From this time on, however, he devoted himself chiefly to teaching, which he had already undertaken with remarkable results before his depar-ture for America. Among his most celebrated pupils were his two daughters, María and Pauline, and his son Manuel. He was also the teacher of Adolphe Nourrit. He died at Paris in 1832, in his fifty-eighth year.

While her father's troupe was in New York, María Felicidad García (she was born in Paris in 1808) married an elderly French banker named Malibran, a name that she was to make famous throughout the musical world. The marriage was an unhappy one, however, and when Malibran soon afterward became bank-rupt she left him and returned to Paris. Thereafter she sang regularly in Paris and London, as well as in Italy (her Italian tour with Lablache in 1832 was a tremendous triumph). Mean-while, she had fallen in love with the Belgian violinist Charles de Bériot, who reciprocated her feelings. But she was still legally married to Malibran, and his unexpected arrival in Paris caused much suffering and sorrow for María. It was not until 1836 that she was able to obtain a divorce and marry de Bériot, with whom she had been living since 1830. Her short span of life was then nearing its end. While riding in London one day, her horse ran away and threw her to the ground. Although she sustained severe head injuries, she nevertheless made light of her accident and sang in a concert that same evening, afterward continuing to fill other engagements. She sang for the last time in Manchester on September 14, 1836. Ten days later she was dead. Soon afterward her remains were taken to Brussels and reinterred there in a mausoleum erected by de Bériot, for which the noted sculptor Geefs made a bust of the singer and Lamartine wrote an inscription declaring that "Beauty, genius, and love were in her look, her heart, and her voice."

María Malibran's voice was a contralto, but with much of the soprano register superadded. Her beauty and her vivid personality contributed to the fascination of her art. She stands with Jenny Lind as one of the most beloved and romantic figures in the annals of song. The Marquis de La Fayette and Alfred de Musset were among her most enthusiastic admirers—de Musset voiced his grief for her death in a passionately eloquent poem.

María's younger sister, Pauline (born in Paris, 1821), was taught singing chiefly by her mother. She also studied counterpoint with Reicha and piano with Meyssenberg and Liszt; the latter wanted her to become a professional pianist. The mother, however, insisted that she should uphold the family tradition by becoming a singer. Pauline Viardot-García (as she was known after her marriage to the French impresario Louis Viardot in 1841) did indeed bear aloft the García standard with honor, her long and distinguished career bringing her laurels in virtually every country of Europe (she did not sing in America, though she was there as a child). One of her most notable triumphs was in the role of Orpheus, in the revival of Gluck's opera prepared by Berlioz for the Théâtre Lyrique in 1859; she sang the part one hundred and fifty times that season. Her voice was a mezzo-soprano with an exceptionally wide range (from c to f^3). She retired from the stage in 1863, but lived to be nearly ninety, dying at Paris in 1910.

THE DISCOVERER OF THE LARYNGOSCOPE

Another long-lived member of this remarkable family was Manuel García's son, Manuel Patricio Rodríguez García (born in Madrid, 1805), who lived to be over a hundred. He began his career as an operatic basso, but from 1829 he devoted himself to teaching, first in Paris and later in London (from 1850–1895 he was professor of singing at the Royal Academy of Music). He developed and codified his father's teaching method, embodying its principles in his fundamental *Traité Complet de l'Art du Chant* (Paris, 1847). His scientific bent caused him to investigate the physiological aspects of vocal production, with results of vast importance for science. In 1840 he presented to the French Academy of Sciences his *Mémoire sur la Voix Humaine*. His major scientific contribution was the invention of the laryngoscope (1854), which made it possible for the first time to look into the human throat. While interesting himself in these scientific matters, García denied the value of anatomical and physiological studies for those who wished to learn singing. His *Hints on Singing*, published posthumously in 1904, is a comprehensive catechism of the vocal art.

Manuel García the younger was the teacher of Jenny Lind, as well as of Henriette Nissen, Julius Stockhausen, and Charles Santley. On the occasion of his hundredth anniversary (March 17, 1905) he was showered with honors, including the Insignia of a Commander of the Royal Victorian Order bestowed by King Edward VII. He died on July 1 of the following year. The vocal tradition of the Garcías has been carried on by his son, Gustave García (1837–1925), and by his grandson, Albert García (born in London, 1875), both of whom sang in opera and settled in London as teachers.

In the second half of the nineteenth century the outstanding Spanish singer was the tenor Julián Gayarre (1844–1890), who triumphed in all the principal opera houses of Europe. In more recent times the tenors Miguel Fleta and Hipólito Lázaro, the baritone Rafael Sagi Barba, the basso José Mardones, the sopranos María Barrientos and Lucrezia Bori,[9] the contralto María Gay, and the mezzo-soprano Conchita Supervía,[10] have helped to maintain the prestige of Spain's vocal art.

From the time of Felipe Libón (1775–1838), who was chamber musician to the Empress Josephine in Paris, Spain has not lacked eminent masters of the violin. One of these, Jesús Monasterio (1836–1903), in addition to winning acclaim as a virtuoso throughout Europe—his success was such that he was offered the post of court *Kapellmeister* at Weimar—played a very important part in the development of symphonic and chamber music in Spain. He was a pupil of Charles de Bériot at the Brussels Conservatory, where he won the Prix d'Honneur at the age of fourteen. As teacher of violin and ensemble playing at the Madrid Conservatory (of which he was for a time director), as founder in 1863 of the Sociedad de Cuartetos (for performing the masterpieces of chamber music), and as conductor, from 1869–1876, of the Sociedad de Conciertos (out of which grew the Madrid Symphony Orchestra), Monasterio raised the standard of musical performance and appreciation in the Spanish capital far above what it had previously been. Among his pupils was Pablo Casals.

SARASATE, THE SUPREME VIRTUOSO

In the annals of violin playing two names stand out above all others: Nicolo Paganini and Pablo de Sarasate. Four years after Paganini's death Pablo Martín Melitón Sarasate y Navascuez— he wisely dropped a few of his names when he began his public career—was born in the ancient Navarrese capital of Pamplona (March 10, 1844). Receiving his first violin lessons from his father, a military bandmaster, he made his concert debut at La Coruña when he was eight. Two years later he became a pupil of Manuel Rodríguez at Madrid, and when he was twelve he gave a concert in the Royal Opera House there. He then set out for Paris, accompanied by his mother, who died on the way, at Bayonne. Befriended by the Spanish Consul in that city, and with financial assistance from Queen Isabel and others, he was able to proceed to Paris, where he studied with Alard at the Conservatoire, winning the First Prize for violin playing in the following year (1857). For a while he studied composition under Reber, but he was born to be a virtuoso, and he knew it.

It has been said of Sarasate that he was neither a great artist nor a great musician, but simply a great fiddler. All agree, however, that he carried fiddling to superlative heights. In the early years of his career, his repertoire consisted almost exclusively of extremely difficult "showpieces," mostly operatic fantasias arranged by himself. Later (from about 1870) his musical interests broadened and he began to play the great masterpieces of violin literature, chiefly of the Romantic period. He also played a number of works written especially for him by contemporary composers, notably Lalo's First Concerto and *Symphonie Espagnole,* Bruch's Second Concerto and *Schottische Fantasie,* Saint-Saëns's *Concertstück* in A, *Rondo Capricioso* (in Spanish style), and Concerto in B minor, and Mackenzie's *Pibroch Suite.* Sarasate is reputed to have had a hand in writing the violin parts of most of these works.

From 1861, when he appeared for the first time in England, until the very last years of his life, Sarasate's career was a succession of triumphs.[11] His tours extended not only throughout Europe, but also in North and South America, Africa, and the Orient. He first visited the United States in 1870; his last American tour was in 1889. Each year he faithfully revisited his native city, his arrival being celebrated with public rejoicings. The violin on which he played was a Stradivarius of 1724, known as the "Boissier de Genève," which he bought in 1866 and which he bequeathed to the Paris Conservatoire. He also owned another Stradivarius, dated 1713 and called "Le Rouge" because of its red color, which he bought in 1888 for 20,000 francs (this he bequeathed to the Madrid Conservatory).

The nonchalant manner in which Sarasate performed the most dazzling technical feats enhanced the fascination he exerted over his audiences. His sense of touch, as evidenced by the unequaled dexterity of his left hand, was marvelous—so marvelous that one writer has called it "supernatural." His platform manner was the embodiment of grace and elegance: a typical pose is that in which Whistler has so strikingly portrayed him. He was every inch the virtuoso.

As a composer, Sarasate wrote with extreme effectiveness for his instrument, and he was, moreover, one of those who contributed most efficaciously to popularizing "the Spanish idiom" abroad, sharing honors with Albéniz in this respect. His numerous

Spanish Dances (both for violin alone, and for violin with piano) will long remain in the violinistic repertoire, for they are full of color and charm, as well as of technical brilliancy.

CASALS, WIZARD OF THE CELLO

Pre-eminent among all modern masters of the violoncello is Pablo Casals, whom Catalonia justly claims as one of her greatest musical glories. Born at Vendrell in 1876, the son of a local organist and choirmaster, he is said to have joined his father's choir at the age of four. When he was about eleven, he went to Barcelona to study the cello under José García and, as his family was poor, he earned money by playing in cafés. The story is told that when he was twelve and a half he came upon Bach's suites for cello alone while looking over some music in a store. He was fascinated by the mystery of this new type of composition, whose existence he had hitherto never even suspected. According to his biographer, "He went from the shop in a trance, carrying his precious 'discovery' with him, and immediately upon reaching home began to read through these suites. He studied and worked at them every day for ten years, and was nearly twenty-five before he felt he dared play one of them in public." [12] Casals eventually made history with his interpretation of Bach's suites for cello alone.

Among those who heard the boy Casals and predicted a great future for him was Isaac Albéniz. Armed with a letter of introduction from Albéniz to Count Morphy, Pablo and his mother went to Madrid. There Pablo gave several concerts in the Royal Palace, at which some of his own compositions, including a string quartet, were performed. For two years he studied chamber music with Monasterio and composition with Bretón at the Madrid Conservatory. Count Morphy, who took a keen interest in the boy's career, believed that he should become a composer rather than a cellist. With this end in view, the Count obtained a royal stipend for Casals to study at the Brussels Conservatoire under Gevaert. Casals, however, found the atmosphere in Brussels uncongenial (it seems that the cello instructor indulged in some foolish sarcasm at his expense) and soon left for Paris. Thereupon his stipend was discontinued and he had to join a vaudeville orchestra in order to support himself and his mother, who had come to look after him. Before long, hardship and illness forced them to return to Barcelona, where Pablo was fortunate enough to obtain the teaching post at the Municipal School which his former teacher García had just relinquished. He also became first cellist at the Liceo Opera, and formed a string quartet with Crickboom (a Belgian musician residing in Barcelona) as first violinist.

After sojourns in Portugal and Madrid, he went to Paris again, this time bearing a letter of introduction to the conductor Charles Lamoureux. As soon as the latter heard Casals play he engaged him as soloist for the opening concert of the Lamoureux Orchestra that season (1898). His success was phenomenal, and from then on engagements followed rapidly. His first tour to the United States was in 1901–1902, and in 1903–1904 he toured both North and South America.

THE ORQUESTA PAU CASALS

But Casals was not content to rest upon his laurels as a virtuoso. Retaining strong spiritual ties with his homeland, he desired to contribute in some effective way to the dissemination of musical culture in Catalonia. This ambition was realized when, in 1919, he founded the Orquesta Pau Casals [13] in Barcelona. This was the first permanent symphony orchestra established in that city (various other orchestras had proved short-lived). For nearly twenty years—until the downfall of the Republic made him an exile—Casals gave a part of each season to the task of conducting this orchestra. A movement into which he threw himself heart and soul was the founding of a Workingman's Concert Association, so that people of the working class could hear symphonic concerts regularly at minimum prices. The project was immensely successful and served as a model and inspiration for similar undertakings in other countries.

In the course of his busy life Casals has found time to compose works that entitle him to serious consideration as a creative artist. His compositions comprise not only pieces for cello and piano, but also the symphonic poem *The Vision of Fray Martin* for solos, chorus, organ, and orchestra, and several large orchestral works.

PIANISTS AND GUITARISTS

The two most celebrated pianists of modern Spain, Isaac Albéniz and Enrique Granados, were even more famous as composers, and to them we have already devoted a chapter. By a curious coincidence, the pioneer pianist of the modern Spanish school was also named Albéniz, though he does not appear to have been related to the composer of *Iberia*. He was Pedro Albéniz, born at Logroño (Castile) in 1795. After studying with Kalkbrenner and Henri Herz in Paris, he became professor of piano at the Madrid Conservatory in 1830. He was the author of a Piano Method which was officially adopted at the Conservatory, and the composer of numerous piano pieces, among them a *Rondo brillante* on the theme of *La Tirana del Trípili* (*cf.* Chapter VIII). He died at Madrid in 1855.

Ricardo Viñes (born at Lérida, Catalonia, in 1875), José Arriola (born at La Coruña, 1896), and José Iturbi (born at Valencia, 1895) are among the most notable of contemporary Spanish pianists. Viñes was the first to play the piano pieces of Debussy and Ravel. To him Falla dedicated the *Nights in the Gardens of Spain*. Arriola began his career as a child prodigy and is reputed to have made his debut in public at the age of two. Iturbi, who graduated from the Paris Conservatoire in 1912, is well known to American audiences, for he has long made his home in the United States. He has lately given much time to conducting and in 1936 was appointed conductor of the Rochester Philharmonic Orchestra.

As may well be imagined, Spain has produced the world's most famous guitarists. Building on the work of his predecessors Basilio and Moretti (*cf.* Chapter III), Dionisio Aguado (1784–1849) established the principles of modern guitar technique in a Method which he published in 1825 and which has never been superseded. His contemporary Fernando Sor (1778-1839), who aroused the admiration of such men as Méhul and Cherubini in Paris—the historian Fétis called him "the Beethoven of the guitar"—provided the basic modern repertoire for the guitar with his numerous brilliant compositions for that instrument. Finally, Francisco Tárrega (1852–1909), the greatest of all the modern masters of the guitar, initiated the present-day renascence of the instrument both as interpreter and as composer, raising it to the level at which it has been maintained by such artists as Miguel Llobet, Emilio Pujol, and Andrés Segovia, whose world-wide triumphs have revealed to many music lovers the full artistic possibilities of the guitar as a concert instrument.

CHAPTER XV

Iberian Folk Music

IT is generally agreed that Spanish folk music is the richest in the world. This is partly because so many cultures have mingled in the Iberian Peninsula, each contributing its share to the development of the popular *melos*, and partly because the Spaniards are so strongly attached to their native traditions that they tend to keep them alive longer than is the case in those countries where life has become more standardized by modern civilization. The mere fact that Spain to a large extent remained outside the path of European "progress" helped to sustain the vitality of her folk traditions. Moreover, the natural conformation of the land, its topography, characterized by mountain chains and river systems dividing the country into well-defined sectors, tended to accentuate the individuality of the different regions and thereby to heighten the variety of the musical folklore.

By folk music we mean music that seems to be the natural and instinctive expression of the people, without benefit of scholastic elaboration, and which is handed down from generation to generation by oral tradition rather than in written or printed form. The fact that it is anonymous does not mean that it is self-generated, but simply that the name of the musician who first thought of the tune has not been preserved. Furthermore, the process of transmission by oral tradition involves a continual process of transformation, so that in the course of time the song or tune becomes a collective rather than a personal creation. It was not until the latter part of the nineteenth century that folk music began to be systematically studied and collected, and it is only within the present century that really scientific methods (chiefly with the aid of recording machines) have been applied to this field.[1] Slowly in some communities, rapidly in others, traditional folk music is disappearing from the world, largely due to the standardization imposed by the radio, the phonograph, and the distribution of printed sheet music. The folk will always have their music, but it will be "popular" rather than traditional.

We have already observed to what extent the Andalusian musical idioms predominate in the foreign conception of Spanish music. This is the region upon which the Arabs left their deepest imprint; consequently its musical exoticism is more pronounced than in any other section of the peninsula. The word "Andalusia" comes from the Arab *al-Andalus* (i.e., "land of the Vandals"), the name which the Moslems gave to Spain, and which they also applied specifically to the four kingdoms of Seville, Córdova, Jaén, and Granada, comprising the southern part of the peninsula. When the modern provincial demarcations of Spain were established in 1833, Andalusia was divided into the eight administrative provinces of Almería, Cádiz, Córdova, Granada, Huelva, Jaén, Málaga, and Seville—names which also designate their respective capitals. The mountains known as the Sierra Morena form the northern boundary of Andalusia proper, making a natural barrier between it and the rest of Spain.

As outlined by Manuel de Falla, who has made a profound study of the subject,[2] the three main factors in the development of Andalusian folk music were (1) the adoption of many elements of Byzantine chant by the primitive church in Spain; (2) the Moslem invasion and occupation; and (3) the immigration into Spain of numerous bands of Gypsies, most of whom settled in Andalusia.[3] Chronologically, these three influences manifested themselves in the order named. Another authority, Medina Azara, gives much importance to a fourth factor, the Hebraic, attempting to show a strong analogy between Andalusian *cante jondo* and the Jewish synagogical chant. There was unquestionably a considerable Jewish influence in Moslem Spain.[4]

THE "DEEP SONG" OF ANDALUSIA

The oldest and most characteristic type of Andalusian folk music is that known by the generic name of *cante jondo* (or *cante hondo*),[5] and the most genuine representative of this type is the *seguiriya gitana*,[6] in which the survival of Byzantine-Oriental influences may be clearly perceived. Following the analysis of Falla, this influence manifests itself, first, in the use of enharmonism as a means of expressive modulation;[7] that is to say, certain functional notes are divided and subdivided into intervals smaller than a semitone, obeying inflections of the voice which in turn are determined by the expression that the words of the song demand. There is also the frequent use of the vocal *portamento*, the practice of "sliding" the voice from one note to another through a series of infinitesimal gradations.

The melodies of *cante jondo* generally move within the compass of a sixth, but the use of enharmonism naturally extends the number of tones available within this interval considerably beyond the nine semitones into which the sixth of the ordinary European scale system is divided. Another markedly Oriental feature is the repeated insistence, amounting almost to an obsession, on a single note, usually accompanied by appoggiaturas from above and below. This produces the effect of a sort of incantation, such as may have been sung by primitive man in prehistoric times.[8]

An element that *cante jondo* shares in common with Byzantine chant is that of ornate melodic embellishment, which, however, is never a merely extraneous ornamentation, but a result of lyrical expansiveness induced by the emotive force of the words. These embellishments lose their essential character when an attempt is made to transcribe them within the fixed intervals of the European tempered scale.[9]

Also of Oriental origin is the custom of encouraging and stimu-

Pablo de Sarasate, from the Portrait by Whistler

lating the singers and instrumentalists by shouting conventional words or phrases, such as the familiar *Olé!*, and of clapping the hands to accompany the rhythm of the dance, as is done in the Andalusian *cuadro flamenco*.[10]

The word *seguiriya*[11] is an Andalusian-Gypsy corruption of the Castilian term "seguidilla," but as metrical compositions the two are not identical. The *seguiriya gitana* of Andalusia is also known as *playera*, which is derived from the verb *plañir*, "to lament." And, in effect, the *seguiriya* or *playera* is fundamentally a lament, imbued with the ineradicable pessimism, the profound fatalism that stamps the most genuine manifestations of *cante jondo*. The *copla* (stanza), like all the verse of *cante jondo*, concentrates within a few lines a wealth of emotional experience. For forceful imagery and compact intensity, no popular verse form excels the Andalusian *copla*.

We have already intimated that it is virtually impossible to convey a faithful impression of *cante jondo* melody through the medium of our modern European musical notation, because of the chromatic inflections and subdivisions, and because of the free rhythm which does not conform to regular measurement. Hearing a good *cante jondo* singer, such as "La Niña de los Peines," is the only way of becoming acquainted with the real spirit of this "deep song."

It is also very difficult to capture the rhythms of this music, particularly of the *seguiriya gitana*, which is marked by the alternation of measures in 3/8 and 3/4 time. The accompanying instrument, of course, is the guitar, which at the end of the verse plays what the Spaniards call *falsetas*, a sort of instrumental interlude. The *falsetas* for the *seguiriya gitana* quoted on the next page (Example 16) were transcribed by Martínez Torner from the playing of the Andalusian guitarist Campillo. This composite rhythm is frequently to be met with in Spanish music from the earliest times. Among examples that have been preserved in print are a ballad, *Retraída está la Infanta*, cited by Salinas in the sixteenth century, and a *zarabanda* included in the guitar

Example 16.

book of Gaspar Sanz, dating from the seventeenth century.

Derived from the *seguiriya gitana* are other forms of *cante jondo*, such as the *polo*, the *martinete*,[12] and (more remotely) the *soleá*. An excellent example of the *polo*, though with a stylized accompaniment, is that contained in Falla's collection *Seven Spanish Popular Songs*. The *soleá* (from *soledad*, "solitude") is another plaintive song of sorrow and loneliness. The loneliness of one who has no mother and father, and nobody to remember him, is expressed in the *soleá* from which we quote.

Example 17.

Those who think of Andalusia as a land of perpetual gaiety will be disillusioned to learn that suffering and sorrow are the chief burden of most of the songs of that region, at least of those which have their roots in the Arabic-Hebraic-Gypsy strains.

FLAMENCO SONGS AND DANCES

In the songs of more modern origin, however, to which the term *cante flamenco* should properly be applied,[13] the general

tone is less somber and we encounter more of that vivacious quality which makes people think of Spain as "the land of joy."
Among the multitude of songs that come under the denomina-
tion of flamenco some of the best known are the *granadinas,*
malagueñas, peteneras, rondeñas, sevillanas, alegrías, bulerías,
and the fandango. Many of these are danced as well as sung.[14] It
is through songs and dances of this type that most people form
their conception of "the Spanish idiom" in music, because they
have been so widely popularized. Almost everyone, for instance,
is familiar with the tune and rhythm of the *sevillanas,* which is
the Andalusian version of the Castilian seguidillas. It begins as
follows:

Example 18.

Scarcely less familiar is the *granadina,* which belongs to the same
group as the *rondeña* and *malagueña* (all these take their names
from cities).

The *peteneras* is one of those forms—the tango is another [15]—
which were brought from Spain to the New World (in this case,
Cuba) and then returned to the mother country modified by
Negro and Creole influences. Like the Cuban *guajira,* it alternates
3/4 time with 3/8. The *bulerías,* in 3/8 time, and the *alegrías,*
in lively 3/4 time, are the most joyful of the flamenco forms.
The fandango, or *fandanguillo,* is found in many parts of Andalusia, each region having its own characteristic version.

Closely associated with the popular religious processions of
Corpus Christi and Holy Week in Seville is the *saeta,* an "arrow
of song" sent forth by the spectators and addressed to an image
of Christ, or of the Virgin Mary, as these are borne along the
streets. It is sung slowly, with great intensity of expression, and is

the only one of the *cante jondo* forms that does not include the characteristic melismatic *Ay!* Also, it is sung without accompaniment.

The ancient kingdom and modern province of Murcia lies between Andalusia and Valencia and forms a connecting link between the folk music of both regions. The *murcianas, tarantas,* and *cartageneras* are related to the *malagueña* of the flamenco group. The *aguinaldos*—songs of Christmas and New Year—with their simple melodies in triple time and their major tonality, are more akin to the Valencian-Catalan group, and so is the *parranda,* the typical dance of the region, also in triple time and in major. In Murcia there are especially interesting reapers' songs, such as the following.

Example 19.

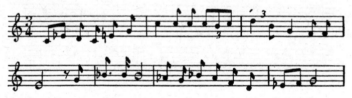

Turning now to the west, we find the region of Extremadura, which lies just north of Andalusia along the Portuguese border. The chief city is Badajoz. Long under Moslem domination, Extremadura reveals in its folk music some of the same Arabian-Oriental traits that are found in the music of Andalusia. This is apparent in the following dance tune (for the feast of the *Virgen de la Salud*), played on a vertical flute with three holes and a *tambor* or small side drum. The melody is in C major, but the tendency to flatten the *b* (the flutist is accustomed to playing in the key of F) is not entirely overcome in spite of an extra compression of the lips; hence the intended *b* natural always sounds a little flat (melody recorded by Bonifacio Gil; Example 20).

The folk music of Extremadura also partakes somewhat of the character of the music belonging to those regions which bor-

Example 20.

der it on the north and east: León, and Old and New Castile. It is rich in traditional ballads, children's singing games, and Christmas carols. The Extremadurian version of the fandango is the most typical dance of the region.

NEW AND OLD CASTILE

To the east of Extremadura lies the region of New Castile, divided into five administrative provinces, including those of Madrid and Toledo. Most of this region is known as La Mancha (from the Arabic *Al Mansha*, meaning "the dry land") and consists of a bare yet strangely beautiful plateau. Don Quixote, it will be recalled, came from La Mancha, and so, according to Cervantes, did the widely popular seguidillas. The following example, at any rate, comes from La Mancha and warmly sings the praises of that region.

Example 21.

Proceeding northward we enter Old Castile, which extends all the way to the Bay of Biscay. In 1833 it was divided into the provinces of Avila, Burgos, Logroño, Palencia, Santander, Segovia, Soria, and Valladolid. Each of these provinces has its more or less well-defined regional music. The folk songs of Old Castile show a strong modal tendency and reflect the influence of plain song both melodically and rhythmically in their lack of conformity to isometric patterns, as may be seen in this bridal song from Burgos, taken from the collection of Federico Olmeda.

Example 22.

There are many semireligious songs that seem to stem directly from the *Cantigas de Santa María*. Many songs are also strongly reminiscent of the villancicos found in the *cancioneros* of the fifteenth and sixteenth centuries.

Many Castilian folk songs terminate on the fifth degree of the scale, producing the "dominant cadence" effect that is so prevalent in Spanish music. The melodic phrases and periods are seldom symmetrical. The following pastoral song from Salamanca is thoroughly Castilian.

Example 23.

In the second half of this song the melodic pattern changes and a triplet is substituted for the group of four sixteenth notes.

An important group of Castilian songs is formed by the *canciones de ronda*, a kind of nocturnal serenade sung by youths to their sweethearts (or sometimes simply to their friends) on all the principal feast days. Sometimes the serenaders go from one house to another, in which case their songs are called *pasacalles* (from *pasar*, "to pass"; and *calle*, "street"). They are generally sung without accompaniment, though in some places the *gaita* (rustic flute) and *tambor* are used. A peculiarity of these songs (as of Castilian dance songs also) is that at the end the singer emits a series of sharp cries, somewhat in the manner of a forced laugh beginning on a high note and cascading downward. This curious custom, of Celtic origin, is also found in the Basque provinces, and in some Latin-American countries.

Among the dance songs of Old Castile the most characteristic is the *rueda*, in 5/8 time (some are also in 2/4 and 3/8). The following *rueda* (literally, "wheel") is from the vicinity of Burgos:

Example 24.

An _da more _ m _ta re _co _ ge _te e _se pañuelo _____

Si le a _rras _tro que le arras _ tre

The *ruedas* are accompanied on the *pandereta* (tambourine), as are also the dance songs called *Al Agudo* and *A lo Llano*. The *Baile a lo Llano* resembles the *jota* of Aragon. The bolero, the seguidillas, the *jota* and the fandango are also danced and sung in Old Castile. The Castilian fandango is very similar to the *jota*. Especially associated with the province of Salamanca is a dance called the *charrada*, which has this type of melody:

Example 25.

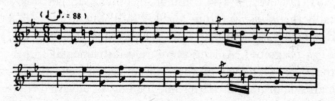

This is accompanied by the castanets and the tambourine.

The traditional ballads and the occupational songs of Castile are also of exceptional interest. The songs of the farm laborers, with their melismatic flourishes, are the only songs that show any kinship with those of Andalusia, perhaps indicating a common Byzantine-Arabic influence.

LEÓN, GALICIA, AND ASTURIAS

The province of León, to the west of Old Castile, is another transitional region, its folk music being partly related to Castile and partly to its northern neighbors, Galicia and Asturias. It is sparsely populated, has no large cities, and most of the inhabitants earn their living as muleteers or carriers. In the vicinity of Astorga live the *Maragatos,* who wear a distinctive costume and do not marry outside their own group. These curious people are thought to be a remnant of the original Celtiberian inhabitants of the peninsula. For a picture of *Maragatos* playing their typical instruments see Plate XIV.

In the extreme northwest corner of the peninsula is Galicia, which comprises the modern provinces of La Coruña, Lugo, Orense, and Pontevedra. We know what an important role Galicia played in the early development of Hispanic musicopoetic forms (*cf.* Chapter I). Modern Galicia has lost much of its cultural importance, but it preserves a distinctive musical folklore whose regional character is accentuated by the use of the Galician dialect (akin to Portuguese). The most characteristic melodic type is the *alalá,* most often in duple time, which takes its name from the syllables used in the refrain. This syllabic refrain (*la, la, la*), however, is also common in other Galician folk songs, notably the *muiñeira* (from *muiño,* "mill"), which is in 6/8 time and is both sung and danced to the accompaniment of the *gaita gallega* (bagpipe). Among the purely instrumental forms there is the *alborada,* played on the Galician bagpipe and the *tamboril* (small side drum), the latter maintaining an unvaried rhythm.

Immediately to the east of Galicia is the nominal principality of Asturias, which is separated from the rest of Spain by mountain ranges on three sides and bounded by the sea on the north. Typical of this region is the *giraldilla* (from *girar*, "to move in a circle"), which, like the Castilian *ruedas*, are sung while dancing around in a circle. The term, however, is also applied to a song which repeats the same melody indefinitely, or which has an *estribillo* (refrain) based on the same pattern as the melody but with a more strongly accented rhythm and a faster tempo.

Of great interest in Asturian folklore is the *danza prima*. This is a communal round dance, supposedly of great antiquity, for it is believed to have had its origin in religious ceremonies of the pre-Christian era. It is danced to the accompaniment of a ballad sung usually by two persons (a man and a woman), of which almost every line begins with the exclamation *Ay!* After every line, moreover, the chorus of dancers interpolates a religious interjection, such as *Viva la Virgen del Carmen!*, and the ballad proceeds in this manner for many verses, recounting a complicated tale of love which seems to be derived from one of the old novelesque *romances*.

Example 26.

The Cantabrian coastal region near Santander, dominated by the lofty mountain known as *Picos de Europa*, is called La Montaña, and its folk music is referred to as *montañés* (Falla's piano piece entitled *Montañesa* evokes the folk songs of this region). P. Nemesio Otaño, who has made a special study of *montañés* folk music, points out that the well-known song *La vi llorando* (I Saw Her Weeping) begins and ends with a melodic formula of

Gregorian character, which was frequently found in the court songs of the fifteenth and sixteenth centuries and which, passing through the tonadilla and the zarzuela, became a commonplace of "the Spanish idiom."

Example 27.

BASQUE PROVINCES, ARAGON, AND CATALONIA

As a race, the Basques are distributed between Spain and France, and their folk music partakes somewhat of this intermediate character. The influence of plain song is prominent and a considerable number of modal melodies are found (chiefly in the Aeolian, Dorian, and Mixolydian modes). The major and minor modes, however, prevail in most of the songs. The following is a characteristic Basque melody.

Example 28.

The most famous of all the Basque dances (it is also sung) is the *zortzico*, which has a curious 5/8 rhythm:

Example 29a.

Later this is varied as follows:

Example 29b.

The *arin-arin*, the rapid dance that terminates the traditional *aurresku* (*cf.* Chapter XVI), has this vivacious duple rhythm:

Example 30.

Aragon, which lies between the Basque provinces and Catalonia, owes its musical fame to the *jota*. No one knows exactly where or when this dance originated, and it is found in various parts of Spain, but the *jota* of Aragon is the best known of all the regional varieties. It is in rapid triple time and the harmony alternates between the dominant and tonic, usually four measures of each. Guitars of various sizes and *bandurrias* (a kind of mandolin) are the principal accompanying instruments, marking the rhythm strongly with strummed chords (*rasgueado*). The following example is a typical *jota* melody from the vicinity of Calatayud.

Example 31.

The strong regional feeling in Catalonia has led to a very thorough study of the folk songs in that territory, the most notable results being embodied in the publications of the *Obra del Cançoner de Catalunya*. Like the Basque provinces in the north, Catalonia formerly overlapped into what is now France, and the Catalan language is more closely related to the Provençal than to any of the peninsular languages. The Moslem penetration in Catalonia was brief and left few traces. However, one finds occasionally the interval of the augmented second, which is an Arabian characteristic. But this is common also to Byzantine chant, which may have been the original source of influence. Certain it is that the ecclesiastical chant has left a deep imprint upon the folk songs of Catalonia, as upon those of so many other Iberian regions.

The frequent use of chromaticism is one of the distinguishing traits of Catalan folk song. The third step of the scale, both in major and minor, is frequently altered, and the tonic is often raised or lowered. The following melody, one of numerous versions of the famous folk song *La Presó de Lleida* (*cf.* Chapter XI), shows some of this chromatic alteration.

Example 32.

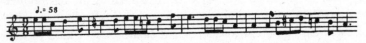

Certain folk songs are widespread in Catalonia and exist in innumerable local variants. The best known of all these is probably the old round of *El Comte Arnau,* based on a medieval Catalan legend, which is sung slowly and solemnly (Pedrell based one of his most important lyrico-dramatic works on this theme and legend). *El Tres Segadors* (The Three Sowers) is another favorite Catalan folk song.

When one thinks of Catalonia, however, one has in mind above all the *sardana,* which is virtually the national emblem of that country. In the strictest sense of the term, the *sardana* is not a folk dance, since both the music and choreography have been created by known individuals in recent times (*cf.* Chapter XVI). But it is strongly rooted in folk traditions and the music is always composed on the basis of popular elements. The following *sardana* is from the *Obra del Cançoner*.

Example 33.

The Balearic Islands come within the orbit of Catalonia and have much the same type of folk music. In Mallorca are to be found interesting songs of field laborers, many of which have a rich and profuse ornamentation.

The region of Valencia, where a variant of Catalan is spoken, has a local version of the *jota* which is almost as famous as that of Aragon. It is a somewhat slower dance than that of Aragon, and there is more freedom and flexibility in the vocal melody, which usually enters ad libitum.

The songs known elsewhere in Spain as *alboradas* are called *albaes* in Valencia. The accompanying instruments for this are the *dulzaína* (rustic oboe) and the *tamboril* (small drum), which play a lively tune (*estribillo*) before and after the singing. When the voice enters, the *dulzaína* stops playing and the *tamboril* maintains an unvaried rhythm, the player tapping very softly with his stick on the rim of the drum, as follows.

Example 34.

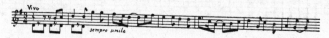

THE FOLK MUSIC OF PORTUGAL*

An expression which appeared very early in Portuguese poetry is the word *saudade*, considered the most beautiful word in the Portuguese language, and one which cannot be translated exactly into any other language. It denotes many things to a Portuguese: longing; longing for someone or something; longing for the past, or even for the future; nostalgia, yearning, wistfulness. This quality, *saudade*, is present in much of the popular and folk music of the Portuguese.

Rural folk music in Portugal is particularly interesting. In many sections of the country the people sing and dance on festival days, in singing matches, at pilgrimages, and on special church occasions. The song dances go under various names in different regions, such as the *vira* and *verdegaio* in the north, the *rabela* and *rusga* in the Douro River region, the *malhão* in the Beiras, the *bailarico* in the Estremadura, the fandango in the Alemtejo, and the *corridinho* in Algarve. Many of these songs are in two parts, the first one a relatively slow movement, rather balladlike, the second a fast dance movement.

In the north of Portugal, near Galicia, the people sing and dance the *vira do minho*, at the same time clapping their hands, snapping their fingers, and rubbing two shells together. The following *vira* is well known throughout Portugal. Its characteristic rhythm is that of the Galician *muiñeira:*

Example 35.

* By Albert T. Luper.

There are some phases of the study of the music and literature of Portugal which cannot very well be divorced from that of Galicia. Galicians, particularly those of the south, have much more in common with northern Portugal than they do with other Spaniards. Thus it is that many of the same songs may be heard on both sides of the border, particularly near the Minho River. The following song, sung for this writer by the Galician scholar Ramón Martínez Lopez,[16] has Portuguese words, and is said by the Galicians themselves to be of Portuguese origin. It is written in the familiar two parts, a slow section followed by a choreographic refrain (*estribilho*):

Example 36.

The southern provinces of Alemtejo and Algarve are those in which the Moors remained for the longest time. Whereas Moorish influence is not nearly as prevalent as it is in Spain, vestiges of the music still remain. The Semitic undulation of the melody may be noted in the chant from Serpa, near the Spanish border, quoted below. The first notes of this melody, entitled "Death comes, and it delays not," are curiously similar to the opening phrase of J. S. Bach's beautiful hymn "Come, Sweet Death." The scale oscillates between the major mode (with low d-sharp) and the Mixolydian mode (high d-natural).[17]

Folk songs in the major portion of the country show to a large degree the modifying influence of modern tonality. However, there is a section of the country, the middle eastern region nearest Spain (provinces of Beira Alta and Beira Baixa), which has remained aloof from modern tendencies and which shows to a

Example 37.

remarkable degree the influence of the church and of medieval tonalities. Rodney Gallop found here some of his most interesting examples. In the next example,[18] not only is the effect of plain chant clearly seen, but of interest also is the employment of the medieval "hochet" (a pause for breath in the middle of a syllable).

Example 38.

The pilgrimage festivals (called *romarias*) are great events in the lives of the people. On the appointed day the peasants and villagers dress up in their most colorful clothes and journey to the shrine, singing the various songs which have become traditional for the particular pilgrimage. Sometimes one may hear several versions of the same song. Such is the case with the hymn of the great *romaria* of the Sunday of Pentecost to the shrine of

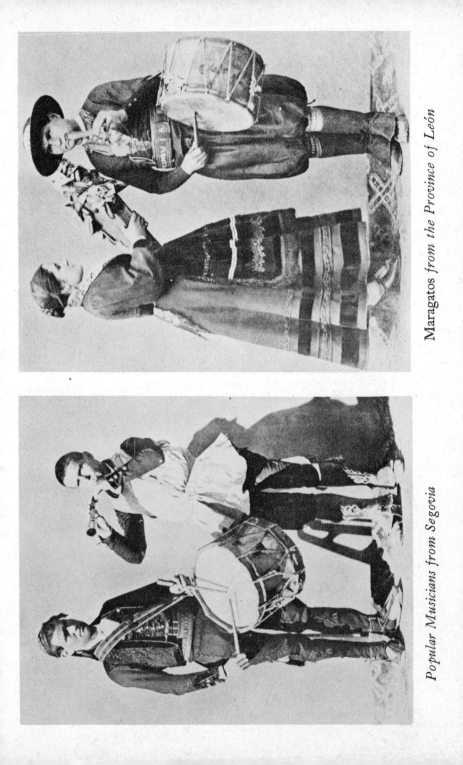

Maragatos from the Province of León

Popular Musicians from Segovia

Our Lady of Póvoa at Val-de-Lobo (in Beira Baixa), three variants of which were taken down by Rodney Gallop [19] on one of his trips into the interior of Portugal.

THE *FADO*

The *fado* is the popular music par excellence of the cities of Portugal. It has been termed the "urban folk song" of Portugal, although traveling musicians and mechanical means have spread it to all sections of the country. The greater portion of the *fados* are sad and melancholic love songs, and are always accompanied on the guitar. Some of the *fados*, however, take on the character of the balladlike chronicle, telling of current happenings, and in this regard they may be compared with certain types of the Mexican *corrido*. The harmonic content of the *fado* is very meager, the phrases in most *fados* alternating between the tonic and the dominant seventh chords, to which is somet. 1es added the subdominant chord at the approach to the caden

The origin of the *fado* is a disputed poin   authorities claiming variously that it is of Moorish, African, Brazilian, or Spanish origin. Others see in it the descendant of the *modinha* (very popular among all classes of people in Portugal and Brazil in the eighteenth and beginning of the nineteenth centuries), or of the *lumdúm* (an African chant), or maintain that it is of maritime origin. There is probably some measure of truth in all these assertions, the *fado* being a form evolved from several sources.

There are two main types of *fado*: the *fado* of Lisbon, sung in the cafés, on the streets, and in the poorer quarters of the city; and the *fado* of Coimbra, the favorite serenade of the students of the University of Coimbra, sung to their sweethearts as they walk the streets of the city or along the banks of the Mondego River.

The following *fado* is typical of the songs of the university students at Coimbra. Although the word *saudade* does not occur in the quatrain, the feeling of *saudade* is very strong.

Example 39.

Lin-das se-nho-ras d'Es-pa-nha, Lem-brai-vos al-gu-mas ve-zes.

Des-ta gui-ta-rra que cho-ra Nos bra-ços dos por-tu-gue-ses,

Des-ta gui-ta-rra que cho-ra Nos bra-ços dos por-tu-gue-ses.

Lindas senhoras d'Espanha,	Lovely ladies of Spain,
Lembrai-vos algumas vezes	Remember sometimes
Desta guitarra, que chora	This guitar, which weeps
Nos braços dos portugueses.	In the arms of the Portuguese.

The *fado* of Lisbon has much of the musical character of the Argentine tango. We present next a portion of a well-known Lisbon *fado* (*Fado Trinta-e-um*) together with the instrumental *estribilho* or refrain (usually played on the small guitar resembling the mandolin, with chordal accompaniment on a *violão*—the ordinary Spanish guitar) which precedes and follows many of the *fados*.

Example 40.

(ESTRIBILHO)

(FADO)

The instruments used for accompanying the various songs and dances of Portugal are quite varied. A brief account of the most common types in use will be of value in completing the picture of Portuguese folk music.

In the northern section of the country a dance song such as the *chula* is accompanied by violins, guitars, a tambour, a triangle, and sometimes by a flute or a clarinet.[20]

The bagpipe (*gaita-de-foles* or *gaita galega*) is common in the northern and central regions. In the central and upper-south regions the *zé pereira*, a sort of fife-and-drum corps, made up mostly of a large number of various-sized drums, is much in use. In Trás-os-Montes and Beira (the most remote regions, near Spain) the *adufe*, of Arabic origin, is quite common. It is a square-shaped drum of one or two inches' thickness, covered with skins on both sides, in between which are placed tin disks and other objects which rattle when the *adufe* is hit in beating the rhythm of the dance.

The guitar family is a very large one, consisting of various types and sizes ranging from the small *cavaquinho, guitarra,* and *rajão* to the large *viola braguesa, viola madeirense, viola micaelense,* and *violão.*

The literary aspects of Portuguese folk song have been studied for many years, even centuries, and systematic collections have been made of the poems. The music, however, has been grossly neglected, and only a few occasional individual studies had been made until the last few years. To remedy this situation, the government has instituted a department of research for collecting, recording, and publishing the beautiful folk music of Portugal before the older examples become extinct under the encroachment of modern forms of popular music.

CHAPTER XVI

Dances of Spain

IN Spain, said Cervantes, the newborn babe comes dancing forth from its mother's womb. Certain it is that the Spaniards are a dancing people and have been famed as such from earliest times to the present. The Roman patricians imported their dancing girls from Cádiz, and while that city itself is no longer noted for its dancers the region of Andalusia remains "the classic home of the dance." [1] Universal tributes to the power and fascination of Spanish dancing could be multiplied indefinitely. The Kinneys [2] give it as their opinion that "in pure decorative beauty; variety and force of expression; scope of motive; happy contrasts of treatment—briefly, in the art of the dance, Andalusia speaks the final word." Waldo Frank [3] declares: "The Spanish dance is organic and essential. It is the one great classic dance surviving in our modern world." André Levinson calls the Spanish dance *le plus ancien et le plus noble des exotismes européens.* [4] And for Havelock Ellis [5] "the highest manifestations of beauty he had seen were the slow movements of certain Spanish dances."

In Spanish dancing may be seen the same fusion of diverse elements that we have observed in Iberian folk music. Castanets were used by the Greeks and Romans, and there is some similarity between Spanish dancing and the movements of the ancient Greek dance. Havelock Ellis thinks that the custom of having the spectators keep time by clapping their hands may be a survival of

Greek dancing, in which case the practice may have been borrowed by the Arabs instead of having been introduced into the peninsula by them. The same authority maintains that "the famous statue of the so-called Venus Callipyge, representing a woman who turns her head around as she bends backward . . . is undoubtedly the image of a Cádiz dancer in a characteristic movement of a Spanish dance." [6]

The iconography of dancing in Spain goes back much further than the Greco-Roman period. It goes back, in fact, to prehistoric times. There is a paleolithic rock painting from Cogul, near Lérida (Catalonia), representing nine women dancing around a young man.[7] The women are clothed but the man is not; the painting depicts a phallic dance. By comparison, the examples of early Iberian ceramic art discovered at Llivia in 1934 seem comparatively modern, though they date from the third century B.C. One of these vases is particularly interesting, for it is decorated with figures of musicians and dancers, the former playing a variety of the Greek aulos.[8] The dancers comprise three men and three women, all holding hands; curiously, instead of alternating, the three women are together, and so are the men. Except for this feature, the manner of dancing is similar to that of the Catalan *sardana*.

Havelock Ellis divides dancing as a whole into three general types. The first is that in which the legs are the chief performers (this type prevails in Europe). In the second the action is confined exclusively to the arms and hands (prevalent in Java and Japan). The third type is that in which the muscles of the body itself play the chief part (Africa and western Asia). Among European dances the Spanish alone includes elements of all three types. The movements of arms and hands and the play of the body muscles are especially prominent in the dances of Andalusia, which conform more closely to the principles of Eastern than of Western dancing. André Levinson points out that the main difference between the Western and the Eastern dance is that the former is *excentric*, that is, tending to deviate or depart from a given center, whereas the latter is *concentric*, tending to converge upon itself. The European dance, especially as developed in the ballet, is based primarily on a displacement of the limbs; the arms and legs are detached from the body in extended movements, and the body itself is usually in movement from one place to another. In the Oriental dance all movements of the arms and legs must appear not to be detached from the body, but to converge upon it, to be a single harmonious line. So it is with the Andalusian dances, in some of which the performer will scarcely move from a given spot, but will employ every muscle in an intense concentration of dynamic movement in which the decorative element is the sinuous arabesque of arms and hands, never angular, but ever winding and curving and turning.

The same contrast appears in the costumes. The dress of the ballet dancer aims above all at freeing the limbs for that detached movement which is essential to her art. Her short skirt and bodice are a mere gesture to modesty; the play of limb must be always visible and palpable. The dress of the Spanish dancer—it is of the woman we speak—is voluminous and unrevealing. The body is definitely covered, even though in some of the flamenco dances the dress may cling to the figure and show its contours. Spanish dancers who dispense with petticoats and make a point of kicking their legs high in the air belong only to the music-hall variety. Like the Oriental woman who veils her face, the Spanish dancer preserves inviolate the mystery of her femininity, being thereby all the more seductive.

Again, there is an absolute physical contrast between the genuine Spanish dancer—particularly the Andalusian—and her standard European or American counterpart. A girlish figure, movie-actress features, and the usual allurements of beauty-contest winners are no more a part of the Spanish dancer's physical equipment than is the lean and agile hardness of the trained ballerina. The most authentic Spanish dancer is a matronly figure; she is a symbol of matriarchal power, of fertility and fulfillment rather than of enticement. She is neither romantic nor frivolous, but performs her dances with a ritualistic intensity that even in moments of apparent abandon retains its inward core of dignity. As Waldo Frank has very truly said, "a 'romantic' Andalusian dance is nonsense."

It is customary to divide Spanish dances into two main groups, the classic and the flamenco, the latter being largely dominated by Gypsy influences. Still another class might be constituted by the communal dances, such as the *sardana* of Catalonia and the *danza prima* of Asturias. Among the classic dances, the bolero, the *sevillanas,* and the *jota* are the best known, while the most popular flamenco types are the tango, the *farruca,* and the *garrotín.* In the eighteenth century the fandango was very popular but later fell into disuse in society, though dances with that name survive in the Basque provinces and elsewhere, being closely related to the *jota.* Another dance popular with Spanish society in the eighteenth century was the seguidillas, of which there were many varieties. The main elements of this dance have survived in the *sevillanas,* which takes its name from Seville, being an Andalusian version of the classic seguidillas. Some of its features have also been incorporated in the bolero, which is often found in the combination *boleras-sevillanas.*

THE BOLERO

The bolero was one of the dances that helped to spread the fame of Spanish dancing abroad, for, championed by the brilliant and enthusiastic pen of Théophile Gautier—fresh from his travels in Spain—it captivated Paris in the early nineteenth century.[9] It is said to have been invented by Sebastián Cerezo, a celebrated dancer of Cádiz, around 1780, and the name is supposedly derived from the verb *volar,* meaning "to fly" (in Spanish the "b" and "v" are practically interchangeable). The bolero was danced either by a single person, or by two dancers, who alternated in displaying their skill in complicated steps. The dance as a whole was divided into three sections, in the second of which the performers executed their difficult solo steps, while in the other two they danced in conjunction with each other. The middle section allowed wide scope for individual skill and invention. Two distinctive features of the bolero, which are also characteristic of Spanish dancing as a whole, are the *paseo* and the *bien parado*. The former is a sort of promenade which serves as an introduction to the dance. The dancers merely walk around—but what beauty and fascination there is in the mere walk of a good Spanish dancer! Pride and nobility of bearing are united to the utmost gracefulness of carriage. The greatest of the modern Spanish flamenco dancers, Pastora Imperio, walked in such a way that it was said she had received this gift from God and out of it had made a new art—that of walking.

The *bien parado*, which concludes the dance and also may be introduced at the end of any section, provides one of those sudden transitions and striking attitudes that are so characteristic of Spanish dancing. In the *bien parado* the dancer makes a sudden stop, corresponding to the end of a musical phrase, and assumes a motionless pose, placing one leg slightly forward, bent at the knee and turned outward, the body somewhat twisted and thrown back upon the support of the other leg, while one arm is held arched over the head and the other is crossed in front of the chest. When this figure is skillfully executed, the spectators cry out *Bien parado!*—which means literally "well stopped!" This abrupt immobility is in sharp contrast to the animated steps included in the bolero.

One of the most important of these steps, which is used in the middle or display section, is the *cuarta*, identical with the *entrechat-quatre* of the classical ballet, the swiftest and most dazzling of all the standard steps, in which the performer, jumping into the air, repeatedly crosses his or her feet in apparent defiance of the law of gravity. In the bolero the man gives added vigor and significance to this step by kicking one foot up and backward as he descends, which causes him to make a half-turn in the air. At the same time he heightens the effect by extending his arms outward.

Steps of the "beating" type (*battement*), in which one leg beats against the other, either straight or with bent knee, are prominent in the bolero, which is characterized throughout by vigorous and brilliant action. The dance is accompanied by the incessant clatter of the castanets, which must also be played vigorously and with unfailing rhythm. It is an extremely difficult feat to keep up the strong rhythm of the castanets while performing the fast and energetic footwork.

There is much less "elevation" (i.e., work off the ground) in the *sevillanas,* probably the favorite of all Andalusian dances. The prevailing step here is the *pas de Basque,* presumably of Basque origin but widely diffused throughout Spain. It is an alternating step, in which one foot is always on the floor, and it produces a swaying or swinging movement. This is used in the *paseo* and in the *pasada;* in the latter movement the dancers (a man and a woman, or sometimes two couples) cross over and change places—a basic evolution in the *sevillanas* (as in other dances of the same type), recurring regularly. The principal step used for variety is the *fouetté,* in which one leg is raised (usually to the level of the waist, or higher) and then lowered in a wide curving sweep. Often used also is the *fouetté tour,* in which the foregoing movement is followed by a complete turn. Arms and hands have an important function in this dance, which is performed with castanets.

FLAMENCO DANCES

The dances known as flamenco, primarily associated with the Gypsies of Andalusia, are of comparatively recent origin, though without doubt they incorporate many traditional features of Spanish dancing. In fact, it is certain that the Gypsies did not invent any of these dances but took them up at a time when the Spaniards themselves, under the impulse of modern "progress," tended to neglect them, and thus placed their characteristic stamp upon them. The *gitano* dances of Andalusia are vivid and uninhibited, full of startling contrasts, by turns violent and caressing, and with an expressiveness of pantomime that embraces all emotions, at times even verging on the grotesque. The rhythmic virtuosity of the *zapateado* (stamping and tapping of the feet) and the stimulating accompaniment of the *jaleo*—the encouraging shouts and rhythmic handclapping of the spectators—are vital to the Gypsy dancer.

The Gypsy dances for himself and not for an audience. He has no use for a passive audience, but he needs a group of active spectators who provide the proper atmosphere for his art. This he gets in the *cuadro flamenco*, in which other dancers, a singer, and a couple of guitarists sit around in a semicircle, making music, clapping their subtle accompaniments, and shouting *Olé!* (or any of a hundred other encouraging phrases) after every well-executed step. Flamenco dancing in this setting is, in the words of Havelock Ellis,[10] "the visible embodiment of an emotion in which every spectator takes an active and helpful part; it is a vision evoked by the spectators themselves, and upborne on the continuous waves of rhythmical sound which they generate."

Castanets are not used in the pure flamenco dances. The only exception is the fandanguillo, whose popularity is recent and which is not considered genuinely *gitano*. The Gypsy prefers to use the *pito* (finger snapping), the *palmada* (clapping of the hands with a sharp, dry "clack"; also, slapping of the thighs), and the *taconeo* (rhythmic stamping with the heels), which is one variety of the *zapateado* (from *zapato*, "shoe"). Male dancers in particular set great store by the *zapateado*, for it infuses the dance with a dynamic energy that asserts their virility, a very important point with Spanish *bailadores*. The most famous *gitano* dancer of the present day, Vicente Escudero, is quoted [11] as saying, "If I heard one single person say that my dancing was in any way effeminate, I would never dance again."

The *farruca* is the dance in which the man has the best opportunity to display his virtuosity and his virility. Sometimes it is danced by a man and a woman, but more often by a man alone—everyone remembers the marvelous *farruca* danced by the miller in Falla's *Three-cornered Hat*, in which Massine obtained such a tremendous triumph. Dressed in the tight-fitting trousers and the short jacket with open front (*chaquetilla*) that constitute the typical costume of the flamenco dancer, the man beats out his complex staccato rhythms at a furious speed, varying the dynamic range from soft to loud. In the *caída* (literally, "fall") he suddenly throws himself on the ground full length, but is up again in the same breath-taking moment, performing leaps and pirouettes—which from his stooping position becomes a mighty upward spiral movement—and in the midst of this furious activity, which yet is so rigidly controlled, he comes to a sudden pause. The effect of contrast is electrifying.

If the woman also takes part in the *farruca*, her work is entirely different (it is characteristic of flamenco dancing to emphasize this distinction between the work of the man and the woman). Her principal evolution in this dance is the *vuelta quebrada* (literally, "broken turn"), similar to the *renversé* of the ballet, which involves a complete turn of the body. The Spanish dancer performs this movement in a smooth, flowing manner, keeping the body low and horizontal. It forms a striking contrast with the vigorous, swirling action of the man.

The tango, a name which has become a household word through its universal adoption as a society dance via Argentina, is in Andalusia a solo dance for a woman (very exceptionally for a man) and has nothing in common, save certain rhythmical elements, with the dance as practiced elsewhere. For the Andalusian tango the woman wears a man's hat, the flat-brimmed *sombrero cordobés*, which she holds in her hands and manipulates during the frequent *taconeos* that occur in this thoroughly *gitano* dance. Allied to this, and also in 2/4 time, is the *garrotín*, likewise generally danced by a woman alone, in which the distinctive feature is the use of the hands, whose expressive fluttering seems to run the gamut of coquetry.

One of the most attractive of the flamenco dances, for a woman, is the *alegrías*, partly because of the stunning dress which is worn, with its frills and long train, usually in white trimmed with red.

The music is gay and exhilarating, and the dancer adds her rhythmic counterpoint of finger snapping and handclapping. The rhythmic complexity of the accompaniment for flamenco dancing is one of its most fascinating features. The guitar provides the basic rhythms, but there is a variety of cross rhythms supplied by the *zapateado*, the *pito*, and the *palmadas* of the dancer, and by the *jaleo* of the *cuadro flamenco*. It was this rhythmic complexity that so fascinated Chabrier during his visit to Spain (*cf.* Chapter XIX).

THE *JOTA* OF ARAGON

One has to go to the province of Aragon to find a dance that can compete in fame, though utterly different in character, with those of Andalusia. The *jota* is found in many regions of Spain but finds its most authentic manifestation in Aragon, a region inhabited largely by a hardy peasant stock which takes pride in their muscular agility and physical endurance. Danced by a couple, or by several couples, the *jota* expresses the perennial theme of courtship, but with the unsophisticated vigor of a rustic background. Its steps are rapid, strong, and energetic. The girl wears the full peasant skirt, and over the upper part of her body she wraps a large shawl; the figure is completely concealed. The man wears a waistcoat and black breeches laced at the knee, with a broad, bright-colored sash around his waist and a headdress of vivid hue. His stockings and shirt are white. For both, the footwear is the *alpargata*, cord-soled sandals tied on with black laces.

Speed, emphasized by abrupt pauses in which the dancers hold themselves immobile for a couple of measures, is the very essence of the *jota*. Strongly executed pirouettes and turns are frequent. Facing each other, with castanets held out at arm's length, the dancers swing outward first one leg and then the other. In one figure the girl sits on the ground playing her castanets while the man pirouettes around her. In another they kneel down on one knee opposite each other, and alternately bump the ground with left and right knee, keeping rhythmic count. In the kneeling position the attitude of the *bien parado* is imitated, with one arm held above the head, the other across the front of the body. The Kinneys [12] rightly declare that "in combination of strong movement, with speed and grace, there does not exist in the world a dance form to excel the *jota* of Aragon."

THE SARDANA

Utterly different is the typical dance of Aragon's southern neighbor, Catalonia. It involves no display of virtuosity, no spectacular action, but expresses the satisfaction of communal participation in a traditional pastime. The *sardana* is danced by large groups of men and women who hold hands in a circle and move first to the left and then to the right, at the same time executing certain fairly simple steps. Similar dances are found in Sardinia and in Bretagne (France). Circular dances seem to have been practiced from the earliest times; they were used by the Greeks, and the Greek geographer Strabo (66 B.C.–29 A.D.) wrote that Iberian men and women danced while holding hands. The precursor of the *sardana* was the *ball rodó* of the Middle Ages (*cf.* Chapter I), danced by men and women in the public square. This type of dance is depicted in one of the sculptured capitals of the cloister of the Monastery of Montserrat, dating from the fifteenth century. First written mention of the *sardana* (or *cerdana*) is found in the late sixteenth century. In the seventeenth century it figures prominently as an aristocratic dance, but eventually it was relegated to the populace, whence no doubt it had originally sprung. In its present form the *sardana* is a relatively recent development and its beginnings may be traced to definite individuals.

The father of the modern *sardana* was Josep ("Pep") Ventura (1817–1875), and it all began when he fell in love with the daughter of a popular musician of Figueras, who held that his prospective son-in-law should also be a musician. Up to that time Ventura had not learned a note of music, but now he applied himself assiduously to its study and soon qualified for member-

ship in the local *cobla* (group of musicians who play for the popular dances). He then went from one village to another throughout the countryside, collecting the popular dance tunes of the
sardana, whose musical form he expanded, creating the *sardana
llarga.* The innumerable *sardanas* that he composed upon this
popular foundation became the basic musical repertoire of the
dance, which was subsequently enriched by the compositions of
such musicians as Joan Carreras (1823–1900) and Enric Morera
(*cf.* Chapter XI). Pep Ventura also drastically altered the
make-up of the *cobla,* which he enlarged to comprise eight instruments.[13] An important member of the *cobla* is the musician
who plays the *fluviol* and the *tambori,* the former a diminutive
three-holed pipe, the latter a small drum attached to his elbow.
He not only announces the beginning of the dance, but also keeps
time with the unvarying beat of his drum taps.

On the choreographic side, the form of the modern *sardana*
was established by the dancer Miquel Pardas (1818–1872), who
in 1850 published his *Método per Apendre a Ballar Sardanas
Llargas.*

The musical structure of the *sardana* consists of two parts: the
first, of shorter duration, is generally of a sad and melancholy
character; the second, much longer, is usually gay and festive.
The steps danced during the first part are called *curts* ("shorts"),
those used in the second part, *llargs* ("longs"). Actually, the
steps of the second part are no longer than those of the first, but
in the "longs" twice as many steps are taken. The basic movement
of the *sardana* is simply two steps to the left followed by two to
the right. When the dance gets under way this is varied by
"pointing" the toes of each foot before the steps are taken. In
the "longs" the arms are raised to the level of the shoulder and
four steps instead of two are taken in either direction. The step
is essentially that of the old *contrepas.*

The dance is not particularly exciting, but it is not as easy as
it looks. The difficulty is more mental than physical, for it is
necessary to keep track of the exact number of measures in each

section of the music and to divide the steps in such a manner that each section will end with either two or four steps in the same direction; certain sections, moreover, must always end on the left foot and moving toward the left.

Usually many circles are formed for the *sardana*, men and women holding hands alternately. The circle may be very small to begin with, but new dancers may enter it at will. The *sardana* is danced by people in all stations of life, freely mixing in this truly democratic manifestation of the communal spirit. For the Catalans, the *sardana* is a symbol of their national unity. In the words of Enric Morera,[14] "the Sardana is a Dance, a Hymn, a Song; it is Catalonia."

BASQUE DANCES

There is an endless variety of dances in Spain, for each region, each village almost, has its own distinctive types, whose individuality is accentuated by the corresponding varieties of regional dress and ornament. We have described some of the most characteristic forms, since it is impossible to deal even in a summary manner with each one. Of the remaining regional dances, those of the Basque provinces deserve special mention.

The principal Basque dance is the *aurresku*, a composite communal dance which in its most complete modern form comprises eight sections: *entra, atzescu, zortzico, pasamano, desafío, fandango, arin-arin,* and *galop*. It is essentially a masculine dance, the women taking mostly a passive role. It takes its name from the leader, who is called the *aurresku* (*aurre* in Basque means "before"). The dancers form a line, holding hands, and advance continually forward. The *aurresku* and his opposite number at the other end of the line, the *atzescu*, display their skill in pirouettes and other steps, but without detaching themselves from the line. In the *desafío* (challenge) the line divides into two sections, facing each other, so that the *aurresku* stands opposite the *atzescu*. These try to outdo each other in skill and agility, gradually drawing nearer until they are about three yards apart. They then terminate the figure with a high leap. The *zortzico*, characterized by its irregular 5/8 rhythm, is somewhat similar to the English hornpipe. The Basque fandango is merely a variant of the Aragonese *jota*, but danced without castanets. The *arin-arin*, danced very rapidly, usually brings the *aurresku* to a close, the *galop* being only an occasional addition.

Among the many other varieties of Basque dances, we may mention the *ezpata-dantza*, or sword dance, in which one dancer represents a corpse and the others express a desire to avenge his death in their choreographic pantomime. It is recorded that during the celebration of Corpus Christi at San Sebastián in 1660, the *ezpata-dantza* was danced in the presence of King Philip IV by one hundred men. The Spaniards have always had recourse to the dance in the most solemn as well as in the gayest moments of life. One thinks in this connection of the *seises* (choirboys) of Seville Cathedral, who every year, during the octave of Corpus Christi, dressed in quaint costumes of the time of Carlos III (doublet and hose, plumed hats), dance before a special altar to the sound of their own castanets and the accompaniment of an orchestra. Again, compare the picture, reproduced by Curt Sachs in his *World History of the Dance*, which shows a Spanish peasant family dancing a slow and solemn version of the *jota* around the body of a dead child. Did not the medieval imagination picture the power of death in the form of a dance? Emblem of death, symbol of life—such is the universal scope of the dance in Spain.

El Jaleo, from the Painting by John Singer Sargent

Courtesy of the Isabella Stewart Gardner Museum, Boston

CHAPTER XVII

Hispanic Music in the Americas

A RETROSPECTIVE glance at the course of Spanish music reveals that its artistic apogee coincided with the discovery of America and the colonization of those lands in the Western Hemisphere that came under Hispanic domination. The secular vocal and instrumental music, the polyphonic music of the church, the musicotheoretical writings, and the union of traditional poetry and music in such popular forms as the *romance* and the villancico—all these attained their supreme development in that period. Seeking gold in their arduous expeditions, the conquistadores brought with them a more lasting treasure in the culture of Spain's "Golden Age."

Almost a hundred years before the founding of the first permanent colony in New England, the Spaniards had established schools in Mexico for the teaching of European music. The first of these was founded by Pedro de Gante at Texcoco in 1524, only three years after the capture of Mexico City by Cortés. Pedro de Gante, a native of Flanders, educated at Louvain University, was a Franciscan friar who came to Mexico in 1523. Texcoco, the city in which he established his school, was at that time the flourishing capital of a former Mexican kingdom. With the aid of twelve newly arrived Franciscan missionaries, this pioneer American music teacher proceeded to organize a method of musical instruction especially devised to acquaint the natives with European notation and technique. They began by teaching the Indians to copy music neatly and clearly, and after a year of this preliminary training the study of ecclesiastical chant was taken up. The primary purpose of the instruction, of course, was to train musicians for the service of the church, to whose liturgy music was an indispensable adjunct. Before long, Indian singers and instrumentalists were taking part in church services in virtually every village throughout the territory occupied by the Spaniards.

Pedro de Gante and his colleagues taught the natives not only to play European musical instruments, but also to construct them. A wide variety of wind instruments, as well as drums, guitars, and *vihuelas de arco* (played with a bow), were made by the natives under supervision of their teachers. This was, indeed, but one phase of the program whereby the Indians were taught many kinds of applied arts and skills. Moreover, those who showed special musical aptitude were encouraged to develop their creative ability by composing, usually four-part religious villancicos.

In 1527, Pedro de Gante settled in Mexico City, continuing his labors there with undiminished zeal until his death in 1572.

While religious music naturally received the greatest share of organized effort, secular music was by no means neglected. In 1526 a certain Ortiz, who had been among the companions of Cortés and who is described as *tocador de bihuela y que enseñaba a danzar* (a player of the guitar and a teacher of dancing), established a dancing school in Mexico City. It would be interesting to know where he recruited his pupils. Were the newly arrived soldiery anxious to add to their social accomplishments, or did the native chieftains yearn to master the intricacies of the chaconne and the sarabande? Music for the dances, at all events, would not be lacking, for violinists, flutists, and other instrumentalists were soon sent for from Spain. They were brought expressly, as an old document puts it, *para alegrar la población*—"to make the people merry."

The traditional ballads of Spain were introduced into the New World simultaneously with the arrival of the first soldiers and colonists. In the old chronicles we find numerous references to these *romances*, which, as we have pointed out (*cf.* Chapter II), were the common property of all classes. The chronicler Bernal Díaz del Castillo, in his *Conquista de Nueva España*, recounts that when Cortés was sailing along the coast of Mexico in 1519 those who were already familiar with the country kept on pointing out various landmarks to him, so that they were reminded of the old ballad which says:

> *Cata Francia, Montesinos,*
> *Cata Paris la ciudad,*
> *Cata las aguas del Duero*
> *Do van a dar a la mar.*[1]

And Cortés himself, thinking of the battle for conquest that lay ahead, quoted the words of the Carolingian ballad,

> *Dénos Dios ventura en armas*
> *Como al paladín Roldán.*[2]

THE FIRST MUSIC PRINTED IN AMERICA

The spread of European culture in New Spain ran parallel with the course of conquest and colonization. As early as 1539 a printing press was established in Mexico City and before long books containing music began to be issued from this press. This fact is all the more remarkable when we consider that even in Europe few printing houses were equipped with musical type at that time. The first American printed book containing music was an *Ordinarium*, that is, an Ordinary of the Mass, issued at Mexico City in 1556.[3] In all, seven books with music were printed in Mexico before 1600. The New England *Bay Psalm Book* was issued in 1640, but music was not added to it until the ninth edition, in 1698. Thus it may be seen to what extent we are indebted to Hispanic enterprise for the foundations of musical Americana.

One of the most interesting of the early music books printed in Mexico was the *Liber in quo quattuor passiones Christi Domini continentur*, which came from the press of Diego López Davalos in 1604.[4] It contains music for Holy Week, consisting of settings of the Passion, eight Lamentations, and a prayer from Jeremiah. This has been attributed to a celebrated Spanish church musician named Juan Navarro, a pupil of Fernández de Castilleja at Seville (*cf.* Chapter V) and choirmaster successively at Salamanca, Ciudad Rodrigo, and Palencia (where he died in 1580). But it was actually written by another musician of the same name, Fray Juan Navarro of Michoacán.[5] As far as is known, this is the only music book printed in Mexico during the seventeenth century. For some reason—perhaps the costliness of production due to the difficulties of obtaining materials — books with music began to be imported from Spain rather than manufactured in the colonies.

The yearly shipments of books from Spain contained numerous musical items. A list of shipments for the year 1586, for instance, includes music by Antonio de Cabezón, whose works had been published in Spain only eight years before this (*cf.* Chapter IV). An entry for the year 1605 consists of sixteen cases, each containing *Un libro de Canto de Guerrero con Las Vísperas de Todo el año*, that is, a book of music for the Vespers of the whole year written by the famous composer Francisco Guerrero. The music of the great Spanish religious composers was in use throughout the colonies and much of it has been preserved in the archives of churches and cathedrals throughout Latin America.

The extent of musical culture in New Spain may be gauged by a list of books found in the library of a Mexican architect, Melchor Pérez de Soto, in 1655. Owing to his unholy interest in the "black art" of astrology, this person had the misfortune of falling into the clutches of the Inquisition; but it is from this circumstance that we are able to ascertain the contents of his library, which included several of the most important musical books of that period, mostly theoretical.[6] Among these were Cerone's *El Melopeo y Maestro*, a treatise on plain song by Sebastián Vicente Villegas, Esteban Daza's *Libro de Música en Cifra para Vihuela* (*cf.* Chapter III), and the *Arte de Música Theórica y Práctica* by

Francisco de Montaños, a work containing many valuable examples of Spanish secular music, which first appeared at Valladolid in 1592 and went through numerous editions.

The aborigines of America, of course, had their own music before the arrival of the Spaniards. The early missionaries and chroniclers have left us several accounts of the musicality of the natives, who used music and dancing in all their religious and civic ceremonies and in their public and private festivities. But, precisely because so much of it was associated with religious cults that they regarded as heathenish, the Spaniards frowned upon the indigenous music of the Indians and sought rather to destroy than preserve it. The really efficient and in most ways admirable educational organization of the missions was enlisted for the task of gradually supplanting the native songs and dances with forms of European music derived for the most part from the liturgy of the church. A book that was instrumental in forwarding this process was the *Psalmodia Christiana,* a collection of Christian hymns and psalms translated into the Mexican language by Bernardino de Sahagún, which was printed at Mexico City in 1583. By enabling the Indians to sing these hymns in their own language, an important step was taken toward weaning them from their pagan cults, even though at first many of the natives persisted in singing the words to their own traditional tunes.

The two great radial centers of Spanish culture in the early colonial period were Mexico City in the north and Lima, the brilliant Peruvian capital, in the south. In these two cities, as to a lesser extent elsewhere, the musical art of Spain was duplicated in all its manifestations. The Spanish drama, which, as we know, was almost invariably associated with music, flourished with notable vigor at Lima during the sixteenth and seventeenth centuries. The plays of Calderón, especially, were held in high esteem there, his popularity enduring even longer than it did in Spain. Music for many of Calderón's plays was composed by José Díaz, who from 1663 was prominent as a dramatic composer at Lima. Sometimes plays were performed locally, with music by outstanding composers of the mother country, as was the case when the "harmonic comedy" *El Mejor Escudo de Perseo* (*The Best Shield of Perseus*), written by the viceroy, Marqués de Castell-dos-Ríus, was produced in 1708 with music by the maestros Durón and Torrejón (the latter resided at Lima for some time).

TANGO AND HABANERA

The lyric theater played an important part in disseminating Spanish music throughout Hispanic America.[7] In the second half of the eighteenth century the *tonadilla escénica* (*cf.* Chapter VIII) had its vogue, to be followed in the nineteenth (and twentieth also) by the popular zarzuela, which enjoyed a tremendous diffusion in the Spanish-American countries. The more successful zarzuelas were performed thousands of times and received with enthusiasm in all the principal cities. At Buenos Aires, for instance, Bretón's *La Verbena de la Paloma* was being given in five theaters simultaneously. Since the bulk of the music written for the zarzuelas consisted of arrangements of popular airs and dances from the various regions of Spain, the effect was to keep alive these traditional rhythms and tunes in the New World. Carlos Vega, the eminent authority on Argentine popular music, believes that the music of the Argentine tango (though not its choreography, which is purely a Creole development) reached Buenos Aires from Andalusia via the zarzuela, and he supports this view with a considerable weight of evidence.[8] The Spanish critic and music historian Adolfo Salazar, for the past few years a resident of Mexico, goes further and declares that "the tango of Cádiz, mixed with African and Cuban influences, appears to have engendered nearly the whole of South American music." [9]

The crux of this statement lies in the qualifying clause, which points to a reciprocal influence between the metropolitan and the colonial music. The 2/4 rhythm that forms the basic pattern of the tango, as of the habanera and the *milonga,* was not entirely a product of Creole influences, since it was known in Europe much earlier. An example of a composition with a similar rhythm may be found in the *Cancionero* published by Barbieri, dating from the end of the fifteenth century (*cf.* Chapter II).[10] When the habanera reached Spain from Cuba it had the novel attraction of something exotic, yet its roots undoubtedly sprang from Iberian soil. Paraphrasing what Rodney Gallop said about Mexican art, we may say that Latin-American music is not so much the product of Hispanic influence upon an indigenous foundation as of an indigenous influence upon a Hispanic foundation.

Why this is so should be clear from the background of Spanish colonization, with its strong element of religious proselytism and its vigorous musical infiltration. The music brought over by the Spaniards and Portuguese practically obliterated the indigenous music, and we have no guarantee that the latter has survived anywhere in its primitive form. To be sure, in certain regions where the descendants of the aboriginal population have continued to live more or less unmolested, as in parts of Peru, Bolivia, and Ecuador, the Indians continue to have their own music which reveals peculiarities, such as pentatonic scale forms, not common to Spanish music. But there are no actual musical documents dating from the pre-Columbian period, and, as Pereira Salas remarks,[11] a knowledge of Indian musical customs does not warrant an identification of the past with the present. Examples of indigenous melody that has not undergone some European influence are very rare in Latin America.

Just as the new environment, the new conditions of life, the various racial juxtapositions and admixtures modified and conditioned the social and psychological make-up of the Spanish colonists and their descendants in the New World, so these same factors modified and conditioned the musical forms brought over by the Spaniards. The question of what percentage of the music of any of the Latin-American countries is primarily of native origin and what percentage is primarily of European origin is largely academic, because, as Carlos Chávez [12] points out with regard to the music of Mexico, its qualities do not depend "on its proportion of Indian and Spanish ancestry, but on the existence of many new, local factors—historical, geographic, and ethnic circumstances which work directly on the artistic phenomenon." What is interesting is to observe the manner in which these local factors operate upon the foundation of Iberian music.

SPANISH-AMERICAN BALLADS

One may, for instance, take the case of the Spanish traditional ballads. For a long time the existence of Spanish ballads in the New World was not known, but the recent investigations of scholars in this field, such as Menéndez Pidal, Vicuña Cifuentes, Aurelio Espinosa, and Vicente Mendoza, have uncovered a wealth of interesting material. The work of the last-mentioned writer [13] is truly epoch-making in this connection, for he presents for the first time a detailed study of the popular Mexican ballad, the *corrido,* based on scientific methods of research and analysis, and traces its derivation from the traditional ballads of Spain. As Mendoza writes, "The Mexican *corrido,* a completely popular form . . . is an expression of the sensibility of our people, and its direct ancestor, both literary and musical, is the Spanish *romance.*" [14] The name *corrido* itself is of Spanish origin, for it was the name given to their traditional ballads by the peasants of Andalusia. Mendoza shows that many of the popular Mexican ballads are simply variants of those still sung in the Iberian Peninsula, which in turn are often modified versions of ballads that go back to very olden times. But whereas in Spain the ballad is found only exceptionally and chiefly as an archaic survival, in Mexico it was adopted as one of the principal manifestations of the popular muse, becoming a notable example of what we call "living folklore."

Not only did the Mexican *corrido* incorporate the basic melodic and metrical features of the Spanish *romance;* it also took over the fundamental generative element of the latter, namely, the narration of memorable or unusual events taken from the contemporary scene. Just as the old Spanish ballad makers sang about the exploits of the Cid, and later ones about the taking of Granada, so the Mexican ballad makers sing about episodes of their revolutions, about the fate of some notorious bandit, or the devastation wrought by some great flood. The advent of new inventions is also celebrated in the *corridos:* the opening of the first railroad, the coming of electricity, etc. As a matter of fact, the ballads may deal with everything under the sun—and they usually do.

On the musical side, Mendoza finds that the Mexican ballad is influenced above all by the Andalusian *corrido,* whence the prevalence of ternary rhythms: 3/8, 6/8, and 9/8. There is a considerable amount of syncopation, another Spanish characteristic. In the Mexican ballads the major mode is more prevalent than in those of Spain, but there are nevertheless vestiges of the old liturgical modes in their melodic structure. In general, the *corrido* of Mexico preserves the octosyllabic verse of the Spanish *romance,* in which case the melodic phrase consists of thirty-two basic notes (corresponding to the number of syllables in the quatrain), with four principal accents. There are, however, numerous metrical variants, such as the *corrido* with recurrent refrain (*estribillo*).

As in Spain, the popular instrument par excellence in Mexico and in most of the other Latin-American countries is the guitar,[15] which is generally used to accompany the singing of *corridos* (the harmonization seldom departs from the tonic, dominant, and subdominant chords). The harp is also frequently used. In Jalisco the ballads are often accompanied by the instrumental ensemble known as *mariachi,* comprising violins, harps, *jaranas,* and large and small guitars. They may be sung by one or several voices, and very often the singing is in thirds. Mendoza classifies the *corrido* in thirty-three different types, according to metrical and melodic structure, indicating that it has more variety than is generally supposed. Both because of its ancient traditional roots and its continued vitality, the *corrido* is one of the most significant popular forms upon which the Mexican composer—or American composers on the whole, for that matter—can draw for creative inspiration. Interesting examples of its use by a first-rate Mexican composer may be seen in some of the compositions of Silvestre Revueltas.[16]

CREOLE SONGS AND DANCES

In Chile there are also numerous examples of traditional Spanish ballads, but their musical aspect remains yet to be studied. Spanish ballads in Argentina have been studied by Juan Carrizo. Further investigation would doubtless uncover other specimens in the various South American countries. Thanks to the recent publication of Eugenio Pereira Salas dealing with the origins of musical art in Chile, we are able to trace in considerable detail the Hispanic roots of the popular music of that country. This authority points out that the indigenous music went on its own way, running parallel to the Creole or Spanish-American musical development, but not blending with the latter. And he concludes that "the historical origin of the popular music of Chile must be sought in the successive waves of [Spanish] peninsular influence, transformed by the Creole temperament." [17] The same is true with regard to the music of Peru and Argentina. At this point it might be well to mention that what is meant by the term "Creole music" as used by South Americans is the music of peninsular origin modified by the American milieu. This transformation began to take place in the seventeenth century, and simultaneously the Creole style began to make its influence felt in Spanish peninsular music. Songs and dances with exotic names, such as *La Gayumba, El Cachupino, El Zambápalo,* and with the Spanish rhythms curiously altered, began to appear in Spain. In the eighteenth century these exotic songs and dances made their way into the theatrical tonadillas, contributing in no small measure to the piquancy of these miniature comic operas. Here is a tune showing Creole influence that achieved popularity via the tonadilla:

Example 41 Zarandillo.

The relation between Spanish peninsular and colonial music, then, is that of a mutual give-and-take, though Spain naturally gave more than she took.

The Spanish dances that were most widespread in Chile, Peru, and Argentina during the colonial period were the bolero, the fandango, the seguidilla, the *tirana*, and the *zapateo*. In Chile the seguidilla was known as *sirilla*, and it has been maintained by tradition up to the present day. Upon the basis of these dances most of the traditional choreography of these countries has been formed. It is interesting to note that in the collection of *yaravies*, *cáchuas*, *lauchas*, and other Peruvian native dances collected by Jiménez de la Espada [18] in the eighteen eighties, there are traces of Spanish dance forms such as the *jota* and the *sevillanas*. The *zamacueca*, the national dance of Chile, originated in Peru, but its remoter antecedents are still in the realm of conjecture. Friedenthal upholds its Hispanic origin, considering it a variant of the fandango.[19]

Of course, not all the dances of Latin America are of Iberian origin. The *cuando* of Argentina, for instance, seems to be simply a variant of the gavotte, and other European society dances have exerted their influence upon the popular dances of the Latin-American countries. In general, all the dances have been considerably modified in their choreographic aspect, as is the case with the tango, which acquired an entirely indigenous choreography in Argentina. The castanets are rarely used in Spanish America, but in many of the folk dances, such as the *pericón* and the *zamacueca*, the dancers manipulate in one hand a handkerchief, which plays an expressive role in the choreographic pantomime.

Returning to Mexico, we find that the *sones*, the tunes played for the popular dance festivals known as *huapangos*, show definite traces of Spanish derivation, going back probably to the early colonial period. They have, too, the same rhythmic complexity that we observed in the Andalusian songs and dances (different rhythms rapidly alternating or appearing simultaneously). The most popular of all Mexican dances, the *jarabe*, had its origin in traditional Spanish dance forms such as the seguidilla and the fandango, incorporating the typically Andalusian element of the *zapateado* (*cf.* Chapter XV). The *jarabe* is made up of a succession of movements ranging in tempo from adagio to presto. It is generally in triple time, and the fast movements bear a marked resemblance to the music of the Spanish *jota*. The characteristic costume for the woman in dancing the *jarabe* is the so-called *vestido de china,* in which red and green predominate in the dress, with black and gold ornaments. Very probably this is imitated from the costume of the Andalusian women.

Usually the Creole versions of the peninsular songs and dances acquire new local names, but throughout Latin America there exist many popular musical forms that retain the original Spanish names while incorporating new musical or choreographic elements. Such is the case, for example, with the *malagueña* of Mexico and the bolero of Cuba. Under Cuban influence the original 3/4 time of the bolero is transformed into 2/4, the representative rhythm of Cuban popular music, and acquires the typical syncopations and offbeat accents of that music. In Cuban folk melody the Spanish strain is predominant. Writes Emilio Grenet: [20] "There is no doubt that the Cuban peasant's song is an echo of Spain." More specifically, the rural folk song of Cuba reveals an analogy with the popular music of Andalusia, especially as regards the cadence on the dominant, always found in the Cuban *guajiras* and *puntos*. Regarding the *zapateo,* the typical dance of the Cuban peasants, Grenet writes: [21]

The dance is executed by two couples, man and woman facing each other some distance apart, marking the fluent rhythm with the feet and keeping the body motionless. The heel-strikes on the floor, the short steps of the dancers and the general rhythm of the gestures which accent the dance could not be more eloquent as regards the origin of this dance. In its entirety it is a variation of the choreographic expression of Andalusia.

One of the most famous of all Cuban lyrical forms is the habanera, in the rhythm of which Sebastián Yradier wrote his universally known song *La Paloma*. Its rhythm is analogous to that of the tango; but composers imbued with genuinely Cuban lyrical feeling have composed excellent habaneras without slavish reliance on this rhythmic formula; a case in point is that of the *Cubana* by Eduardo Sánchez de Fuentes.

Much stress has been laid lately upon the Negro element in Cuban music. The Negro influence manifests itself above all rhythmically. The basic melodic elements in so-called Afro-Cuban music seem to be of Hispanic origin, or at least influenced by Hispanic melody, as indicated by certain modal traits. The now-celebrated conga and rumba are the popular forms that reveal the most marked Negro influence. Some of the leading modern composers of Cuba, among them Amadeo Roldán and Alejandro García Caturla, have drawn heavily upon Afro-Cuban music in their works. Throughout the nineteenth century, however, Spanish influence predominated in the art music of Cuba.

SOME BRAZILIAN TYPES

With regard to Brazil, the same general observations that we have made about the rest of Latin America are applicable, save that the point of reference is not Spain but Portugal. The prevailing mood of Brazilian music, like that of Portugal, is melancholy, full of that quality designated by the term *saudade* (*cf.* Chapter XV). This naturally melancholic tendency of Portuguese lyricism was intensified by the conditions the colonists had to face in this immense, untamed country, with its wild jungles and manifold dangers. In the midst of this strange and hostile environment the songs of the settler tended to assume a brooding, tragic undertone, imbued with indefinable longing. The typical lyrical manifestation of Brazil, the *modinha*, probably had its remote antecedents in the ancient Portuguese-Galician lyric of the troubadours, but it came to be the veritable expression of the Brazilian soul. Its general mood is sentimental and full of feeling, the melody being usually in the minor and divided into two sections, the first slow and expressive, the second more animated. In the nineteenth century the *modinha* was taken up by the cultivated composers of Brazil and invaded all the *salons* of the country. Its spirit still pervades the music of more modern composers, including that of Heitor Villa-Lobos.[22]

The Negro element seems predominant in many of the popular dances of Brazil, such as the *samba* and the *lundú*, a modern variant of the latter being the *maxixe*. Some confusion has been caused by the fact that in the south of Brazil the *samba* was known by the name of fandango; the rhythm of the *samba* is binary, not ternary like that of the Spanish fandango. However, the fandango and other Spanish dances were undoubtedly practiced in Brazil in early colonial times. It is curious to observe how certain features of the Catholic religious processions, imported from the peninsula, were blended with voodooistic ceremonies brought by slaves from Africa in the Brazilian *congadas*, processions with dancing, singing, and acting traditionally practiced by the Negroes in Brazil. It is equally interesting to note that European influence is apparent in most of the music associated with the *congadas* or *congos*.[23]

HISPANIC MUSIC IN THE UNITED STATES

Within our own borders there are numerous living traces of Hispanic civilization on this continent. One has only to remember that the entire territory now occupied by the states of Louisiana, Texas, New Mexico, Arizona, and California was formerly a Spanish possession and remained so for several centuries. One of the principal investigators in this field, Arthur Campa, writes:

No other group in the United States is more given to singing, with the possible exception of the Southern Negro, than the Spanish population of the Southwest. They have today a threefold repertoire comprising the traditional ballads brought over by the Conquerors; the *décima* so popular in the 19th century; and the diversified *canción* that in the last fifty years has found its way uɒ from Mexico.[24]

The *décima* mentioned by Campa is one of the variants of the popular ballad, based on a poetic form that began to be cultivated in Spain in the sixteenth century. It was widely diffused in Spanish America, especially in Mexico, Puerto Rico, Chile, and Peru. The *décima* derives its name from the fact that it is made up of ten-line stanzas, preceded by an introductory strophe of four lines. It employs the traditional Spanish octosyllabic verse and is similar in spirit to the old ballads, but deals with a wider variety of subjects and lays less stress on narrative.

Essentially sentimental is the *canción*, the popular Spanish song of the Southwest, closely allied to the Mexican *canción*. These songs have more melodic interest than the *corridos* and *décimas* and they almost invariably treat of love, often of sad and unrequited love. Manuel Ponce divides them into three types: those which have a slow and ample melody; those in rapid tempo; and those in ternary rhythm and moderate tempo.

Children's singing games, Christmas songs (*posadas*), religious songs of praise (*alabados*), and songs of the *vaqueros* (cowboys) are among other types of Spanish music found in the Southwest.

One of the most interesting Hispanic survivals in the Southwest is the religious play with music, which harks back to the Spanish *autos* of the sixteenth century, these being in turn a continuation of the medieval mystery. These plays are divided into two cycles, the first treating of subjects taken from the Old Testament and the second centering around the life of Christ. Among the former is the so-called *Comedia de Adán y Eva*, which had its prototype in one of the first plays to be performed in the New World, an *auto* depicting the life of Adam and Eve presented at Mexico City in 1532.[25] Plays in the second cycle seem to be more popular, and among these the best known is the Christmas play *Los Pastores* (*The Shepherds*) in which the story of the Nativity is enacted.

Of course, we have no exact data about the origin of these plays, whose text and music have been handed down by oral tradition. The text employs traditional Spanish verse meters such as the *romance* and the *décima,* the versions varying considerably in different localities. It may safely be assumed that they are at least to some extent survivals of the religious *autos* introduced by the early Spanish missionaries, and their preservation in the midst of an environment so alien to the primitive Christian spirit that gave birth to the old miracle plays is one further proof of the tenacity with which Hispanic peoples cling to their ancient customs.

Given annually in some communities, at irregular intervals in others, *Los Pastores* is usually enacted against the background of a *Nacimiento,* a decorated altar with figures representing the Nativity. It begins with the singing of a villancico by a chorus of shepherds off stage, and the action thereafter is interspersed with songs. The melodies are simple and flowing and may readily be associated with the traditional Spanish villancicos.[26] Many of the actors wear their ordinary clothes, with the addition of some ornaments for the occasion. Masks are worn only by the Hermit and the Devils, who represent the grotesque element in the play. The performance takes place out of doors.

Iberian folk music within the United States has been kept alive by Spanish and Portuguese communities in various parts of the country. In several New England towns, for instance, and at Provincetown, Cape Cod, in particular, there are colonies of Portuguese immigrants who have preserved many of their traditional songs. In the state of Idaho there is a Basque colony among whom the highly characteristic songs and dances of the Basque provinces may still be heard and seen.[27]

The Corrido *Singer, Mural Painting by Diego Rivera*

CHAPTER XVIII

The Music of Portugal *

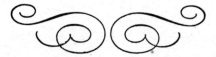

THE early music of Portugal is closely linked with that of the rest of the Iberian Peninsula, and even in later periods there was free exchange of musicians between Spain and Portugal, especially during the sixty years from 1580 to 1640 when Portugal was under the rule of the Castilian kings, Philip II, III, and IV.

The history of music in Portugal may be divided into the following periods: (1) Period of the Troubadours, (2) Period of primitive Renaissance, (3) Period of the domination of church music, (4) Period of Italian influence, (5) Period of French and German influence, and (6) Contemporary period—the Portuguese renascence in music.

The works of the Portuguese troubadours are found, for the most part, in three collections, called *Cancioneiros*: the *Cancioneiro da Ajuda,* also known as *Cancioneiro do Colégio dos Nobres,* in the library of the palace of Ajuda in Lisbon; the *Cancioneiro da Vaticana,* in the Vatican Library in Rome; and the *Cancioneiro Colocci-Brancuti* (now in the National Library at Lisbon), discovered in the library of Count Brancuti and copied for the Italian philologist Colocci in the sixteenth century. Unfortunately, as was the case with many other such collections of the time, we have only the verbal poetry of these troubadours, the music usually

* By Albert T. Luper.

not having been recorded. There is, however, a *Canção do Figueiral*, or "Song of the Fig Orchard," sometimes attributed to the early troubadour Goesto Ansunes, who lived in the twelfth century, and written down in the fifteenth century from oral tradition.

Example 42.

No fi- guei-ral fi-guei-re - do, Lá no fi- guei-ral en-trei, seis ni-ñas en-con-tra-va, seis ni-ñas en-con-trei; pa-ra el — — las an-dá-ra, pa-ra el — — las an-dei, llo-ran-do las a-chá-ra, llo-ran-do las a-chei; ló-go las pes-cu-dá-ra, ló-go las pes-cu-dei, quem las mal-tra-tá ra, ya tan ma-la ley. No fi-guei-ral fi-guei re - do, lá no fi - guei-ral en - trei.

Among the most celebrated Portuguese troubadours were Abril Perez (d. 1245, the author of a *Jocz enamoratz* included in the Vatican collection); Pai Soares de Taveiros (several works in the Vatican and Ajuda collections); Martim Soares (of whom the Colocci-Brancuti collection said that he . . . *trobou melhor ca todos que trobarom e assi foy julgado antr'os outros trobadores*); Afonso Lopes Bayam (works in the *Cancioneiro da Vaticana*); and later the king, D. Diniz, who was educated by the troubadour Aymeric d'Ebrard of Provence.

The role of this king, D. Diniz (d. 1325), in the early development of literature and the arts in Portugal is most significant. He was the first peaceful monarch, his predecessors having concerned themselves mostly with the wars which were necessary in the establishment of the kingdom. Under his tutelage the poetic courtiers developed the Portuguese dialect into a "beautiful and flexible literary language." Diniz also founded the

University of Coimbra (first located at Lisbon) in the year 1290, establishing a chair of music there later.

Besides the troubadours, there appeared in Portugal the *jograis* (Portuguese term for *jongleur*), of which there were three types: *jograis de penola*, for stringed instruments; *jograis de boca*, for wind instruments; and *jograis dos atambores*, for percussion instruments. The instruments most commonly used by the Portuguese troubadours were, as may be seen in illuminations of the *Cancioneiro da Ajuda*, the psaltery (a triangular-shaped plucked instrument with thirteen strings), the viola d'arco (a bowed string instrument), the viola (a member of the guitar family), the harp, castanets, and the tambourin.

THE PRIMITIVE RENAISSANCE

The period of the primitive Renaissance in music in Europe had its counterpart in Portugal. The style of composition for voices with instrumental accompaniment which sprang up in the fourteenth and fifteenth centuries in Italy, France, Flanders, England, and the Iberian Peninsula was a direct outgrowth of the troubadour movement in those countries.

Afonso V, who was interested in furthering the betterment of music in his realm, in 1439 sent musicians to London to get materials for the musical reform of his chapel. The first important Portuguese composer in the accompanied vocal style, Tristão da Silva, was charged by Afonso V with the assemblying of the king's favorite compositions into a volume entitled *Los amables de la musica*, which unfortunately has not survived until our time. Other outstanding Portuguese composers in this style were André de Resende, a great Portuguese antiquarian; Jorge de Montemór (or Monte Mayor), author of the pastoral romance *Diana enamorada*, and important in the literary history of Spain; Gonçalo de Baena, a minstrel of King John III, whose only remaining works are four fragments written in three voices; Damião de Goes (1501–1553), the chronicler, traveler, diplomat, scholar, and musician, of whom we still have three motets: *Ne laeteris* and *In die tribulationis* in three voices, and *Surge propera* in five parts; and, finally, Gil Vicente, the founder of the Portuguese (and to a large extent the Spanish) theater, who, being a musician and composer, interposed *vilancicos* and other musical pieces between the various parts of his *autos* and comedies (*cf.* Chapter VI).

The *vilancico* (in Spanish *villancico*), the peninsular form of the madrigal, was greatly cultivated. Damião de Goes, mentioned above, makes allusions to the vocal and instrumental polyphony of the period. Among the musicians in the service of King John III was João de Badajoz, eight of whose compositions in three and four parts are included in Barbieri's *Cancionero Musical de los Siglos XV y XVI*. The Spanish composer Luis Milán dedicated his celebrated *Libro de vihuela* . . . to the same King John III, as did Fray Juan Bermudo with his *Libro primo de la declaración de instrumentos musicales*.

The cultivation of instrumental music, particularly guitar (*viola* or *vihuela*) music, attained to a high state during this period, beginning with the Royal Prince D. Pedro in the fifteenth century and extending to the time of the Castilian ascendancy in the sixteenth and seventeenth centuries. The most famous Portuguese guitarist was the Franciscan friar Peixoto da Pena, who lived in the early part of the sixteenth century. The favorite forms for instrumental writing during this period were the *glosas* or *diferenças*, the original variation form. Variations were written on the *folía*, considered by many recent authorities as having its origin in Portugal despite the fact that it has been known the world over for centuries as *Folies d'Espagne*; on the *chacona*, which may well have been the successor to the medieval Portuguese dance *chacota*; and on the *vilão*, another medieval dance found in both Spain and Portugal.

As we leave this period mention should be made of a bloodless victory of Portugal over Italy. Vicente Lusitano, a Portuguese musician and theorist living in Rome in the sixteenth century, had an argument with the celebrated Italian musician Nicola Vicentino over whether anyone knew in what genus he wrote: whether in the diatonic, the chromatic, or the enharmonic. After long discussion, substantiated by entire treatises written by each of the disputants, the Portuguese was awarded the victory by a jury of musicians from the papal chapel.

THE GOLDEN AGE OF PORTUGUESE MUSIC

We come now to the golden period in Portuguese music—". . . to the marvelous contrapuntists of the school of Évora, who made of the capital of the Alemtejo—the powerful center of irradiation of the plastic arts—an equal, if not superior, center of musical culture." [1]

There were six great contrapuntists in this school, and many minor ones. The first one of the six, chronologically, is Manuel Mendes, who was born in Évora in the first half of the sixteenth century, dying there in 1605. His style is marked by a simplicity and purity which is severe and constructive rather than expressive. None of his works was published but many exist in codices in the libraries of Lisbon and Évora.

The next in order is Duarte Lobo,[2] probably the greatest Portuguese musician. He was born about 1565, studied in Évora under Manuel Mendes, going later to Lisbon, where he labored as teacher and choirmaster in the Royal Hospital and in the Cathedral. Many of his works were published by the celebrated Plantin house in Antwerp, and in Lisbon by Pedro Craesbeck, a former apprentice of Plantin. These works may be found in widely separated places, such as the libraries and archives at Lisbon, Évora, Valladolid, Munich, Vienna, London, Cambridge, and, as this writer has recently discovered, in the Cathedral Archives in Mexico City. In addition to his published works, several Masses and motets of this composer exist in manuscript. Although in his early works there may have been an element of calculating intellectuality, Lobo's mature compositions show that his technical equipment was not made an end in itself, but rather became a tool or medium of expression. In their intensity of feeling and modernity of expression, his compositions rival those of Victoria in Spain and Palestrina in Italy. Lobo died in 1643, having turned out many works and trained many students, among whom were outstanding Portuguese theorists and composers.

Second in importance to Duarte Lobo in the Portuguese poly-phonic school was the barefoot Carmelite monk Frei Manuel Cardoso (1569–1650), who likewise studied with Manuel Mendes at Évora. The high esteem in which Cardoso was held may be seen by the fact that when he visited Spain King Philip IV, to whom Cardoso dedicated a Mass, publicly honored him and made him Master of his Chapel. Cardoso was also highly considered by King John IV of Portugal, who honored him by placing his portrait in first place in the Royal Library of Music. Cardoso was prolific in composition, leaving a large body of religious works, some of which were published by Lourenço Craes-beck in Lisbon. Four packages of his manuscripts were discovered by the German musicologist Eitner in the Library of Louvain, but these were unfortunately destroyed in the war of 1914. The music of this composer, particularly in the Mass dedicated to the Spanish sovereign, shows a great technical equipment and an ability to make use of every contrapuntal device. Lambertini states that he is perhaps the first well-known Portuguese com-poser who consciously let himself be influenced by the style of Palestrina.

Felipe de Magalhães, the fourth in this group of composers, was born near Lisbon toward the end of the sixteenth century, and therefore did most of his work in the seventeenth century. He studied in Évora with Manuel Mendes, after which he taught and composed in Lisbon, leaving many students and musical works, some of the latter published in Lisbon and Antwerp, others still in manuscript. Magalhães was honored by Philip II of Spain with several important musical posts in Portugal, in-cluding that of choirmaster of the Royal Chapel in Lisbon.

The fifth composer in this group, João Soares Rebello (or João Lourenço Rebello, 1610–1661), was born in the north of

Portugal and was a fellow student of the future King John IV at the Ducal palace at Vila Viçosa. John IV honored Rebello in many ways, dedicating a book to him, bestowing on him a title, and making him the choirmaster of the Ducal and Royal Chapels. Rebello wrote for both small and large numbers of voices, including one composition in thirty-nine voices written for the occasion of the king's thirty-ninth birthday.

The last of the great Portuguese polyphonists was Diogo Dias de Melgaço (or Melgaz, 1638–1700). Melgaço studied at Évora, later became choirmaster of the cathedral of that city and rector of the seminary. His compositions were left in manuscript in Lisbon and Évora, many of them having disappeared by now. Ernesto Vieira tells us that he owned several motets by Melgaço which were magnificent specimens of the style of the epoch, but which showed also "a notable progress in the feeling of modern tonality." [3]

A ROYAL MUSIC LOVER

We have already made mention several times of King John IV (1604–1656). His importance in music, not only in Portugal but also internationally, is such that we must take further notice of him and of his work. He has been much neglected by modern musicologists, who forget that he is the author of one of the oldest books of musical criticism, the *Defensa de la Musica Moderna*, published in Spanish and in Italian, in which he answered Bishop Cirilo Franco, and with great erudition makes a good case for the *a capella* style. He also wrote a pamphlet about the Mass *Panis quem ego dabo* of Palestrina, answering the doubts cast on it by some of the technicians in Rome. Two other didactic works are attributed to him, one a musical concordance, the other a book of rudiments of music. His compositions include both large and small works for church use, of which only two are known to exist today: the motet *Adjuva nos Deus*, sung often in the Lisbon Cathedral during Lent, and a *Crux Fidelis*, in four voices. John IV's greatest contribution to the annals of music is, however, in the field of musical bibliography and library science, for he organized the most complete musical library we know of up to that time and had its Catalogue printed, of which there exist only two copies of Part I, one in Paris, the other in Lisbon. The Portuguese musicologist Joaquim de Vasconcellos republished this first part of the Catalogue in 1874, and it is frequently consulted by music scholars the world over. Unfortunately, this wonderfully rich library was lost to posterity in the famous earthquake and fire of 1755.[4]

In addition to the two centers of contrapuntal music teaching mentioned above, Évora and Vila-Viçosa, both in the southeastern section of the country, there was another important school at Coimbra, the university city, which was unknown until recent years. This school was located at the Monastery of Santa Cruz, and the names of most of the composers here are unknown. However, a large group of manuscripts of these anonymous writers has been discovered in the archives of this monastery, which are now incorporated into the library of the University of Coimbra. Some of this music has been published in a recent edition of works of Portuguese classical composers.[5]

The *vilancico* form (madrigal) was also greatly cultivated by many musicians during this period. At first the *vilancico* was closely allied to the services of the church, being sung more usually at matins, but gradually it became secularized and its employment was so abused that it was prohibited from church use by King John V in 1723. The outstanding Portuguese madrigalists were the Carmelite monk Frei Francisco de Santiago, choirmaster in Seville, where he died in 1646, and who had, among other works, 538 *vilancicos* listed in the Catalogue of John IV; Gabriel Dias (or Dias Besson), in 1624 choirmaster of the Incarnation Convent in Madrid, one of his motets having been highly praised by Lope de Vega; and Marqués Lésbio (1639–1709), a poet-composer born in Lisbon.

ORGANISTS AND THEORISTS

Contemporary with the great school of vocal counterpoint in Portugal was a group of organists who composed a large quantity of keyboard music, and who until recent years have been equally neglected with the composers of vocal music. The most important composer in this group was the priest Manuel Rodrigues Coelho, born in 1583 in Elvas near the Spanish border, where he was church organist, becoming organist in 1603 in the Lisbon Cathedral, and later in the Royal Chapel. Coelho was the author of the oldest Portuguese published work of instrumental music, the *Flores de Musica*, a collection of *tentos* (*ricercari* or preludes) for organ, clavichord, or harp, printed by Craesbeck in Lisbon in 1620. This admirable work should place its author in the front rank of the important group of predecessors of Bach, and should list him alongside such men as Frescobaldi in Italy, Sweelinck in Holland, and Scheidt in Germany. Other prominent composers of keyboard music were Gregório Silvestre de Mesa (1526–1570), organist at the Cathedral in Granada and author of a book of tablature for the organ entitled *Arte de escrever para cifra*; Diogo de Alvarado (d. 1643), co-organist with Coelho at the Royal Chapel; and Francisco Correia de Araújo, famous organist at the church of S. Salvador in Seville (*cf.* Chapter IV).

In connection with this instrumental music it would be well to mention the oldest method for the violin, the *Lyra de Arco ou Arte de tanger rabeca* by Agostinho da Cruz, published in Lisbon in 1639. The only known example of this book was in the National Library at Madrid.

In the province of music theory in this period these two names stand out: João Álvares Frovo (1608–1682) and António Fernandes (15–?–16–?), both of whom were pupils of Duarte Lobo. Frovo, who was librarian and chaplain to John IV, was the author of the treatise *Discursos sobre a perfeição do Diathesaron* (Lisbon, 1662). Fernandes, considered by many of his compatriots as one of the most eminent figures in Portuguese music, wrote several treatises on music. The only one in existence, dedicated to Duarte Lobo, bears the following title: *Arte de Musica de canto dorgam, e canto cham, e Proporçoes de Musica divididas harmonicamente* (Lisbon, 1626). This work, while not highly original, was the first of its kind in the Portuguese language, and as such was a pioneer in leading the way for later writers in Portugal. It summarizes and classifies some of the material presented in the writings of the Italian theorist Zarlino, thereby providing one small link between Zarlino and the revolutionary theories of Rameau.

The next important revival of the arts in Portugal was initiated by King John V, who ascended to the throne in 1706. He was zealous in bringing some of the best Italian musicians to his court to practice their art and to teach, while on the other hand he sent promising young artists to Italy to study, paying for their expenses from his own purse.

The most notable of the Italians to come to Portugal was Domenico Scarlatti, who graced the court from 1721 to 1729 as Master of the Royal Chapel and as teacher of the Infanta Dona Barbara (*cf.* Chapter VII). Scarlatti's influence on the growth of Portuguese music at this time, as a teacher and model of excellence, must have been considerable, particularly so since he helped to guide it in the direction of the Neapolitan school which exerted such a long dominion in the country.

The most notable Portuguese harpsichordist was José António Carlos de Seixas (1709–1742), sometimes called the "Portuguese Scarlatti." Despite his short life he made his name famous in Portugal both as performer and composer, and wrote hundreds of toccatas and sonatas, employing the form of two subjects in contrasting keys, as did Scarlatti.

Of the pensionists sent to Italy by John V one deserves special mention: Francisco António de Almeida, author of the first-known opera by a Portuguese composer, *La Pazienza di Socrate,* performed in Lisbon in 1733. In this same year the first-known opera in the Portuguese language, sung by Portuguese artists, was produced. It was *Vida do grande D. Quixote de la Mancha*, written by António José da Silva, known as "the Jew."

THE GREATEST PORTUGUESE OPERA COMPOSER

John V's successor on the throne, D. José, although not as intensely the lover of music as were several of his predecessors in the Braganza dynasty, continued the policy of encouraging musical activity, particularly in the operatic field. As evidence of the splendor of the court and of the operatic productions of this time is the testimony of the famous English traveler and musician, Dr. Burney, who stated of the magnificent Teatro da Ribeira opened on April 2, 1755, that it ". . . surpassed in magnitude and decorations all that modern times can boast." This from a man who had had the opportunity to view and hear the best that other European countries had to offer. Unfortunately, this sumptuous structure was reduced to ruins only seven months later in that terrible catastrophe which destroyed so much of the rich cultural heritage of Portugal, the earthquake of November 1, 1755.

D. José likewise continued the policy of sending pensionists to Italy for their advanced musical studies. The most productive composer of this group was João de Sousa Carvalho (1709–1798), important not only for his writings but also, and even more, for his success as a teacher. Two of his students became outstanding musicians of their time, exerting their efforts in opposite directions. They were Marcos António Portugal, the greatest Portuguese opera composer, and João Domingos Bomtempo, pianist and composer, the founder and first director of the National Conservatory of Music.

Marcos Portugal (1762–1830) began his studies in the Seminário Patriarcal at Lisbon, and produced his first dramatic work, a farce entitled *A casa de pasto*, in 1784. In 1792 he went to Italy, where, under the influence of the Neapolitan school, he produced twenty-one operas in the principal theaters. In 1800 he returned to Lisbon to become director of the São Carlos Theater and Master of the King's Chapel. Portugal followed the Royal Family and the court to Brazil in 1810 (where they had gone in 1808 to flee the invading army of Napoleon), remaining there until his death in 1830. His remains were returned to Lisbon in 1928 and were buried in the crypt of the church of Santa Isabel in 1931. His compositions, including thirty-five Italian operas, twenty-one Portuguese comic operas (mainly in one act), and over one hundred pieces of church music, were known in many parts of Europe (including Italy, London, and St. Petersburg) and in Brazil. Whereas his work was typical of much of the writing of the times and contained many trivialities, it was better than that of his Portuguese contemporaries who wrote in the same style, and it undoubtedly influenced the development of Portuguese lyric art.

PORTUGAL'S FIRST SYMPHONIST

In contrast to Marcos Portugal and other composers of the Italian style was João Domingos Bomtempo (1775–1842), the founder of modern music in Portugal and Portugal's first symphonist. After a period of study at the Seminário Patriarcal (piano and composition) and with his father (oboe) he spent several years in Paris and London where he obtained great success as a pianist and composer. His works, based on the style of Haydn and Mozart, include symphonies, sonatas and concertos for piano, several Masses, including his greatest work, a *Requiem to the memory of Camões* (the great sixteenth-century poet and author of the epic poem *Os Lusíadas*), chamber music, and the *Variaçóes sobre o Fandango* for the piano. His pedagogical works include a method for piano, a treatise on harmony and counterpoint, and a treatise on composition. Bomtempo's importance is further attested by his creation of the first Portuguese symphony orchestra, the Sociedade Filarmónica, in 1822, with which he performed works of Haydn, Mozart, and Beethoven, and by his founding in 1835 the Conservatório Nacional de Música, which completely transformed the teaching of music in Portugal.

Although the Italian influence in Portuguese music, represented by Xavier Migone (1811–1861), Joaquim Casimiro (1808–1862), Francisco Sá de Noronha (1820–1881), and the Viscount of Arneiro (1838–1903), lasted until near the end of the nineteenth century, Portuguese dramatic music began to throw off the yoke of slavery to Italian standards and turned to a more progressive animating spirit. Leaders in this movement were Augusto Machado (1845–1924), trained under Dannhauser and Lavignac in Paris, who broke with the old traditions in his operas, and who, as director of the Conservatório, exerted a profound influence on musical pedagogy in Portugal; and Alfredo Keil (1850–1907), the composer of the Portuguese National Anthem, *A Portugueza,* who in his first opera set an ideal of musical nationalism from which he never strayed. Keil is further distinguished as the composer of the first opera printed in Portuguese, *A Serrana,* which is a favorite of the Portuguese public.

Other prominent musicians of this period were the opera composer Frederico de Guimarães, a composition professor in the National Conservatory; and Júlio Neuparth, composer of symphonic and chamber music and professor of harmony in the Conservatory, whose pedagogical activities included the writing of a History of Music and the translation into Portuguese of outstanding French didactic works.

THE CONTEMPORARY SCENE

Contemporary music in Portugal is characterized by intense activity along all lines of endeavor. The group of neoclassicist composers, for instance, led by Luís de Freitas Branco (b. 1890), strive to capture in their works the spirit of the great polyphonic school. Of this group the outstanding figure among the younger men is Jorge Croner de Vasconcellos, a pupil of Freitas Branco. Freitas Branco, himself a pupil of Humperdinck and Désiré

Pâque, first introduced French impressionism into Portugal, developing since that time a more personal and more national style. His compositions include three symphonies, four symphonic poems, a violin concerto, a ballad for piano and orchestra, a cantata, an oratorio, songs with orchestra, chamber music, organ music, and several four- and five-part madrigals to words by Camões.

There is another group of composers who look to the marvelous folklore of the country as the basis for a musical nationalism. The oldest man of this group is the venerable José Vianna da Motta (b. 1868), famed pianist, teacher, and composer, the first instrumental virtuoso in Portuguese music, who was for many years the director of the National Conservatory. Vianna da Motta was trained in the German tradition under such teachers as Scharwenka, Liszt, and von Bülow. His compositions include a symphony, a string quartet, *The Lusiads* for choir and orchestra, *Portuguese Scenes* (Opus 9), and *Five Portuguese Rhapsodies* (Opus 10). His other works include transcriptions for pianoforte (two and four hands) of Alkan's pieces for pedal piano, numerous articles written for the most part in German musical journals, and the coeditorship of the complete edition of Liszt's piano works published by the firm of Breitkopf & Härtel.

Still a third group of composers prefer to follow the vanguard in international music. Leaders in this younger group are Frederico de Freitas (b. 1902), who first introduced polytonal and polyrhythmic compositions into Portugal, and Fernando Lopes Graça (b. 1906), outstanding scholar and theorist, a pupil of Schönberg and Alois Haba who has developed a style of his own.

Ruy Coelho (b. 1892) is considered the founder of modern Portuguese opera. After early study at Lisbon and with Humperdinck he studied also with Schönberg, although he does not use the twelve-tone scale. A new work by Coelho was chosen to be produced on December 1, 1940, at the reopening, following its restoration, of Portugal's finest lyric theater, the Teatro de São Carlos (built in 1793). This opera commemorates Portugal's liberation from Spanish rule in 1640, the three hundredth anniversary of which was celebrated in 1940 along with the eight hundredth anniversary of the founding of the kingdom. Coelho has produced the following operas: *Inês de Castro, Crisfal, Belkiss* (Madrid prize in 1924), *Entre Gestas,* and *Tá-Mar,* and is the author of symphonic poems (*Sinfonia Camoniana, Proménade d'Été*), chamber music, works for piano, and songs with piano accompaniment. Coelho's activities also include that of music critic on Lisbon's daily paper *O Diário de Notícias.*

In the field of musical scholarship and journalism, of outstanding relief are Luís de Freitas Branco (music historian and critic for *O Século*), Mário de Sampayo Ribeiro, Gualtério Armando, Júlio Eduardo dos Santos, and Santiago Kastner, the present-day successors to Joaquim de Vasconcellos, Ernesto Vieira, and Michel'Angelo Lambertini, who first began modern Portuguese musicology in the last half of the past century and the first years of this one.

Concerts in Lisbon are numerous, while the audiences are highly discriminating in their support of the best in music from over the world. Two symphony orchestras maintain regular seasons of concerts, Lisbon's population being something over 600,000. One orchestra, of eighty-five men, that of the radio center "Emissora Nacional," is directed by Pedro de Freitas Branco (younger brother of Luís). The "Emissora Nacional" also maintains a chamber orchestra under the direction of Frederico de Freitas, and an orchestra of sixty-two pieces, conducted by Pedro Blanch, for playing light music. The other large orchestra, the *Orquestra Filarmónica de Lisboa,* is conducted by Dr. Ivo Cruz, the present director of the music section of "Conservatório Nacional de Música e de Teatro," [6] most often presenting this group in joint concert with the *Duarte Lobo* choral society. Another group specializing in the presentation of the masterpieces of choral music is the *Sociedade Coral de Lisboa.*

Other cities in Portugal have their musical life, though on a smaller scale. The second city in the nation, Porto (or Oporto), maintains at municipal expense a fine Conservatory under the directorship of Freitas Gonçalves. The leading composer here is Cláudio Carneyro, a professor in the Conservatory, trained under Widor, Dukas, and Pierné. Porto boasts also the oldest choral group in the nation, the *Orfeão do Porto*.

The third city in size is Coimbra, the ancient seat of the great University of Coimbra, where a chair of music has been located since the early part of the fourteenth century. Coimbra maintains also an Academy of Music, a conservatory which offers many of the advantages of the larger schools in Lisbon and Oporto.

CHAPTER XIX

The Spell of Spanish Music

TO borrow and build upon popular tunes of various countries has been a conventional procedure of musical composition since the very dawn of the art. In the polyphonic
period Masses were written on the themes of folk songs not necessarily confined to the geographical limits of the composer's country. Later certain dances of popular origin, incorporated in the
instrumental "suites," became the common property of all composers, constituting a sort of international musical baggage. Notwithstanding their Hispanic origin, little national significance was
eventually attached to such dance forms as the *chacona*, the *zarabanda*, the *pavana*, and the *pasacalle*. Indeed, the development
of musical art preceded that of nationalism, and it is only in the
nineteenth century that the latter term acquires a definite significance with regard to music.

Spanish national music, in spite of its widespread popularity
from the beginning of the nineteenth century, was slow to take
its place in the standard symphonic and operatic repertoire because of the lack of orchestral technique of its composers. Thus it
happened that "the Spanish idiom" in symphonic and operatic
music first attracted serious international attention in the works
of non-Spanish composers. In opera Bizet led the way—and still
holds the lead—with *Carmen* (1875). In the very same year
Lalo's *Symphonie Espagnole* appeared, followed by Chabrier's

España (1883) and Rimsky-Korsakoff's *Capriccio Espagnol* (1887), all three quickly becoming favorite items of the symphonic repertoire.

GLINKA IN SPAIN

Rimsky-Korsakoff was not the first Russian composer to cultivate the Spanish idiom. He was preceded by Michael Glinka, the "father" of Russian music, the man who prepared the way for the "Five" (Balakireff, Borodin, Cui, Mussorgsky, Rimsky-Korsakoff). Already famous as the composer of the first Russian national opera, *A Life for the Czar,* Glinka went to Spain in the spring of 1845 and was immediately fascinated by the popular songs and dances (to say nothing of the pretty singers and dancers, who claimed at least an equal share of his attention). In Valladolid, where he spent the summer, his enthusiasm was aroused by the playing of a guitarist named Castilla, from whom he heard the *Jota de Aragón* with variations. This gave him the idea of writing his *Capriccio Brillant* for orchestra on the same theme, which he composed in Madrid soon after his arrival there in September (the piece was later renamed *Spanish Overture,* No. 1). In Madrid, Glinka listened assiduously to popular singers and guitarists, whose tunes and rhythms he attempted to write down in his notebook.[1] The singing of *seguidillas manchegas* by a muleteer was among the experiences that inspired him to write his *Spanish Overture,* No. 2 *(Night in Madrid).*[2]

Glinka had gone to Spain with the deliberate intention of utilizing the regional melodies in orchestral works which he originally designated as *Fantaisies pittoresques.* In these "picturesque fantasies" his aim was to combine the superior technique of "serious" music, as developed in the modern symphony orchestra, with the popular appeal of folk tunes. He explained that he was attracted toward Spain because of the originality of its regional melodies, rich in unexploited resources. He even toyed with the idea of writing an opera on Spanish themes. His experiences with Spanish music undoubtedly stimulated him to treat the music of his own country in a similar manner, for his famous orchestral fantasy *Kamarinskaya*, "which became the model for all later essays in the symphonic handling of Russian folk melodies," [3] was written shortly after his return from Spain.

It appears that Glinka attempted to write an orchestral piece on Andalusian themes, but did not succeed owing to the difficulty of handling the strange scales and elusive rhythms. He spent the winter of 1845–1846 at Granada, where he passed long hours listening to the flamenco playing of an excellent popular guitarist named Francisco Rodriguez Murciano and to the singing of "a charming Andalusian girl." He also watched the Gypsies dance and even ventured to try the Spanish dances himself. Of this experience he writes, "My feet were all right but I couldn't manage the castanets." [4] After a summer in Madrid, he spent the following winter and spring in Seville, and in May, 1847, departed on his homeward journey.

It was perhaps not by chance that the first foreign composer to exploit in a large way the possibilities of Spanish folk music was a Russian. The two countries meet on the common ground of semi-Oriental exoticism. Though Glinka, who at bottom remained a dilettante in music, may have been baffled as well as fascinated by the exotic Andalusian scales, his followers in the Russian national school owed no small part of their success to the exploitation of equally exotic scales and melodies from the eastern regions of Russia. Thus Rimsky-Korsakoff, though he had spent only three days in Spain—he stopped at Cádiz while cruising as a naval cadet in 1864–1865—felt sufficiently at home in the music of that country to lavish his best efforts on a *Spanish Capriccio* for orchestra which in his own words was meant "to glitter with dazzling orchestral color." Writing about this piece, he continues: [5]

The Spanish themes, of dance character, furnished me with rich material for putting in use multiform orchestral effects. All in all, the *Capriccio* is undoubtedly a purely external piece, but vividly brilliant for all that.

That is a very good estimate of the *Capriccio Espagnol* and leaves little more to be said on the subject. With its *Alborada*, its *Variations*, its *Scene and Gypsy Song*, and its *Fandango of the Asturias*, the work introduces no fundamentally novel conception of pseudo-Spanish music, but merely carries out the concept of Glinka with a more elaborate technical apparatus. The Spanish character of the work is perhaps most apparent in the *Fandango*, which yet remains, like the rest of the composition, on an entirely superficial plane.[6]

It is probably just as well that Rimsky-Korsakoff did not carry out his original intention of writing his *Spanish Capriccio* as a fantasy for violin and orchestra, because in that case he would have had to compete with Lalo's *Symphonie Espagnole*, one of the most effective works in the entire violinistic repertoire. Lalo had Spanish blood in his veins (though he was born at Bordeaux in 1823), and in writing his *Symphonie Espagnole* he profited moreover from the help and advice of Sarasate (*cf.* Chapter XIV), who gave the first performance of the work at Paris on February 7, 1875. Lalo handles his material with skill and imagination, and he has captured in some of his themes that passionate melancholy which is always lurking beneath the outward gaiety of the Spaniards. His Hispanism nevertheless is conventional in form and substance.

BIZET AND *CARMEN*

Less than a month after the first performance of Lalo's *Symphonie Espagnole*, Bizet's *Carmen* was produced at the Opéra-Comique (March 3, 1875). Exactly three months later Georges Bizet died, unaware that he had just written one of the world's most popular operas.[7] From the Hispanic point of view, *Carmen* was in all respects a secondhand affair. The original story was written by a Frenchman (Prosper Mérimée), and the libretto concocted therefrom was by two Parisians, Meilhac and Halévy. Bizet himself had never set foot in Spain.[8] How, then, did he manage to compose a work that, rightly or wrongly, has stood in the minds of millions as the prototype of a "Spanish opera"?

Though he was no traveler—his Italian sojourn as Prix de Rome laureate was his sole taste of foreign life—Bizet had an innate knack for absorbing exotic experiences vicariously. While leading his routine-ridden existence in Paris, his imagination roamed to the far-off places which he made the locales of his operas, and he was often able to free his music from the atmosphere of the boulevards and the *salons,* capturing colors that no Frenchman had been able to seize before. The fact remains that only when he turned his attention to Spain was he able to command the enduring enthusiasm of posterity.

When Bizet decided to write a Spanish opera, he simply went to the Library of the Conservatoire and wrote on a slip of paper, "I request a list of the collections of Spanish songs in the possession of the Library." There were not many available in Paris at the time, and, according to Julien Tiersot, the collection most likely to have been consulted by Bizet was one entitled *Échos d'Espagne,* which had been published in 1872. It includes seguidillas, boleros, *tiranas,* habaneras, a *malagueña,* a *jota aragonesa,* and a *polo.* All but the last are anonymous. This piece, to quote from the preface, is none other than "the admirable *polo* composed by the celebrated García," that is, the song beginning *Cuerpo bueno, alma divina,* included by Manuel García in his theatrical tonadilla *El Criado Fingido* (*cf.* Chapter VIII). Here, then, we have the main source upon which Bizet drew for the Spanish themes in *Carmen.*

The other composition by an identified author embodied in the score is the *Habanera* which Carmen sings after her entrance in the first act. The story goes that Bizet heard this melody sung by a lady in Paris, and, thinking it was a Spanish folk song, wrote it down for use in his opera. After the production of the work the song was recognized as being by Sebastián Yradier,[9] the publisher (Heugel of Paris) protested, and in the printed score acknowledgment of the source was made. Whether Bizet really acquired the song in this manner, or whether he took it from one of the published collections of Yradier's songs, the fact remains that he was greatly indebted to the relatively obscure composer of *La Paloma*, for Carmen's *Habanera*, from the standpoint of popular success, is one of the big moments of the opera. Contrary to his usual practice, Bizet copied the tune almost literally, and such slight changes as he made were not always an improvement on the original (viz., the banality of the final cadence). In the Yradier collection published by Heugel the song in question is entitled *El Arreglito*, and, like *La Paloma*, it is a love song addressed to the ubiquitous "Chinita." [10]

Bizet evidently steeped himself in the spirit of the Spanish popular songs he could secure in Paris, but rarely did he attempt to reproduce them exactly. The nearest he came to doing this was in the seguidillas of Act I, *Près des ramparts de Séville*, a fairly close imitation of the original. He observed that the vast majority of the songs and dances were in triple time and made the most of this observation in his score. He absorbed some of the harmonic and rhythmic traits of the flamenco guitar style, as may be seen, for instance, in the accompaniment of the *Chanson Bohême* in Act II. The places in the score, however, where actual imitations or reminiscences of Spanish themes occur may be counted on the fingers of one hand. We have already mentioned three of them and will presently come to the fourth and most important. Let it be said here that the bulk of the score of *Carmen* is pure Bizet and thoroughly French. The vivid life and passion that he put into his music causes most of it to blend with the Andalusian background, but occasionally, as in José's aria *La fleur que tu m'avais jetée*, he sets us squarely in a Parisian *salon*. The same is true of the music for Micaela, an entirely superfluous character. As for the famous and incredibly vulgar "Toreador Song," which Bizet himself is said to have called a *cochonnerie*, it surely cannot be pinned upon Spain.

THE "GRANDFATHER" OF *CARMEN*

With the entr'acte that precedes Act IV we come to what is really vital and authentic, from a Spanish point of view, in *Carmen*. It is here that the spirit of *cante jondo* suffuses the scene and envelops the characters with colors and moods reflecting no whit of Paris. The real soul of Carmen, as a character, and of *Carmen*, as an opera, springs from the music of this entr'acte. And this music, in turn, springs straight from Andalusia via the *polo* of Manuel García.

For those who wish to compare the actual musical documents, we quote the chief melodic elements of García's *polo*. The first period is as follows:

Example 43a.

Then comes this:

Example 43b.

And finally there are the prolonged melismatic flourishes on the syllable *Ay*, leading always to a cadence on the dominant.

Example 43c.

Bizet handled this song much more freely than he did Yradier's *Habanera*, which, of course, has not half the character of García's

composition. Nevertheless, his entr'acte music has exactly the
same tonality (D minor) and time signature (3/8) as García's
song, and while he introduced certain rhythmic modifications, the
essential notes of the melody are kept intact and the number of
measures is equal in both cases. The vocalization on *Ay* he trans-
fers to the instruments in a higher register, changing only one
chromatic inflection and keeping the characteristic descent to the
dominant. This termination on the dominant is the very essence
of *cante jondo*, and it is in these cadences above all that Bizet leans
most heavily upon his unwitting collaborator. Any musician can
write a cadence on the dominant; only an Andalusian can do it
as though it were in his blood. García's ghostly hand guided Bizet
infallibly here.

Carmen in any case would be an effective opera; if it is also a
great opera, that is due principally to the last act. And the last
act draws its vital sustenance from the entr'acte music. Bizet's
truly marvelous skill in transforming his thematic material so as
to give it new and heightened significance is most apparent in
these pages. For the most significant feature of all, for the kernel
of *Carmen*, we must return to the initial prelude of the opera, and
specifically to the third and final theme included there, that
strangely dramatic and fatalistic theme associated throughout the
work with Carmen, warning always of impending doom.

Example 44.

It is characterized by the interval of the augmented second, which
gives to Andalusian music much of its Oriental character. Observe
that it is in the key of D minor and that the melodic phrase represents a descent to the dominant. Observe, moreover, that its five
notes are embodied in the first phrase from García's *polo*, and
especially in one of the variants of that phrase used by Bizet in

Act IV. Can we doubt that this Carmen-theme, containing the musical essence of the character, has its roots in García's composition? To recognize this is not to detract from Bizet's achievement. To borrow like this is to create. It is genius.

Manuel García has aptly been called "the grandfather of *Carmen*." [11] It is a further title to fame, and not the least.

CHABRIER'S *ESPAÑA*

It is within France that one must continue to look for the most significant specimens of "Spanish music" written by foreign composers. After Bizet and Lalo, the names of Chabrier, Debussy, and Ravel stand pre-eminent in this field. The three last-mentioned composers struck deeper into the heart of Spain than their predecessors, producing works that are not merely Spanish in style but Spanish in essence, even while they mirror the personalities of their respective creators. Emmanuel Chabrier (1841–1894) was more fortunate that Bizet in being able actually to visit Spain, and he made the most of his opportunity. An immensely gifted amateur rather than a professionally trained musician, Chabrier was employed as a clerk in the Ministry of the Interior until 1880, when he resigned in order to devote himself entirely to composition. He had already composed several works but was still an obscure musical figure. In the summer of 1882 he realized a long-cherished wish to visit Spain, perhaps not suspecting that this was to mark the turning point in his career. Of a jovial and expansive nature, full of wit and drollery, he fairly bubbles over with enthusiasm and excitement in his letters from Spain. He entered the country by Irún and San Sebastián, but soon betook himself to Andalusia, where the *bailes flamencos* worked their inevitable spell upon him. His descriptions are vivid:

Those eyes, those flowers in the lovely hair, those shawls knotted around the figure, those feet that strike infinitely varied rhythms, those arms that ripple along the length of a body ever in movement, those undulations of the hand, those flashing smiles, and those ad-

mirable Sevillian haunches that turn in every direction while the rest
of the body seems to remain motionless—and all this to the cries of
Olé, olé, anda la María! Eso es! Baile la Carmen! anda! anda!
shouted by other women and by the public!

Chabrier was accompanied by his wife, so, unlike Glinka's, his
feelings did not pass beyond the stage of verbal admiration. Seville, Málaga, Cádiz, Granada, Valencia—it was a perpetual round
of flamenco guitar playing, singing, and dancing: *malagueñas,
soleares, zapateados, peteneras,* tangos. And through it all Chabrier, notebook in hand, overwhelmed and delighted by the infinite
complexity of the rhythms and the elusive snatches of melody,
was busy writing down the tunes and rhythms as well as he could.[12]
He was particularly intrigued by the *malagueña,* though he affirmed that it was impossible to write it down accurately.

The very fact that he had not imbibed the scholastic prejudices
of the Conservatoire tended to make Chabrier more keenly recep-
tive to these unconventional melodies and rhythms. When he returned to Paris and prepared to use his Spanish jottings and impressions in an orchestral composition—he chose the *malagueña*
and the *jota aragonesa* for his main themes—he gave full scope
to his innate flair for unhackneyed rhythmic and harmonic effects,
and to his unerring instinct for piquantly unorthodox instrumentation. The result was the orchestral rhapsody entitled *España,* first
performed at a Lamoureux Concert on November 6, 1883 and
received with the utmost enthusiasm. It made Chabrier famous.

It may be said of Chabrier's *España* that it was the most thoroughly Spanish orchestral work written up to that time, inside or
outside of Spain, and that within its special genre it has never
been surpassed. On this point we have the testimony of no less
an authority than Manuel de Falla, who writes:

Referring to this model of our folklore [the *jota*], I venture to
say that no Spaniard has succeeded better than Chabrier in giving us,
with such authenticity and genius, the version of a *jota* as it is
"shouted" by the peasants of Aragón in their nocturnal rounds.[13]

THE HISPANISM OF DEBUSSY AND RAVEL

Claude Debussy represents a special case in the realm of pseudo-Spanish music. He was the first to appreciate the full possibilities of Spanish (more specifically, Andalusian) popular music and to raise its inherent values to the category of the highest art. Chabrier, with all his keenness of perception, failed to realize the marvelous resources of the guitar as a popular instrument,[14] whereas Debussy intuitively recognized and exploited these resources. He never visited Spain except to attend a bullfight at San Sebastián, but he had occasion to hear authentic *cante jondo* singers and guitarists at the Exposition Universelle of 1889–1890 in Paris. There were many reasons why the traditional music of Spain made a strong appeal to him, apart from his innate love for the exotic. The survival of the medieval modes, the lack of isometric regularity in the melodies, the shifting and conflicting rhythms, the unorthodox harmonization, with its frequent recourse to consecutive fourths and fifths, the strong contrasts of mood—all these were in line with his own creative instincts. Hence it happened that there are Hispanic elements not only in such of his works as are specifically Spanish in style and subject—*Ibéria, La Soirée dans Grenade, La Puerta del Vino*—but also in several other works, notably *Sérénade Interrompue, Fantoches, Mandoline, Masques, Danse Profane*, and the second movement of the String Quartet, which, according to Manuel de Falla, "might pass for one of the finest Andalusian dances ever written." [15]

The largest of Debussy's Hispanic compositions is the orchestral *Ibéria*, one of the three pieces entitled collectively *Images*. It consists of three sections, played without pause: *Par les Rues et par les Chemins; Les Parfums de la Nuit;* and *Le Matin d'un Jour de Fête*. The locale is unmistakably established by the castanets and tambourines, used, however, with admirable discretion. The generative theme of the whole composition is a kind of *sevillana*, whose native characteristics become considerably attenuated in the course of the development. In his *Ibéria* Debussy is truly the impressionist; he gives us no virtuoso handling of popular themes, but transmutes the poetic essence of Spain in the subtle alembic of his imagination. His vision of Spain is the most personal that any composer has given us. The expressive power of Debussy's music may be summed up in the single word "atmosphere." With a few phrases he can evoke "the intoxicating spell of Andalusian nights" or "the festive gaiety of a people dancing to the joyous strains of a band of guitars and *bandurrias*" (Falla).

A colored post card sent to him from Granada by Manuel de Falla inspired Debussy to write his piano prelude, *La Puerta del Vino*, in which the sinuous melody of *cante jondo* is so skillfully suggested. Its rhythm, that of the habanera, is also employed in another prelude, *La Soirée dans Grenade*, of which Falla has written:

The force of imagination concentrated in the few pages of *La Soirée dans Grenade* approaches the marvelous when it is borne in mind that they were written by a stranger guided almost exclusively by the visions of his genius. The work takes us away from those "Serenades," "Madrilènes" and "Boleros" wherewith so-called Spanish music-makers used to regale us; here it is Andalusia itself that we see; truth without authenticity, so to speak, since there is not a bar directly borrowed from Spanish folk-music and yet the whole piece to its smallest detail is redolent of Spain.[16]

This principle of essential truth without recourse to the actual folklore document was the aesthetic basis of Albéniz's *Iberia* and for most of Falla's music. It brings Debussy very close to the ideals of the modern Spanish school and renews in modern terms the conceptions already implied in the art of Domenico Scarlatti.

Maurice Ravel's approach to Spanish music was somewhat similar, though the factor of personal contact figured more prominently in his case. Both his parents had lived for a long time in Spain and were extremely attached to that country. Falla attributes much of Ravel's Hispanism to the influence of his mother, who frequently sang Spanish songs to him. Ravel himself was born but a few miles from the Spanish border, in the

French-Basque town of Ciboure. An acute French writer, André Suarès, saw in Ravel, both artistically and personally, the embodiment of many Spanish traits:

Parisian to his finger tips, he is even so the most Spanish of artists. He answers better than another to one's idea of a great musician in the Spanish cast; he has something of Goya and the picaresque. . . . And let no one think that it was by chance that he made his entrance into music by way of Spain. . . . I recognize Spain in every part of Ravel—in what he is and in what he does. This little man is so dry, so sensitive, at once frail and resistant, caressing and inflexible, supple as tempered steel; his large nose and hollow cheeks, his angular and lean figure; his air at once a little distant and yet always courteous— these traits are reminiscent of Spain. And his art, still more decidedly, is of the French tongue touched with a Spanish accent.[17]

One of Ravel's earliest and most characteristic compositions, in which his originality appeared full fledged, was the *Habanera* for two pianos (1895), which he later orchestrated and incorporated in the *Rapsodie Espagnole* (1907), the three other sections of this work being *Prélude à la Nuit*, *Malagueña*, and *Feria*. With the exception of the *jota* that appears in the last section, Ravel does not use actual folk themes in his rhapsody, but employs freely the rhythms, the modal melodies, and the ornamental traits of Spanish folk music.

In contrast to the impressionistic imagery of Debussy, the *Spanish Rhapsody* of Ravel is aglow with smoldering intensity, with violent contrasts of mood and dynamic impact, with the sensuous warmth of Andalusia and the ardent aridity of Castile. The flame and the ecstasy flash amid the infinite precision of Ravel's superbly controlled instrumentation.

Ravel's only opera, *L'Heure Espagnole* (1907), has a Spanish setting, but its piquant fantasy is of no particular country. His famous *Boléro* for orchestra, which created such a furor—it was first performed as a ballet at the Paris Opéra in 1928—has little in common with the traditional Spanish dance of that name. But its unitonal intensity and rhythmic persistence are general Spanish traits. One finds more marked Hispanic coloring in the earlier orchestral piece, *Alborada del Gracioso* (1912),[18] with its alternating 6/8 and 9/8 rhythms and its flashing arpeggios. Ravel included a harmonization of a Spanish folk song in his *Quatre Chants Populaires*, and the last composition he wrote before he was stricken with the brain disease that led to his death a few years later was an evocation of the Spain of Don Quixote, three songs for baritone solo and small orchestra entitled *Don Quichotte à Dulcinée* (1934). A temporary alleviation of his ailment enabled Ravel to visit once more, in 1935, the country from which he had drawn so much of his inspiration. But not even the cherished colors and images of Spain could revive the creative spark in a mind so tragically ravaged.

Before leaving France we must mention Louis Aubert's admirable *Habanera* for orchestra (1919) and the Spanish operas of the French-Basque composer Raoul Laparra: *La Habanera* (1908), *La Jota* (1911), *Las Torreras* (zarzuela, 1929), and *L'Illustre Fregona* (after Cervantes, 1931). Of these, the most successful has been *La Habanera*, performed at Boston in 1910 and at the Metropolitan Opera House, New York, in 1924. Starkly tragic in plot, it depicts the musical atmosphere of Castile with impressive fidelity.

SOME AMERICAN COMPOSERS

In the United States the tradition of pseudo-Spanish composition begins with Louis Moreau Gottschalk, a native of New Orleans who died at Rio de Janeiro in 1869 during one of his extensive tours as pianist. A brilliant virtuoso, Gottschalk composed copiously for his instrument, cultivating not only Spanish peninsular themes such as the *jota aragonesa*, but also many types of Ibero-American popular music. His compositions have fallen into almost total neglect, but he was the first North American musician to make an impression in Latin America, and his influence there was considerable.

Another American composer of French extraction, Charles Martin Loeffler, continued the tradition with his *Divertissement Espagnol* for orchestra and saxophone (1900), of which Carl Engel writes: "His music concentrates, with agonizing intensity, the rays of a sun that scorches the mind and stirs the sap to a point of fatal irresponsibility." [19] Loeffler also wrote a one-act Spanish opera, *The Passion of Hilarion,* after the play by William Sharp.[20]

Obviously, American composers do not have to seek beyond the Atlantic Ocean for music of Hispanic character. It abounds in our own midst, as well as among our neighbors in the southern part of the hemisphere. A composer who has utilized the Hispanic aspect of America's cultural tradition is Harl McDonald, in his Symphony No. 1, *The Santa Fe Trail* (1934). The first movement, *The Explorers,* depicts the American pioneers arriving in the Southwest. Of the second movement, *The Spanish Settlements,* the composer writes:

This movement (an *allegro scherzando,* with a trio, *molto moderato,* of Hispanic-Jota patterns) reflected the spirit of the life in the Spanish settlements, where the explorers come upon a kind of life which is beyond their comprehension. At first these cold men of the North and East are dimly aware of the gaiety and indolence of the Hispanic life, but soon it becomes the pulse of their existence.[21]

The third and last movement, *The Wagon Trails of the Pioneers,* "represents the many influences—Hispanic, Nordic, and American Indian—that combined to build the spirit and substance of the Southwest."

In his *Rumba Symphony* (1935), McDonald uses rumba themes in the third movement "because they seem to be a part of the pulse of our times."

Aaron Copland, in his extremely effective orchestral piece *El Salón México,* has shown what can be done by the clever use of Mexican folk tunes and rhythms. In his vivid impression of a popular dance hall in Mexico City he has caught a bit of color and movement that strikes like a flash of lightning through the drab cerebralism of academic modernism.

Compositions of Hispanic character figure prominently among the works of Emerson Whithorne, who has written the symphonic poems *España* and *Sierra Morena*, a *Fandango* for orchestra, and the piano suite *El Camino Real*. Among the younger composers, Paul Bowles has an alert ear for the tunes and rhythms of Hispanic America.

To include here a catalogue of all the pseudo-Spanish compositions that have been written would be to extend this chapter beyond all reasonable limits. In addition to those whose works we have discussed, many other composers—among them Chopin, Corelli, d'Indy, Elgar, Glazunoff, Gluck, Humperdinck, Ibert, Liszt, Carl Loewe, Massenet, Moszkowski, Mozart, Pierné, Rossini, Anton Rubinstein, Saint-Saëns, Schumann, Spohr, Richard Strauss, Stravinsky, Widor, Hugo Wolf—have contributed, in greater or lesser degree, to that unique body of music which owes its existence to the everlasting fascination of Spain.

Spanish Music Since 1941

NOT a great deal, creatively, has happened in Spanish music since this book was first published seventeen years ago; but a great deal has happened *to* Spanish music. The publication, performance, and recording of Spanish music — of all types and all periods, from *villancicos* to *zarzuelas*, and from polyphony to flamenco — has reached proportions that are quite staggering if viewed from the perspective of 1940. Perhaps the continuing interest in the present book is another straw in the wind to indicate that the perennial fascination of Spain's music, far from decreasing with familiarity, has steadily grown by feeding on a generous supply of publications, performances, and recordings.

Actually, the events most worthy of note in the Spanish musical scene during the past two decades or so, are concerned not so much with the appearance of new talents—though some of these may certainly be discerned—as with the disappearance of eminent figures whose work and fame have loomed large in the twentieth century. Among them are Manuel de Falla (d. 1946), Joaquín Turina (d. 1949), Joaquín Nin (d. 1949), and Conrado del Campo (d. 1953). For more about Falla's last work and posthumous influence, the reader is referred to what follows in this chapter. As for the others, Conrado del Campo never achieved abroad any acceptance comparable to what he received at home, where his prestige was great both as composer and pedagogue. In the case of Joaquín Nin, whose last years were spent in Havana, I have long felt that he should have been given more importance in this book, perhaps not as a composer, but surely as one of those who helped to bring about the latter-day renaissance of Spanish music through his skillful and sensitive arrangements of songs and keyboard pieces of the past. The number of recordings of Turina's music issued in recent years—always a good index of public acceptance—indicates that this composer's posthumous reputation has suffered no diminution.

FALLA'S DEATH AND POSTHUMOUS INFLUENCE

Manuel de Falla died in Alta Gracia de Córdoba, Argentina, on November 14, 1946, at the age of seventy. With him to the last was his sister María del Carmen. All his papers and manuscripts, including the unfinished score of *L'Atlántida,* were placed in a sealed valise, delivered to the Spanish Embassy in Buenos Aires, and transmitted thence to Spain by diplomatic pouch. Copies of his last will and testament were released to the Argentine press. In two sections, dated respectively August 9, 1935, and August 4, 1936, the will is more concerned with spiritual and moral matters than with material dispositions (his few worldly goods were left to his brother and sister). He requested that Masses be said for the souls of all his teachers, whom he mentions by name, including Felipe Pedrell and José Tragó. He demanded that, unless the royalties were strictly necessary for the support of his brother and sister, none of his works be performed on the stage after his death—and he insisted that this prohibition be scrupulously observed even after his stage works had entered the public domain! A truly quixotic will, worthy of a medieval Spanish saint.

After being exposed to public view in Buenos Aires, Falla's remains were transported to Spain for burial in the Cathedral of Cádiz. The funeral took place on January 9, 1947, with the participation of the "Capella Classica" of Palma de Mallorca, which sang Victoria's *Requiem* under the direction of Falla's friend, Juan María Thomás. By his express wish, his tomb was inscribed with these words: TO GOD ALONE HONOR AND GLORY.

The unfinished score and sketches of *L'Atlántida* were entrusted for completion to Falla's former pupil, Ernesto Halffter, with the hope that the work might be completed in time to receive its first world performance in connection with the commemoration of the third millennium of the city of Cádiz, in the summer of 1956. But the trimillennium passed and the expectations of the musical world were not fulfilled. Falla once suggested that *L'Atlántida* might be called a "Mystery," little suspecting how unfortunately apt that designation would prove to be.

It was in 1926 that Falla became acquainted with Verdaguer's epic poem *L'Atlántida*, when the Madrid newspaper *El Sol* published some excerpts from it in a Spanish translation by Eduardo Marquina. Falla was then seeking a suitable subject for a lirico-dramatic work of epic proportions in which choral music would be a preponderant element. Some years previous he had considered writing a lyric drama based on the novel *La Gloria de Don Ramiro* by the Argentine writer and ardent Hispanophile, Enrique de Larreta. Then he had thought of composing an *auto sacramental* with a libretto adapted from Calderón de la Barca. But when he read the fragments from *L'Atlántida*, and soon afterwards the complete poem in the Catalan language (which he took pains to learn), Falla felt that he need seek no further for a subject that fired his imagination, for it embraced the whole of Spain, from the Pyrenees to the Atlantic; it dealt with the founding of Barcelona, a city to which he had become strongly attached of late (he selected it for the première of the Harpsichord Concerto in 1926); the action centered around the exploits of Hercules, legendary founder of Cádiz, the city of Falla's birth, and maker of the Strait of Gibraltar, through which Columbus and his caravels were to sail in search of the New World, the beginning of Spain's maximum historical adventure, and the culmination of Verdaguer's great epic poem.

Falla worked on the score of *L'Atlántida* as much as the precarious state of his health permitted. But when he arrived in Buenos Aires in October, 1939, he told a newspaper reporter, "Much still remains to be done." Yet in that same interview he revealed a gleam of optimism: "It is certain that my coming to America, so magnificently evoked in the poem of the illustrious Catalan, should lead to the more rapid termination of this work." This optimism, as we know, was not justified. What we never could have foreseen is that in 1958, twelve years after the master's death, *L'Atlántida* would still remain, not only unfinished, but also unpublished and unperformed.

According to the available information *L'Atlántida* is scored for vocal quartet of soloists (soprano, alto, tenor, baritone), one solo boy's voice, several other singers for minor rôles, and two mixed choruses (one of children's voices); two pianos, harpsichord, a large percussion section, a "formidable" brass section, including eight horns and a fanfare of eight trombones; and the usual woodwinds and strings. In addition, Falla in some places uses his favorite device of a chamber orchestra made up of soloists. The total duration of the work is said to be about two hours.

In an interview printed in "ABC" of Madrid in 1957, Halffter stated that "several important sections" of *L'Atlántida,* including the Prologue (duration: eighteen minutes) were completely orchestrated by the composer; other sections had the vocal parts written in full and the orchestration indicated with guides to the upper and lower parts; still other sections consisted merely of rough sketches, with several ver-

sions of some parts, making a definite selection difficult. This
third state applies in particular to Part II of the work, which
contains the core of the action. Part III, like the Prologue,
is stated to be quite complete, and Part I requires completion
of the instrumentation.

The general plan of the work (subject to rectification in
detail, especially in the confused Part II) is as follows:

PROLOGUE.	1.	The Submerged Atlántida.
	2.	Hispanic Hymn.
PART I.	1.	The Conflagration of the Pyrenees.
	2.	The Founding of Barcelona.
PART II.	1.	Hercules in Cádiz.
	2.	The Garden of the Hesperides.
	3.	Combat with Geryon and the Dragon.
	4.	The Pleiades.
	5.	The Atlantides.
	6.	Titans Pursue Hercules.
	7.	The Voice Divine.
	8.	Opening of the Strait.
	9.	The Archangel.
	10.	Messengers' Voices.
	11.	The Cataracts.
	12.	The Sinking.
	13.	*Non Plus Ultra.*
PART III.	1.	The Pilgrim (Christopher Columbus).
	2.	Isabella's Dream in the Alhambra.
	3.	The Caravels.
	4.	The *Salve Regina* at Sea.
	5.	The Supreme Night (Meditation of Columbus).

Falla definitely envisioned *L'Atlántida* as a "scenic" cantata, to be produced with appropriate stage settings, which

he had discussed with the painter José María Sert, including the use of film projection for certain scenes. As previously stated, he had been contemplating a major stage work for several years before his choice settled upon Verdaguer's poem. His correspondence with Don Enrique Larreta regarding the project for a lyrical version of the latter's historical novel of the reign of Philip II, *La Gloria de Don Ramiro*, reveals something of his aims and aspirations in this respect. Wrote Falla: "Obviously, I never had the intention of writing an opera in the sense that is usually given to this term. What I propose to write is a musical work for the stage *(una obra musical escénica)* in which the characters will *sing* whatever they need to say, and nothing else, and will mime everything for which the intervention of words is not necessary. The chorus will have an almost preponderant rôle, not to comment on the action, but to participate in it whenever this is appropriate; or to serve as background for the action itself; or, again, as a purely musical element which, contributing to the evocation of the setting *(ambiente)*, will *envelope* the characters: something akin to a reflection of the different spiritual states of the characters themselves. (In these last instances the chorus will be invisible and wordless.) . . . My desire is to represent all of this through music that is intensely expressive and evocative and which would have its origins in all that is greatest in the musical heritage of our race, be it in a *natural* or an *artistic* manner. And all this realized in a form absolutely foreign to the Wagnerian or Italian operatic procedures. *Natural* music, energetic or mysterious according to the situation, but always *ours*."

This, then, is Falla's statement of his aspirations as a Spanish composer. He takes up Pedrell's doctrine of the dual source of great national music, the popular and the artistic traditions; stresses the need for a *natural* mode of musical expression, intense or mysterious, but always sincere because, however universal in aspiration, it remains profoundly Spanish in essence. We have every reason to believe that *L'Atlántida* was intended to be the ultimate musical manifestation of this artistic creed.

The crowning irony of Falla's creative evolution is that, having raised the Andalusian idiom to unprecedented heights of artistic expression in his most popular works, he thereafter devoted himself to the creation of works in an entirely different vein, marked by a much more profound and all-embracing Hispanism, whose originality, compelling character, and increasing influence have completely overshadowed (save in popular acceptance, which is unimportant) the works of the Andalusian period. The measure of Falla's influence on Spanish music over the past twenty years is to be sought in *El Retablo de Maese Pedro* and the Harpsichord Concerto. These are the scores in which the younger composers have looked for guidance and inspiration. They carry the ascending curve of Falla's musical nationalism towards its summit. Eventually, together with *L'Atlántida*, they will reveal to the world a genuine musical image of the Spain that endures while fake flamenco dancers cavort in American night clubs. Though Falla's Andalusian works remain as paradigms of their kind, the Andalusian idiom today, for all artistic purposes, is simply a parody of itself. The final evidence of Manuel de Falla's greatness is that, having perfected the Andalusian idiom in art-music, he was able to transcend it, and in the process to emerge as the most representative Spanish composer since the Golden Age of Spain's music.

IN THE FOOTSTEPS OF FALLA

Fifteen years ago, Ernesto Halffter appeared to be Falla's most promising pupil, but it cannot be said that this promise has been entirely fulfilled. Since his Portuguese Rhapsody for piano and orchestra (1939), which received its Madrid première in 1941, Halffter has produced no major work. And even the Rhapsody, for all its brilliance as a repertory piece, merely exploits accepted folkloristic formulas without breaking any new ground. Only in the deeply expressive second movement does the composer transcend the limitations of local color. In spite of its ostensible Portuguese character, including the evocation of a *fado*, critics have remarked that the style and structure of the Rhapsody are basically Spanish.

In addition, Halffter has written a Concerto for violin and orchestra, a *Suite Antigua* for wind instruments, and an elegy on the death of the famous pianist Ricardo Viñes, *Llanto a la muerte de Ricardo Viñes*, for piano. He has revised the early *Habanera* and has composed several film scores, including *Bambu*. He has also orchestrated Falla's *Seven Spanish Popular Songs* and was planning a version for 'cello and orchestra of the *Fantasía Bética*. Perhaps this is his way of accomplishing what he has stated to be his "major ambition," namely, "never to depart, in my life and in my work, from the path that Falla traced for me as an ideal."

The blind Valencian composer Joaquín Rodrigo has been extremely productive. Stemming directly from the line Pedrell-Albéniz-Falla, he has cultivated a many-sided nationalism, drawing sparingly upon folklore but endeavoring to embrace the whole tradition of Hispanic music and the whole scope of Spanish culture, both in time (historically) and in space (geographically). With the *Concierto de Aranjuez* (1939) for guitar and orchestra he achieved an immense popular success as well as an artistic triumph in finding an ideal solution for the difficult problem of form and balance involved in this combination.

This was the first of five concertos written by Rodrigo, the others being *Concierto Heroíco* for piano and orchestra (1941-42), *Concierto de Estío* for violin and orchestra

(1943), *Concierto Galante* for 'cello and orchestra (1949), and *Concierto-Serenata* for harp and orchestra (1954). He has also written another concerted work for guitar and orchestra, titled *Fantasía para un Gentilhombre* (1954).

The catalogue of Rodrigo's works to date is already so large that only a summary of it can be given here, indicating something of the range of his musical Hispanism. His piano music, after bowing to Albéniz in such pieces as the *Tres Danzas de España* (1941) and *A l'Ombre de Torre Bermeja* (1945), reaches its present culmination in the *Cinco Sonatas de Castilla con Toccata a modo de Pregón* (1950-51), in which Rodrigo, taking up the one-movement Scarlattian pattern, renews the tradition of the Spanish sonata as exemplified in the music of Antonio Soler, Mateo Albéniz, Rafael Anglés, and other peninsular keyboard composers of the 18th century. The subtitle of the fourth Sonata, *"como un Tiento,"* underlines the intent to revive the former spirit of the sonata as a unified "sound-piece." The placing of the Five Sonatas under the egis of Castile signifies that turning inward upon the core of Spanish character, away from the exotic Andalusian periphery, that Falla initiated with *El Retablo de Maese Pedro*.

This tendency reaches a creative peak in another Castillian evocation, the *Música para un Códice Salmantino sobre letra de Miguel de Unamuno* (1953), being a setting of Unamuno's "Ode to Salamanca" for bass solo, four-part mixed chorus, and eleven instruments (two violins, viola, 'cello, double-bass, piccolo, flute, English horn, trumpet, French horn, and harp), written to commemorate the Seven Hundredth Anniversary of the founding of the University of Salamanca. The composition, which lasts about twelve minutes, has the general structure of a motet, with (in the words of the composer) an occasional "involuntary lyrical escapade." The introductory instrumental section was conceived by the composer as a kind of "Introit," expressing a feeling of jubilant gratitude. It consists, formally, of a canon at the octave in eight parts. The soloist sings in an *arioso* style of "free melody," while the pervading melodic atmosphere derives partly from Gregorian chant and partly from Castillian folksong. As the composer writes: "The generative harmonic factor is the perfect chord which stretches itself lazily up to the major seventh that punctuates the Sapphic cadence of Unamuno's verse. This whole harmonic atmosphere is maintained in the same 'climate' to the end, extended over the bimodalism of an ambiguous tonality . . ."

The musical genealogy of this work may be traced in an unbroken line from some of Rodrigo's earliest compositions, such as the settings for voice and piano of the *Cantiga* by Gil Vicente, "Muy graciosa es la Doncella" (1925); of the *Serranilla* by the Marqués de Santillana (1928); of the *Cantico de la Esposa* by St. John of the Cross (1934); and of the *Cuatro Madrigales Amatorios* based on well-known love-songs of the 16th century, among them "Vos me matasteis" and "De los álamos vengo" (1947; orchestrated in 1948). Its direct antecedent is probably to be found in the *Ausencias de Dulcinea*, with texts from the *Don Quixote* of Cervantes, composed for large orchestra, bass solo voice and four sopranos (1948), which is one of Rodrigo's most impressive scores.

Again like Falla, Rodrigo has turned to the Catalan language and the poetry of Jacinto Verdaguer, in his setting of the latter's *Triptic de Mossen Cinto* (1946) and in his *Cuatre cançons en llengua catalana* (1946), both for voice and orchestra. Among his numerous evocations of the great age of Spanish poetry are his settings of Lope de Vega's *Romance del Comendador de Ocaña* (1947-48) and of the *romance* "Triste Estaba el Rey David" (for chorus, 1950), and his incidental music for Calderón's *La Vida es Sueño* (1954).

In 1955 he composed the score of a ballet, *Pavana Real*, inspired by the music of Luis Milán. For solo guitar he has written a *Tiento* (1942) and *Tres piezas españolas* (1954).

Since 1939 Rodrigo has lived in Madrid, where he teaches the history of music at the Faculty of Philosophy and Letters of the University. In 1944 he obtained the National Music Prize for his work as a whole; in 1950 he was elected a member of the Academy of Fine Arts of San Fernando; and, in 1953, he was awarded the Grand Cross of the Order of Alfonso the Wise. Not an innovator, but a sincere and sensitive artist, Rodrigo continues and intensifies, with a profound sense of tradition, the cycle of enlightened nationalism initiated by Barbieri and Pedrell.

ANOTHER HALFFTER

Cristóbal Halffter (nephew of Ernesto and Rodolfo), was born in Madrid on March 24, 1930. Like Ernesto he was precocious and began to compose at the age of thirteen. From 1947 to 1951 he was a pupil of Conrado del Campo at the Madrid Conservatory, twice winning the "Extraordinary Prize" for harmony and composition. Since 1951 he has been on the staff of the Spanish National Radio as musical commentator. In 1953 he won the National Music Prize for his Concerto for piano and orchestra, which was first performed in Madrid by the National Orchestra under the direction of Eduardo Toldrá, with the pianist Manuel Carra. In 1956 he received the International Prize of the "Jeunesses Musicales" (UNESCO) for his *Two Movements* for kettle drum and string orchestra. He is the regular conductor of the "Orquesta Manuel de Falla" (chamber orchestra).

Besides the works already mentioned, Halffter has written a sonata for piano (1951); *Antifona Regina Coeli* for four solo voices, mixed chorus and orchestra (1952); two motets for chorus *a capella* (1954); three pieces for string quartet

(1955); concertino for string orchestra (1956); the ballet *Saeta* (produced by the Ballets of the Marqués de Cuevas, Paris, 1955); various songs for voice and piano (also orchestrated); and the *Misa Ducal* for mixed chorus and organ (or orchestra), first performed in Madrid at the inauguration of the renovated "Palacio de Liria" (home of the Dukes of Alba). This Mass was commissioned by the present Duke and Duchess of .Alba, to whom the score is dedicated. The first public performance was given in Madrid on October 26, 1956, with the Orquesta Nacional conducted by the late Ataulfo Argenta (d. 1958).

In Halffter's *Misa Ducal* the scoring is for two flutes, piccolo, two oboes, English horn, three clarinets, violas *a tre*, 'cellos, and double-basses. The writing is tonal, but freely so, with modal passages and serial or twelve-tone influences.

THE DISPERSED GENERATION

Writing of "The Younger Generation" in 1941, I asked, "Will these young composers ever be able to reincorporate themselves into the musical life of Spain? Will they not rather be absorbed into the cultural stream of the countries in which they are now residing?" The composers in question were those whose lives had been disrupted by the Civil War of 1936-39, which forced them into exile in various parts of the world. Of the "dispersed" musicians mentioned in that chapter, only one, to my knowledge, has returned to Spain. He is Enrique Casal Chapí, who went from the Dominican Republic to Uruguay, whence he returned to his native country in 1956. Of the others, Gustavo Durán became a citizen of the United States, served in the American diplomatic corps and later joined the staff of the United Nations. He has not been active musically. Gustavo Pittaluga has devoted his energies chiefly to conducting in various Latin American countries. Rosa García Ascot, Rodolfo Halffter, and Adolfo

Salazar have remained in Mexico City, taking a very active part in the musical life of that capital. Salazar's work as critic and historian has overshadowed his work as a composer, which nonetheless deserves at least passing mention. His output includes some orchestral scores, chamber music, piano pieces, and songs. In 1955 a breakdown in health sent him into permanent seclusion. He died in 1958. Julián Bautista has remained in Buenos Aires, Argentina, active in the Argentine League of Composers, writing film scores, and composing steadily. His recent production merits attention.

The Argentine critic Roberto García Morillo, in a valuable monograph on Bautista, suggests that four different "manners" (not chronological phases) may be discerned in that composer's music: impressionistic, nationalist *("españolista")*, neoclassical, and contemporaneous. As in the case of Falla, the conjunction of traditional (Hispanic) and contemporary (international) factors is decisive in some of his most significant works, such as *Tres Ciudades* for voice and orchestra, on poems of García Lorca (1937); the *Fantasía española* for clarinet and orchestra (1945-46); the *Catro poemas galegos* for voice and orchestra (also arranged for piano, 1946); and the *Romance del Rey Rodrigo* for mixed chorus *a cappella* (1955-56). Of his works in neoclassical vein, the most important are the first and second *Sonata concertata a quattro* (1933-34 and 1938), the *Sonate à quattre, d'après Giovanni Battista Pergolesi* (1939), and the *Sinfonía Breve* for orchestra (1956).

In *Tres Ciudades (Three Cities)*, Bautista pays his tribute to Andalusia, as most Spanish composers have done in one form or another. The music is analogous to the poetry of García Lorca, in that it extracts the essence of the vernacular, preserving the latter's primitive strength and expressiveness, and distils this essence in an artistically controlled formal structure while preserving the semblance of spontaneity. The work is in three contrasting sections: (1) *Malagueña,* intense and tragic; (2) *Barrio de Córdoba* (Nocturne), emotion mysteriously veiled; (3) *Baile* (Seville), passionate, dramatic, sensuous and exultant. The first performance took place at the Festival of the International Society for Contemporary Music in 1938.

The *Catro Poemas Galegos (Four Galician Poems)* are scored for solo voice, flute, oboe, clarinet, viola, 'cello and harp. The text, in the Galician language, consists of poems by Lorenzo Varela *(Maria Pita and Three Medieval Portraits)*. These poems evoke the heroic past of Spain, from the ninth to the sixteenth centuries, through episodes related to celebrated figures of Galician history: Maria Pita, who defended the city of La Coruña against the forces of Sir Frances Drake; the Bishop Adaulfo II of Santiago de Compostela, who proved his innocence by taming a brave bull in the ring; Ruy Xordo, leader of a peasant uprising against feudalism; and María Balteira, gay companion in love and war of troubadours and jongleurs in the reign of Alfonso the Wise. This composition, tense with confrontations of the archaic and the modern, the rustic and the sophisticated, the lyrical and the dramatic; textured with supreme economy of means; strong and harsh at need, and always powerfully evocative, places Bautista unmistakably within the great, authentic tradition of Hispanic music.

Bautista's position within the creative mainstream of Spanish music is further confirmed by his setting of the *Romance del Rey Rodrigo* for chorus *a cappella,* which received its world première at Buenos Aires on August 3, 1956, sung by the "Conjunto Madrigalista" of the Association of Chamber Music Concerts, which commissioned the work. The text is taken from the anonymous cycle of the traditional *Romancero Español* dealing with the defeat by the Moors of the last Visigothic King of Spain. According to the legend, King

Roderick was betrayed by "La Cava," whose love he had forced and whose father, Count Julian, made a treacherous pact with the Moors. The work is divided into three main sections: "The Phophecy," "The Letter" (written by "La Cava" to her father) and "The Betrayal," each preceded by a brief "Imprecation" or lament for the betrayal and downfall of Spain. The music rejoins the great polyphonic tradition of Spanish music within the framework of twentieth century dissonant and polyrhythmic writing, avoiding mere grandiloquence in an expressive atmosphere marked by both sobriety and vehemence, by dramatic intensity and soaring lyricism.

Thus Bautista, while physically far removed from Spain, continues to be deeply conscious of his mission as a Spanish composer and appears determined to fulfill his destiny as one of the chief continuators of the national tradition in contemporary Spanish music.

Rodolfo Halffter, who became a Mexican citizen, is director of a publishing firm, Ediciones Mexicanas de Música, and for several years edited the review *Nuestra Música*. His most important work written after he left Spain is the Concerto for violin and orchestra (1939-40), first performed by Samuel Dushkin (for whom it was written) in June, 1942, with the Mexican Symphony Orchestra conducted by Chávez. Later, Halffter made a thorough revision of this score.

Halffter's music for piano written during this period includes *Homenaje a Antonio Machado* (1944), composed in memory of the great contemporary Spanish poet; two piano sonatas (1949 and 1951); and *Eleven Bagatelles* (1949), composed primarily as study pieces but thoroughly representative of his mature style, marked by systematic use of polytonality. An ingratiating *Pastorale* for violin and piano dates from 1940, and in 1946 he made settings for voice and piano of two sonnets by Sor Juana Inés de la Cruz.

Halffter has shown a continuing interest in the ballet, as demonstrated by three scores: *La Madrugada del Panadero* (*The Baker's Early Rising*, 1940), a ribald and macabre tale of a baker's flirtatious wife; *Elena la Traicionera* (1945), on a Mexican subject; and *Tonantzintla* (1952), based on the keyboard sonatas of Antonio Soler and named after a celebrated Baroque church in Puebla, Mexico.

The method of composing with twelve tones has attracted Halffter in recent years. He has utilized this idiom in *Tres Hojas de Album* for piano, in Three Pieces for String Orchestra (1956), and in the String Quartet (1957) commissioned by the University of Michigan.

Halffter's continued Hispanism is evidenced in the style of his two piano sonatas, which follow the Scarlatti-Soler tradition in a modern idiom; and also by his orchestration of three sonatas by Padre Antonio Soler. His *Three Epitaphs* for mixed chorus (for Don Quixote, for Dulcinea, and for Sancho Panza), with texts by Cervantes, were performed with notable success at the Inter-American Music Festival in Washington, D. C., in April, 1958.

COMPOSERS OF CATALONIA

Federico Mompou, born in Barcelona on April 16, 1893, is now generally recognized as one of the most distinctive voices in contemporary music. Although limited in scope and tenuous in texture, his compositions, which are mostly for piano, possess a genuine poetic quality and an emotional freshness that derive from their very simplicity. Mompou himself has defined his aesthetic ideal as tending toward an intimate type of musical expression, the cultivation of music in a state of purity, motivated by a purposeful reaction against the "cerebralism" dominant in our epoch. He reacts against the "music of the laboratory," seeking a true form of expression in a lyrical feeling enriched by the musical experience of the past. His musical style has been called "New Primitivism" and the composer characterizes it by the term *recomien-zo*, a recommencing or beginning afresh. Harmonic modulation and thematic development are reduced to a minimum, in favor of sheer evocation and sonorous sensibility.

Mompou's compositions for piano include *Canço i Dança, Cants Magics, Dialogues, Charmes,* and Preludes. He has also written a number of songs, to both Catalan and Castillian texts, such as *L'Hora grisa, Combat del somni,* and *Llueve sobre el río* (text by Juan Ramón Jiménez). Since 1941 Mompou has lived in Barcelona.

Xavier Montsalvatge Bassols, born in Gerona on March 11, 1912, has made his reputation largely with his songs, although his works in other forms have not lacked recognition, especially his numerous ballets and the opera buffa *Puss in Boots* (after the story by Perrault), which was produced at the Liceo of Barcelona in 1947. He studied at the Municipal School of Music in Barcelona, where his teachers in composition were Enric Morera and Jaime Pahissa. At the age of twenty-four he won the "Felipe Pedrell Prize" for his *Little Burlesque Suite* for violin and woodwind quartet. In 1949, the prize of the Municipality of Barcelona was awarded to him for the *Mediterranean Symphony,* and in 1952 he obtained another prize for his *Indian Quartet.* Other instrumental compositions include the symphonic suite *La Muerte enamorada* and *Variations on an Españoleta by Giles Farnaby* for violin and piano. Among his songs the most famous are the *Cinco canciones negras (Five Negro Songs),* with texts by Rafael Alberti, Nestor Luján, Nicolas Guillén, and Ildefonso Pereda Valdés. These songs have been orchestrated by the composer. Montsalvatge has also written a vocal-symphonic poem for chorus, soli and orchestra, titled *Égloga del Tajo (Eclogue of the River Tagus).*

Narciso Bonet, born in Barcelona on January 22, 1933, studied in his native city with a number of teachers, among whom he considers Juan Massià and Eduardo Toldrá as most

decisive for his musical formation. Later, from 1949, he
studied composition with Nadia Boulanger at the American
Conservatory in Fontainebleau, obtaining first prizes for composition in 1952 and 1953. Beginning in 1949, he has appeared
frequently as pianist. In May, 1957, one of his most important works, the *Missa in Epiphanie Domini*, for chorus, soli
and orchestra, received its première in Barcelona under the
direction of Alain Milhaud. Among his other works are a
Suite for string orchestra (1952), Four Nocturnes for piano
(1951), *Canço de bressol de la Verge*, for chorus and orchestra (1951), Sonata for violin and piano (1956), and *Retablo
de Nativitate Christi* (1957). He has also made arrangements of Catalonian folksongs for mixed chorus.

TWO "SPANISH" COMPOSERS OF THE
UNITED STATES

Joaquín Nin-Culmell and Carlos Surinach are both citi-
zens of the United States and make their permanent home
in this country, yet both are entitled to be considered as "Spanish" composers because, in spite of their completely cosmopolitan backgrounds, they have maintained profound musical
ties with Spain in their creative work.

As a pupil of Manuel de Falla and as the son of the eminent pianist and composer Joaquín Nin y Castellanos (born
in Cuba when that country belonged to Spain, of Catalan
ancestry), Joaquín Nin-Culmell can claim both physical and
spiritual kinship with Spain. He was born in Berlin (where
his father happened to be teaching at the time) on September 5, 1908. As a child he was brought to the United States,
where he received his early schooling; and as an adolescent
he was taken to Paris, where he studied piano and theory at
the Schola Cantorum and composition with Paul Dukas at
the Conservatoire. During several summers he also studied
composition with Manuel de Falla in Granada. In 1936 he

returned to the United States, in 1940 joined the music faculty of Williams College, and in 1948 went to the University of California in Berkeley, where he holds the rank of Professor of Music. On leave of absence, he spent two years (1956-58) in Spain, composing and concertizing. He has toured widely as pianist and has also been active as a conductor.

Nin-Culmell's most important scores to date are the Quintet for piano and string quartet (1938) and the Concerto for piano and orchestra (1955). The former was first performed at the festival of the International Society for Contemporary Music at London in 1938. The Piano Concerto received its première with the Rochester Philharmonic Symphony Orchestra under the direction of Erich Leinsdorf, with the composer as soloist. For piano he has written *Three Impressions* (1930) and a sonata (1934, reprinted as *Sonata Breve* in 1955); for guitar, *Six Variations on a Theme by Milan;* and for orchestra, *Eight Variations on a Theme by Sanz* (the 17th-century Spanish guitarist, Gaspar Sanz). His vocal compositions and arrangements include Three Poems of Gil Vicente for soprano and piano, Two Poems of Jorge Manrique for soprano and string quartet, Twelve Catalonian Folksongs for soprano and piano, and Three Traditional Cuban Songs for mixed chorus. In 1956 he commenced a series of *Tonadas* for piano, based on folk tunes from different regions of Spain, ranging from the Balearics to Galicia. One of these, the *Diferencia sobre la arada de Salamanca* (No. 5), recalls the *diferencias* or variations on folk tunes written by Cabezón and other 16th-century Spanish composers. In 1958, while living in Barcelona, Nin-Culmell completed the score of a three-act ballet on the theme of Don Juan.

Carlos Surinach has made his home in New York City since 1951, but he continues to be a "Spanish" composer, not by citizenship, but by his music, which achieves an effect of novelty by exploiting all the familiar clichés of the "Spanish idiom" with new technical resources and with a completely non-impressionistic sensibility. Sharply etched lines, dissonant clashes, emphasis on the sheer primitive power of rhythm, and strong reliance on percussion, give to his music a mid-twentieth century accent that contrasts with the post-impressionistic language prevalent in most contemporary Spanish composition. Surinach breaks with the tradition that has made France the chïef breeding-ground for Spanish composers since Albéniz and Granados. Although he made Paris his professional headquarters for several years, his decisive musical training (after initial studies with Morera in Barcelona) was received in Germany, specifically in Berlin, Duesseldorf and Cologne. Unlike other Spanish composers who underwent marked German influence (e.g., Conrado del Campo and Oscar Esplá), Surinach brought his disciplined technique to bear mainly on the Andalusian idiom, which he galvanized into new life by treating it not as romantic atmosphere but as raw material for firmly structured and tautly textured scores, in which individual instrumental lines are thrust into sharp relief against a strongly percussive rhythmic base. His stress on the "Moorish" associations of Spanish music are also in line with the present cult of the exotic, the general interest in primitive and non-European musics. Typical of this aspect of Surinach's music are the *Three Berber Songs* of 1952, for flute, oboe, clarinet, viola, 'cello and harp.

The title of a set of piano pieces for children, *Tales From the Flamenco Kingdom* (1955), might be taken as symbolic of Surinach's production as a whole. He has made the "Flamenco Kingdom" his musical domain. The *Danza Andaluza* (1946) for small orchestra, the *Flamenquerías* (1951) for two pianos, the *Tientos* (1953) for chamber ensemble, the *Sinfonietta Flamenca* for orchestra in four movements (1953), and the ballet *Ritmo Jondo* (1953), are all landmarks in this kingdom. *Ritmo Jondo* was originally written, characteristically, for clarinet, trumpet, timpani (alternating with tamburo), xylophone, and three hand-clappers. The inclusion of hand clapping as part of the percussion was a very clever stroke. The composer kept this feature, so evocative of the traditional *cuadro flamenco*, when he revised this score as a ballet, commissioned by the Bethsabée de Rothschild Foundation and first performed by José Limon and his company in New York City on April 15, 1953.

Surinach has also writen a number of "abstract" or non-representational works, such as the Quartet for piano and strings (1944), the *Passacaglia Symphony* (1945), the Second Symphony in four movements (1949), the *Doppio Concertino* in three movements for violin, piano and chamber orchestra (1954), the Concerto for piano, strings and cymbals (1956) and the *Short Symphony* (1957), proving that he has no intention of restricting himself to the "Flamenco Kingdom." And yet even these scores would not be what they are, would not have that peculiar and fascinating symbiosis of Teutonic technique and Mediterranean temperament, if Surinach had not lingered, in spirit, near that mythical Andalusian kingdom whose symbols are the Alhambra and the Giralda and whose geographical boundaries are not to be measured but imagined.

Notes

NOTES FOR CHAPTER I

[1] The same codex contains another secular Latin song, *Disticon Filomelaicum*, also written by St. Eugene. These melodies, written in Visigothic neumes, are as yet intranscribable. The transcription of S. Tafall (*Bolétin de la Real Academia Gallega*, 1915, p. 327), reproduced by Trend (*The Music of Spanish History*, p. 201), is entirely arbitrary.

[2] Catalonia's musical importance dates from somewhat later. The monastery of Santa María de Ripoll in Catalonia was a flourishing musical center in the tenth and eleventh centuries.

[3] As many as ten Christian churches functioned in Toledo and its environs during the Moslem occupation of that city.

[4] The Mozarabic rite was allowed to continue up to the present time in a special chapel of Toledo Cathedral dedicated to that purpose by Cisneros.

[5] All that we know about Hispano-Arabic music is derived from theoretical and literary sources, since no actual musical documents have been preserved. Ribera's theory concerning the Arabic derivation of medieval secular music in Europe rests upon no solid foundation.

[6] The *Cantigas* have been preserved in four codices (three with music) copied at the court of Alfonso X. The *Codex princeps* is that of the Escorial Monastery, with 417 compositions.

[7] As Gustave Reese (*Music in the Middle Ages*, p. 247) writes, the transcriptions of Ribera, "with their drawing-room accompaniments, are quite fantastic." Higini Anglès has a modern edition of the *Cantigas* in preparation; this should be definitive. Ribera's edition (see Bibliography) is useful only for the facsimiles and the illustrations.

[8] The rectangular psaltery was introduced into Spain by the Arabs under the name of *qânûn*.

[9] Reproduced in facsimile by Vindel (see Bibliography). The transcriptions by Tafall (reprinted by Trend, *op. cit.*) are not authoritative. Somewhat better results were achieved by Isabel Pope (see Bibliography).

[10] Quoted by Menéndez Pidal, *Poesia Juglaresca y Juglares*, p. 376.

NOTES FOR CHAPTER II

[1] Cited by Mitjana, *La Musique en Espagne*, p. 1955.

[2] *Cf.* Chapter VI.

[3] This was the Spaniard Rodrigo Borgia, who bestowed upon Ferdinand and Isabel the title of "Catholic Kings," by which they are known in Spanish history.

[4] Published in 1890 as *Cancionero Musical de los Siglos XV y XVI*. Before the discovery of this collection, no music by Encina was known.

[5] After the eighteenth century the term "villancico" retained only its religious associations, being applied usually to songs celebrating the Nativity (Spanish equivalent of the Christmas carol).

[6] Juan Díaz Rengifo, *Arte Poética Española* (Salamanca, 1592).

[7] *Cf*. Chapter V.

[8] Dr. Alfred Einstein was kind enough to call to my attention, and to copy out for me, nine Spanish villancicos published anonymously in an Italian collection of part songs dating from 1516 (*Frottole Libro Secondo*), probably printed by J. A. de Laneto at Naples (*cf*. E. Vogel, *Bibliothek der gedruckten weltlichen Vocalmusik Italiens aus den Jahren 1500–1700*, II. Band, pp. 373–374), which is in the Biblioteca Marucelliana at Florence. Among them is this villancico by Encina, identified from the Barbieri *Cancionero*, the two versions differing but slightly.

[9] This villancico evidently was long and widely known, for Luis Milán mentions it in his *El Cortesano* (1561).

[10] Compare especially the villancico *De Monzón venía el mozo* with the melody of the Mozarabic plain song *Pange lingua* (which in its extant version, incidentally, cannot be dated earlier than the fifteenth century).

[11] It is interesting to note that several Spanish villancicos appear in the collections of Petrucci, including the *Odhecaton* (1501), the first printed collection of part music. The villancico *Nunca fué pena mayor*, found in the *Odhecaton*, is also in Barbieri's *Cancionero* (No. 1), where the text is attributed to Don García Alvarez de Toledo, first Duke of Alba, and the music to Juan Urrede. Pierre de la Rue, who came to Spain in the suite of Philip the Handsome, wrote a Mass on this song.

[12] Notes for the *Anthologie Sonore*, Vol. II, p. 20.

[13] *Cf*. Chapter XII.

[14] *La Musique en Espagne*, p. 1947.

[15] The text and music were published by Gaston Paris in *Chansons du XVe Siècle* (Société des Anciens Textes Français, Paris, 1875). See also *Romania*, Tome I, p. 363.

[16] *Cf*. Chapter III.

[17] Paul Henry Láng, *Music in Western Civilization* (New York, 1941), p. 262.

NOTES FOR CHAPTER III

[1] *Cf*. Janet Dodge, "Lute Music of the XVIth and XVIIth Centuries," in *Proceedings of the Musical Association*, London, 34th Session (1907–1908), p. 126.

[2] *Cf*. *Instrumentos Músicos del Duque de Calabria*, in *Revista de Archivos*, Tomo I (1871), pp. 187 ff.

[3] *Cf*. H. Collet, *Le Mysticisme Musical Espagnol au XVIe Siècle*, p. 107.

[4] Pedrell was under the erroneous impression that *El Cortesano* was a translation of Castiglione's work. Cf. *Cancionero Musical*, III, p. 31.

[5] *Analytical and Historical Notes* for the *Anthologie Sonore*, Vol. IV, p. 27.

[6] Valderrábano wrote 120 variations on this tune, Pisador 37, Mudarra 12, and Venegas de Henestrosa 5.

[7] W. Apel, in *The Musical Quarterly*, Vol. XX, No. 3, p. 301.

[8] *Cf. Revista Musical Catalana*, Any XXXIII, No. 388, pp. 140–143.

[9] There is some uncertainty as to the actual date of the first edition of this work.

[10] An English translation of *Marcos de Obregón* was published at London in 1816.

[11] A woodcut in Amat's treatise also shows the neck of the guitar bent back near the top; but early drawings, such as those of Milán and Bermudo, show a virtually straight neck.

NOTES FOR CHAPTER IV

[1] *The Musical Quarterly*, Vol. XX, No. 3, p. 298.

[2] Published by La Mara in *Briefe hervorragender Zeitgenossen an Franz Liszt* (Leipzig, 1895), Vol. I, p. 256; quoted by Mitjana in *La Musique en Espagne*, p. 1992.

[3] Quoted by Pedrell, Introduction to Vol. III of *Hispaniae Schola Musica Sacra*.

[4] In the Archives of Simancas (No. 1345) there is a list of the musicians who accompanied Philip II to England, and Antonio de Cabezón is included therein.

[5] This title requires some explanation. The term "tecla" was used in Spain to designate all the keyboard instruments known at that time (organ, clavichord, harpsichord, etc.). The use of the term "vihuela" has already been explained (*cf.* Chapter III), and "arpa," of course, was the word for harp. It is evident that Cabezón wrote primarily for the organ, and the inclusion of the terms "vihuela" and "arpa" was primarily a concession to the popular taste of the day.

[6] Pedrell, *Diccionario Bio-Bibliográfico de los Músicos Españoles*, article on Bermudo, p. 179.

[7] Most of the tunes given by Salinas were transcribed and reproduced in Pedrell's *Lírica Nacionalizada* (see Bibliography). Dr. Burney also included some of these tunes in his *History of Music* (Vol. III, pp. 293 ff.).

[8] F. T. Arnold, *The Art of Accompanying from a Thorough-Bass* (London, 1931), p. 5.

[9] *Historical Organ Recitals*, VI, Preface.

NOTES FOR CHAPTER V

[1] *Critical and Bibliographical Notes on Early Spanish Music*, pp. 3–4.

[2] *Estudios Sobre Algunos Músicos del Siglo XVI*, p. 183.

[3] Also in Italy; J. B. Trend mentions an unpublished Mass by Morales on the tune of the Spanish folk song *Tristezas me matan*, which is in the Sistine Chapel at Rome, and quotes from it in his article on Morales (*cf.* Bibliography).

[4] *Nouvelle Histoire de la Musique*, I, p. 287.

[5] The facts of Victoria's life given here differ considerably from those generally accepted. They are based largely upon the researches of Rafael Casimiri (*cf.* Bibliography), upon which the author also drew in preparing the article on Victoria for the 4th edition of *Baker's Biographical Dictionary of Musicians*.

[6] For an account of musical activity in the Congregation of the Oratory, see *The History of the Popes from the Close of the Middle Ages*. From the German of Ludwig, Freiherr von Pastor. Edited by Ralph Francis Kerr. Vol. XIX, Ch. IV (London, 1930).

[7] *The International Cyclopedia of Music and Musicians* (New York, 1939), p. 1352.

[8] *Histoire de l'Opéra en Europe Avant Lully et Scarlatti*, p. 29.

[9] *Nouvelle Histoire de la Musique*, I, p. 289.

[10] The importance of the role that Spanish musicians played in the development of the so-called "Roman School" cannot be overemphasized. This point was strongly brought out by Dr. Southgate, when he remarked, "I think there would have been no Palestrina if there had been no Morales to show what could be done in church music." Cf. *Proceedings of the Musical Association*, London, 34th Session (1907–1908), p. 43.

[11] *Lira Sacro-Hispana*.

NOTES FOR CHAPTER VI

[1] The word *auto* is derived from the Latin *actus* and was originally a forensic term. It came to be applied to solemn public acts, such as the *Autos de Fé* of the Inquisition or the *Autos Sacramentales*, the religious plays celebrating the mystery of the Eucharist, which at first were performed in the streets during the feast of Corpus Christi. Spanish dramatists, and Calderón in particular, developed the *Auto Sacramental* into an artistic dramatic form. Music played an important part in the performance of these *Autos Sacramentales*. But in the eighteenth century they degenerated and were forbidden by royal decree. The term *auto* was also loosely applied to any short dramatic work, secular or sacred.

[2] Reprinted by Morphy, *Les Luthistes Espagnols*, Vol. II.

[3] Cf. *Gil Vicente, Obras Completas. Anotadas por Marques Braga* (Coimbra, 1933), Vol. I, p. 88, footnote.

[4] Otto Gombosi (*Acta Musicologica*, Vol. VIII, 1936) attempts to show that the *folía* was of Italian origin.

[5] The earliest known musical example of the *folías* in Spain is contained in Salinas's *De musica libri septem* (1577).

[6] Cervantes, *Prólogo al lector*, in his *Comedias y Entremeses* (Madrid, 1615).

[7] *La Selva sin Amor* was first printed in 1630; it is found in Vol. 5 (first series) of the *Obras Completas* of Lope de Vega published by the Academia Española.

[8] *Zarza* in Spanish means bramblebush. La Zarzuela was a common name for villages and hamlets in Spain. It was near one of these villages that the Palace of La Zarzuela stood; hence its name.

[9] The *loa* was a prologue, sometimes in the form of a dialogue spoken by two or more actors. In the *loa* for *Hipómenes y Atalanta* (1659) by Antonio de Solís there was acting, singing, and dancing.

[10] The *mojiganga* was originally a popular festival at carnival time, a sort of burlesque masquerade, accompanied by the music of flutes, castanets, and side drum. After the middle of the seventeenth century it was generally

replaced, as conclusion for a dramatic performance, by the *Fin de Fiesta*, less crude in character.

[11] Pedrell published four musical numbers (two 4-part choruses and two solos) from *El Jardín de Falerina* in his *Catàlech* of the Barcelona Library (Vol. II, pp. 287–291) and reprinted them in his *Cancionero*, IV.

[12] This comedy, based on the fable of Cephalus and Procris in Ovid's *Metamorphoses*, was not included in any of the original editions of Calderón's works; but it is found in Part 19 of *Comedias Nuevas y Escogidas de los Mejores Ingenios de España* (Madrid, 1663).

[13] Music for these two plays is included in Pedrell's *Teatro Lírico*, IV and V. But Pedrell erroneously attributes the text of *Los Celos Hacen Estrellas* to Luis Vélez de Guevara (father of Juan Vélez), who died in 1644; moreover, the sixth number included by Pedrell among the musical examples from this play is in reality from another work.

[14] *Cf*. Pedrell, *Cancionero*, IV (No. 93).

[15] Cited by Cotarelo y Mori, *Historia de la Zarzuela*, p. 70. In the original Spanish the word "opera" is used, curiously, to mean orchestra.

[16] This song, and another by Marín, *Desengañémonos ya* (*Let Us Be Undeceived*), are included in Joaquín Nin's *Sept Chants Lyriques Espagnols* (freely harmonized).

[17] An admirable *jácara*, for three sopranos and chorus, is in Pedrell's *Cancionero*, IV (No. 101). The *jácara* was also a dance, and as such we find it incorporated in collections of instrumental music along with other old dance forms.

[18] Cited by Subirá, in *Las Ciencias*, II, Año II, No. 1 (1935), pp. 166 ff.

[19] Compare the anecdote told about Durón, p. 121. Evidently the devil was held in high esteem as a musician by all Spaniards.

NOTES FOR CHAPTER VII

[1] Domenico Scarlatti died in Madrid on July 23, 1757, as proved by a document discovered in 1936 by Dr. Luise Bauer and described in an unpublished thesis. Cf. *Archiv für Musikforschung* (1938), p. 335, footnote.

[2] Some writers claim that he visited Dublin in 1740–1741.

[3] Yet Farinelli apparently took some interest in Scarlatti's music, for it was he who brought to Bologna the principal MS. collection of Scarlatti's keyboard compositions, that which originally belonged to Queen María Barbara and was later deposited in the Biblioteca Marciana, Venice.

[4] Cf. *Annual Report of the Librarian of Congress*, 1940 (Washington, 1941), pp. 142–143.

[5] For the best estimate of Boccherini's music, see the article on that composer in *Cobbett's Cyclopedic Survey of Chamber Music*.

[6] *Cf.* the article on Spanish Chamber Music in *Cobbett's Cyclopedic Survey of Chamber Music*, Vol. II, pp. 439–444.

[7] The first volume of J. Nin's *Classiques Espagnols du Violon* (Paris, 1937) contains ten pieces by Herrando with the bass "realized" for piano.

NOTES FOR CHAPTER VIII

[1] Reprinted by Eslava, *Lira Sacro-Hispana*.

[2] These numbers were printed by Cotarelo y Mori in *Don Ramón de la Cruz* (Madrid, 1899). Teresa's air was also printed by Mitjana, *La Musique en Espagne*, pp. 2164-2166.

[3] This, and another famous *polo* by García, *Cuerpo bueno, alma divina*, from the tonadilla *El Criado Fingido* (*The Pretended Servant*), were reprinted by Mitjana, *La Musique en Espagne*, pp. 2293-2299. See also Chapter XIX.

[4] He was the son of Francesco Basili, who as director of the Milan Conservatory refused Verdi admittance to that institution, and who was later choirmaster of St. Peter's in Rome.

[5] Chueca has aptly been called "the barrel organ of his generation." His *Marcha de Cádiz*, from the zarzuela *Cádiz*, became the national hymn of Spain under the monarchy.

NOTES FOR CHAPTER IX

[1] A legend has it that Terradellas drowned himself in the Tiber owing to the failure of his opera *Sesostri*. There is no factual support for this.

[2] Copies of six operas by Martín y Soler are in the Library of Congress. A new edition of *Una Cosa Rara* was brought out by L. Sachse (Halle, 1922).

[3] Quoted by Pedrell, *Diccionario Bio-Bibliográfico de los Músicos Españoles*, article on Asenjo Barbieri, p. 131.

[4] *Historia de la Zarzuela* (Prologue).

[5] Quoted by E. Istel in *The Musical Quarterly* (see Bibliography).

[6] Eximeno (b. Valencia, 1729; d. Rome, 1808) was an eminent Jesuit writer on music. In his *Dell'Origine e delle Regole della Musica* (Rome, 1774; Spanish translation, 1776) he protested against pedantic rules in musical theory. His satirical novel *Don Lazarillo Vizcardi* (edited by Barbieri, 2 vols., 1872-1873) gives a vivid picture of musical life in eighteenth-century Spain.

[7] April 15, 1893.

[8] For Pedrell's relation to the Catalan school, see Chapter XI.

NOTES FOR CHAPTER X

[1] Arbós later made brilliant orchestral transcriptions of several numbers from the *Iberia* of Albéniz, namely, *Evocación*, *Fête-Dieu à Seville*, *Triana*, *El Puerto*, and *El Albaicín*.

[2] The Tango in D is almost invariably played in the elaborate arrangement by Godowsky, which destroys the simple charm of the original version.

[3] Albéniz left unfinished two other pieces for piano, *Navarra* (completed by Déodat de Sévérac) and *Azulejos* (completed by Granados). The former was orchestrated by Fernández Arbós in 1926.

[4] *Revue Musicale S.I.M.* (December 1, 1913), p. 43. See also L. Vallas, *Les Idées de Claude Debussy* (Paris, 1927; English translation as *The Theories of Claude Debussy*, London, 1929).

[5] A term applied to the more flamboyant element of the Madrid populace.

[6] Some of these sketches are reproduced in Subirá's book on Granados (see Bibliography), and in the *Diccionario de la Música Ilustrado* (Barcelona, 1930), Vol. I, p. 559.

[7] This is a beautiful and finely wrought work, well worth the attention of orchestral conductors. The score was published by G. Schirmer in 1915.

[8] This is reproduced on the cover of the vocal score of the opera, published by G. Schirmer in 1915 (with an English translation of the libretto).

[9] Kolodin, *The Metropolitan Opera* (New York, 1940), p. 223.

[10] Granados wrote several other operas besides *Goyescas*, among them *María del Carmen* (1898), which Spanish critics consider his most important dramatic work.

[11] *Dictionary of Modern Music and Musicians* (ed. A. Eaglefield Hull), p. 197.

[12] *The Musical Times* (August, 1917).

NOTES FOR CHAPTER XI

[1] *Cf.* the author's article of that title in the New York *Times Magazine* (March 26, 1939). See also E. Allison Peers, *Catalonia Infelix* (New York, 1938).

[2] Born in 1893, pupil of Koechlin and Ravel in Paris. His orchestral works include 3 *Dances Valencianes*, *Escenes i Paisatges Valencians*, *Coplas de mi Tierra*, and *Gongoriana*. For piano: *Valencia*, *Muntanyesa*, *Breves Preludios*, etc.

[3] Best known for his *Pinceladas Goyescas* for orchestra.

[4] *Cf.* Chapter XIII.

[5] *Revue Musicale S.I.M.* (December, 1913).

[6] At the time of writing (1941) these last two works had not yet been performed.

[7] His operas include *La Adúltera Penitente* (1917) and *Jardín de Oriente* (1923).

[8] Villa (1873–1935), who was conductor of the Municipal Band of Madrid, also wrote a *Rapsodia Asturiana* for violin and orchestra, first performed by Sarasate.

[9] The most famous musician produced by Navarre was, of course, Pablo de Sarasate, who figures among the virtuosi in Chapter XIV.

[10] Also known as Padre Donostia (the Basque name for San Sebastián). He is a member of the Franciscan Order and studied composition with E. Cools in Paris. For his folklore publications, see the Bibliography for Chapter XV.

[11] Born in Madrid, but of Basque parentage, was Vicente Arregui (1871–1925), composer of a strongly regional Basque Symphony, and of the successful opera *Iolanda* (Madrid Royal Opera, 1923).

[12] *La Música Contemporánea en España*, p. 223.

NOTES FOR CHAPTER XII

[1] Henry Prunières, in the New York *Times*, April 8, 1928.

[2] Where no other source is given, the quotations in this chapter are from autobiographical notes supplied to the author by Falla under date of April 23, 1939.

[3] Falla (*loc. cit.*) remarks that the first of these works, *Los Amores de la Inés*, deserved its fate, but that he retains a better recollection of the second, *La Casa de Tócame Roque*.

[4] *Collected Essays* (London, 1932), p. 14.

[5] *Cf.* Chapter XIX.

[6] For a fuller discussion of these pieces than it is possible to give here, see the author's article on *Falla's Music for Piano Solo* in *The Chesterian*, Vol. XXI, No. 148 (January–March, 1940).

[7] Five more years elapsed between the completion of the work and its first performance, which took place at London in 1921, with the composer at the piano.

[8] It was given at Madrid (Teatro de la Zarzuela) on November 14, 1914, and thereafter in all the principal cities of Spain. The American première took place at the Metropolitan Opera House, New York, on March 7, 1926; only four performances were given.

[9] The titles of the seven songs are as follows: *El Paño Moruno, Seguidilla Murciana, Asturiana, Jota* (extremely popular), *Nana, Canción, Polo*. Six of the songs have been arranged for violin and piano by Kochanksi under the title of *Suite Populaire Espagnole*.

[10] In the composer's own highly effective piano transcription, the *Ritual Fire Dance* has become a favorite encore number with concert pianists.

[11] *Cf.* A. Bonilla y San Martín, *Los Orígenes de El Sombrero de Tres Picos*, in *Revue Hispanique*, Tome XIII, No. 43 (1905), pp. 5–17. The same story was used by Hugo Wolf for his opera *Der Corregidor*.

[12] The first concert performance was given at Seville on March 23, 1923.

[13] The Concerto was first performed at Barcelona on Nov. 5, 1926, with Wanda Landowska at the harpsichord and the composer conducting.

[14] The principal work written and released since that date is the suite *Homenajes* (1938) for orchestra, comprising *Pour le Tombeau de Debussy* (originally composed for guitar in 1920), *Fanfare pour Arbós* (1933), *Pour le Tombeau de Paul Dukas* (originally written for piano, 1935), and *Pedrelliana*. Other works by Falla not mentioned in this chapter are: *Trois Mélodies* (Théophile Gautier) for voice and piano (1909) and *Psyché*, for mezzo-soprano, flute, harp, violin, viola, and cello (1924).

[15] For a more detailed account of the subject matter of *La Atlántida*, see "An Interview with Manuel de Falla," by Raymond Hall, in the New York *Times*, November 23, 1930.

NOTES FOR CHAPTER XIII

[1] Quoted in the *Christian Science Monitor* (August 8, 1925).
[2] Formerly music critic of *El Sol* in Madrid; since 1939 living in Mexico.
[3] Reprinted in *Musicalia* (Havana), Nos. 15–16 (January–April, 1931).
[4] Pittaluga was on the staff of the Spanish Embassy in Washington from 1937–1939, after which he went to France.

NOTES FOR CHAPTER XIV

[1] His real family name was Rodríguez, but he adopted the conventional Spanish name of García for professional use.
[2] In 1822, Rossini married the celebrated Spanish soprano Isabel Colbrán (1785–1845), for whom he had written the title role of his opera *Elisabetta, Regina d'Inghilterra* (Naples, 1815). At the time of their meeting she was the mistress of the impresario Domenico Barbaja and of King Ferdinand of Naples, but she soon forsook them both for Rossini. After 1832 they were estranged.
[3] Which, however, was composed mostly of Spaniards.
[4] Quoted by Odell, *Annals of the New York Stage,* III, p. 182.
[5] Odell, *loc. cit.*
[6] Contemporary account in the *American,* quoted by Odell, *op. cit.,* p. 190.
[7] The author of the libretto of *Don Giovanni,* Lorenzo da Ponte, was then professor of Italian at Columbia College; he may, therefore, have been present at this performance.
[8] García's daughter María did not accompany him to Mexico.
[9] A native of Valencia, Lucrezia Bori is known to Americans through her long and brilliant career at the Metropolitan Opera of New York, from which she retired in 1936. Her real family name is Borgia.
[10] Possessing a voice of exceptional range and an extraordinary command of coloratura, Supervia sang several of the soprano roles in Rossini's operas with striking success. She died (in childbirth) at the untimely age of thirty-seven, in 1936.
[11] He died at Biarritz in 1908.
[12] L. Littlehales, *Pablo Casals* (New York, 1929), p. 34.
[13] "Pau" is the Catalan form of "Pablo."

NOTES FOR CHAPTER XV

[1] The first collection of Spanish and Portuguese folk music based on mechanical recordings is that of the late Kurt Schindler, published by the Hispanic Institute in the United States, 1941 (see Bibliography). Not all regions are represented, but there are many songs from regions hitherto neglected.

[2] In 1922, together with the poet García Lorca, Falla organized a memorable festival of *cante jondo* at Granada.

[3] The first Gypsies arrived in Spain in 1449. The Gypsy element seems preponderant in *cante jondo* and *cante flamenco*.

[4] The Jews were expelled from Spain in 1492. They carried with them many of the songs they had learned in Spain, and these have been traditionally preserved among the Sephardic (Spanish-Jewish) communities of the Near East. The Spanish composer Manrique de Lara (d. 1929) collected several thousand such songs, which as yet remain unpublished. Consult the works of Máximo Kahn and A. Hemsi cited in the Bibliography for this chapter. Recordings of traditional Spanish songs sung by Sephardic Jews residing in New York are in the archives of the Casa Hispánica, Columbia University.

[5] The word *hondo* in Spanish means "deep." The strongly aspirated "h" of and Andalusians leads to the phonetic spelling *jondo* (the "h" in Spanish is always silent; "j" is pronounced like our initial "h" in *home*, though the Castilians give it a harsher, more guttural sound). Those who uphold the Jewish origin of *cante jondo* maintain that the term does not mean "deep song," but that it is derived from the Hebrew *Jom Tov*, meaning feast day.

[6] *Gitano* (feminine, *gitana*) is the Spanish word for Gypsy.

[7] Not to be confused with the modern meaning of the term, which refers to the transition from one key to another.

[8] Falla has effectively exploited this trait in his *Ritual Fire Dance*.

[9] It is also true that the instrumental accompaniment of *cante jondo* and *cante flamenco* becomes quite denatured when transcribed for the piano. The guitar is the only instrument on which this music can authentically be performed.

[10] The *cuadro flamenco* consists of a group of singers, dancers, and instrumentalists who sit around in a semicircle and take turns in performing as soloists, the others providing the accompaniment (*cf.* Chapter XVI).

[11] The verse form of the *seguiriya* consists of a four-line stanza in which the third line is much longer than the others and has a characteristic "break" (*quiebro*) in the middle.

[12] The *martinete* is a prison song, without accompaniment, in which the loss of liberty is vehemently lamented.

[13] Some writers make no distinction between *jondo* and *flamenco;* our classification is based on the studies of Manuel de Falla.

[14] The same is true of nearly all the forms of Spanish folk music (obviously, this does not apply to occupational songs, etc.). For this reason we have not thought it advisable to treat folk songs and dance music separately. In Chapter XVI we deal with the choreographic aspect of the dance, and these two chapters should be read in conjunction with each other.

[15] For further discussion of the tango, see Chapter XVII.

[16] Dr. Martínez Lopez, a friend of the writer, has lived in Portugal for several years and is now on the faculty of the University of Texas. I am indebted to him also for other examples (A. T. Luper).

[17] Gallop, *Cantares do Povo Português* (Lisbon: Instituto para a Alta Cultura, 1937), p. 43.

[18] *Op. cit.*, p. 69.

[19] *Op. cit.*, pp. 100–101.

[20] Section on "Portugal" by M. Lambertini in the *Encyclopédie de la Mu-*

sique et Dictionnaire du Conservatoire, ed. by A. Lavignac (Paris, 1920), p. 2465.

NOTES FOR CHAPTER XVI

[1] R. Johnstone, *A History of the Dance.*
[2] *The Dance,* p. 155.
[3] *Virgin Spain,* p. 88.
[4] "The oldest and most noble of European exoticisms" (*La Argentina, Essai sur la Danse Espagnole,* p. 11).
[5] Quoted by E. Porter, *Music Through the Dance* (London, 1937), p. 119.
[6] H. Ellis, *The Soul of Spain,* new edition, p. 174.
[7] The painting is reproduced by Curt Sachs, *World History of the Dance* (American edition), plate I.
[8] Reproduced in the *Revista Musical Catalana,* Any XXXIII, Num. 385.
[9] The bolero was used by Auber in *Masaniello,* by Carl Maria von Weber in *Preciosa,* and by Méhul and Delibes.
[10] *Op. cit.,* p. 180.
[11] Quoted by Cyril Rice, *Spanish Dancing,* p. 18.
[12] *Op. cit.,* p. 155. Slower versions of the *jota* are danced in lower Aragon and Valencia.
[13] The modern *cobla* generally comprises four wood winds, four brass, and a double bass. The solo instrument is the *tenora,* a combination of wood and brass.
[14] Quoted by J. Langdon-Davies, *Dancing Catalans,* p. 34.

NOTES FOR CHAPTER XVII

[1] Gaze upon France, Montesinos,
  Behold the city of Paris.
  Behold the waters of the Duero,
  Where they empty into the sea.
[2] God give us fortune in arms,
  As unto the Knight Roldán.
[3] A copy is in the New York Public Library.
[4] A copy is in the John Carter Brown Memorial Library, Providence, R.I.
[5] Cf. *The Musical Quarterly,* Vol. XXXI, No. 2 (April, 1945).
[6] These facts are cited by Pereira Salas, *Los Orígenes del Arte Musical en Chile,* p. 9.
[7] One should, however, bear in mind that the Spanish lyric theater was largely dominated by Italian influences (*cf.* Chapter IX) and that this influence was thereby spread to the Spanish-American countries, leaving its imprint on many of their popular songs.
[8] C. Vega, *Danzas y Canciones Argentinas.*
[9] *The International Cyclopedia of Music and Musicians,* edited by Oscar Thompson (New York, 1939), p. 583.

[10] *Cancionero Musical de los Siglos XV y XVI*, No. 78.

[11] *Op. cit.*, p. 1.

[12] *Mexican Music* (The Museum of Modern Art, New York, 1940), p. 10.

[13] Mendoza was the first to approach the study of the Spanish-American ballad from the musical rather than the literary angle.

[14] Mendoza, *El Romance Español y el Corrido Mexicano*, p. 4.

[15] The Indian, however, prefers the violin, though it is believed that previous to the Conquest he had only wind and percussion instruments. Generally he plays on a homemade fiddle.

[16] See *The Musical Quarterly*, Vol. XXVII, No. 2 (April, 1941).

[17] Pereira Salas, *op. cit.*, p. 171.

[18] Published in the *Actas* of the *Congreso Internacional de Americanistas*, 1881, Vol. II (Madrid, 1883).

[19] Humberto Allende holds essentially the same view, though he associates it with the Moorish *zambra*. Cf. *Revista Ercilla* (September 16, 1938).

[20] *Popular Cuban Music*, p. 14.

[21] *Op. cit.*, p. 19.

[22] The *Preludio* from this composer's *Bachianas Brasileiras* No. 1, for example, is a *modinha*.

[23] Cf. Mario de Andrade, *Os Congos*, in *Boletín Latino Americano de Música*, Año I, Tomo I (April, 1935).

[24] A. Campa, *The Spanish Folksong in the Southwest*, p. 5.

[25] Cf. C. E. Castañeda, "The First American Play," in *The Catholic World* (January, 1932).

[26] Recordings of music from *Los Pastores*, as of other Spanish and Portuguese songs from the United States, are in the Archive of American Folk Song at the Library of Congress.

[27] Basque folk music in Idaho has been studied and recorded by Miss Kjösness Valborg of Boise.

NOTES FOR CHAPTER XVIII

[1] Freitas Branco, *Elementos de Sciências Musicais*, 1st ed. (Lisbon, Sassetti & Cia., 1923), p. 106. He goes on: "The forgetfulness in which this admirable period of Portuguese art is held, and the glorification of our noisy mediocrities of the eighteenth and beginning of the nineteenth centuries, make it possible for it to be said, save honorable exceptions, that the history of music in Portugal is made backwards."

[2] Lobo's name may be found listed variously as Lobo, Lupus, Lupi, and Lopez. The first name is often given as Eduardus and Eduardo. Lobo's birth date is usually given as 1540, which would have made him 103 when he died. But recent investigations by the Portuguese scholar Sampayo Ribeiro seem to establish that he was born between 1565 and 1570.

[3] Ernesto Vieira, *Diccionario Biographico de Músicos Portuguezes* (Lisbon, 1900), pp. 80–81.

[4] Vasconcellos says: "The Music Library of King D. John IV may be considered the richest that has existed, and in spite of the musical treasures of the libraries of Paris, London, Munich, Berlin, Vienna, and the Vatican it would

still be the most opulent in musical literature up to the middle of the XVIIth century, judging only by the *First Part of the Catalogue* (all that is published); and let it also be noted that the treasures of the above-mentioned capitals were not collected by only one individual, whereas it is probable that the Libraria de Musica was put together in its best and greater part by King John IV." Joaquim de Vasconcellos, *Ensaio Crítico sobre o Catálogo d'El-Rey D. João IV,* in the *Archeologia Artistica* (Porto: Imprensa Portugueza, 1873), p. 51.

5 *A Polifonia Clássica Portuguesa,* ed. by Júlio Eduardo dos Santos (Lisbon, 1937).

6 About one thousand students are regularly enrolled in the Conservatório, which also undertakes to examine about the same number of other students who study under private teachers. It is modeled along the same lines as the Paris Conservatoire.

NOTES FOR CHAPTER XIX

1 Glinka's notebooks from Spain are preserved in the manuscript section of the Leningrad Public Library.

2 Originally called *Recuerdos de Castilla* (*Memories of Castile*).

3 Calvocoressi and Abraham, *Masters of Russian Music,* p. 53.

4 *Ibid.,* p. 51.

5 Rimsky-Korsakoff, *My Musical Life* (English translation, New York, 1923), p. 246. The composer originally intended to write a fantasia on Spanish themes for violin and orchestra, but instead used the material for his *Capriccio Espagnol.*

6 Other members of the Russian "Five" who wrote music in Spanish style were Balakireff (Overture on a theme from a Spanish March) and Borodin (*Serenata Espagnole*).

7 Contrary to a persistent legend, *Carmen* was not a "failure" upon its first performance. But it was received with comparative indifference.

8 A slight doubt exists on this point. The most authoritative biographical opinion is that he never went to Spain.

9 Sebastián Yradier was born in Sauciego (province of Álava) in 1809 and died in Vitoria in 1869. He was singing master to the Empress Eugénie in Paris, where several collections of his songs were published. He lived for some time in Cuba, and his famous song in habanera rhythm, *La Paloma,* is probably the best-known song associated with Latin America.

10 For the music of this song, see R. Laparra, *Bizet et l'Espagne,* p. 18.

11 By Raoul Laparra.

12 Some of Chabrier's musical jottings from Spain are reproduced in J. Desaymard, *Chabrier d'après ses lettres,* pp. 80–83.

13 *La Revue Musicale* (March, 1939).

14 He said of the guitar that it was an instrument which one spent fifty minutes tuning in order to play on it for ten minutes.

15 *The Chesterian* (January, 1921).

16 *Ibid.*

17 Quoted in *Boston Symphony Orchestra Program Notes,* 1936–37, pp. 673–74.

[18] Originally written for piano as one of the five pieces comprised in *Miroirs* (1905). The title cannot be readily translated. *Alborada* means "morning serenade" and *gracioso* is a jester; Ravel doubtless had in mind a witty and ironic character rather than a simple buffoon.

[19] *International Cyclopedia of Music and Musicians* (New York, 1939), p. 1036.

[20] Holograph score in the Library of Congress. Facsimile edition limited to thirty-two copies (Boston, 1936).

[21] Quoted in *The Victor Book of the Symphony* (New York, 1941), p. 319.

A Note on Recordings for the Second Edition. The list of recordings given in the first edition is now mainly of historical interest, as is also the obsolete discography by William Sewall March, *Musical Spain From A to Z as Exemplified on Phonograph Records* (Providence, R. I., 1929). Since the advent of the long-playing record, numerous new recordings of Spanish music, of all periods and all kinds, from the *Cantigas* of Alfonso the Wise and the songs of the *Cancionero de Palacio* to almost the entire standard repertory of *zarzuelas*, have become available. The reader is advised to consult the record lists published in such publications as *The Musical Quarterly, Notes of the Music Library Association, Saturday Review, High Fidelity Magazine*, etc.; also the monthly Long Playing Record Catalogues and the catalog of Montilla, "Music from Spain" (New York City). Among record guides that may be consulted are *The World's Encyclopedia of Recorded Music*, edited by Clough & Cuming (Third Supplement, 1953-55), *High Fidelity Record Annual*, and *Record Ratings, The Music Library Association's Index of Record Reviews*, compiled by Kurtz Myers, edited by Richard S. Hill (New York, 1956).

Bibliography

(Note: Books and articles that contain musical examples are marked with a single asterisk; those that are primarily collections of music are marked with a double asterisk.)

GENERAL

Anglès, Higini: *Catàleg dels Manuscrits Musicals de la Collecció Pedrell* (Barcelona, 1920).*

Burney, Charles: *A General History of Music*, 4 vols. (London, 1776–89). New edition in 2 vols., edited by F. Mercer (London and New York, 1935).*

López Chavarri, Eduardo: *Historia de la Música*, 2 vols., 3rd edition (Barcelona, 1929).*

Mitjana, Rafael: "La Musique en Espagne," in *Encyclopédie de la Musique et Dictionnaire du Conservatoire*, Part I, vol. 4 (Paris, 1920).*

Oxford History of Music, new edition, 7 vols. (London, 1929–34).*

Pedrell, Felipe: *Catàlech de la Biblioteca Musical de la Diputació de Barcelona*, 2 vols. (Barcelona, 1908–09).*

——— *Diccionario Biográfico y Bibliográfico de Músicos y Escritores de Música Españoles, Portugueses e Hispano-Americanos antiguos y modernos* (Barcelona, 1897). [Incomplete]

Prunières, Henry: *Nouvelle Histoire de la Musique*, 2 vols. (Paris, 1933, 1936).*

Saldoni, Baltasar: *Diccionario Biográfico de Efemérides de Músicos Españoles*, 4 vols. (Madrid, 1869–81).

Soriano Fuertes, Mariano: *Historia de la Música Española desde la Venida de los Fenecios hasta el Año de 1850*, 4 vols. (Madrid, 1855–59).*

Soubies, Albert: *Histoire de la Musique: Espagne*, 3 vols. (Paris, 1900).

Trend, J. B.: "The Performance of Music in Spain," in *Proceedings of the Musical Association*, Session 55 (Leeds, 1929).*

Ursprung, Otto: "Musikkultur in Spanien," in *Handbuch der Spanienkunde* (Frankfurt a. M., 1932).*

Van Vechten, Carl: *The Music of Spain* (New York, 1918).

Wolf, Johannes: *Historia de la Música. Traducción de Roberto Gerhard. Con un estudio crítico de la historia de la música española por Higinio Anglès* (Barcelona, 1934).*

CHAPTER I

Anglès, Higini: "Cantors und Ministrers in den Diensten der Koenige von Katalonien-Aragonien im 14. Jahrhunderts," in *Bericht über den musikwissenschaftlichen Kongress in Basel* (Leipzig, 1925).

Anglès, Higini: "Die merstimmige Musik in Spanien vor dem 15. Jahrhunderts," in *Kongressbericht* of the "Beethoven-Zentenarfeir" (1927).
———— *El Codex de Las Huelgas* (*música a veus dels segles XIII-XIV*). Introducció, facsimil i transcripció, 3 vols. (Barcelona, 1931).**
———— "Hispanic Musical Culture from the 6th to the 14th Century," in *The Musical Quarterly*, vol. XXVI, No. 4 (October, 1940).* An adaptation of part of the Introduction to the preceding.
———— *La Música a Catalunya fins al segle XIII* (Barcelona, 1935).*
———— "La Música Medieval en Toledo Hasta el Siglo XI," in *Gesammelte Aufsätze zur Kulturgeschichte Spaniens*, 7. Band (Münster in Westfalen, 1938).
———— "La Musique aux Xe et XIe Siècles. L'École de Ripoll," in *La Catalogne à l'Époque Romane* (Paris, 1932).
———— *Les "Cantigas" del Rei N'Anfós el Savi* (Barcelona, 1927).*
———— "Les Mélodies del Trobador Guiraut Riquier," in *Estudis Universitaris Catalans*, XI (1926).*
Aubry, Fierre: "Iter Hispanicum," in *Sammelbände der internationalen Musik-Gesellschaft*, VIII (1907) and IX (1907–08).*
Beichert, E. A.: *Die Wissenschaft der Musik bei Al-Farabi* (Regensburg, 1931). Also published in *Kirchenmusikalisches Jahrbuch*, 1932–33.
Bishop, W. C.: *The Mozarabic and Ambrosian Rites* (London, 1924).
Brehaut, Ernest: *An Encyclopaedist of the Dark Ages, Isidore of Seville* (New York, 1912).
Carreras, Joseph Rafel: "Idea del que Foren Musicalment els Joglars, Trobadors y Ministrils en Terres de Parla Provensal y Catalana," in *Revista Musical Catalana*, Any V, Nos. 52–54 and 57 (April–September, 1908).*
Collet, Henri, and Luis Villalba: "Contribution à l'Étude des 'Cantigas' d'Alphonse le Savant," in *Bulletin Hispanique*, Tome XIII (1911).*
Daux, Camille: *Les Chansons des Pèlerins de Saint-Jacques* (Montauban, 1899).*
Erlanger, Baron Rodolphe d': *La Musique Arabe*, 4 vols. (Paris, 1930–39).*
Farmer, Henry George: *A History of Arabian Music to the XIIIth Century* (London, 1929).
———— *Al-Fārābī's Arabic-Latin Writings on Music* (Glasgow, 1934).
———— *Historical Facts for the Arabian Musical Influence* (London, 1930).
Fleischer, Oskar: "La Música Cristiana més Antiga de l'Espanya," in *Revista Musical Catalana*, Any XXIII, Nos. 267–268 (March–April, 1926).
Menéndez Pidal, Ramón: *Poesia Juglaresca y Juglares* (Madrid, 1924).
Milá y Fontanals, Manuel: *De los Trovadores en España* (Barcelona, 1889).
Olmeda, Federico: *Memoria de un Viaje a Santiago de Compostela, o examen crítico musical del códice del Papa Calisto II* (Burgos, 1895).*
Pedrell, Felipe: "Jean I d'Aragon, Compositeur de Musique," in *Riemann-Festschrift* (Leipzig, 1909).
Pope, Isabel: "Medieval Latin Background of the 13th-century Galician Lyric," in *Speculum, A Journal of Medieval Studies*, IX (1934).*
Prado, Germán: "Mozarabic Melodics," in *Speculum*, III (1928).*
———— "Un 'Gloria in excelsis' Mozarabe," in *Revue Grégorienne*, Année 18, No. 1 (1933).*
Reese, Gustave: *Music in the Middle Ages* (New York, 1940).*
Riaño, Juan F.: *Critical and Bibliographical Notes on Early Spanish Music* (London, 1887).
Ribera, Julián: *Disertaciones y Opúsculos*, 2 vols. (Madrid, 1928).*

———— *La Música Árabe y su Influencia en la Española* (Madrid, 1927).*

———— *La Música Andaluza Medieval en las Canciones de Trovadores, Troveros y Minnesinger*, 3 vols. (Madrid, 1923–25).**

———— *La Música de las Cantigas* (Madrid, 1922).**

———— *Music in Ancient Arabia and Spain* (London, 1929). An abridged translation of the commentary in the preceding.*

Rojo, Casiano, and Germán Prado: *El Canto Mozárabe* (Barcelona, 1929).*

Rubio Piqueras, F.: *Códices Polifónicos Toledanos* (Toledo, 1925).*

Schindler, Kurt: *Two Miracles and Three Nativity Songs of Medieval Spain*, for mixed voices (New York, c. 1917).**

Serrano Fatigati, Enrique: *Instrumentos Músicos en las Miniaturas de los Códices Españoles, siglos X al XIII* (Madrid, 1901).

Solalinde, Antonio G.: "El Códice Florentino de las 'Cantigas' y su Relación con los demás manuscritos," in *Revista de Filología Española*, Tomo V, No. 2 (April–June, 1918).

Spanke, Hans: "Die Theorie Riberas über Zusammenhänge zwischen frühromanischen Strophenformen und andalusisch-arabischer Lyrik des Mittelalters," in *Volkstum und Kultur der Romanen*, III (1930).

———— "Zur Geschichte der spanischen Musik des Mittelalters," in *Historische Vierteljahrschrift*, Jahrg. 28 (1934).

Stegemeier, Henri: *The Dance of Death in Folksong*. University of Chicago dissertation (Chicago, 1939).

Suñol, Gregorio: "Els Cants dels Romeus," in *Analecta Montserrantensia*, I (1917).*

Trend, J. B.: *Alfonso the Sage and other Spanish Essays* (London, 1926).

———— *The Music of Spanish History to 1600* (London, 1926).*

Ursprung, Otto: "Spanische-Katalanische Liedkunst des 14. Jahrhunderts," in *Zeitschrift für Musikwissenschaft*, Jahrg. 4, Heft 3 (December, 1921).*

———— "Um die Frage nach dem arabischen bzw. maurischen Einfluss auf die abendländische Musik des Mittelalters," in *Zeitschrift für Musikwissenschaft*, Jahrg. 16, Heft 3 (March, 1934).

Wagner, Peter: "Der mozarabische Kirchengesang und seine Überlieferung," in *Gesammelte Aufsätze zur Kulturgeschichte Spaniens*, I (1928).

———— "Untersuchungen zu den Gesangstexten und zur responsorialen Psalmodie der altspanischen Liturgie," in *Gesammelte Aufsätze zur Kulturgeschichte Spaniens*, II (1930).

Whyte, F.: *The Dance of Death in Spain and Catalonia*. Bryn Mawr dissertation (Baltimore, 1931).

Wiener, Leo: *Contributions Towards a History of Arabico-Gothic Culture*, 2 vols. (New York, 1917).

CHAPTER II

Anglès, Higini: "Die spanische Liedkunst im 15. und am Anfang des 16. Jahrhunderts," in *Theodor Kroyer-Festschrift* (Regensburg, 1933).

Anglès, H., and F. Pedrell: *Els Madrigals i la Missa de Difunts d'En Brudieu, Transcripció i Notes Historiques i Critiques* (Barcelona, 1921).**

Bal y Gay, Jesús: *Romances y Villancicos Españoles del Siglo XVI* (Mexico, 1939).**

Bal y Gay, Jesús: *Treinta Canciones de Lope de Vega.* Special number of *Residencia, Revista de la Residencia de Estudiantes* (Madrid, 1935).**

Barbieri, Francisco Asenjo: *Cancionero Musical de los Siglos XV y XVI* (Madrid, 1890).**

Carrera, Rafael: "La Biografia d'En Mateu Flecha, Monjo Carmelita," in *Revista Musical Catalana,* Any III, No. 28 (April, 1906).

Chase, Gilbert: "Juan del Encina, Poet and Musician," in *Music & Letters,* vol. XX, No. 4 (October, 1939).

Collet, Henri: *Catorce Cantos Españoles del Siglo XV* (Paris, 1935).**

Durán, Agustín: *Romancero General (Romances Castellanos Anteriores al Siglo XVIII),* 2 vols. (Madrid, 1926, 1930).

Encina, Juan del: *Cancionero. Primera Edición,* 1496. *Publicada en facsimile por la R. Academia Española* (Madrid, 1928).

Geiger, Albert: "Bausteine zur Geschichte des iberischen Vulgar-Villancico," in *Zeitschrift für Musikwissenschaft,* Jahrg. 4, Heft 2 (November, 1921).*

——— "Spezielles über Form und Inhalt der Spanischen Münchener Kodizes," in *Zeitschrift für Musikwissenschaft,* Jahrg. 6, Heft 4/5 (January–February, 1924).*

Haraszti, Emile: "Mattheo Flecha le Jeune, Abbé de Tyhon," in *Acta Musicologica,* vol. VII, Fasc. 1 (1935).

Istel, Edgar: "The Music in 'Don Quixote,'" in *The Musical Quarterly,* vol. XIII, No. 3 (July, 1927).*

Maeso, Ricardo Espinosa: "Nuevos Datos Biográficos de Juan del Encina," in *Boletín de la Real Academia Española,* Año VIII, Tomo VIII (December, 1921).

Martínez Torner, Eduardo: *Cancionero Musical* (Madrid, 1927).**

——— *Cuarenta Canciones Españolas Harmonizadas* (Madrid, 1924).**

——— "Ensayo de una Clasificación de los Romances," in *Homenaje Ofrecido a Menéndez Pidal,* vol. II (Madrid, 1925).*

Mendoza, Vicente T.: *El Romance Español y el Corrido Mexicano* (Mexico, 1939).*

Menéndez Pidal, Jimena: *Romancero* (Madrid, 1933).*

Menéndez Pidal, Ramón: *El Romancero; Teorías e Investigaciones* (Madrid, 1928).

——— *Flor Nueva de Romances Viejos* (Madrid, 1928).*

Michaëlis de Vasconcellos, Carolina: "Nótulas Sobre Cantares e Vilhancicos Peninsulares e a Respeito de Juan del Encina," in *Revista de Filología Española,* Tomo V, No. 4 (October–December, 1918).

Mitjana, Rafael: *Cincuenta y Cuatro Canciones Españolas del Siglo XVI* (Uppsala, 1909).**

——— "Comentarios y Apostillas al Cancionero de Sablonara," in *Revista de Filología Española,* Tomo VI, Nos. 1 and 3 (1919).

——— *Estudios Sobre Algunos Músicos Españoles del Siglo XVI* (Madrid, 1918).

——— "Nuevas Notas al Cancionero Musical de los Siglos XV y XVI Publicado por el Maestro Barbieri," in *Revista de Filología Española,* Tomo V, No. 2 (April–June, 1918).

Pedrell, Felipe: *Cancionero Musical Popular Español,* vols. III and IV (Valls, 1918–22).**

——— "Musichs Vells de la Terra: Flecha," in *Revista Musical Catalana,* Any

I, Nos. 4–12 (April–December, 1904), Any II, Nos. 14–16 (February–April, 1905), and Any III, Nos. 28–31 (April–July, 1906).*

―――― "Musichs Vells de la Terra: Joan Brudieu," in *Revista Musical Catalana*, Any II, Nos. 17 and 19 (May–July, 1905), and Any III, Nos. 32–35 (August–November, 1906).*

―――― "Musichs Vells de la Terra: Pere Albert Vila," in *Revista Musical Catalana*, Any I, Nos. 1–3 (January–March, 1904).

Riemann, Hugo: *Handbuch der Musikgeschichte*, zweiter Band, erster Teil (Leipzig, 1907).*

Roda, Cecilio de: *Los Instrumentos, las Danzas y las Canciones en el Quixote* (Madrid, 1905).

Ruetz, Manfred: *Spanische Lieder um 1500* (Kassel, 1933).**

St. Amour, Sister Mary Paulina: *A Study of the Villancico up to Lope de Vega* (Washington, 1940).

Trend, J. B.: "A Note on Spanish Madrigals," in *Report of the First Congress*, International Society for Musical Research, Liège, 1930 (Durham, 1931).

―――― *Catalogue of the Music in the Biblioteca Medinaceli, Madrid* (New York, 1927). Detached from the *Revue Hispanique*, Tome LXXI, No. 160.

Villalba Muñoz, Luis: *Diez Canciones Españolas de los Siglos XV y XVI.***

CHAPTER III

Anglès, Higini: "Dades Desconegudes Sobre Miguel de Fuenllana, Vihuelista," in *Revista Musical Catalana*, Any XXXIII, No. 388 (1936).

Bal, Jesús: "Fuenllana and the Transcription of Spanish Lute-Music," in *Acta Musicologica*, vol. XI, Fasc. I–II (1939).*

Brondi, Maria Rita: *Il Liuto e la Chitarra* (Turin, 1926).

Contreras, Segundo N.: *La Guitarra* (Buenos Aires, 1927).

Koczirz, Adolf: "Die Gitarrekompositionen in Miguel de Fuenllana's Orphénica Lyra," in *Archiv für Musikwissenschaft*, Jahrg. IV, Heft 2 (April, 1922).*

Martínez Torner, Eduardo: *Colección de Vihuelistas Españoles del Siglo XVI. Composiciones Escogidas de El Delphín de Música de Narváez* (Madrid, 1923).**

―――― *Colección de Vihuelistas Españoles del Siglo XVI. Estudios y Transcripciones de las Ediciones Originales. Cuaderno I: Narváez, El Delphín de Música* (Madrid, 1923).**

Morphy, Guillermo, Conde de: *Les Luthistes Espagnols du XVIème Siècle*, 2 vols. (Leipzig, 1902).**

Pedrell, Felipe: *Emporio Científico e Histórico de Organografía Musical Antigua Española* (Barcelona, 1901).

―――― "Musichs Vells de la Terra: Joan Carles Amat," in *Revista Musical Catalana*, Any II, Nos. 25–26 (January–February, 1906).

Prat, Domingo: *Diccionario Biográfico, Bibliográfico, Histórico, Crítico, de Guitarras, Guitarristas . . .* (Buenos Aires, 1934).

Pujol, Emilio: *La Guitarra y su Historia. Conferencia* (Buenos Aires, 1932).

―――― "La Guitare," in *Encyclopédie de la Musique et Dictionnaire du Conservatoire*, Part II, vol. 3 (Paris, 1927).*

Riemann, Hugo: "Das Lautenwerk des Miguel de Fuenllana," in *Monatshefte für Musikgeschichte,* Jahrg. 27, No. 6 (1895).*

Schrade, Leo: *Libro de Música de Vihuela de Mano, Intitulado El Maestro, compuesto por Luys Milan; in der Originalnotation und einer Übertragung* . . . (Leipzig, 1927).**

Tagliapietra, Gino: *Antologia di Musica Antica e Moderna per Pianoforte,* vol. I (Milan, 1931).**

Trend, J. B.: *Luis Milan and the Vihuelistas* (London, 1925).*

Villalba Muñoz, Luis: "La Orphénica Lyra de Fuenllana," in *Musica Sacro-Hispana* (1910).*

CHAPTER IV

Anglès, Higini: *Musici Organici Johannis Cabanilles Opera Omnia,* 3 vols. (Barcelona, 1927–36).**

―――― "Orgelmusik der Schola Hispanica vom XV. bis XVII. Jahrhundert," in *Peter Wagner-Festschrift* (Leipzig, 1926).

Apel, Willi: "Early Spanish Music for Lute and Keyboard Instruments," in *The Musical Quarterly,* vol. XX, No. 3 (July, 1934).*

Arnold, Frank T.: *The Art of Accompanying From a Thorough-Bass* (London, 1931).*

Bonnet, Joseph: *Historical Organ Recitals,* vols. I and VI (New York, 1917, 1940).**

Collet, Henri: "Contribution a l'Étude des Théoriciens Espagnols de la Musique au XVIᵉ Siècle," in *L'Année Musicale, 1912* (Paris, 1913).

―――― *Le Mysticisme Musical Espagnol au XVIᵉ Siècle* (Paris, 1913).*

Hill, A. G.: "Medieval Organs in Spain," in *Sammelbände der internationalen Musik-Gesellschaft,* Jahrg. XIV (1912–13).

Kinkeldey, Otto: *Orgel und Klavier in der Musik des 16. Jahrhunderts* (Leipzig, 1910).*

Pedrell, Felipe: *Antología de Organistas Clásicos Españoles* (Madrid, 1908).**

―――― *El Organista Clásico Español* (Barcelona, 1905).**

―――― "Folk-lore Musical Castillan du XVIᵉ Siècle," in *Sammelbände der internationalen Musik-Gesellschaft,* Jahrg. I (1900).*

―――― *Hispaniae Schola Musica Sacra,* vols. 3, 4, 6, 7, and 8 (Barcelona, 1894–98).**

―――― *Lírica Nacionalizada* (Paris, 1909).*

Pirro, André: "L'Art des Organistes," in *Encyclopédie de la Musique et Dictionnaire du Conservatoire,* Part II, vol. 2 (Paris, 1926).*

Trend, J. B.: "A Sixteenth Century Collector of Folk Songs" [Francisco Salinas], in *Music & Letters,* vol. VIII, No. 1 (January, 1927).*

Villalba Muñoz, Luis: *Antología de Organistas Clásicos Españoles.***

―――― *El Órgano, su Invención e Historia y su Cultivo en España por Organistas del Siglo XV y Primera Mitad del XVI* (Segovia, n. d.).

Wolf, Johannes: *Musica Practica Bartolomei Rami de Pareia.* Publikationen der internationalen Musik-Gesellschaft (Leipzig, 1910).

CHAPTER V

Anglès, Higini: *Johannis Pujol . . . Opera Omnia*, 2 vols. (Barcelona, 1926, 1932).**

——— "La Polyphonie Religieuse Péninsulaire Antérieure à la Venue des Musiciens Flamands en Espagne," in *Report of the First Congress*, International Society for Musical Research, Liège, 1930 (Durham, 1931).

Baixuli, M.: "Las Obras Musicales de San Francisco de Borja," in *Razón y Fé*, Tomo III (October, 1902).

Casimiri, Raffaele: *"Il Vittoria," Nuovi Documenti per una Biografia Sincera de Tommaso Ludovico de Victoria* (Rome, 1934). Extracted from *Note d'Archivo per la Storia Musicale*, Anno 1934, Fasc. 2.

——— *Societas Polyphonica Romana* (Rome, 1925–34).**

Collet, Henri: *Le Mysticisme Musical Espagnol au XVIe Siècle* (Paris, 1913).*

——— *Victoria* (Paris, 1914).

Elústiza, Juan B.: "Del Viaje y Estancia en Roma del Maestro Guerrero," in *Revista Musical de México*, vol. I, No. 11 (1920).

Elústiza, Juan B., and G. Castrillo Hernández: *Antología Musical; Siglo de Oro de la Música Litúrgica de España* (Barcelona, 1933).**

Eslava, Miguel Hilarión: *Lira Sacro-Hispana* (Madrid, 1869 ff.).**

Mitjana, Rafael: *Cristóbal de Morales, Estudio Crítico-biográfico* (Madrid, 1920).

——— *Estudios Sobre Algunos Músicos Españoles del Siglo XVI* (Madrid, 1918).

Pedrell, Felipe: *Hispaniae Schola Musica Sacra*, vols. 1, 2, 5, and 6 (Barcelona, 1894–98).**

——— *La Festa d'Elche; ou Le Drame Lyrique Liturgique Espagnol* (Paris, 1906).*

——— *Thomae Luduvici Victoria Abulensis Opera Omnia . . .* , 8 vols. (Leipzig, 1902–13).**

——— *Tomás Luis de Victoria, Abulense* (Valencia, 1918).

Ponnelle, Louis, and L. Bordet: *St. Philip Neri and the Roman Society of His Times* (English translation; London, 1932).

Proske, Karl: *Musica Divina* (Ratisbon, 1853–69).**

Pujol, David: *Mestres de l'Escalonia de Montserrat; Obres Musicals del Monjos del Monestir de Montserrat, 1500–1800*, 2 vols. (Barcelona, 1934, 1936).**

Ripolles Pérez, Vicente: *El Villancico i la Cantata del Segle XVIII a Valencia* (Barcelona, 1935).*

Rubio Piqueras, F.: *Música y Músicos Toledanos* (Toledo, 1922).

Trend, J. B.: "Cristóbal Morales," in *Music & Letters*, vol. VI, No. 4 (January, 1925).*

——— *The Music of Spanish History to 1600* (London, 1926).*

——— "Thomé Luis de Victoria," in *Musical Times*, vol. 66 (April, 1925).

Wagner, Peter: *Geschichte der Messe* (Leipzig, 1913).*

CHAPTER VI

Chase, Gilbert: "Lucas Fernández, Poet and Musician," in *The Chesterian*, vol. XX, No. 146 (July–August, 1939).

Cotarelo y Mori, Emilio: *Colección de Entremeses, Loas, Bailes, Jácaras y Mojigangas desde fines del Siglo XVI a mediados del XVIII*, 2 vols. (Madrid, 1911).

——— "Juan del Encina y los Orígenes del Teatro Español," in *Estudios de Historia Literaria de España*, Tomo I (Madrid, 1901).

——— *Historia de la Zarzuela* (Madrid, 1934).

———: *Orígenes y Establecimiento de la Ópera en España hasta 1800* (Madrid, 1917).

Crawford, J. P. Wickersham: *Spanish Drama Before Lope de Vega*, revised edition (Philadelphia, 1937).

Díaz de Escovar, Narciso: *Historia del Teatro Español*, 2 vols. (Barcelona, 1924).

Encina, Juana del: *Teatro Completo*. Edición de la R. Academia Española (Madrid, 1893).

Milegro, Julio: *El Teatro en Toledo Durante los Siglos XVI y XVII* (1909).

Pedrell, Felipe: *Cancionero Musical Popular Español*, vols. III and IV (Valls, 1918–22).**

——— "La Musique Indigène dans le Théâtre Espagnol du 18e Siècle," in *Sammelbände der internationalen Musik-Gesellschaft*, Jahrg. V (1903–04).

——— *Teatro Lírico Español Anterior al Siglo XIX*, 5 vols. (La Coruña, 1896–98).**

Reiff, A.: "Die Anfänge der Oper in Spanien," in *Spanien, Zeitschrift für Auslandskunde* (Hamburg), Jahrg. I, Heft 3 (1919).

Salazar, Adolfo: "Music in the Primitive Theatre Before Lope de Vega," in *Papers . . . of the American Musicological Society*. Annual Meeting, Washington, 1938 (1940).

Subirá, José: *Celos aun del Aire Matan; Ópera del Siglo XVII. Texto de Calderón y Musica de Juan Hidalgo* (Barcelona, 1933).*

——— *El Operista Español D. Juan Hidalgo* (Madrid, 1934).

——— *La Participación Musical en el Antiguo Teatro Lírico Español* (Barcelona, 1930).

——— "Una Tonada del Operista D. Juan Hidalgo," in *Las Ciencias*, Año II, No. 1 (1935).*

Trend, J. B.: *A Picture of Modern Spain: Men and Music* (Boston and New York, 1921).

Vincent, C. E.: "Du Rôle de la Musique Dans le Théâtre Espagnol," in *Revue Internationale de Musique*, No. 10 (August, 1898).*

CHAPTER VII

Bonaventura, Arnaldo: *Boccherini* (Milan and Rome, 1931).

Bouvet, Charles: "Boccherini Inconnu," in *Revue de Musicologie*, Année 13, No. 32 (November, 1929).

Luciani, S. A.: "Domenico Scarlatti," in *La Rassegna Musicale* (December, 1938; January and February, 1939). Also reprinted separately.

Malipiero, Francesco: "Domenico Scarlatti," in *The Musical Quarterly*, vol. XIII, No. 3 (July, 1927).*

Mitjana, Rafael: *Discantes y Contrapuntos* (Valencia, 1905).

Nin, Joaquín: *Cinq Commentaires pour violon et piano* (Paris, 1929).**

—— *Classiques Espagnols du Violon: Dix Pièces de Herrando* (Paris, 1939).**

—— *Dix-sept Sonates et Pièces Anciennes d'Auteurs Espagnols* (Paris, 1929).**

—— *Seize Sonates Anciennes d'Auteurs Espagnols* (Paris, 1925).**

—— "The Bi-centenary of Antonio Soler," in *The Chesterian*, vol. 11, No. 84 (January–February, 1930).

Picquot, L.: *Boccherini. Notes et Documents Nouveaux par Georges de Saint-Foix* (Paris, 1930).*

Searle, Humphrey: "Boccherini's 'Ballet Espagnol,'" in *Monthly Musical Record*, vol. 68, No. 798 (July–August, 1938).

Sitwell, Sacheverell: *A Background for Domenico Scarlatti* (Lonaon, 1935).

Soler, Antonio: *Sis Quintets per a Instruments d'Arc i Orgue o Clave Obligat. Transcripció i Revisió per Robert Gerhard. Introducció i Estudi d'Higini Anglès* (Barcelona, 1933).**

Subirá, José: *La Música en la Casa de Alba* (Madrid, 1927).

Trend, J. B.: "Spanish Chamber Music," in *Cobbett's Cyclopedic Survey of Chamber Music*, vol. II (London, 1930).

CHAPTER VIII

Cotarelo y Mori, Emilio: *Don Ramón de la Cruz y sus Obras* (Madrid, 1899).*

—— *Historia de la Zarzuela* (Madrid, 1934).

Gómez, Julio: "Don Blas de Laserna," in *Revista de la Biblioteca, Archivo y Museo del Ayuntamiento de Madrid* (1925–26).

Hamilton, Mary Neal: *Music in Eighteenth Century Spain* (Urbana, 1937).* University of Illinois, *Studies in Language and Literature*, vol. XXII.

Nin, Joaquín: *Sept Chansons Picaresques* (Paris, 1926).**

—— *Sept Chants Lyriques Espagnols Anciens* (Paris, 1926).**

Pedrell, Felipe: *Teatro Lírico Español Anterior al Siglo XIX*, 5 vols. (La Coruña, 1896–98).**

Picón, Jacinto O.: "Prohibición de Pan y Toros en Tiempo de Isabel II," in *Revue Hispanique*, Tome XL, No. 97 (1917).

Salazar, Adolfo: "La Música Española en Tiempos de Goya," in *Revista de Occidente*, vol. 22, No. LXVI (December, 1928).

Subirá, José: *La Tonadilla Escénica*, 3 vols. (Madrid, 1928–30).*

—— *Los Maestros de la Tonadilla Escénica* (Barcelona, 1933).**

—— *Tonadillas Satíricas y Picarescas* (Madrid, 1927).

—— *Tonadillas Teatrales Inéditas* (Madrid, 1932).*

CHAPTER IX

Al Maestro Pedrell. Escritos Heortásticos (Tortosa, 1911).

Barbieri, Francisco Asenjo: *El Teatro Real y el Teatro de la Zarzuela* (Madrid, 1877).

Bellaigue, Camille: *Études Musicales*, 2ème série (Paris, 1903).
———— *Notes Brèves* (Paris, 1911).
Blom, Eric: *Step-children of Music* (London, 1923).
Carreras y Bulbena, José Rafael: *Domenech Terradellas* (Barcelona, 1908).
Curzon, Henri de: *Felipe Pedrell et Les Pyrénées* (Paris, 1902).
———— "Un Maître de la Musique Espagnole: F. Pedrell," in *Nouvelle Revue*, Tome 25, Série 3 (1912).
Esperanza y Sola, José María: *Treinta Años de Crítica Musical*, 3 vols. (Madrid, 1906).
Falla, Manuel de: "Felipe Pedrell," in *La Revue Musicale*, Année 4, No. 4 (February, 1923).
Fernández Nuñez, Manuel: *La Vida de los Músicos Españoles* (Madrid, 1925).
Istel, Edgar: "Felipe Pedrell," in *The Musical Quarterly*, vol. XI, No. 2 (April, 1925).*
Mitjana, Rafael: *Para Música Vamos!* (Valencia, 1909).
Moller, Heinrich: "Felipe Pedrell und das Spanische Volkslied," in *Die Musik*, Jahrg. 15, Heft 10 (July, 1923).*
Pedrell, Felipe: "Musics Vells de la Terra: Domingo Miquel Bernabé Tarradellas [sic]," in *Revista Musical Catalana*, Any V, Nos. 54–56 (June–August, 1908).
———— *Por Nuestra Música* (Barcelona, 1891).
Peña y Goñi, Antonio: *La Ópera Española en el Siglo XIX* (Madrid, 1881).
Reiff, Alfred: "Felipe Pedrell," in *Zeitschrift für Musikwissenschaft*, Jahrg. 3, Heft 5 (February, 1921).
Salazar, Adolfo: *El Siglo Romántico* (Madrid, 1936).
———— *La Música Contemporánea en España* (Madrid, 1930).
Salcedo, Angel S.: *Tomás Bretón, su Vida y sus Obras* (Madrid, 1924).
Tebaldini, Giovanni: *Filippo Pedrell ed il Dramma Lirico Spagnuolo* (Turin, 1897). Extracted from *Revista Musicale Italiana*, vol. IV, Fasc. 2 and 3 (1897).
Villalba Muñoz, Luis: *Felipe Pedrell* (Segovia, 1922).

CHAPTER X

Boladeres Ibern, G. de: *Enrique Granados* (Barcelona, 1921).
Collet, Henri: *Albéniz et Granados* (Paris, 1926).*
Grew, Sydney: "The Music of Albéniz for Pianoforte," in *The Chesterian*, vol. VI, No. 42 (November, 1924).
Istel, Edgar: "Isaac Albéniz," in *The Musical Quarterly*, vol. XV, No. 1 (January, 1929).*
Jean-Aubry, G.: "Enrique Granados," in *The Musical Times*, vol. 57, No. 886 (December, 1916).
———— "Isaac Albéniz," in *The Musical Times*, vol. 58, No. 898 (December, 1917).
———— *La Musique et les Nations* (Paris, 1922; English translation, 1923).
Klein, Herman: "Albéniz's Opera 'Pepita Jiménez,'" in *The Musical Times*, vol. 59, No. 901 (March, 1918).
Marliave, Joseph de: *Études Musicales* (Paris, 1917).

Newman, Ernest: "The Granados of the 'Goyescas,'" in *The Musical Times*, vol. 58, No. 894 (August, 1917).*

Revista Musical Catalana, Any XIII, No. 150 (June 15, 1916). Special issue devoted to Granados.

Salazar, Adolfo: *La Música Contemporánea en España* (Madrid, 1930).

Subirá, José: *Enrique Granados* (Madrid, 1926).

———— "En Memoria de Enrique Granados," in *Música*, No. 5 (May–June, 1938).*

Villar, Rogelio: *Los Músicos Españoles*, first series (Madrid, 1918).

CHAPTER XI

Bertrán, Marcos Jesús: *El Gran Teatro del Liceo de Barcelona, 1837–1930* (Barcelona, 1931).

Bosch, Carlos: *Impresiones Estéticas* (Madrid, 1918).

Collet, Henri: *L'Essor de la Musique Espagnole au XXᵉ Siècle* (Paris, 1929).

———— "La Renaissance Musicale," in *Encyclopédie de la Musique et Dictionnaire du Conservatoire*, Part I, vol. 4 (Paris, 1920).

Elústiza, Juan B.: *Estudios Musicales* (Seville, 1917).

Eresalde, Juan de: *Los Esclavos Felices, Ópera de J. C. de Arriaga* (Bilbao, 1935).

Gallop, Rodney: "Father Donostia," in *Monthly Musical Record*, vol. LXVII, No. 789 (September, 1937).

Grew, Sydney: "Modern Spanish Music," in *Spain, A Companion to Spanish Studies*, edited by E. Allison Peers (New York, 1929).*

Iglesias, I.: *Enric Morera* (Barcelona, 1921).

Lamaña, Luis: *Barcelona Filarmónica* (Barcelona, 1927).

Millet, Lluis: "La Celestina del Mestre Felip Pedrell," in *Revista Musical Catalana*, Any I, Nos. 1–10 (March–October, 1904).*

———— *Pel Nostre Ideal* (Barcelona, 1917).

Nadal, Lluis B.: "Francisco Alió," in *Revista Musical Catalana*, Any V, No. 55 (July, 1908).

Salazar, Adolfo: "Die Moderne: Spanier," in *Handbuch der Musikgeschichte*, edited by Guido Adler, 2nd edition, vol. 2 (Berlin, 1930).

———— *La Música Actual en Europa* (Madrid, 1935).

———— *La Música Contemporánea en España* (Madrid, 1930).

———— *Música y Músicos de Hoy* (Madrid, 1928).

Schindler, Kurt: *Seven Songs of Catalonia for Mixed Chorus* (Barcelona, 1919).**

Subirá, José: "La Música Española Contemporánea," in *Nuestro Tiempo*, Año 22 (1922).

———— *El Músico-Poeta Clavé* (Madrid, 1924).

Trend, J. B.: "A New Goyesque Opera," in *A Picture of Modern Spain* (Boston and New York, 1921).

Turina, Joaquín: "Bartolomé Pérez Casas," in *La Gaceta Musical* (September, 1928).

Villalba, Luis: *Últimos Músicos Españoles del Siglo XIX* (Madrid, 1914).

Villar, Rogelio: *El Sentimiento Nacional en la Música Española* (Madrid, 1918).

CHAPTER XII

Altermann, J. P.: "Manuel de Falla," in *La Revue Musicale*, Année 2, No. 8 (June, 1921).

Castelnuovo-Tedesco, Mario: "Manuel de Falla," in *Il Pianoforte*, Anno 4, No. 1 (January, 1923).

Chase, Gilbert: "Manuel de Falla," in *The International Cyclopedia of Music and Musicians*, edited by Oscar Thompson (New York, 1939).

Ewen, David: *Twentieth Century Composers* (New York, 1937).

Fraser, Andrew: *Essays in Music* (London, 1930).

Istel, Edgar: "Manuel de Falla," in *The Musical Quarterly*, vol. XII, No. 4 (October, 1926).*

Jean-Aubry, G.: " 'El Retablo' by Manuel de Falla," in *The Chesterian*, New Series, No. 34 (October, 1923).

———— *La Musique et les Nations* (Paris, 1922).

———— "Manuel de Falla," in *The Musical Times*, vol. 58, No. 890 (April, 1917).

Lliurat, Federico: "El Concerto para Clavicémbalo y Cinco Instrumentos, de Manuel de Falla," in *Musicalia*, Año II, No. 8 (September–October, 1929).*

Manuel, Roland: *Manuel de Falla* (Paris, 1930).

Pannain, Guido: *Modern Composers* (English translation; London, 1933).

Trend, J. B.: *Manuel de Falla and Spanish Music* (New York, 1929; new edition, 1935).*

Turina, Joaquín: "Manuel de Falla," in *The Chesterian*, New Series, No. 7 (May, 1920).

Villar, Rogelio: *Falla y su Concierto de Cámara* (Madrid, 1932).

CHAPTER XIII

Chase, Gilbert: "A View of the Younger Genius of Spain," in *Musical America*, vol. 56, No. 14 (September, 1936).

Collet, Henri: *L'Essor de la Musique Espagnole au XXᵉ Siècle* (Paris, 1929).

Jean-Aubry, G.: "And Now a Spanish Carmen," in *The Christian Science Monitor* (December 4, 1926).

———— "Ernesto Halffter Escriche," in *The Christian Science Monitor* (August 8, 1925).

Salazar, Adolfo: *La Música Contemporánea en España* (Madrid, 1930).

CHAPTER XIV

Altadill, Julio: *Memorias de Sarasate* (Pamplona, 1909).

Cotarelo y Mori, Emilio: *María del Rosario Fernández, La Tirana* (Madrid, 1897).

———— *María Ladvenant y Quirante* (Madrid, 1896).

Flament, Albert: *L'Enchanteresse Errante, la Malibran* (Paris, 1937).

Gibert, Vicente M. de: "Francesc Tàrrega," in *Revista Musical Catalana*, Any XXXII, No. 380 (August, 1935).

González, Anselmo: *Gayarre* (Paris, c. 1930).

Hartmann, Theodore: "The Perfect Virtuoso [Sarasate]," in *Musical America*, vol. LX, No. 6 (March 25, 1940).

Héritte de la Tour, Louis: *Mémoires de Louise Héritte-Viardot* (Paris, 1923).

Lanquine, Clément: *La Malibran* (Paris, 1912).

Levien, John M.: *The García Family* (London, 1932).

Littlehales, Lilian: *Pablo Casals* (New York, 1929).*

Lorenzi de Bradi, Michel: *La Brève et Merveilleuse Vie de la Malibran* (Paris, 1936).

Mackinlay, Malcolm Sterling: *Garcia the Centenarian and His Times* (London, 1908).

Pougin, Arthur: *Marie Malibran* (London, 1911).

Prod'homme, J. J.: "La Fayette and Maria-Felicia Malibran," in *The Chesterian*, New Series, No. 1 (September, 1919).

Rogers, Francis: *Some Famous Singers of the 19th Century* (New York, 1914).

Villar, Rogelio: *Músicos Españoles*, 2nd series (Madrid, n. d.).

CHAPTER XV

Alford, Violet: "Cantabrian Calendar Customs and Music," in *The Musical Quarterly*, vol. XX, No. 4 (October, 1934).*

Anglès, Higini: "Das Spanische Volkslied," in *Archiv für Musikforschung*, Jahrg. 3, Heft 3 (1938).*

Arnandas Larrodé, Miguel: *Colección de Cantos Populares de la Provincia de Teruel* (Saragossa, 1927).**

Arxiu d'Etnografia i Folklore de Catalunya, Estudis i Materials, 2 vols. (Barcelona, 1916–17).*

Azkue, Resurrección M. de: *Cancionero Popular Vasco*, in 12 parts (Barcelona, 1923–24).**

Baldelló, Francesc: *Cançoner Popular Religiós de Catalunya* (Barcelona, 1932).**

Brown, George Boylston: *A Survey of Iberian Folksong and a Study of the Jota Aragonesa*. Master's thesis, Eastman School of Music (University of Rochester), 1935.*

Brown, Irving: *Deep Song. Adventures with Gypsy Songs and Singers in Andalusia and Other Lands* (New York, 1929).*

Caba, Carlos: *Andalucía, su Comunismo y su Cante Jondo* (Madrid, 1933).

Calleja, Rafael: *Cantos de la Montaña* (Madrid, 1901).**

Camps y Mercadal, Francisco: *Folklore Menorquí: De la Pagesia* (Mahon, 1918).*

Carreras y Candi, F.: *Folklore y Costumbres de España*, vol. II (Barcelona, 1931).*

Castrillo Hernández, Gonzalo: *Estudio Sobre el Canto Popular Castellano* (Palencia, 1925).*

Chottin, Alexis: *Chants Arabes d'Andalousie* (Paris, n. d.).*

Cortés, Narciso Alonso: "Cantares Populares de Castilla," in *Revue Hispanique*, Tome XXXII, No. 81 (October, 1914).*

Danckert, Werner: *Das Europäische Volkslied* (Berlin, 1939).*

Donostia, J. A.: *Euskel Eres-Sorta, Cancionero Vasco* (Madrid, 1919).**

———— *Gure Herria* (Paris, 1928).**

Duff, Donald: "Flamenco," in *Modern Music*, vol. XVII, No. 4 (May–June, 1940).

Elústiza, Juan B.: *Estudios Musicales* (Seville, 1917).*

Esquerrá, Adriá: *Nadales Populars* (Madrid, 1917).**

Falla, Manuel de: *El Cante Jondo (Canto Primitivo Andaluz)*. Pamphlet (Granada, 1922). Italian translation published in *La Rassegna Musicale*, Anno 11, No. 10 (October, 1938).

———— *Siete Canciones Populares Españolas* (Paris, 1922).

Federico García Lorca, by F. de Onís and others. Hispanic Institute in the United States (New York, 1941).*

Fernández Núñez, Manuel: *Folklore Leonés* (Madrid, 1931).*

Gay, Joan: *Cançons Populars de Catalunya* (Paris, c. 1901).**

Gallop, Rodney: *A Book of the Basques* (London, 1930).*

Gil García, Bonifacio: *Cancionero Popular de Extremadura* (Valls, 1931).**

González Pastrana, Eduardo: *La Montaña de León; 100 Canciones Leonesas* (Madrid, 1929).**

Hanssen, Federico: "La Seguidilla," in *Anales de la Universidad de Chile* (September–October, 1909).

Hemsi, A.: *Coplas Sefardies (Chansons Judeo-Espagnoles)*, 3 vols. (Alexandria, 1932–34).**

Inzenga, José: *Cantos y Bailes de España*, 3 vols. (Madrid, 1888).**

Kahn, Máximo José: "Chant Populaire Andalou et Musique Synagogale," in *Cahiers d'Art*, Nos. 5–10 (Paris, 1939).

Laparra, Raoul: "La Musique et la Danse Populaires en Espagne," in *Encyclopédie de la Musique et Dictionnaire du Conservatoire*, Part I, vol. 4 (Paris, 1920).*

Ledesma, Dámaso: *Folk-lore o Cancionero Salmantino* (Madrid, 1907).**

Llorens de Serra, Sara: *El Cançoner de Pineda* (Barcelona, 1931).**

López Chavarri, Eduardo: *Música Popular Española* (Barcelona, 1927).*

Lozano González, Antonio: *La Música Popular, Religiosa y Dramática en Zaragoza desde el Siglo XVI hasta Nuestros Días* (Saragossa, 1895).

Marcial-Dorado, Carolina: *España Pintoresca* (Boston, 1917).*

Martínez Hernández, Antonio: *Antología Musical de Cantos Populares Españoles* (Barcelona, 1930).**

Martínez Torner, Eduardo: *Cancionero Musical* (Madrid, 1928).**

———— *Cancionero Musical de la Lírica Popular Asturiana* (Madrid, 1920).**

———— *Metodología del Canto y la Música* (Madrid, 1935).*

———— *Temas Folklóricos* (Madrid, 1935).* With an extensive bibliography.

Menéndez Pidal, Juan: *Poesía Popular: Colección de los Viejos Romances que se Cantan por los Asturianos en la Danza Prima* (Madrid, 1885).

Milá y Fontanals, Manuel: *Romancerillo Catalan* (Barcelona, 1882).*

Millet, Lluis: *De la Cançó Popular Catalana* (Barcelona, 1917).*

Nin, Joaquín: *Vingt Chansons Populaires Espagnoles*, 2 vols. (Paris, 1923–1924).**

Noguera, Antonio: *Memoria Sobre Cantos, Bailes y Tocatas Populares en la Isla de Mallorca* (Barcelona, 1893).*

Obra del Cançoner Popular de Catalunya, Materials, 3 vols. (Barcelona, 1926–29).**

Olmeda, Federico: *Cancionero Popular de Burgos* (Seville, 1903).**

Onís, Federico de, and Emilio de la Torre: *Canciones Españolas* (New York, 1931).**

Otaño, Nemesio: *El Canto Popular Montañés* (Santander, 1915).*

Pedrell, Felipe: *Cancionero Musical Popular Español,* 4 vols. (Valls, 1918–1922).** New edition in 2 vols., Barcelona, 1936.

——— *La Cansó Popular Catalana* (Barcelona, 1906).*

——— *Lírica Nacionalizada* (Paris, 1909).*

Pelay Briz, Francesch: *Cansons de la Terra,* 5 vols. (Barcelona, 1866–77).**

Pol, A.: *Folk-lore Musical Mallorquín* (Barcelona, 1925).**

Pujol, Francesco: *L'Œuvre du Chansonnier Populaire de la Catalogne* (Barcelona, 1927).**

Puyol y Alonso, Julio: "Cantos Populares Leoneses," in *Revue Hispanique,* Tome XII, No. 41 (1905).*

Ribera, Julián: *La Música de la Jota Aragonesa* (Madrid, 1928).*

Rodríguez Marín, Francisco: *Cantos Populares Españoles,* 5 vols. (Seville, 1882–83).*

——— *El Alma de Andalucía en sus Mejores Coplas Amorosas* (Madrid, 1929).

Schindler, Kurt: *Folk Music of Spain and Portugal* (New York, 1941).**

——— *Songs of the Spanish Provinces,* 2 series (Boston, 1922–23).**

Serrá i Boldú, Valeri: *Llibre d'Or del Rosari a Catalunya* (Barcelona, 1925).*

Starkie, Walter F.: *Don Gypsy, Adventures with a Fiddle in Barbary, Andalusia and La Mancha* (London, 1936).*

——— *Spanish Raggle-Taggle* (London, 1934).*

Trend, J. B.: "Music in Spanish Galicia," in *Music & Letters,* vol. V, No. 1 (January, 1924).*

——— *Spain From the South* (London, 1928).

Varela y Silvari, José María: *La Música Popular Española* (Mondoñedo, 1883).

CHAPTER XVI

Alford, Violet: *Pyrenean Festivals* (London, 1937).*

——— "The Dance of the Gipsies in Catalonia," in *Journal of the English Folk Dance and Song Society,* vol. 1 (1934).

Arnaudas Larrodé, Miguel: *La Jota Aragonesa* (Saragossa, 1933).

Capdevila, Manuel: *De la Sardana* (Barcelona, 1925).

Capmany, Aurelio: *La Dansa a Catalunya* (Barcelona, 1930).

Carreras y Candi, F.: *Folklore y Costumbres de España,* vol. II (Barcelona, 1931).*

Cordelier, Suzanne F.: *La Vie Brève de La Argentina* (Paris, 1936).

Ellis, Havelock: *The Soul of Spain,* new edition (Boston, 1937).

Gallop, Rodney: *A Book of the Basques* (London, 1930).*

Gascue, Francisco: "L'Aurresku Basque," in *La Revue Musicale S. I. M.* (September–October, 1912).*

Kinney, Troy and Margaret West: *The Dance,* new edition (New York, 1935).

Langdon-Davies, John: *Dancing Catalans* (London and New York, 1929).

Levinson, André: *La Argentina, Essai sur la Danse Espagnole* (Paris, 1928).
———— "The Spirit of the Spanish Dance," in *Theatre Arts Monthly*, vol. 9 (1925).
Llano, Aurelio de: *Del Folklore Asturiano* (Madrid, 1922).
Martínez Torner, Eduardo: *Temas Folklóricos* (Madrid, 1935).* With bibliography.
Mas y Prat, Benito: *La Tierra de María Santísima* (Barcelona, 1891).
Moreira, Joan: *Del Folklore Tortosí* (Tortosa, 1934).*
Nadal, Luis B.: "Balls Populars Catalans," in *Revista Musical Catalana*, Any I, No. 4 (April, 1904).*
Otero Aranda, José: *Tratado de Bailes de Sociedad Regionales Españoles* (Seville, 1912).*
Pabanó, F. M.: *Historia y Costumbres de los Gitanos* (Barcelona, 1915).
Parnac, Valentin: *Histoire de la Danse* (Paris, 1932).
Pericot, Lluis: "Una Representació de Dansa Ibèrica," in *Revista Musical Catalana*, Any XXXIII, No. 385 (January, 1936).
Rice, Cyril: *Dancing in Spain* (London, 1931).
Sachs, Curt: *World History of the Dance* (English translation; New York, 1937).*

CHAPTER XVII

Almeida, Renato: *Historia da Musica Brasileira* (Rio de Janeiro, 1926).
Alvarez, Juan: *Orígenes de la Música Argentina* (Rosario, 1908).*
Andrade, Mario de: *Ensaio Sobre Musica Brasileira* (São Paulo, 1928).*
———— *Modinhas Imperiaes* (São Paulo, 1930).*
Arzeno, Julio: *Del Folk-lore Musical Dominicano* (Santo Domingo, 1927).*
Bernal Jiménez, Miguel: *El Archivo Musical del Colegio de Santa Rosa de Santa María de Valladolid, Siglo XVIII* (Morelia, 1939).*
Berrien, William: "Some Considerations Regarding Contemporary Latin American Music," in *Concerning Latin American Culture*, edited by C. C. Griffin (New York, 1940).
Boggs, Ralph S.: *Bibliography of Latin American Folklore* (Washington and New York, 1940).
Boletín Latino-Americano de Música, edited by Francisco Curt Lange (director of Instituto Interamericano de Musicología, Montevideo).* Four volumes published, 1935–38, with musical supplements (vol. V to be published, 1941).
Brito Mendes, Julia de: *Canções Populares do Brasil* (Rio de Janeiro, 1911).*
Cadilla de Martínez, María: *Juegos y Canciones Infantiles de Puerto Rico* (San Juan, 1940).*
Calcaño, José Antonio: *Contribución al Estudio de la Música en Venezuela* (Caracas, 1939).*
Campa, Arthur L.: *A Bibliography of Spanish Folk-lore in New Mexico* (Albuquerque, 1930).
———— *Spanish Folksong in the Southwest* (Albuquerque, 1933).
———— *Spanish Religious Folk Theatre in the Southwest* (Albuquerque, 1934).
University of New Mexico Bulletin, Language Series, vol. V, Nos. 1 and 2.
Campos, Rubén M.: *El Folklore Musical de las Ciudades* (Mexico, 1930).*

────── *El Folklore y la Música Mexicana* (Mexico, 1928).*

Carrizo, Juan Alfonso: *Cancionero Popular de Tucumán* (Buenos Aires, 1937).*

────── *Cantares Tradicionales del Tucumán* (Buenos Aires, 1939).*

Chacón y Calvo, José María: *Literatura Cubana; Ensayos Críticos* (Madrid, 1922).

Chase, Gilbert: *Annotated Bibliography of the Dance in Latin America* (Washington, 1941).

────── *Partial List of Latin American Music . . .* Compiled in the Music Division, Library of Congress (Washington, 1941). Mimeographed.

Chávez, Carlos: "Mexican Music," in *Renascent Mexico*, edited by H. Herring and H. Weinstock (New York, 1935).

Cole, M. R.: *Los Pastores. A Mexican Miracle Play. Memoirs of the American Folklore Society*, vol. IX (New York, 1907).*

Contreras, Segundo N.: *Disertaciones Musicales* (Buenos Aires, 1931).

Cortijo Alahija, L.: *La Música Popular y los Músicos Célebres de la América Latina* (Barcelona, 1919).*

Curtis, F. S., Jr.: *Spanish Songs of New Mexico* (Austin, 1925). Publications of the Texas Folk-lore Society, No. IV.*

Espinosa, Aurelio M.: "Romancero Nuevomejicano," in *Revue Hispanique*, Tome XXXIII, No. 84 (1915).* See also Tome XL, No. 97 (1917), for Addenda.

────── "Romances de Puerto Rico," in *Revue Hispanique*, Tome XLIII, No. 104 (1918).

────── "Traditional Ballads From Andalucía," in *Flügel Memorial Volume* (Stanford University, California, 1916).

Freire-Marreco, Barbara: "New-Mexican Spanish Folk-lore," in *Journal of American Folk-Lore*, vol. XXIX, No. CXIV (October–December, 1916).

Friedenthal, A.: *Musik, Tanz und Dichtung bei den Kreolen Amerikas* (Berlin, 1911).*

Furt, Jorge M.: *Coreografía Gauchesca* (Buenos Aires, 1927).*

Galindo, Miguel: *Nociones de Historia de la Música Mejicana* (Colima, 1933).*

Gallet, Luciano: *Estudos de Folklore* (Rio de Janeiro, 1934).**

Gallop, Rodney: Mexican Mosaic (London, 1939).*

Garay, Narciso: *Tradiciones y Cantares de Panamá* (Brussels, 1930).*

Garfías, Carlota: "Mexican Folklore Collected in New York City," in *Journal of American Folk-Lore*, vol. 51 (1938).*

González Sol, Rafael: *Datos Históricos Sobre el Arte de la Música en El Salvador* (San Salvador, 1940).

Grenet, Emilio: *Popular Cuban Music* (Havana, 1939).**

Hague, Eleanor: *Folk Songs From Mexico and South America.* Piano accompaniments by Edward Kilenyi (New York, 1914).**

────── *Latin American Music, Past and Present* (Santa Ana, Calif., 1934).

────── "Spanish-American Folk Songs," in *Journal of American Folk-Lore*, vol. XXIV, No. XCIII (September, 1911).**

────── *Spanish-American Folk Songs.* Publication of the American Folk-Lore Society (New York, 1917).**

Handbook of Latin American Studies, an annual bibliography edited in the Library of Congress and published by the Harvard University Press, Cambridge, Mass.

Hare, Maud Cuney: "Portuguese Folk-songs from Provincetown, Cape Cod, Mass.," in *The Musical Quarterly*, vol. XIV, No. 1 (January, 1928).*

Henríquez Ureña, Pedro: "Música Popular de América," in *Biblioteca del Colegio Nacional de la Universidad de la Plata*, vol. I (1930).

—— "Romances de América," in *Cuba Contemporánea* (December, 1913).

Laval, Ramón A.: "Sobre Dos Cantos Chilenos Derivados de un Antiguo Romance Español," in *Revista Chilena de Historia y Geografía*, No. 67 (December, 1929).

Leonard, Irving A.: *Romances of Chivalry in the Spanish Indies* (Berkeley, 1933).

Lohmann Villena, Guillermo: "Apuntaciones Sobre el Arte Dramático en Lima Durante el Virreinato," in *Tres* (Lima), No. 7 (December, 1940).

Luce, Allena: *Canciones Populares* (Boston, 1921).**

Lucero-White, Aurora: *Folk-dances of the Spanish-Colonials of New Mexico*, 2nd revised edition (Santa Fe, 1940).*

Lummis, Charles F.: *Spanish Songs of Old California* (Los Angeles, 1925).**

—— *The Land of Poco Tiempo* (New York, 1925).*

Lynch, Ventura R.: *Cancionero Bonaerense* (Buenos Aires, 1925).*

McCoy, William J.: *Folk Songs of the Spanish Californians* (San Francisco, 1926).**

Mason, J. Alden: "Porto-Rican Folk-lore. Décimas, Christmas Carols, Nursery Rhymes, and Other Songs," in *Journal of American Folk-Lore*, vol. 31, No. 121 (July–September, 1918).

Mattfeld, Julius: *The Folk Music of the Western Hemisphere*. A list of references in the New York Public Library (New York, 1925).

Mendoza, Vicente T.: *El Romance Español y el Corrido Mexicano* (Mexico, 1939).*

—— "Los Cantos de Arada en España y México," in *Revista Mexicana de Sociología*, Año 2, No. 1 (1940).*

Menéndez Pidal, Ramón: "Las Primeras Noticias de Romances Tradicionales en America," in *Homenaje a Enrique José Varona* (Havana, 1935).

—— *Los Romances de América, y Otros Ensayos* (Buenos Aires, 1939).

Muñoz Sanz, Juan Pablo: *La Música Ecuatoriana* (Quito, 1938).

Nolasco, Flérida de: *La Música en Santo Domingo* (Ciudad Trujillo, 1939).*

Ortiz y San Pelayo, Felix: *Nuestra Música; o, La Música Española* (Buenos Aires, 1920).

Pereira de Mello, Guilherme T.: *A Música no Brasil* (Bahia, 1908).*

Pereira Salas, Eugenio: *Los Orígenes del Arte Musical en Chile* (Santiago, 1941).*

Ponce, Manuel M.: *Escritos y Composiciones Musicales* (Mexico, 1917).*

Poncet, Carolina: *El Romance en Cuba* (Havana, 1914).

Ramirez, Serafín: *La Habana Artística* (Havana, 1891).*

Ribera, Julián: "Para la Historia de la Música Popular," in *Boletín de la Real Academia de la Historia*, Tomo 80 (January–March, 1927).

Rodrigues Valle, Flausino: *Elementos de Folk-lore Musical Brasileiro* (São Paulo, 1936).*

Saldívar, Gabriel: *El Jarabe, Baile Popular Mexicano* (Mexico, 1937).*

—— *Historia de la Música en Méjico* (Mexico, 1934).*

Sánchez de Fuentes, Eduardo: *El Folk-lore en la Música Cubana* (Havana, 1923).*

Schianca, Arturo C.: *Historia de la Música Argentina* (Buenos Aires, c. 1933).*

Schwendener, Norma: *Legends and Dances of Old Mexico* (New York, 1934).*

Seeger, Charles: "Inter-American Relations in the Field of Music," in *Music Educators Journal* (March–April, 1941).

Slonimsky, Nicolas: "South America's Constellation of Composers," in *Musical America* (February 10, 1940). Also reprinted separately.

Spell, Lota M.: "Las Canciones Populares Hispano-Americanas en los Estados Unidos," in *Boletín Latino-Americano de Música*, Tomo V (Montevideo, 1941).

———— *Music in Texas* (Austin, 1936).*

———— *Music Teaching in New Mexico in the 17th Century* (Santa Fe, 1927). Reprinted from *New Mexico Historical Review*, vol. II, No. 1 (January, 1927).

———— "The First Music Books Printed in America," in *The Musical Quarterly*, vol. XV, No. 1 (January, 1929). Also reprinted separately.

Spizzy, Mable Seeds: *La Fiesta, A Unit of Early California Songs and Dances* (Lincoln, Neb., 1939).*

Valtón, Emilio: *Impresos Mexicanos del Siglo XVI (Incunables Americanos)* . . . (Mexico, 1935).*

Van der Voort, A.: *Old Spanish Songs* . . . (Santa Barbara, 1928).**

Van Stone, Mary R., and E. R. Sims: "Canto del Niño Perdido" [New-Mexican religious folk play], in *Publications of the Texas Folk-lore Society*, No. XI (Austin, 1933).*

Vázquez Santa Ana, Higinio: *Historia de la Canción Mexicana* (Mexico, 1931).*

Vega, Carlos: *Danzas y Canciones Argentinas* (Buenos Aires, 1936).*

Vicuña Cifuentes, Julio: *Romances Populares y Vulgares, Recogidos de la Tradición Oral Chilena* (Santiago, 1912).

CHAPTER XVIII

Armando, Gualtério: "Musik und Musiker in Portugal," in *Die Musik*, Jahrg. XXX, Heft 9 (June, 1938).

Carneyro, Katherine Hickel: "Music in Portugal," in *The International Cyclopedia of Music and Musicians*, edited by Oscar Thompson (New York, 1939).

Coelho, P. Manuel R.: *Tentos*, edited by Santiago Kastner (Mainz and Leipzig, 1936).**

Cravistas Portugueses, edited by Santiago Kastner (Mainz and Leipzig, 1935).**

Diogo Correia, J.: *Cantares de Malpica, Beira Baixa* (Lisbon, 1938).*

Freitas Branco, Luís de: *Elementos de Sciências Musicais*, first edition (Lisbon, 1923). Second edition (Leipzig, 1931).*

Gallop, Rodney: *Cantares do Povo Português* (Lisbon, 1937).**

———— *Portugal, A Book of Folk-ways* (Cambridge, England, 1936).*

———— "The Fado (The Portuguese 'Song of Fate')," in *The Musical Quarterly*, vol. XIX, No. 2 (April, 1933).*

———— "The Folk Music of Eastern Portugal," in *The Musical Quarterly*, vol. XX, No. 1 (January, 1934).*

Inventário de Inéditos e Impressos Musicais (Subsídios para um Catálogo), Publicações da Biblioteca da Universidade, Fasc. I (Coimbra, 1937).

Kastner, Santiago: "La Musique de Clavier Portugaise," in special number of *La Revue Musicale* (February–March, 1940).

——— *Música Hispânica, O Estilo do Padre Manuel R. Coelho* (Lisbon, 1936).*

Lambertini, Michel'angelo: "Portugal," in *Encyclopédie de la Musique et Dictionnaire du Conservatoire*, Part I, vol. 4 (Paris, 1920).*

Lopes Dias, Jaime: *O que a Nossa Gente Canta. Etnografia da Beira*, vol. II (Lisbon, 1927).**

Luper, Albert T.: *Portuguese Music Theory in the Early Seventeenth Century*. Master's thesis, Eastman School of Music (Rochester), 1938.*

Moreira de Sá, B. V.: *Compêndio de Música* (Porto, 1921).*

Neuparth, Júlio: *Os Grandes Períodos da Música* (Lisbon, 1911).

Novello, Vincent: *The Fitzwilliam Music* (London, 1825).**

Pinto, Alfredo: *Música Moderna Portuguesa e os Seus Representantes* (Lisbon, 1930).

Pires de Lima, Fernando de Castro: *Cantares do Minho* (Barcelos, 1937).**

Recueil des Morceaux de Musique Ancienne, edited by Le Prince de Moskowa, vol. 6 (Paris, 1842).**

Ritter, A. G.: *Zur Geschichte des Orgelspiels* (Leipzig, 1884).*

Sampayo Ribeiro, Mário de: *Achegas para a História da Música em Portugal*.
Part I: *A Obra Musical do Padre Antonio Pereira de Figueiredo* (Lisbon, 1932). Reprint from *Estudos Portugueses do Integralismo Lusitano*, vol. I, Fasc. VII, VIII, and IX.
Part II: *Damião de Góes na Livraria Real de Música* (Lisbon, 1935). Reprint from *Trabalhos da Associação dos Arqueólogos Portugueses*, vol. I.

——— "A Música em Lisboa," in *Revista Municipal*, Ano I, No. 4 (1940).

Santos, Júlio Eduardo dos: *A Polifonia Clássica Portuguesa* (Lisbon, 1937).**

Soubies, Albert: *Histoire de la Musique: Portugal* (Paris, 1898).

Vasconcellos, Joaquim de: *Ensaio Crítico Sobre o Cátalogo d'el Rey D. João IV* (Porto, 1873).

——— *Os Músicos Portuguezes*, 2 vols. (Porto, 1870).

——— *Primeira Parte do Index da Livraria de Música do Rey Dom João IV* (Porto, 1874).

Vasconcellos, J. Leite de: *Poesia Amorosa do Povo Português* (Lisbon, 1890).

Vianna da Motta, José, and Luís de Freitas Branco: "La Musique Portugaise," in special number of *La Revue Musicale* (February–March, 1940).

Vieira, Ernesto: *Diccionario Biographico de Músicos Portuguezes*, 2 vols. (Lisbon, 1900).

CHAPTER XIX

Abraham, Gerald, and M. D. Calvocoressi: *Masters of Russian Music* (London, 1936).

Calvocoressi, M. D.: *Glinka* (Paris, 1913).*

Desaymard, Joseph: *Chabrier d'Après ses Lettres* (Paris, 1934).*

Falla, Manuel de: "Claude Debussy and Spain," in *The Chesterian*, New Series, No. 12 (January, 1921).

——— "Notes sur Ravel," in *La Revue Musicale*, Année 20, No. 189 (March, 1939).

Jankélevitch, J.: *Maurice Ravel* (Paris, 1939).*

Laparra, Raoul: *Bizet et l'Espagne* (Paris, 1935).*

Lockspeiser, Edward: "L'Influence de l'Espagne sur la Musique," in *Mercure Français* (Sept. 1, 1937).

Manuel, Roland: *Maurice Ravel* (Paris, 1938).*

O'Connell, Charles: *The Victor Book of the Symphony*, revised edition (New York, 1941).*

Subirá, José: *Richard Strauss, su Hispanismo . . .* (Madrid, 1925).

Tiersot, Julien: "Bizet and Spanish Music," in *The Musical Quarterly*, vol. XIII, No. 4 (October, 1927).*

Vallas, Léon: *Les Idées de Claude Debussy* (Paris, 1927; English translation as *The Theories of Claude Debussy*, 1929).

ADDENDA

GENERAL

Kastner, Santiago: *Contribución al Estudio de la Música Española y Portuguesa* (Lisbon, 1941).*

CHAPTER V

Mitjana, Rafael: *Don Fernando de las Infantas, Teólogo y Músico* (Madrid, 1918).*

CHAPTER IX

Mitjana, Rafael: *La Música Contemporánea en España y Felipe Pedrell* (Madrid, 1901).

CHAPTER XV

Azara, Medina: "Cante Jondo y Cantares Sinagogales," in *Revista de Occidente*, Año VIII, No. 88 (October, 1930).

Correia Lopes, Edmundo Arménio: *Cancioneirinho de Fozcoa* (Coimbra, 1926).*

Fernandes Thomas, Pedro: *Canções Populares da Beira*, 2nd edition (Coimbra, 1923).**

────── *Velhas Canções e Romances Populares Portuguêses* (Coimbra, 1913).**

Folklore Musical; Répertoire International des Collections et Centres de Documentation . . . (Paris: Institut International de Coopération Intellectuelle, 1939). Section on Spain by Jesús Bal y Gay, with extensive bibliography.

Gallop, Rodney: *Eight Portuguese Folksongs*. Arranged for voice and piano (London and Lisbon, 1936).**

Rodríguez Gómez, Fernando [Fernando el de Triana]: *Arte y Artistas Flamencos* (Madrid, 1935).

(For Portuguese folk music, consult also the bibliography for Chapter XVIII.)

Supplementary Bibliography
to Second Edition

PUBLICATIONS OF THE "INSTITUTO ESPAÑOL DE MUSICOLOGIA"

SERIES I. — Monuments of Spanish Music.

1. La Música en la Corte de los Reyes Católicos. vol. I. *Polifonía religiosa.* Por Higinio Anglès. Madrid, 1941.
2. La Música en la Corte de Carlos V, con la transcripción del *Libro de Cifra Nueva para Tecla, Arpa y Vihuela,* de Luys Venegas de Henestrosa (Alcalá de Henares, 1557). Por H. Anglès. Barcelona, 1944.
3. *Los Seys Libros del Delphin de Música de Cifra para Tañer Vilhuela,* de Luys de Narváez (Valladolid, 1538). Transcripción y estudio por E. Pujol. Barcelona, 1945.
4. *Recopilación de Sonetos y Villancicos a Quatro y a Cinco,* de Juan Vázquez (Sevilla, 1560). Transcripción y estudio por H. Anglès. Barcelona, 1946.
5. *El Cancionero Musical de Palacio (Siglo XV).* Transcripción y estudio por H. Anglès. vol. I. Barcelona, 1947.
6. *Facultad Orgánica,* de Francisco Correa de Arauxo (Alcalá de Henares, 1626). Transcripción y estudio por S. Kastner. vol. I. Barcelona, 1948.
7. *Tres Libros de Música en Cifra para Vihuela,* de Alonso Mudarra (Sevilla, 1546). Transcripción y estudio por E. Pujol. Barcelona, 1949.
8-9. *Cancionero Musical de la Casa de Medinaceli.* Transcripción y estudio por M. Querol. vol. I. Barcelona, 1949. vol. II, Barcelona, 1950.
10. *El Cancionero Musical de Palacio.* vol. II. Transcripción y estudio de H. Anglès. Barcelona, 1951.
11. *Opera Omnia,* de Cristóbal de Morales. vol. I: *Missarum Liber I* (Roma, 1544). Transcripción y estudio por H. Anglès. Roma, 1952.
12. *Facultad Orgánica,* de Francisco Correa de Arauxo (Alcalá, 1626). Transcripción y estudio de S. Kastner. vol. II. Barcelona, 1952.
13. *Opera Omnia,* de Cristóbal de Morales. vol. II: *Motetes, I, XXV.* Transcripción y estudio por H. Anglès. Roma, 1953.
14. El Cancionero Musical de Palacio. vol. III. *Estudio preliminar* por Jorge Rubio. Introducción y edición crítica de los textos literarios por J. M. Figueras.
15. *Opera Omnia,* de Cristóbal de Morales. vol. III: *Missarum Liber II* (Roma, 1544). Transcripción y estudio por H. Anglès. Roma, 1954.
16. *Opera Omnia,* de Francisco Guerrero. vol. I: *Canciones y Villanescas Espirituales* (Venecia, 1589). 1.ª parte. Transcripción por V. García. Revisión y estudio por M. Querol. Barcelona, 1955.
17. *Opera Omnia,* de Cristóbal de Morales. vol. IV: XVI *Magníficat* (Venecia, 1545). Transcripción y estudio por H. Anglès. Roma, 1956.
18. *Romances y Letras a tres voces (Siglo XVII).* Transcripción y estudio por M. Querol. Barcelona, 1956.

SERIES II. — Anuario Musical.
Musical yearbooks, published annually since 1946. They contain important studies of Spanish music.

SERIES III. — Musical Catalogues.
1-3. Catálogo Musical de la Biblioteca Nacional de Madrid. Por H. Anglès y J. Subirá. vol. I: *Manuscritos.* Barcelona, 1946. vol. II: *Impresos.* Barcelona, 1949. vol. III: *Impresos; Música práctica.* Barcelona, 1951.

SERIES IV. — Monographs.
1. *El Origen Musical de los Animales-Símbolos en la Mitología y la Escultura Antiguas.* Por Marius Schneider. Barcelona, 1946.
2. *El Quijote en la Música.* Por Victor Espinós. Barcelona, 1947.
3. *La Danza de Espadas y la Tarantela: Contribución Musical, Etnográfico-Arqueológica al Problema de los Ritos de Medicina.* Por M. Schneider. Barcelona, 1948.
4. *El Poeta-Compositor Iriarte y el Cultivo Español del Melólogo* (Melodrama). Por José Subirá. 2 vols. Barcelona, 1949 and 1950.
5. *El Teatro del Real Palacio.* (1849-1851). Por José Subirá. Madrid, 1950.

SERIES V. — Collections of Spanish Folksong.
1-2. *Cancionero Musical de la Provincia de Madrid.* Materiales recogidos por Manuel Garciá Matos. Edición crítica por Marius Schneider y José Romeu Figueras. 2 vols. Barcelona-Madrid, 1951 and 1952.
3. *Cancionero Musical de las Provincias de Cádiz y Huelva.* Materiales recogidos por M. García Matos y A. de Larrea. Edición crítica por Juan Tomás y J. Romeu Figueras.

Música Hispana

SERIES A: Folk Music
1. *Doce Canciones Populares Españolas, con acompañamiento de piano,* por J. Rodrigo. Barcelona, 1952.

SERIES B: Polyphony.
1. *Misa "De Beata Virgine," a cuatro voces mixtas,* por Cristóbal de Morales. Transcripción por H. Anglès. Barcelona, 1953.
2. *Antología Polifónica Española Profana (Siglos XV-XVII),* por Miguel Querol.

SERIES C: Chamber Music.
1. Soler, P. Antonio: *III Concierto para dos instrumentos de tecla.* Transcripción por Santiago Kastner. Barcelona, 1952.
2. Manalt, Francisco: *Sonatas N.ᵇ I y II para violín y piano.* Transcripción y realización por P. J. A. Donostia. Barcelona, 1955.
3. Soler, P. Antonio: *I Concierto para dos instrumentos de tecla.* Transcripción por S. Kastner. Barcelona, 1956.
4. Soler, P. Antonio: *II Concierto para dos instrumentos de tecla.* Transcripción por Santiago Kastner. Barcelona, 1957.

GENERAL

Anglès, Higini: "La Música en España," in J. Wolf, *Historia de la Música* (Barcelona, 1944).

———*Antifonario Visigótico Mozarabe de la Catedral de León.* Edición facsimil. (Madrid, 1953). Centro de Estudios e Investigaciones S. Isidro.

Araiz, Andrés: *Historia de la Música Religiosa en España* (Barcelona and Madrid, 1942).

Bermudo, Juan: *Declaración de Instrumentos Musicales, 1555,* Faksimile-Nachdruck hrsg. von Macario Santiago Kastner (Kassel & Basel, Barenreiter-Verlag 1957).

Borras, Tomás: *Conrado del Campo* (Madrid, 1954). With a complete list of works.

Cabezón, Antonio de: *Obras de Música para Tecla, Arpa y Vihuela* (Claviermusik). Revised and edited by Santiago Kastner (London and New York, 1951).

Cancionero Musical Español de los Siglos XV y XVI. Transcripto y comentado por F. Asenjo Barbieri (Buenos Aires, 1945).

Capmany, Aurelio: *El Ball i la Dansa Popular a Catalunya* (Barcelona, 1948).

Chase, Gilbert: *A Guide to Latin American Music* (The Library of Congress, 1945).

———"Juan Navarro Hispalensis and Juan Navarro Gaditanus", in *The Musical Quarterly,* vol. XXXI, No. 2 (1945).

Cimorra, Clemente: *El Cante Jondo; Origen y Realidad Folklórica* (Buenos Aires, 1943).

Cobas Pazos, V: *Esbozo de un Estudio Sobre la Gaita Gallega* (Santiago de Compostela, 1955).

Cruz, María Antonieta de Lima: *Historia da Música Portuguesa* (Lisboa, 1955).

Diego, Gerardo, Joaquín Rodrigo, and Federico Sopeña: *Diez Años de Música en España: Musicología — Intérpretes — Compositores* (Madrid, 1949).

Donostía, José Antonio de: *Música y Músicos en el País Vasco* (San Sebastián, 1951).

Esplá y Triay, Oscar: *Función Musical y Música Contemporánea.* Discurso . . . leído en el acto de su recepción pública el día 4 de mayo de 1955 (Madrid, 1955).

Falla, Manuel de: *Escritos Sobre Música y Músicos* (Buenos Aires — México, 1950). Introduction and notes by Federico Sopeña. Includes an essay on "Cante jondo."

Freitas Branco, Luis de: *D. João IV, Músico* (Lisboa, 1956).

González Ruiz, Nicolás: *La Caramba; Vida Alegre y Muerte Ejemplar de una Tonadillera del Siglo XVIII* (Madrid, 1944).

Henriques, Mário Ventura: *Fernando Lopes Graça na Música Portuguesa Contemporánea* (Sacavem, 1956).

Jaenisch, Julio: *Manuel de Falla und die Spanische Musik* (Zürich, 1952).

Kirkpatrick, Ralph: *Domenico Scarlatti* (Princeton, N. J., 1953).

López Chavarri, Eduardo: *Folklore Musical Español* (Madrid, 1955).

Manrique de Lara, Manuel: "Romances Españoles en los Balkanes," in *Blanco y Negro,* año 26, No. 1285. (Jan. 2, 1916).

Martínez Torner, Eduardo: "Indicaciones Prácticas Sobre la Notación Musical de los Romances," in *Rev. de filología española,* vol. X (1923).

Mingote, Angel: *Manuel Palau, Músico Contemporáneo* (Valencia, 1946).

Pahissa, Jaime: *Sendas y Cumbres de la Música Española* (Buenos Aires, 1955).

———*Vida y Obra de Manuel de Falla* (Buenos Aires, 1947).

Pedrell, Felipe: "Conferencia-Audicion Sobre Folklore Musical Hispano," in *Arxiu d'Etnografia i Folklore de Catalunya*, vol. I (1916), pp. 23-48.

Pope, Isabel: "The Musical Development and Form of the Spanish Villancico," in *Papers of the American Musicological Society for 1940* (Published by the Society, 1946).

———"The 'Spanish Chapel' of Philip II," in *Renaissance News*, vol. V, No. 1 (1952).

Prado, Dom Germán, and W. M. Whitehall: *Liber Sancti Jacobi: Codex Calixtinus* (Santiago de Compostela, 1944).

Ribera, Julián: "La Música Andaluza Antigua y su Influencia," in *Boletín de la Real Academia de Córdoba*, vol. VIII (1929), pp. 221-232.

Rodríguez Gómez, Fernando: *Arte y Artistas Flamencos.* 2nd edition (Madrid, 1952).

Roland-Manuel: *Manuel de Falla.* Seguido de un Ensayo de Vicente Salas Viu Sobre Falla y el Futuro de la Música Española (Buenos Aires, 1945).

Sagardia, Angel: *Jesús Guridi; Ensayo Crítico de su Vida y de sus Obras* (Madrid, 1950).

Sainz de la Maza, Regino: *La Guitarra y su Historia* (Madrid, 1955).

Salazar, Adolfo: *El gran siglo de la Música Española en el Cuarto Centenario de la Muerte de Cristóbal de Morales* (Santiago de Chile, 1955).

———"El Laúd, lá Vihuela y la Guitarra," in *Nuestra Música* (México), Año 1, No. 4 (Sept. 1946).

———*La Música de España (La Música en la Cultura Española)* (Buenos Aires and México, 1953).

———*La Música Contemporánea en Espana*, 2nd edition (Buenos Aires, 1952).

———*La Música en la Sociedad Europea*, 4 vols. (México, D. F., 1942-46).

———"Música, Instrumentos y Danzas en las Obras de Cervantes," in *Nueva Revista de Filología Española*, vol. II, Nos. 1 & 2 (México, D. F., 1948).

———"Poesía y Música en las Primeras Formas de Versificación Rimada en Lengua Vulgar y sus Antecedentes en Lengua Latina en la Edad Media (con una bibliografía)," in *Filosofía y Letras* (Universidad Nacional de México), No. 8 (Oct.-Dec. 1942).

Sanchis Guarner, Manuel: *El Cant de la Sibil-la; Antiga Cerimonia Nadalenca* (Valencia, 1956).

Sopeña, Federico: *Joaquín Rodrigo* (Madrid, 1946).

———*Historia de la Música Española Contemporánea* (Madrid, 1958).

Subirá, José: *Historia de la Música Española e Hispano-Americana* (Barcelona, 1953).

———*Historia de la Música Teatral en España* (Barcelona — Madrid, 1945).

Thomás, Juan María: *Manuel de Falla en la Isla* (Palma de Mallorca, n.d.).

Wilkes, J. T., and I. Guerrero Cárpena: *Formas Musicales Rio-Platenses: su Génesis Hispánica* (Buenos Aires, 1946).

Index

DOVER BOOKS

SPINNING TOPS AND GYROSCOPIC MOTION, John Perry. A classic elementary text of the dynamics of rotation — the behavior and use of rotating bodies such as gyroscopes and tops. In simple, everyday English you are shown how quasi-rigidity is induced in discs of paper, smoke rings, chains, etc., by rapid motions; why a gyrostat falls and why a top rises; precession; how the earth's motion affects climate; and many other phenomena. Appendix on practical use of gyroscopes. 62 figures. 128pp. 5⅜ x 8. T416 Paperbound **$1.00**

THE EVOLUTION OF SCIENTIFIC THOUGHT FROM NEWTON TO EINSTEIN, A. d'Abro. A detailed account of the evolution of classical physics into modern relativistic theory and the concommitant changes in scientific methodology. The breakdown of classical physics in the face of non-Euclidean geometry and the electro-magnetic equations is carefully discussed and then an exhaustive analysis of Einstein's special and general theories of relativity and their implications is given. Newton, Riemann, Weyl, Lorentz, Planck, Maxwell, and many others are considered. "Model of semi-popular exposition," NEW REPUBLIC. 21 diagrams. 482pp. 5⅜ x 8. T2 Paperbound **$2.00**

THE RISE OF THE NEW PHYSICS (formerly THE DECLINE OF MECHANISM), A. d'Abro. This authoritative and comprehensive 2 volume exposition is unique in scientific publishing. Written for intelligent readers not familiar with higher mathematics, it is the only thorough explanation in non-technical language of modern mathematical-physical theory. Combining both history and exposition, it ranges from classical Newtonian concepts up through the electronic theories of Dirac and Heisenberg, the statistical mechanics of Fermi, and Einstein's relativity theories. "A must for anyone doing serious study in the physical sciences," THE FRANKLIN INSTITUTE. 97 illustrations. 991pp. 2 volumes.
T3 Vol. 1, Paperbound **$2.00**
T4 Vol. 2, Paperbound **$2.00**

A CONCISE HISTORY OF MATHEMATICS, D. Struik. A lucid, easily followed history of mathematical ideas and techniques from the Ancient Near East up to modern times. Requires no mathematics but will serve as an excellent introduction to mathematical concepts and great mathematicians through the method of historical development. 60 illustrations including Egyptian papyri, Greek mss., portraits of 31 eminent mathematicians. Bibliography. xix + 299pp. 5⅜ x 8. T255 Paperbound **$1.75**

THE NATURE OF PHYSICAL THEORY, P. W. Bridgman. A Nobel Laureate's clear, non-technical lectures on difficulties and paradoxes connected with frontier research in the physical sciences. Concerned with such central concepts as thought, logic, mathematics, relativity, probability, wave mechanics, etc., he analyzes the contributions of such men as Newton, Einstein, Bohr, Heisenberg, and many others. "Lucid and entertaining . . . recommended to anyone who wants to get some insight into current philosophies of science," THE NEW PHILOSOPHY. Index. xi + 138pp. 5⅜ x 8. S33 Paperbound **$1.25**

THE RESTLESS UNIVERSE, Max Born. A remarkably lucid account by a Nobel Laureate of recent theories of wave mechanics, behavior of gases, electrons, and ions, waves and particles, electronic structure of the atom, nuclear physics, and similar topics. "Much more thorough and deeper than most attempts . . . easy and delightful," CHEMICAL AND ENGINEERING NEWS. **SPECIAL FEATURE:** 7 animated sequences showing such phenomena as gas molecules in motion, the scattering of alpha particles, etc. 11 full-page plates of photographs. Total of nearly 600 illustrations. 315pp. 6⅛ x 9¼.
T412 Paperbound **$2.00**

WHAT IS SCIENCE?, N. Campbell. The roll of experiment and measurement, the function of mathematics, the nature of scientific laws, the difference between laws and theories, the limitations of science, and many similarly provocative topics are treated clearly and without technicalities by an eminent scientist. "Still an excellent introduction to scientific philosophy," H. Margenau in PHYSICS TODAY. 192pp. 5⅜ x 8. S43 Paperbound **$1.25**

FADS AND FALLACIES IN THE NAME OF SCIENCE, Martin Gardner. Formerly entitled IN THE NAME OF SCIENCE, this is the standard account of the various cults, quack systems, and delusions which have masqueraded as science: hollow earth fanatics, Reich and orgone sex energy, dianetics, Atlantis, multiple moons, Forteanism, flying saucers, medical fallacies like iridiagnosis, zone therapy, etc. A new chapter has been added on Bridey Murphy, psionics, and other recent manifestations in this field. "Should be read by everyone, scientist and non-scientist alike," R. T. Birge, Prof. Emeritus of Physics, Univ. of California; Former President, American Physical Society. Index. x + 365pp. 5⅜ x 8.
T394 Paperbound **$1.50**

EXPERIMENT AND THEORY IN PHYSICS, Max Born. A Nobel Laureate examines the nature of experiment and theory in theoretical physics and analyzes the advances made by the great physicists of our day: Heisenberg, Einstein, Bohr, Planck, Dirac, and others. The actual process of creation is detailed step-by-step by one who participated. 44p. 5⅜ x 8. S308 Paperbound **60¢**

A HISTORY OF ASTRONOMY FROM THALES TO KEPLER, J. L. E. Dreyer. Formerly titled A HISTORY OF PLANETARY SYSTEMS FROM THALES TO KEPLER. This is the only work in English which provides a detailed history of man's cosmological views from prehistoric times up through the Renaissance. It covers Egypt, Babylonia, early Greece, Alexandria, the Middle Ages, Copernicus, Tycho Brahe, Kepler, and many others. Epicycles and other complex theories of positional astronomy are explained in terms nearly everyone will find clear and easy to understand. "Standard reference on Greek astronomy and the Copernican revolution," SKY AND TELESCOPE. Bibliography. 21 diagrams. Index. xvii + 430pp. 5⅜ x 8. S79 Paperbound **$1.98**

THE STUDY OF THE HISTORY OF MATHEMATICS, THE STUDY OF THE HISTORY OF SCIENCE, G. Sarton. Two books bound as one. A long introduction to methods and philosophy, skills of the historian, concepts of history and science, psychology of idea-creation, and the purpose of history of science. More than 80 pages of classified bibliography. Complete and unabridged. Indexed. 10 illustrations. 188pp. 5⅜ x 8. T240 Paperbound **$1.25**

SCIENCE THEORY AND MAN, Erwin Schrödinger. Complete unabridged reissue of SCIENCE AND THE HUMAN TEMPERAMENT plus an additional essay: "What Is an Elementary Particle?" Nobel Laureate Schrödinger discusses such topics as nature of scientific method, the nature of science, chance and determinism, science and society, conceptual models for physical entities, elementary particles and wave mechanics. Presentation is popular. "Fine practical preparation for a time when laws of nature, human institutions . . . are undergoing a critical examination without parallel," Waldemar Kaempffert, N. Y. TIMES. 192pp. 5⅜ x 8.   T428 Paperbound **$1.35**

BRIDGES AND THEIR BUILDERS, D. B. Steinman & S. R. Watson. Engineers, historians, and every person who has ever been fascinated by great spans will find this book an endless source of information and interest. Greek and Roman structures, Medieval bridges, modern classics such as the Brooklyn Bridge, and the latest developments in the science are retold by one of the world's leading authorities on bridge design and construction. BRIDGES AND THEIR BUILDERS is the only comprehensive and accurate semi-popular history of these important measures of progress in print. New, greatly revised, enlarged edition. 23 photos; 26 line-drawings. Index. xvii + 401pp. 5⅜ x 8.   T431 Paperbound **$1.95**

BIOLOGY, NATURAL HISTORY & TRAVEL

TREES OF THE EASTERN AND CENTRAL UNITED STATES AND CANADA, W. M. Harlow. A revised edition of a standard middle-level guide to native trees and important escapes. More than 140 trees are described in detail, and illustrated with more than 600 drawings and photographs. Supplementary keys will enable the careful reader to identify almost any tree he might encounter. xiii + 288pp. 5⅜ x 8.
T395 Paperbound **$1.35**

INTRODUCTION TO THE STUDY OF EXPERIMENTAL MEDICINE, Claude Bernard. The only major work of Claude Bernard now available in English, this classical records Bernard's efforts to transform physiology into an exact science. He examines the roles of chance and error and incorrect hypothesis in leading to scientific truth and describes many classic experiments on the action of curare, carbon monoxide, and other poisons, the functions of the pancreas, the glycogenic function of the liver, and many others. Introduction. Foreword by I. B. Cohen. xxv + 266pp. 5⅜ x 8.   T400 Paperbound **$1.50**

THE ORIGIN OF LIFE, A. I. Oparin. The first modern statement of the theory that life evolved from complex nitro-carbon compounds. A historical introduction covers theories of the origin of life from the Greeks to modern times and then the techniques of biochemistry as applied to the problem by Dr. Oparin. The exposition presupposes a knowledge of chemistry but can be read with profit by everyone interested in this absorbing question. Bibliography. Index. xxv + 270pp. 5⅜ x 8.
S213 Paperbound **$1.75**

A SHORT HISTORY OF ANATOMY AND PHYSIOLOGY FROM THE GREEKS TO HARVEY, C. Singer. An intermediate history formerly entitled THE EVOLUTION OF ANATOMY, this work conveys the thrill of discovery as the nature of the human body is gradually clarified by hundreds of scientists from the Greeks to the Renaissance. Diogenes, Hippocrates, and other early workers, up to Leonardo da Vinci, Vesalius, Harvey, and others, with 139 illustrations from medieval manuscripts, classical sculpture, etc. Index. 221pp. 5⅜ x 8.   T389 Paperbound **$1.75**

THE BEHAVIOUR AND SOCIAL LIFE OF HONEYBEES, Ronald Ribbands. The most comprehensive, lucid, and authoritative book on bees. How bees communicate, how they tell fellow workers exactly how far away stores of food are, how individual bees learn their duties in the hive, and all the complex patterns and motivations. Much of the material is the result of very recent research by Mr. Ribbands and others. "A 'MUST' for every scientist, experimenter, and educator, and a happy and valuable selection for all interested in the honeybee," AMERICAN BEE JOURNAL. 690 item bibliography. Indices. 127 illustrations; 11 photographic plates. 352pp.   S410 Clothbound **$4.50**

TRAVELS OF WILLIAM BARTRAM, edited by Mark Van Doren. One of the 18th century's most delightful books; an excellent source of first-hand material on American geography, anthropology, and natural history. Many descriptions of early Indian tribes are our only source of information. "The mind of a scientist with the soul of a poet," John Livingston Lowes. 13 original illustrations and maps. Edited with an introduction by Mark Van Doren. 448pp. 5⅜ x 8.   T13 Paperbound **$2.00**

SAILING ALONE AROUND THE WORLD, Captain Joshua Slocum. A great modern classic in a convenient inexpensive edition. Captain Slocum's account of his single-handed voyage around the world in a 34 foot boat which he rebuilt himself. A nearly unparalled feat of seamanship told with vigor, wit, imagination, and great descriptive power. "A nautical equivalent of Thoreau's account," Van Wyck Brooks. 67 illustrations. 308pp. 5⅜ x 8.   T326 Paperbound **$1.00**

EARTH SCIENCES

THE BIRTH AND DEVELOPMENT OF THE GEOLOGICAL SCIENCES, F. D. Adams. The most complete and thorough history of the earth sciences in print. Geological thought from earliest recorded times to the end of the 19th century — covers over 300 early thinkers and systems: fossils and hypothetical explanations of them, vulcanists vs. neptunists, figured stones and paleontology, generation of stones, and similar topics. 91 illustrations, including medieval, renaissance woodcuts, etc. 632 footnotes and bibliographic notes. Index. 511pp. 5⅜ x 8.   T5 Paperbound **$2.00**

URANIUM PROSPECTING, H. L. Barnes. A clear, practical book about uranium prospecting by a professional geologists with first-hand field experience. Hundreds of important facts about minerals, geological occurrence, tests, detectors, sampling, assays, claiming and developing, government regulations. Index. Glossary of technical terms. Annotated bibliography. x + 117pp. 5⅜ x 8.
T309 Paperbound **$1.00**

DE RE METALLICA, Georgius Agricola. Written over 400 years ago, for 200' years the most authoritative work on production of metals; still one of the most beautiful and fascinating volumes in the history of science. 12 books, exhaustively annotated, give a wonderfully lucid and vivid picture of the history of mining, selection of sites, types of deposits, excavating pits, sinking shafts, ventilating, pumps, crushing machinery, assaying, smelting, refining metals, making salt, alum, nitre, glass, and many other topics. This definitive edition contains all 289 of the 16th century woodcuts which made the original an artistic masterpiece. A superb gift for geologists, engineers, libraries, artists, and historians. Biographical, historical introductions. Translated by Herbert & L. H. Hoover. Bibliography, survey of ancient authors. Indices. 289 illustrations. 672pp. 6¾ x 10¾. Deluxe library edition.
S6 Clothbound **$10.00**

MUSIC

A GENERAL HISTORY OF MUSIC, Charles Burney. A detailed coverage of music from the Greeks up to 1789, with full information on all types of music: sacred and secular, vocal and instrumental, operatic and symphonic. Theory, notation, forms, instruments, innovators, composers, performers, typical and important works, and much more in an easy, entertaining style. Burney travelled over much of Europe and spoke with hundreds of authorities and composers so that this work is more than a compilation of records . . . it is a living work of careful and first-hand scholarship. A recent NEW YORK TIMES review said, "Surprisingly few of Burney's statements have been invalidated by modern research . . . still of great value." Edited and corrected by Frank Mercer. 35 figures. Indices. 1915pp. 5½ x 8½.
2 volumes. T36 The set, Clothbound **$12.50**

JOHANN SEBASTIAN BACH, Philipp Spitta. The complete and unabridged text of the definitive study of Bach. Written some 70 years ago, it is still unsurpassed for its coverage of nearly all aspects of Bach's life and work. There could hardly be a finer non-technical introduction to Bach's music than the detailed, lucid analyses which Spitta provides for hundreds of individual pieces. 26 solid pages are devoted to the B minor mass, for example, and 30 pages to the glorious St. Matthew Passion. This monumental set also includes a major analysis of the music of the 18th century: Buxtehude, Pachelbel, etc. "Unchallenged as the last word on one of the supreme geniuses of music," Hohn Barkham, SATURDAY REVIEW SYNDICATE. Total of 1819pp. 2 volumes. Heavy cloth binding. 5⅜ x 8.
The set, T252 Clothbound **$10.00**

A DICTIONARY OF HYMNOLOGY, John Julian. This exhaustive and scholarly work has become known as an invaluable source of hundreds of thousands of important and often difficult to obtain facts on the history and use of hymns in the western world. More than 30,000 entries on individual hymns, giving authorship, date and circumstances of composition, publication, textual variations, location of texts, translations, denominational and ritual usage, etc. Biographies of more than 9,000 hymn writers, and essays on important topics such as Christmas carols and children's hymns, and much other unusual and valuable information. A 200 page double-columned index of first lines — the largest in print. Total of 1786 pages in two reinforced clothbound volumes. 6¼ x 9¼. The set, T333 Clothbound **$15.00**

STRUCTURAL HEARING: TONAL COHERENCE IN MUSIC, Felix Salzer. Written by a pupil of the late Heinrich Schenker, this is not only the most thorough exposition in English of the Schenker method but also extends the Schenker approach to include modern music, music of the middle ages, and renaissance music. It explores the phenomenon of tonal organization by means of a detailed analysis and discussion of more than 500 musical pieces. It casts new light for the reader acquainted with harmony upon the understanding of musical compositions, problems of musical coherence, and connection between theory and composition. "Has been the foundation on which all teaching in music theory has been based at this college," Leopold Mannes, President of The Mannes College of Music. 2 volumes. Total of 658pp. 6½ x 9¼. The set, S418 Clothbound **$8.00**

PUZZLES, ENTERTAINMENT, ETC.

MATHEMATICS, MAGIC AND MYSTERY, Martin Gardner. Why do card tricks work? How do magicians perform astonishing mathematical feats? How is stage mind-reading possible? This is the first book length study explaining the application of probability, set theory, theory of numbers, topology, etc., to many startling tricks. Non-technical, accurate, detailed. 115 sections discuss tricks with cards, dice, coins, knots, geometrical vanishing illusions, how a Curry square "demonstrates" that the sum of the parts may be greater than the whole, and dozens of others. 135 illustrations. xii + 174pp. 5⅜ x 8.
T335 Paperbound **$1.00**

MATHEMATICAL PUZZLES FOR BEGINNERS AND ENTHUSIASTS, G. Mott-Smith. 188 mathematical puzzles based on algebra, dissection of plane figures, permutations and probability, that will test and improve your powers of inference and interpretation. The Odic Force, The Spider's Cousin, Ellipse Drawing, theory and strategy of card and board games. 100 pages of detailed mathematical explanations. Appendix of primes, square roots, etc. 135 illustrations. 2nd revised edition. 248pp. 5⅜ x 8.
T198 Paperbound **$1.00**

LEARN CHESS FROM THE MASTERS, F. Reinfeld. Formerly titled CHESS BY YOURSELF, this book contains 10 games which you play against such masters as Marshall, Bronstein, Najdorf, and others, and an easy system for grading each move you make against a variety of other possible moves. Detailed annotations reveal the principles of the game through actual play. 91 diagrams. viii + 144pp. 5⅜ x 8.
T362 Paperbound **$1.00**

REINFELD ON THE END GAME IN CHESS, F. Reinfeld. Formerly titled PRACTICAL END-GAME PLAY, this book contains clear, simple analyses of 62 end games by such masters as Alekhine, Tarrasch, Marshall, Morphy, Capablanca, and many others. Primary emphasis is on the general principles of transition from, middle play to end play. This book is unusual in analyzing weak or incorrect moves to show how error occurs and how to avoid it. Covers king and pawn, minor piece, queen endings, weak squares, centralization, tempo moves, and many other vital factors. 62 diagrams. vi + 177pp. 5⅜ x 8. T417 Paperbound **$1.25**

101 PUZZLES IN THOUGHT AND LOGIC, C. R. Wylie, Jr. Brand new problems you need no special knowledge to solve! Take the kinks out of your mental "muscles" and enjoy solving murder problems, the detection of lying fishermen, the logical identification of color by a blindman, and dozens more. Introduction with simplified explanation of general scientific method and puzzle solving. 128pp. 5⅜ x 8. T367 Paperbound **$1.00**

THE COMPLETE NONSENSE OF EDWARD LEAR. This is the only complete edition of this master of gentle madness available at a popular price. A BOOK OF NONSENSE, NONSENSE SONGS, MORE NONSENSE SONGS AND STORIES in their entirety with all the old favorites that have delighted children and adults for years. The Dong With A Luminous Nose, The Jumblies, The Owl and the Pussycat, and hundreds of other bits of wonderful nonsense. 214 limericks, 3 sets of Nonsense Botany, 5 Non-sense Alphabets, 546 drawings by Lear himself, and much more. 320pp. 5⅜ x 8. T167 Paperbound **$1.00**

28 SCIENCE FICTION STORIES OF H. G. WELLS. Two full unabridged novels, MEN LIKE GODS and STAR BEGOTTEN, plus 26 short stories by the master science-fiction writer of all time! Stories of space, time, invention, exploration, future adventure. PARTIAL CONTENTS: Men like Gods, The Country of the Blind, In the Abyss, The Crystal Egg, The Man Who Could Work Miracles, A Story of the Days to Come, The Valley of Spiders, and 21 more! 5⅜ x 8. T265 Clothbound **$3.95**

SEVEN SCIENCE FICTION NOVELS, H. G. Wells. Full unabridged texts of 7 science-fiction novels of the master. Ranging from biology, physics, chemistry, astronomy, to sociology and other studies, Mr. Wells extrapolates whole worlds of strange and intriguing character. "One will have to go far to match this for entertainment, excitement, and sheer pleasure," NEW YORK TIMES. Contents: THE TIME MACHINE, THE ISLAND OF DR. MOREAU, THE FIRST MEN IN THE MOON, THE INVISIBLE MAN, THE WAR OF THE WORLDS, THE FOOD OF THE GODS, IN THE DAYS OF THE COMET. 1015pp. 5⅜ x 8. T264 Clothbound **$3.95**

FIVE ADVENTURE NOVELS OF H. RIDER HAGGARD. All the mystery and adventure of darkest Africa captured accurately by a man who lived among Zulus for years, and who knew African ethnology and folkways as did few of his contemporaries. They have been regarded as examples of the very best high adventure by such critics as George Orwell, Andrew Lang and Kipling. Contents: SHE, KING SOLOMON'S MINES, ALLAN QUATERMAIN, ALLAN'S WIFE, MAIWA'S REVENGE. 821pp. 5⅜ x 8. T108 Clothbound **$3.95**

MATHEMAGIC, MAGIC PUZZLES, AND GAMES WITH NUMBERS, R. V. Heath. More than 60 new puzzles and stunts based on the properties of numbers. Easy techniques for multiplying large numbers men-tally, revealing hidden numbers magically, finding the date of any day in any year, and dozens more. Edited by J. S. Meyer. 76 illustrations. 128pp. 5⅜ x 8. T110 Paperbound **$1.00**

WIN AT CHECKERS, M. Hopper. (Formerly CHECKERS). The former World's Unrestricted Checker Cham-pion discusses the principles of the game, expert's shots and traps, problems for the beginner, standard openings, locating your best move, the end game, opening "blitzkrieg" moves, ways to draw when you are behind your opponent, etc. More than 100 detailed questions and answers anticipate your problems. Appendix. 75 problems with solutions and diagrams. Index. 79 figures. xi + 107pp. 5⅜ x 8. T363 Paperbound **$1.00**

HOUDINI ON MAGIC, Harry Houdini. One of the greatest magicians of modern times explains his most prized secrets. How locks are picked, with illustrated picks and skeleton keys; how a girl is sawed into twins; how to walk through a brick wall — Houdini's explanations of 44 stage tricks with many diagrams. Also included is a fascinating discussion of great magicians of the past and the story of his fight against fraudulent mediums and spiritualists. Edited by W. B. Gibson and M. N. Young. Bibliography. 155 figures, photos. xv + 280pp. 5⅜ x 8. T384 Paperbound **$1.00**

THE BOOK OF MODERN PUZZLES, G. L. Kaufman. A completely new series of puzzles as fascinating as crossword and deduction puzzles but based upon different principles and techniques. Simple 2-minute teasers, word labyrinths, design and pattern puzzles, logic and observation puzzles — over 150 brainrackers. Answers to all problems. 116 illustrations. 192pp. 5⅜ x 8. T143 Paperbound **$1.00**

NEW WORD PUZZLES, G. L. Kaufman. 100 ENTIRELY NEW puzzles based on words and their com-binations. Chess words, based on the moves of the chess king; design-onyms, symmetrical designs made of synonyms; rhymed double-crostics; syllable sentences; addle letter anagrams; alphagrams; linkograms; and many others all brand new. Full solutions. Space to work problems. 196 figures. vi + 122pp. 5⅜ x 8. T344 Paperbound **$1.00**

MATHEMATICAL RECREATIONS, M. Kraitchik. One of the most thorough compilations of unusual mathe-matical problems for beginners and advanced mathematicians. Historical problems from Greek, Me-dieval, Arabic, Hindu sources. 50 pages devoted to pastimes derived from figurate numbers, Mersenne numbers, Fermat numbers, primes and probability. 40 pages of magic, Euler, Latin, panmagic squares. 25 new positional and permutational games of permanent value: fairy chess, latruncles, reversi, jinx, ruma, lasca, tricolor, tetrachrome, etc. Complete rigorous solutions. Revised second edition. 181 illustrations. 330pp. 5⅜ x 8. T163 Paperbound **$1.75**

MATHEMATICAL EXCURSIONS, H. A. Merrill. Even if you hardly remember your high school math, you'll enjoy the 90 stimulating problems. Little effort. Many useful shortcuts and diversions not generally known are included: division by inspection, Russian peasant multiplication, memory systems for pi, building odd and even magic squares, square roots by geometry, dyadic systems, and many more. Solutions to difficult problems. 50 illustrations. 145pp. 5⅜ x 8.   T350 Paperbound **$1.00**

PUZZLE QUIZ AND STUNT FUN, J. Meyer. The solution to party doldrums. 238 challenging puzzles, stunts and tricks. Mathematical puzzles like The Clever Carpenter, Atom Bomb; mysteries and deductions like The Bridge of Sighs, The Nine Pearls, Dog Logic; observation puzzles like Cigarette Smokers, Telephone Dial; over 200 others including magic squares, tongue twisters, puns, anagrams, and many others. All problems solved fully. 250pp. 5⅜ x 8.   T337 Paperbound **$1.00**

MAGIC TRICKS & CARD TRICKS, W. Jonson. Two books bound as one. 52 tricks with cards, 37 tricks with coins, bills, eggs, smoke, ribbons, slates, etc. Details on presentation, misdirection, and routining will help you master such famous tricks as the Changing Card, Card in the Pocket, Four Aces, Coin Through the Hand, Bill in the Egg, Afghan Bands, and over 75 others. If you follow the lucid exposition and key diagrams carefully, you will finish these two books with an astonishing mastery of magic. 106 figures. 224pp. 5⅜ x 8.   T909 Paperbound **$1.00**

CRYPTANALYSIS, H. F. Gaines. Formerly entitled ELEMENTARY CRYPTANALYSIS. The best book in print on cryptograms and their solution. Covers all major techniques of the past, and contains much that is not generally known except to experts. Full details about concealment, substitution, and transposition ciphers; periodic mixed alphabets, multafid, Kasiski and Vignere methods, Ohaver patterns, Playfair, and scores of other topics. 6 language letter and word frequency appendix. 167 problems, now furnished with solutions. Index. 173 figures. vi + 230pp. 5⅜ x 8.
T97 Paperbound **$1.95**

FLATLAND, E. A. Abbott. A science-fiction classic of life in a 2-dimensional world that is also a first-rate introduction to such aspects of modern science as relativity and hyperspace. Political, moral, satirical, and humorous overtones have made FLATLAND fascinating reading for thousands. 7th edition. 16 illustrations. 128pp. 5⅜ x 8.   T1 Paperbound **$1.00**

PARTY GAMES, M. Moyes. Over 80 old favorites and new entertainments in this sparkling collection for adults and children. All are easy, safe, fun, and require no special equipment. Organizing the party, warming-up games, performing, games, dance games, children's games, forfeits, and others. Large and small groups, family and guest, everybody loves games! 26 illustrations. 80pp. 5 x 7¼.
T941 Paperbound **75¢**

WIN AT CHESS, F. Reinfeld. 300 practical chess situations from actual tournament play to sharpen your chess eye and test your skill. Traps, sacrifices, mates, winning combinations, subtle exchanges, show you how to WIN AT CHESS. Short notes and tables of solutions and alternative moves help you evaluate your progress. Learn to think ahead playing the 'crucial moments' of historic games. 300 diagrams. Notes and solutions. Formerly titled CHESS QUIZ. vi + 120pp. 5⅜ x 8.
T438 Paperbound **$1.00**

HOW TO FORCE CHECKMATE, F. Reinfeld. Formerly titled CHALLENGE TO CHESSPLAYERS, this is an invaluable collection of 300 lightning strokes selected from actual masters' play, which will demonstrate how to smash your opponent's game with strong decisive moves. No board needed — clear, practical diagrams and easy-to-understand solutions. Learn to plan up to three moves ahead and play a superior end game. 300 diagrams. 111pp. 5⅜ x 8.   T439 Paperbound **$1.25**

MORPHY'S GAMES OF CHESS, edited by Philip W. Sergeant. You can put boldness into your game by following the brilliant, forceful moves of the man who has been called the greatest chess player of all time. 300 of Morphy's best games, carefully annotated, reveal Morphy's principles. Unabridged reissue of the latest revised edition. Bibliography. New introduction by Fred Reinfeld. Annotations and introduction by Sergeant. Index. 235 diagrams. x + 352pp. 5⅜ x 8.
T386 Paperbound **$1.75**

THE ART OF THE STORY-TELLER, M. L. Shedlock. Regarded by librarians, story-tellers, and educators as the finest, most lucid book on the subject. The nature of the story, difficulties of communicating stories to children, artifices used in story-telling, how to obtain and maintain the effect of the story, and the elements to seek or avoid in selecting material. A 99 page selection of most effective stories. Extensive bibliography of further material. xxi + 320pp. 5⅜ x 8.   T245 Paperbound **$3.50**

CRYPTOGRAPHY, L. D. Smith. An excellent introductory work on ciphers and their solution, the history of secret writing, and actual methods and problems in such techniques as transposition and substitution. Appendices describe the enciphering of Japanese, the Baconian biliteral cipher, and contain frequency tables and a bibliography for further study. Over 150 problems with solutions. 160pp. 5⅜ x 8.   T247 Paperbound **$1.00**

LANGUAGE

NEW RUSSIAN-ENGLISH AND ENGLISH-RUSSIAN DICTIONARY, M. A. O'Brien. Over 70,000 entries in new orthography! Idiomatic uses, colloquialisms. Irregular verbs, perfective and imperfective aspects, regular and irregular sound changes, and other features. One of the few dictionaries where accent changes within the conjugation of verbs and the declension of nouns are fully indicated. "One of the best," Prof. E. J. Simmons, Cornell. First names, geographical terms, bibliography, etc. 738pp. 4½ x 6¼.   T208 Paperbound **$2.00**

MONEY CONVERTER AND TIPPING GUIDE FOR EUROPEAN TRAVEL, C. Vomacka. Currency regulations and tipping for every European country including Iron Curtain countries, Israel, Egypt, and Turkey. Complete conversion tables for every country from U.S. to foreign and vice versa. Only source of such information as phone rates, postal rates, clothing sizes, duty-free imports, and dozens of other valuable topics. 128pp. 3½ x 5¼.
T260 Paperbound **65¢**

MONEY CONVERTER AND TIPPING GUIDE FOR TRAVEL IN THE AMERICAS (including the United States and Canada), C. Vomacka. The information you need for informed and confident travel in North and South America. U. S. to foreign and foreign to U. S. currency conversion tables for every country. Special section covers over 250 tipping situations in the U. S. Tipping, postal and telephone rates, customs regulations, and much more is covered for all countries. 128pp. 3½ x 5¼.
T261 Paperbound **65¢**

DUTCH-ENGLISH AND ENGLISH-DUTCH DICTIONARY, F. G. Renier. For travel, literary, scientific or business Dutch; the most convenient, practical and comprehensive dictionary on the market. More than 60,000 entries, shades of meaning, colloquialisms, idioms, compounds and technical terms. Dutch and English·strong and irregular verbs. This is the only dictionary in its size and price range that indicates the gender of nouns. New orthography for use with older books. xviii + 571pp. 5½ x 6¼.
T224 Clothbound **$2.50**

LEARN DUTCH!, F. G. Renier. The most satisfactory and most easily used grammar of modern Dutch. The student is gradually led from simple lessons in pronunciation, through translation, finally to a mastery of spoken and written Dutch. Grammatical principles are clearly explained while a useful, practical vocabulary is introduced in easy exercises and readings. It is used and recommended by the Fulbright Committee in the Netherlands. Phonetic appendices. Over 1200 exercises; Dutch-English, English-Dutch vocabularies. 181pp. 4¼ x 7¼.
T441 Clothbound **$1.75**

LISTEN & LEARN

FRENCH   SPANISH   GERMAN   ITALIAN

LISTEN & LEARN is the only language record course designed especially to meet your travel and everyday needs. It is available in separate sets for FRENCH, SPANISH, GERMAN, or ITALIAN, and each set contains 3 ten-inch 33-1/3 rpm long-playing records — 1½ hours of recorded speech by eminent native speakers who are professors at Columbia, New York University, Queens College.
Check the following special features found only in LISTEN & LEARN:

- **Dual-language recording. 812 selected phrases and sentences,** over 3200 words, spoken first in English, then in their foreign language equivalents. A suitable pause follows each foreign phrase, allowing you time to repeat the expression. You learn by unconscious assimilation.

- **128-page manual** contains everything on the records, plus a simple phonetic pronunciation guide.

- **Indexed for convenience. The only set on the market** that is completely indexed. No more puzzling over where to find the phrase you need. Just look in the rear of the manual.

- **Practical.** No time wasted on material you can find in any grammar. LISTEN & LEARN covers central core material with phrase approach. Ideal for the person with limited learning time.

- **Living, modern expressions,** not found in other courses. Hygienic products, modern equipment, shopping — expressions used every day, like "nylon" and "air-conditioned."

- **Limited objective.** Everything you learn, no matter where you stop, is immediately useful. You have to finish other courses, wade through grammar and vocabulary drill, before they help you.

- **High-fidelity recording.** LISTEN & LEARN records equal in clarity and surface-silence any record on the market costing up to $6 per record.

41 different categories covering all your travel wants — Greetings, introductions, social conversations . . . Making yourself understood . . . Useful words, phrases, sentences . . . Passing customs, checking baggage . . . Buying travel tickets . . . Flying, train travel, boats, buses, streetcars, taxis, subways . . . Automobile travel, repairs, parts . . . At a nightclub, restaurant . . . Menus: breakfast, soups, entrees, vegetables, salads, fruits, drinks, desserts . . . Sports, sightseeing, concerts, dancing . . . Cashing checks . . . Cameras, photography, films . . . Drugstores, doctors, dentists, medicines . . . Barber shops, beauty parlors, laundries, dry cleaning . . . Telephoning, postal services . . . Time, numbers, dates, months, seasons . . . and many more, including the largest collection of street and shop signs in print anywhere.

"Excellent . . . the spoken records . . . impress me as being among the very best on the market," **Prof. Mario Pei,** Dept. of Romance Languages, Columbia University. "Inexpensive and well-done . . . it would make an ideal present," CHICAGO SUNDAY TRIBUNE. "More genuinely helpful than anything of its kind which I have previously encountered," **Sidney Clark,** well-known author of "ALL THE BEST" travel books.

UNCONDITIONAL GUARANTEE. Try LISTEN & LEARN, then return it within 10 days for full refund if you are not satisfied. The only course on the market guaranteed after you actually use it.

LISTEN & LEARN comes in 4 useful modern languages — FRENCH, SPANISH, GERMAN, or ITALIAN — one language to each set of 3 ten-inch records, (33-1/3 rpm). 128 page manual. Album.

Spanish	the set **$4.95**	German	the set **$4.95**
French	the set **$4.95**	Italian	the set **$4.95**

SAY IT language phrase books

These handy phrase books (128 to 196 pages each) make grammatical drills unnecessary for an elementary knowledge of a spoken foreign language. Covering most matters of travel and everyday life each volume contains:

Over 1000 phrases and sentences in immediately useful forms — foreign language plus English.
Modern usage designed for Americans. Specific phrases like, "Give me small change," and "Please call a taxi."
Simplified phonetic transcription you will be able to read at sight.
The only completely indexed phrase books on the market.
Covers scores of important situations: — Greetings, restaurants, sightseeing, useful expressions, etc.

These books are prepared by native linguists who are professors at Columbia, N.Y.U., Fordham and other great universities. Use them independently or with any other book or record course. They provide a supplementary living element that most other courses lack. Individual volumes in:

French 60¢	**German 60¢**	**Italian 60¢**
Russian 60¢	**Portuguese 75¢**	**Spanish 60¢**
Hebrew 60¢	**Norwegian 75¢**	**Swedish 60¢**
Japanese 60¢	**Polish 75¢**	**Modern Greek 60¢**
Dutch 75¢	**Esperanto 75¢**	**Yiddish 75¢**

English for Spanish-speaking people 60¢
English for Italian-speaking people 60¢
English for German-speaking people 60¢
Turkish 75¢

Large clear type. 128-196 pages each. 3½ x 5¼.
Sturdy paper binding.

LITERATURE

WORLD DRAMA, B. H. Clark. 46 plays from Ancient Greece, Rome, Medieval Europe, France, Germany, Italy, England, Russia, Scandinavia, India, China. Japan, etc. — including classic authors like Aeschylus, Sophocles, Euripides, Aristophanes, Plautus, Marlowe, Jonson, Farquhar, Goldsmith, Cervantes, Moliere, Dumas, Goethe, Schiller, Ibsen, and many others. This creative collection avoids hackneyed material. Over 1/3 of this material is unavailable in any other current edition! "The most comprehensive collection of important plays from all literature available in English," SAT. REV. OF LITERATURE. Introduction. Reading lists. 2 volumes. 1364pp. 5⅜ x 8.

Vol. 1, T57 Paperbound **$2.00**
Vol. 2, T59 Paperbound **$2.00**

MASTERS OF THE DRAMA, John Gassner. The most comprehensive history of the drama in print, covering drama in every important tradition from the Greeks to the Near East, China, Japan, Medieval Europe, England, Russia, Italy, Spain, Germany, and dozens of other drama producing nations. This unsurpassed reading and reference work encompasses more than 800 dramatists and over 2000 plays, with biographical material, plot summaries, theatre history, etc. "Best of its kind in English," NEW REPUBLIC. Exhaustive 35 page bibliography. 77 photographs and drawings. Deluxe edition with reinforced cloth binding, headbands, stained top. xxii + 890pp. 5⅜ x 8.
T100 Clothbound **$5.95**

THE DRAMA OF LUIGI PIRANDELLO, D. Vittorini. All 38 of Pirandello's plays written between 1918 and 1935 are summarized and analyzed in this authorized study. Their cultural background, place in European dramaturgy, symbolic techniques, and plot structure are carefully examined. Foreword by Pirandello. Biography. Bibliography. xiii + 350pp. 5⅜ x 8.
T435 Paperbound **$1.98**

ARISTOTLE'S THEORY OF POETRY AND THE FINE ARTS, edited by S. H. Butcher. The celebrated Butcher translation of this great classic faced, page by page, with the complete Greek text. A 300 page introduction discussing Aristotle's ideas and their influence in the history of thought and literature, and covering art and nature, imitation as an aesthetic form, poetic truth, art and morality, tragedy, comedy, and similar topics. Modern Aristotelian criticism discussed by John Gassner. lxxvi + 421pp. 5⅜ x 8.
T41 Clothbound **$3.95**
T42 Paperbound **$2.00**

EUGENE O'NEILL: THE MAN AND HIS PLAYS, B. H. Clark. No source-book has previously been published on O'Neill's life and work. Clark analyzes each play from the early THE WEB to the recently produced MOON FOR THE MISBEGOTTEN and THE ICEMAN COMETH, revealing the environmental and dramatic influences necessary for a complete understanding of these important works. Bibliography. Appendices. Index. ix + 182pp. 5⅜ x 8.
T379 Paperbound **$1.25**

EPIC AND ROMANCE, W. P. Ker. Written by one of the foremost authorities on medieval literature, this is the standard survey of medieval epic and romance. It covers Teutonic epics, Icelandic sagas, Beowulf, French chansons de geste, the Roman de Troi, and many other important works of literature. It is an excellent account of a body of literature whose beauty and value has only recently come to be recognized. Index. xxiv + 398pp. 5⅜ x 8.
T355 Paperbound **$1.95**

FOUNDERS OF THE MIDDLE AGES, E. K. Rand. The best non-technical discussion of the transformation of Latin pagan culture into medieval civilization. Tertullian, Gregory, Jerome, Boethius, Augustine, the Neoplatonists, and many other literary men, educators, classicists, and humanists. A storehouse of information presented clearly and simply for the intelligent non-specialist. "Thoughtful, beautifully written," AMERICAN HISTORICAL REVIEW. "Extraordinarily accurate," Richard McKeon, THE NATION. ix + 365pp. 5⅜ x 8.
T369 Paperbound **$1.85**

ORIENTALIA

CHRISTIAN AND ORIENTAL PHILOSOPHY OF ART, A. K. Coomaraswamy. A unique fusion of philosopher, orientalist, art historian, and linguist discusses the true function of aesthetics in art, symbolism, intellectual and philosophic backgrounds, the role of traditional culture in enriching art, the nature of medieval art, the nature of folklore, the beauty of mathematics, and similar topics. 2 illustrations. Bibliography. 148pp. 5⅜ x 8. T378 Paperbound **$1.25**

TRANSFORMATION OF NATURE IN ART, A. K. Coomaraswamy. Unabridged reissue of a basic work upon Asiatic religious art and philosophy of religion. The theory of religious art in Asia and Medieval Europe (exemplified by Meister Eckhart) is analyzed and developed. Indian Medieval aesthetic manuals, symbolic language in philosophy, the origin and use of images in India, and many other fascinating and little known topics. Glossaries of Sanskrit and Chinese terms. Bibliography. 41pp of notes. 245pp. 5⅜ x 8. T368 Paperbound **$1.75**

ORIENTAL RELIGIONS IN ROMAN PAGANISM, F. Cumont. A study of the cultural meeting of east and west in the Early Roman Empire. Important eastern religions from their first appearance in Rome, 204 B.C., when the Great Mother of the Gods was first brought over from Syria. The ecstatic cults of Syria and Phrygia — Cybele, Attis, Adonis, their orgies and mutilatory rites; the mysteries of Egypt — Serapis, Isis, Osiris; the dualism of Persia, the elevation of cosmic evil to equal stature with the deity, Mithra; worship of Hermes Trismegistus; Ishtar, Astarte; the magic of the ancient Near East, etc. Introduction. 55pp. of notes; extensive bibliography. Index. xxiv + 298pp. 5⅜ x 8. T321 Paperbound **$1.75**

THE MYSTERIES OF MITHRA, F. Cumont. The definitive coverage of a great ideological struggle between the west and the orient in the first centuries of the Christian era. The origin of Mithraism, a Persian mystery religion, and its associaion with the Roman army is discussed in detail. Then utilizing fragmentary monuments and texts, in one of the greatest feats of scholarly detection, Dr. Cumont reconstructs the mystery teachings and secret doctrines, the hidden organization and cult of Mithra. Mithraic art is discussed, analyzed, and depicted in 70 illustrations. 239pp. 5⅜ x 8. T323 Paperbound **$1.85**

YOGA, H. P. Shastri. A disciple of the Indian saint Shri Dada, and founder of an important center of classical Yoga, the author gives a lucid, comprehensive account of yoga as practised according to Shankara's Ideal Monism. This is neither an occult book nor a shallow popularization; it is a careful introduction to one of the most important Indian philosophical methods of achieving self-discipline and self-understanding through mental and physical exercise. Glossary. Passages from yoga literature. 6 figures. 96pp. 5 x 7¼. T975 Paperbound **75¢**

ANTHROPOLOGY, SOCIAL SCIENCES, ETC.

THE IDEA OF PROGRESS, J. B. Bury. Practically unknown before the Reformation, the idea of progress has since become one of the central concepts of western civilization. Prof. Bury analyzes its evolution in the thought of Greece, Rome, the Middle Ages, the Renaissance, to its flowering in all branches of science, religion, philosophy, industry, art, and literature, during and following the 16th century. Introduction by Charles Beard. Index. xl + 357pp. 5⅜ x 8. T39 Clothbound **$3.95** / T40 Paperbound **$1.95**

PRIMITIVE MAN AS PHILOSOPHER, P. Radin. A standard anthropological work covering primitive thought on such topics as the purpose of life, marital relations, freedom of thought, symbolism, death, resignation, the nature of reality, personality, gods, and many others. Drawn from factual material gathered from the Winnebago, Oglala Sioux, Maori, Baganda, Batak, Zuni, among others, it interprets strictly within the original framework. Extensive selections of original primitive documents. Bibliography. Index. xviii + 402pp. 5⅜ x 8. T392 Paperbound **$2.00**

PRIMITIVE RELIGION, P. Radin. A thorough treatment of the supernatural and the influences that have shaped religious expression in primitive societies. Ranging over Arunta, Ashanti, Aztec, Bushman, Crow, Fijian, etc., Africa, Australia, Pacific Islands, the Arctic, North and South America, Prof. Radin integrates modern psychology, comparative religion, and economic thought with first-hand accounts gathered by himself and other scholars of primitive initiations, training of the shaman, and other fascinating topics. "Excellent," NATURE (London). New author's preface. Bibliographic notes. Index. x + 322pp. 5⅜ x 8. T393 Paperbound **$1.85**

THE GIFT OF LANGUAGE, M. Schlauch. Formerly titled THE GIFT OF TONGUES, this is a middle-level survey that avoids both superficiality and pedantry. It covers such topics as linguistic families, word histories, grammatical processes in such foreign languages as Aztec, Ewe, and Bantu, semantics, language taboos, and dozens of other fascinating and important topics. Especially interesting is an analysis of the word-coinings of Joyce, Cummings, Stein and others in terms of linguistics. 232 bibliographic notes. Index. viii + 342pp. 5⅜ x 8. T243 Paperbound **$1.85**

PHILOSOPHY

GUIDE TO PHILOSOPHY, C. E. M. Joad. Does free will exist? Is there plan in the universe? How do we know and validate our knowledge? Such opposed solutions as subjective idealism and realism, chance and teleology, vitalism and logical positivism, are evaluated and the contributions of the great philosophers from the Greeks to moderns like Russell, Whitehead, and others, are considered in the context of each problem. "The finest introduction," BOSTON TRANSCRIPT. Index. Classified bibliography. 592pp. 5⅜ x 8.   T297 Paperbound **$2.00**

THE PHILOSOPHY OF HEGEL, W. T. Stace. The first detailed analysis of Hegel's thought in English, this is especially valuable since so many of Hegel's works are out of print. Dr. Stace examines Hegel's debt to Greek idealists and the 18th century and then proceeds to a careful description and analysis of Hegel's first principles, categories, reason, dialectic method, his logic, philosophy of nature and spirit, etc. Index. Special 14 x 20 chart of Hegelian system. x + 526pp. 5⅜ x 8.
T253 Clothbound **$3.95**
T254 Paperbound **$2.00**

ARISTOTLE, A. E. Taylor. A brilliant, searching non-technical account of Aristotle and his thought written by a foremost Platonist. It covers the life and works of Aristotle; classification of the sciences; logic, first philosophy, matter and form; causes; motion and eternity; God; physics; metaphysics; and similar topics. Bibliography. New index compiled for this edition. 128pp. 5⅜ x 8.
T279 Clothbound **$2.75**
T280 Paperbound **$1.00**

HISTORY OF ANCIENT PHILOSOPHY, W. Windelband. Perhaps the clearest survey of Greek and Roman philosophy. Discusses ancient philosophy in general, intellectual life in Greece in the 7th and 6th centuries B.C., Thales, Anaximander, Anaximenes, Heraclitus, the Eleatics, Empedocles, Anaxagoras, Leucippus, the Pythagoreans, the Sophists, Socrates, Democritus (20 pages), Plato (50 pages), Aristotle (70 pages), the Peripatetics, Stoics, Epicureans, Sceptics, Neo-platonists, Christian Apologists, etc. 2nd German edition translated by H. E. Cushman. xv + 393pp. 5⅜ x 8.   T357 Paperbound **$1.75**

LANGUAGE AND MYTH, E. Cassirer. Analyzing the non-rational elements in culture, Cassirer demonstrates that beneath both language and myth lies an unconscious "grammar" of experience whose categories and canons are not those of logical thought. His analyses of seemingly diverse phenomena such as Indian metaphysics, the Melanesian "mana," the Naturphilosophie of Schelling, modern poetry, etc., are profound without being pedantic. Introduction and translation by Susanne Langer. Index. x + 103pp. 5⅜ x 8.   T51 Paperbound **$1.25**

SUBSTANCE AND FUNCTION, EINSTEIN'S THEORY OF RELATIVITY, E. Cassirer. In this double-volume, Cassirer develops a philosophy of the exact sciences that is historically sound, philosophically mature, and scientifically impeccable. Such topics as the concept of number, space and geometry, non-Euclidean geometry, traditional logic and scientific method, mechanism and motion, energy, relational concepts, degrees of objectivity, the ego, Einstein's relativity, and many others are treated in detail. Authorized translation by W.C. and M. C. Swabey. xii + 465pp. 5⅜ x 8.   T50 Paperbound **$2.00**

THE PHILOSOPHICAL WORKS OF DESCARTES. Definitive English edition of all major philosophical works and letters of René Descartes. All of his revolutionary insights, from his famous "Cogito ergo sum" to his detailed account of contemporary science and his astonishingly fruitful concept that all phenomena of the universe (except mind) could be reduced to clear laws by the use of mathematics. An excellent source for the thought of men like Hobbes, Arnauld, Gassendi, etc. Translated by E. S. Haldane and G. Ross. Introductory notes. Index. Total of 842pp. 5⅜ x 8.
T71 Vol. 1, Paperbound **$2.00**
T72 Vol. 2, Paperbound **$2.00**

ESSAYS IN EXPERIMENTAL LOGIC, J. Dewey. Based upon the theory that knowledge implies a judgement, which in turn implies an inquiry, these papers consider the inquiry stage in terms of: the relationship of thought and subject matter, antecedents of thought, data and meanings. 3 papers examine Bertrand Russell's thought, while 2 others discuss pragmatism and a final essay presents a new theory of the logic of values. Index. viii + 444pp. 5⅜ x 8.   T73 Paperbound **$1.95**

THE PHILOSOPHY OF HISTORY, G. W. F. Hegel. One of the great classics of western thought which reveals Hegel's basic principle: that history is not chance but a rational process, the realization of the Spirit of Freedom. Ranges from the oriental cultures of subjective thought to the classical subjective cultures, to the modern absolute synthesis where spiritual and secular may be reconciled. Translation and introduction by J. Sibree. Introduction by C. Hegel. Special introduction for this edition by Prof. Carl Friedrich. xxxix + 447pp. 5⅜ x 8.   T112 Paperbound **$1.85**

THE WILL TO BELIEVE and HUMAN IMMORTALITY, W. James. Two complete books bound as one. THE WILL TO BELIEVE discusses the interrelations of belief, will, and intellect in man; chance vs. determinism, free will vs. fate, pluralism vs. monism; the philosophies of Hegel and Spencer, and more. HUMAN IMMORTALITY examines the question of survival after death and develops an unusual and powerful argument for immortality. Two prefaces. Index. Total of 429pp. 5⅜ x 8.
T294 Clothbound **$3.75**
T291 Paperbound **$1.75**

INTRODUCTION TO SYMBOLIC LOGIC, S. Langer. No special knowledge of math required. You start with simple symbols and advance to a knowledge of the Boole-Schroeder and Russell-Whitehead systems. Forms, logical structure, classes, the calculus of propositions, logic of the syllogism, etc., are all covered. "One of the clearest and simplest introductions," MATHEMATICS GAZETTE. Second enlarged, revised edition. 368pp. 5⅜ x 8.   S164 Paperbound **$1.75**

MIND AND THE WORLD-ORDER, C. I. Lewis. Building upon the work of Peirce, James, and Dewey, Professor Lewis outlines a theory of knowledge in terms of "conceptual pragmatism." Dividing truth into abstract mathematical certainty and empirical truth, the author demonstrates that the traditional understanding of the a priori must be abandoned. Detailed analyses of philosophy, metaphysics, method, the "given" in experience, knowledge of objects, nature of the a priori, experience and order, and many others. Appendices. xiv + 446pp. 5⅜ x 8.   T359 Paperbound **$1.95**

THE GUIDE FOR THE PERPLEXED, Maimonides. One of the great philosophical works of all time and a necessity for everyone interested in the philosophy of the Middle Ages in the Jewish, Christian, and Moslem traditions. Maimonides develops a common meeting-point for the Old Testament and the Aristotelian thought which pervaded the medieval world. 2nd revised edition. Complete unabridged Friedländer translation. 55 page introduction to Maimonides' life, period, etc., with an important summary of the GUIDE. Index. lix + 414pp. 5⅜ x 8.   T351 Paperbound **$1.85**

THE PHILOSOPHICAL WRITINGS OF PEIRCE, edited by J. Buchler. Formerly THE PHILOSOPHY OF PEIRCE), a carefully integrated exposition of Peirce's complete system composed of selections from his own work. Symbolic logic, scientific method, theory of signs, pragmatism, epistemology, chance, cosmology, ethics, and many other topics are treated by one of the greatest philosophers of modern times. xvi + 386pp. 5⅜ x 8.
T216 Clothbound **$5.00**
T217 Paperbound **$1.95**

SCEPTICISM AND ANIMAL FAITH, G. Santayana. To eliminate difficulties in the traditional theory of knowledge, Santayana distinguishes between the independent existence of objects and the essence our mind attributes to them. Scepticism is thereby established as a form of belief, and animal faith is shown to be a necessary condition of knowledge. Belief, classical idealism, intuition, memory, symbols, literary psychology, and much more, discussed with unusual clarity and depth. Index. xii + 314pp. 5⅜ x 8.
T235 Clothbound **$3.50**
T236 Paperbound **$1.50**

THE ANALYSIS OF MATTER, B. Russell. Logical analysis of physics, prerelativity physics, causality, scientific inference, Weyl's theory, tensors, invariants and physical interpretations, periodicity, and much more is treated with Russell's usual brilliance. "Masterly piece of clear thinking and clear writing," NATION AND ATHENAEUM. "Most thorough treatment of the subject," THE NATION. Introduction. Index. 8 figures. viii + 408pp. 5⅜ x 8.   T231 Paperbound **$1.95**

THE SENSE OF BEAUTY, G. Santayana. A revelation of the beauty of language as well as an important philosophic treatise, this work studies the "why, when, and how beauty appears, what conditions an object must fulfill to be beautiful, what elements of our nature make us sensible of beauty, and what the relation is between the constitution of the object and the excitement of our susceptibility." "It is doubtful if a better treatment of the subject has since been published," PEABODY JOURNAL. Index. ix + 275pp. 5⅜ x 8.
T237 Clothbound **$2.85**
T238 Paperbound **$1.00**

THE CHIEF WORKS OF SPINOZA. Spinoza's most important philosophical works. Vol. I: The Theologico-Political Treatise and the Political Treatise. Vol. II: On The Improvement Of Understanding, The Ethics, Selected Letters. Profound and enduring ideas on God, the universe, pantheism, society, religion, the state, democracy, the mind, emotions, freedom, and the nature of man, which influenced Goethe, Hegel, Schelling, Coleridge, Whitehead, and many others. Introduction. 2 volumes. 862pp. 5⅜ x 8.
T249 Vol. I, Paperbound **$1.50**
T250 Vol. II, Paperbound **$1.50**

TRAGIC SENSE OF LIFE, M. de Unamuno. The acknowledged masterpiece of one of Spain's most influential thinkers. Between the despair at the inevitable death of man and all his works and the desire for something better, Unamuno finds that "saving incertitude" that alone can console us. This dynamic appraisal of man's faith in God and in himself has been called, "A masterpiece," by the ENCYCLO-PAEDIA BRITANNICA. xxx + 332pp. 5⅜ x 8.   T257 Paperbound **$1.95**

PHILOSOPHY AND CIVILIZATION IN THE MIDDLE AGES, M. de Wulf. This semi-popular survey covers aspects of medieval intellectual life such as religion, philosophy, science, the arts, etc. It also covers feudalism vs. Catholicism, rise of the universities, mendicant orders, monastic centers, and similar topics. Unabridged. Bibliography. Index. viii + 320pp. 5⅜ x 8.   T284 Paperbound **$1.75**

AN INTRODUCTION TO SCHOLASTIC PHILOSOPHY, Prof. M. de Wulf. Formerly entitled SCHOLASTICISM OLD AND NEW, this examines the central scholastic tradition from St. Anslem, Albertus Magnus, Thomas Aquinas, up to Suarez in the 17th century. The relation of scholasticism to ancient and medieval philosophy and science is clear and easily followed. The second part of the book considers the modern revival of scholasticism, the Louvain position, relations with Kantianism and Positivism. Unabridged. xvi + 271pp. 5⅜ x 8.
T296 Clothbound **$3.50**
T283 Paperbound **$1.75**

HISTORY OF MEDIAEVAL PHILOSOPHY, M. de Wulf. An unabridged reproduction of this standard history of medieval philosophy from the 4th to 12th centuries A.D. Covers St. Augustine, Boethius, John Scotus Erigena, St. Anselm, the school of Chartres, Abelard, Hugh of St. Victor, John of Salisbury, Peter Lombard, and scores of others including dualists, canonists, jurists, mystics like Dionysius Areopagitica, St. Bernard, Joachim of Flores, and others. Byzantine, Arabic and Jewish philosophy, and the scholastic tradition covered in detail. Classified bibliography of thousands of items. "The best treatment of the subject in English," Richard McKeon. Recommended by SHAW'S LIST OF BOOKS FOR COLLEGE LIBRARIES; STANDARD CATALOG FOR PUBLIC LIBRARIES. Indexed. xviii + 317pp. Volume 1 only.
T285 Clothbound **$4.00**

A HISTORY OF MODERN PHILOSOPHY, H. Höffding. An exceptionally clear and detailed coverage of western philosophy from the Renaissance to the end of the 19th century. Major and minor men such as Pomponazzi, Bodin, Boehme, Telesius, Bruno, Copernicus, da Vinci, Kepler, Galileo, Bacon, Descartes, Hobbes, Spinoza, Leibniz, Wolff, Locke, Newton, Berkeley, Hume, Erasmus, Montesquieu, Voltaire, Diderot, Rousseau, Lessing, Kant, Herder, Fichte, Schelling, Hegel, Schopenhauer, Comte, Mill, Darwin, Spencer, Hartmann, Lange and many others are discussed in terms of theory of knowledge, logic, cosmology, and psychology. Index. 2 volumes, total of 1159pp. 5⅜ x 8.
T117 Vol. 1, Paperbound **$2.00**
T118 Vol. 2, Paperbound **$2.00**

LANGUAGE, TRUTH AND LOGIC, A. J. Ayer. A clear, careful analysis of the basic ideas of Logical Positivism. Building on the work of Schlick, Russell, Carnap, and the Viennese School, Mr. Ayer develops a detailed exposition of the nature of philosophy, science, and metaphysics; the Self and the World; logic and common sense, and other philosophic concepts. An aid to clarity of thought as well as the first full-length development of Logical Positivism in English. Introduction by Bertrand Russell. Index. 160pp. 5⅜ x 8.
T10 Paperbound **$1.25**

PSYCHOLOGY

SEX IN PSYCHO-ANALYSIS (formerly CONTRIBUTIONS TO PSYCHO-ANALYSIS), S. Ferenczi. Written by an associate of Freud, this volume presents countless insights on such topics as impotence, transference, analysis and children, dreams, symbols, obscene words, masturbation and male homosexuality, paranoia and psycho-analysis, the sense of reality, hypnotism and therapy, and many others. Also includes full text of THE DEVELOPMENT OF PYSCHO-ANALYSIS by Ferenczi and Otto Rank. Two books bound as one. Total of 406pp. 5⅜ x 8.
T324 Paperbound **$1.85**

THE PRINCIPLES OF PSYCHOLOGY, William James. The full long course, unabridged, of one of the great classics of Western literature and science. Wonderfully lucid descriptions of mental activity, the stream of thought, consciousness, time perception, memory, imagination, emotions, reason, abnormal phenomena, and similiar topics. Original contributions are integrated with the work of such men as Berkeley, Binet, Mills, Darwin, Hume, Kant, Royce, Schopenhauer, Spinoza, Locke, Descartes, Galton, Wundt, Lotse, Herbart, Fechner and scores of others. All contrasting interpretations of mental phenomena are examined in detail — introspective analysis, philosophical interpretation, and experimental research. "A classic," JOURNAL OF CONSULTING PSYCHOLOGY. "The main lines are as valid as ever," PSYCHOANALYTICAL QUARTERLY. "Standard reading . . . a classic of interpretation," PSYCHIATRIC QUARTERLY. 94 illustrations. 1408pp. 2 volumes. 5⅜ x 8.
Vol. 1, T381 Paperbound **$2.00**
Vol. 2, T382 Paperbound **$2.00**

ARTS AND CRAFTS

STICKS AND STONES, Louis Mumford. A survey of forces that have conditioned American architecture and altered its forms. The medieval tradition in early New England villages; the Renaissance influence and rise of the merchant class; the classical influence of Jefferson's time; the "Mechanicsvilles" of Poe's generation; the Brown Decades; the philosophy of the Imperial facade; and finally the modern machine age   "A truly remarkable book," SAT. REV. OF LITERATURE. 2nd revised edition. 21 illustrations. xvii + 228pp. 5⅜ xx 8.
T202 Paperbound **$1.60**

THE AUTOBIOGRAPHY OF AN IDEA, Louis Sullivan. The pioneer architect whom Frank Lloyd Wright called "the master" records the crystallization of his opinions and theories, the growth of his organic theory of architecture that still influences American designers and architects. This volume contains 34 full-page plates of his finest architecture. Unabridged reissue of 1924 edition. New introduction by R. M. Line. Index. xiv + 335pp. 5⅜ x 8.
T281 Paperbound **$1.85**

THE MATERIALS AND TECHNIQUES OF MEDIEVAL PAINTING, D. V. Thompson. Based on years of study of medieval manuscripts and laboratory analysis of medieval paintings, this book discusses carriers and grounds, binding media, pigments, metals used in painting, etc. Considers relative merits of painting al fresco and al secco, the processing of coloring materials, burnishing, and many other matters. Preface by Bernard Berenson. Index. 239pp. 5⅜ x 8.
T327 Paperbound **$1.85**

WILD FOWL DECOYS, J. Barber. The standard work on this fascinating branch of folk art, this book describes duck decoys of all sorts ranging from Indian mud and grass devices to the realistic carved wooden decoys invented in Revolutionary days and still in use. Collectors information about styles, types, and periods as well as detailed information on producing your own decoys is given in a lucid and entertaining style. Seven decoy paintings and sets of plans (14 new plates) have been added, making a total of 140 unusual and valuable illustrations (4 in color) for handycrafters, artists, hunters, and students of folk art. 281pp. 7⅞ x 10¾. Deluxe edition.
T11 Clothbound **$8.50**

METALWORK AND ENAMELLING, H. Maryon. Probably the best book ever written on the subject. Prepared by Herbert Maryon, F.S.A., of the British Museum, it tells everything necessary for home manufacture of jewelry, rings, ear pendants, bowls, and dozens of other objects. Clearly written chapters provide precise information on such topics as materials, tools, soldering, filigree, setting stones, raising patterns, spinning metal, repoussé work, hinges and joints, metal inlaying, damascening, overlaying, niello, Japanese alloys, enamelling, cloisonné, painted enamels, casting, polishing coloring, assaying, and dozens of other techniques. This is the next best thing to apprenticeship to a master metalworker. 363 photographs and figures. 374pp. 5½ x 8½. **T183 Clothbound $7.50**

PRINCIPLES OF ART HISTORY, H. Wölfflin. Analyzing such terms as "baroque," "classic," "neoclassic," "primitive," "picturesque," and 164 different works by artists like Botticelli, van Cleve, Dürer, Hobbema, Holbein, Hals, Rembrandt, Titian, Brueghel, Vermeer, and many others, the author shows what really occurred between the 14th century primitives and the sophistication of the 18th century in terms of basic attitudes and philosophies. "A remarkable lesson in the art of seeing," SAT. REV. OF LITERATURE. Translated from the 7th German edition. 150 illustrations. 254pp. 6⅛ x 9¼. **T276 Paperbound $2.00**

SHAKER FURNITURE, E. D. and F. Andrews. Far and away the most illuminating study of Shaker furniture and the principles of Shaker craftsmanship ever written. The results of 15 years of research in Shaker communities, archives, and collections, Chronology, craftsmanship, furniture, houses, shops, etc., of Shaker culture. Over 200 chairs, tables, desks, clocks, beds, benches, are illustrated by clear photographs. For everyone interested in Americana, antiques, art, American culture of fine arts. "Mr. & Mrs. Andrews knows all there is to know about Shaker furniture," MARK VAN DOREN, NATION. 48 full page plates. 192pp. Deluxe cloth binding. 7⅞ x 10¾. **T7 Clothbound $6.00**

HANDBOOK OF ORNAMENT, F. S. Meyer. One of the largest collections of copyright-free traditional art. Over 3300 line cuts of Greek, Roman, Medieval, Islamic, Renaissance, Baroque, 18th and 19th century objects. 180 plates illustrate networks, Gothic tracery, geometric elements, flower and animal motifs, etc., while 100 plates illustrate decorative objects: chairs, thrones, cabinets, crowns, weapons, utensils, vases, jewelry, armor, heraldry, bottles, altars, and scores of other objects. Full text. 3300 illustrations. xiv + 548pp. 5⅜ x 8. **T302 Paperbound $2.00**

THREE CLASSICS OF ITALIAN CALLIGRAPHY, edited by Oscar Ogg. Complete reproductions of three famous calligraphic works by the greatest writing masters of the Renaissance: Arrighi's OPERINA and IL MODO, Tagliente's LO PRESENTE LIBRO, and Palatino's LIBRO NUOVO. These books present more than 200 complete alphabets and thousands of lettered specimens. The basic hand is Papal Chancery, but scores of other alphabets are also given: European and Asiatic local alphabets, foliated and "art" alphabets, scrolls, cartouches, borders, etc. Text is in Italian. Introduction. 245 plates. x + 272pp. 6⅛ x 9¼. **T212 Paperbound $1.95**

THE HISTORY AND TECHNIQUES OF LETTERING, A. Nesbitt. The only thorough inexpensive history of letter froms from the point of view of the artist. Mr. Nesbitt covers every major development in lettering from the ancient Egyptians to the present and illustrates each development with a complete alphabet. Such masters as Baskerville, Bell, Bodoni, Caslon, Koch, Kilian, Morris, Garamont, Jenson, and dozens of others are analyzed in terms of artistry and historical development. The author also presents a 65 page practical course in lettering, besides the full historical text. 89 complete alphabets; 165 additional lettered specimens. xvii + 300pp. 5⅜ x 8. **T427 Paperbound $2.00**

LETTERING AND ALPHABETS, J. A. Cavanagh. This unabridged reissue of LETTERING offers a full discussion, analysis, illustration of 89 basic hand lettering styles — styles derived from Caslons, Bodonis, Garamonds, Gothic, Black Letter, Oriental and many others. Upper and lower cases, numerals and common signs pictured. Hundreds of technical hints on make-up, construction, artistic validity, strokes, pens, brushes, white areas, etc. May be reproduced without permission! 89 complete alphabets; 72 lettered specimens. 121pp. 9¾ x 8. **T53 Paperbound $1.25**

THE HUMAN FIGURE IN MOTION, Eadweard Muybridge. The largest selection in print of Muybridge's famous high-speed action photos of the human figure in motion. 4789 photographs illustrate 162 different actions: men, women, children — mostly undraped — are shown walking, running, carrying various objects, sitting, lying down, climbing, throwing, arising, and performing over 150 other actions. Some actions are shown in as many as 120 photographs each. More than 500 action strips at shutter speeds as high as 1/6000th of a second! These are not posed shots, but true stopped motion. They show bone and muscles in situations that the human eye is not fast enough to capture. Earlier, smaller editions of these prints have brought $40 and more on the out-of-print market. "A must for artists," ART IN FOCUS. "An unparalled dictionary of action for all artists," AMERICAN ARTIST. 390 full-page plates, with 4789 photographs. Printed on heavy glossy stock. Reinforced binding with headbands. 7⅞ x 10⅝. **T204 Clothbound $10.00**

ANIMALS IN MOTION, Eadweard Muybridge. This is the largest collection of animal action photos in print. 34 different animals (horses, mules, oxen, goats, camels, pigs, cats, guanacos, lions, gnus, deer, monkeys, eagles — and 21 others) in 132 characteristic actions. The horse alone is shown in more than 40 different actions. All 3919 photographs are taken in series at speeds up to 1/6000th of a second. You will see exactly how a lion sets his foot down; how an elephant's knees are like a human's — and how they differ; the position of a kangaroo's legs in mid-leap; how an ostrich's head bobs; details of the flight of birds — and thousands of facts of motion taken only the fastest cameras can catch. Neither semiposed artificial shots nor distorted telephoto shots taken under adverse conditions. Artists, biologists, cartoonists, will find this book indispensable for understanding animals in motion. "A really marvelous series of plates," NATURE (London). "The dry plate's most spectacular early use was by Eadweard Muybridge," LIFE. 3919 photographs; 380 full pages of plates. 440pp. Printed on heavy glossy paper. Deluxe binding with headbands. 7⅞ x 10⅝. **T203 Clothbound $10.00**

THE BOOK OF SIGNS, Rudolf Koch. 493 symbols from ancient manuscripts, medieval cathedrals, coins, catacombs, pottery, etc. Crosses, monograms of Roman emperors, astrological, chemical, botanical, runes, housemarks, and 7 other categories. Invaluable for handycraft workers, illustrators, scholars, etc., this material may be reproduced without permission. 493 illustrations by Fritz Kredel. 104pp. 6⅛ x 9¼. Sewn binding. T162 Paperbound **$1.00**

A HANDBOOK OF EARLY ADVERTISING ART, C. P. Hornung. The largest collection of copyright-free early advertising art ever compiled. Vol. I contains some 2,000 illustrations of agricultural devices, animals, old automobiles, birds, buildings, Christmas decorations (with 7 Santa Clauses by Nast), allegorical figures, fire engines, horses and vehicles, Indians, portraits, sailing ships, trains, sports, trade cuts — and 30 other categories! Vol. II, devoted to typography, has over 4000 specimens: 600 different Roman, Gothic, Barnum, Old English faces; 630 ornamental type faces; 1115 initials, hundreds of scrolls, flourishes, etc. This third edition is enlarged by 78 additional plates containing all new material. "A remarkable collection," PRINTERS' INK. "A rich contribution to the history of American design," GRAPHIS.
Volume 1, Pictorial Volume. Over 2000 illustrations. xlv + 242pp. 9 x 12. T122 Clothbound **$10.00**
Volume II, Typographical Volume. Over 4000 specimens. vii + 312pp. 9 x 12. T123 Clothbound **$10.00**
Two volume set, Clothbound, only **$18.50**

DESIGN FOR ARTISTS AND CRAFTSMEN, L. Wolchonok. The most thorough course on the creation of art motifs and designs. Create your own designs out of things around you — from geometric patterns, plants, birds, animals, humans, landscapes, and man-made objects. It leads you step by step through the creation of more than 1300 designs, ranging from near representationalism to the most advanced forms of abstraction. The material in this book is entirely new, and combines full awareness of traditional design with the work of such men as Miro, Leger, Picasso, Moore, and others. 113 detailed exercises, with instruction hints, diagrams, and details to enable you to apply Wolchonok's methods to your own work. "A great contribution to the field of design and crafts," N. Y. SOCIETY OF CRAFTSMEN. More than 1300 illustrations. xv + 207pp. 7⅞ x 10¾. T274 Clothbound **$4.95**

HANDBOOK OF DESIGNS AND DEVICES, C. P. Hornung. Indispensable to the designer, commercial artist, and hobbyist. It is not a text-book but a working collection of 1836 basic designs and variations, which may be used without permission. Variations of circle, line, band, triangle, square, cross, diamond, swastika, pentagon, octagon, hexagon, star, scroll, interlacement, shields, etc. Supplementary notes on the background and symbolism. "A necessity to every designer who would be original without having to labor heavily," ARTIST AND ADVERTISER. 204 plates. 240pp. 5⅜ x 8. T124 Clothbound **$3.95**
T125 Paperbound **$1.90**

THE UNIVERSAL PENMAN, George Bickham. This beautiful book, which first appeared in 1743 contains 212 full-page plates drawn from the work of such 18th century masters of English roundhand as Dove, Champion, and Bland. They contain 22 complete alphabets, over 2,000 flourishes, and 122 illustrations, each drawn with a stylistic grace impossible to describe. This book is invaluable to anyone interested in the beauties of calligraphy, or to any artist, hobbyist, or craftsman who wishes to use the very best ornamental handwriting and flourishes for decorative purposes. Commercial artists, advertising artists, have found it unexcelled as a source of material suggesting quality. "An essential part of any art library, and a book of permanent value," AMERICAN ARTIST. 212 plates. 224pp. 9 x 13¾.
T20 Clothbound **$10.00**

AN ATLAS OF ANATOMY FOR ARTISTS, F. Schider. A new 3rd edition of this standard text enlarged by 52 new illustrations of hands, anatomical studies by Cloquet, and expressive life studies of the body by Barcsay. 29 plates show all aspects of the skeleton, with closeups of special areas, while 54 full-page plates, mostly in two colors, give human musculature as seen from four different points of view, with cutaways for important portions of the body. 14 full-page plates provide photographs of hand forms, eyelids, female breasts, and indicate the location of muscles upon models. 59 additional plates show how great artists of the past utilized human anatomy! Michelangelo, Leonardo da Vinci, Goya, and 15 others. This is a lifetime reference work which will be one of the most important books in any artist's library. "The standard reference tool," AMERICAN LIBRARY ASSOCIATION. "Excellent," AMERICAN ARTIST. Third enlarged edition. 189 plates, 647 illustrations. xxvi + 192pp. 7⅞ x 10⅝.
T241 Clothbound **$6.00**

FOUNDATIONS OF MODERN ART, A. Ozenfant. An illuminating discussion of the interrelationship of all forms of human creativity, from painting to science, writing to religion. The creative process is explored in all facets of art, from paleolithic cave painting to modern French painting and architecture, and the great universals of art are isolated. Expressing its countless insights in aphorisms accompanied by carefully selected illustrations, this book is itself an embodiment in prose of the creative process. Enlarged by 4 new chapters. 226 illustrations. 368pp. 6⅛ x 9¼. T215 Paperbound **$1.95**

AN ATLAS OF ANIMAL ANATOMY FOR ARTISTS, W. Ellenberger, H. Baum, H. Dittrich. The largest, richest animal anatomy for artists available in English. 99 detailed anatomical plates of such animals as the horse. dog, cat, lion, dear, seal, kangaroo, flying squirrel, cow, bull, goat, monkey, hare, and bat. Surface features are clearly indicated, while progressive beneath-the-skin pictures show musculature, tendons, and bone structure. Detailed cross-sections are given for heads and important features. The animals chosen are representative of specific families so that a study of these anatomies will provide knowledge of hundreds of related species. "Highly recommended as one of the very few books on the subject worthy of being used as an authoritative guide," DESIGN. Second revised, enlarged edition with new plates from Cuvier, Stubbs, etc. 288 illustrations. 153pp. 11⅜ x 9.
T82 Clothbound **$6.00**